UNIVERSITIES AND INNOVATION ECONOMIES

This book is dedicated to my father, Harry, who was a gifted engineer and who imparted to me something of the engineer's respect for how things are rather than what we might wish them to be. If an engineer ignores the reality of the forces of nature, the bridge falls down. So it is with society. If we ignore what is possible and what is practical, our social bridges collapse under their own weight.

Universities and Innovation Economies

The Creative Wasteland of Post-Industrial Society

PETER MURPHY

James Cook University, Australia

Routledge
Taylor & Francis Group

LONDON AND NEW YORK

First published 2015 by Ashgate Publishing

2 Park Square, Milton Park, Abingdon, Oxfordshire OX14 4RN
52 Vanderbilt Avenue, New York, NY 10017

Routledge is an imprint of the Taylor & Francis Group, an informa business

First issued in paperback 2020

British Library Cataloguing in Publication Data
A catalogue record for this book is available from the British Library

The Library of Congress has cataloged the printed edition as follows:
Murphy, Peter, 1956–
    Universities and innovation economies : the creative wasteland of post-industrial
society / by Peter Murphy.
        pages cm.
    Includes bibliographical references and index.
    ISBN 978-1-4724-2535-5 (hardback)
1. Education, Higher—Economic aspects. 2. Postmodernism
and higher education. 3. Educational change. I. Title.
    LC67.6.M88 2015
    338.4'3378–dc23

                                                                    2014028902

ISBN 978-1-4724-2535-5 (hbk)
ISBN 978-0-367-59966-9 (pbk)

Contents

List of Figures and Tables

Figures

Tables

Acknowledgements

My sincere thanks to: Greg Melleuish, Ken Friedman, Vrasidas Karalis, and David Roberts, who read and commented on the book in manuscript. Warm thanks to Simon Marginson with whom I worked on a research project about universities while I wrote *Universities and Innovation Economies*. Other colleagues have also been generous with their thoughts about universities, creation and innovation—among them Anders Michelsen, Agnes Heller, Dominique Bouchet, Eduardo de la Fuente, John Carroll, Chris Hay, Paul Collits, Ian Atkinson, Wayne Cristaudo, Doug Kirsner, Celia Lury, Andrea Vestrucci, Mujadad Zaman, Warwick Powell, Tina Besley, Ryan Daniel, Scott Lash, John Rundell, Xinxin Deng, Ron Barnett, Suzi Adams, Gerard Puccio, Peter Beilharz, Katja Fleischmann, Hong Chengwen, David Salisbury, Craig Browne, Glenn Porter, Susanne Maria Weber, Michael Peters, Andrew Benjamin, Brian Nelson, and Trevor Hogan. I am grateful to those colleagues for their observations and reflections—and to Robin Gauld and Sian Supski who assisted me in the collection of data for this volume.

Introduction

The Creative Wasteland of Post-Industrial Society

The global financial crisis of 2008 signaled the beginning of the end of the post-industrial age. The prolonged stagnation that followed 2008—accompanied by sovereign debt, low productivity and high unemployment in major economies—was an indication of the failure of many of the claims that had been made since the 1970s about the economic power of post-industrial economies and knowledge societies. Economic failure translated into fiscal contraction. This affected all kinds of government spending including on a super-sized university sector. During the post-modern era, mass higher education had grown ferociously. Philosophies of post-industrialism legitimated a relentless expansion of government budgets for education along with other social sectors. The resulting levels of sovereign debt and government budget deficits were not sustainable—not least because the economic promise of post-industrial economies was never realized.

The promise of post-industrialism was innovation. The primary cause of modern economic growth, the theory went, was innovation. Innovation is the social application of the power of creation. Modern societies that lack the capacity for creation struggle socially and flounder economically. The theory was not wrong. The extended economic stagnation in many OECD countries that followed 2008 was a symptom of depressed innovation. But this despondent state pointed to a deeper problem: namely that the post-industrial 'knowledge society' and the post-modern 'information society' had stopped innovating on a large scale—or rather it had never lived up to its self-image as an innovating epoch. The 'bio technology revolution' that was promised in the 1990s failed to happen. The 2000s saw mass consumer enthusiasm for social media, computer applications and smart phones. Yet the last significant productivity increase in the OECD occurred in the late 1990s and that was short-lived. The university was the symbolic core of the post-modern age. It embodied its desires. It represented its aspirations. It was emblematic of the knowledge and information that, supposedly, elicited the technological and sociological innovations that energized economies and enlarged social prosperity. It was an institutional source of concepts that animated and unscored the ideas-driven growth that supposedly typified post-industrial economies. Yet in reality growth, prosperity and ideas proved to be much scarcer than in the industrial age.

Part of the explanation of this is bureaucracy. The post-modern age promised to replace inflexible 'Fordist' organizations with flexible 'post-Fordist' institutions. In reality, post-Fordism out-did Fordism in its fascination with administration. This was, above all, true of universities. Post-modern bureaucratic organization contributed much to the failure of contemporary innovation and the paltry nature of its idea-generation. Large and medium-sized organizations dominate today's economic and social landscape. Yet, whatever their virtues, these organizations are typically poor innovators and miserable concept-producers. Smaller enterprises and informal milieu for the most part are better at substantive innovation and genuine creation. That does not stop large formal organizations touting their innovation prowess in ways that are both self-serving and self-deluding. A specious rhetoric of innovation deployed by bureaucratic organizations and bureaucratic societies took off in the early 1970s. This coincided with the rapid expansion of universities. The peak of social discussion about universities occurs in the period between 1967 and 1974.[1] This was one of the harbingers of the post-modern society. The effect of this interest and its concomitant rhetoric was perverse. It contributed to hollowing out the inner substance of innovation and creation while appropriating its legitimating properties. Large organizations not least of all the ever-expanding universities proclaimed (without much evidence) their own impressive novelty and freshness. This shameless booster mentality belied an underlying reality of exhaustion and entropy. All round there was much sound and fury that signified nothing.

Modern economies are cyclical. The most important cycles are the long economic waves. These last 70–80 years and define the world's mega-trends. We have just come to the conclusion of one of those waves. It began in 1950 and ended in 2010. It started on an upswing and terminated in chronic stagnation. There were good times during the era but sluggish periods as well. Some of the good times hid bad practices. Consequently a good portion of the wealth created in the 1990s and the 2000s was fictional. It was the product of speculation rather than ingenuity and hard work. The overlapping long economic waves of 1900–1970 and 1950–2010 were notably less impressive in real terms than the waves of 1780–1870 and 1850–1920. While the global economy is wealthier today than it was in the nineteenth century, its creative energy is less.

Where do we go from here? What can help restart the stalled engine of creation and re-engage yet another long cycle of creative capitalism? Can the spirit of the nineteenth century be recaptured, or will the world's next long economic wave prove to be more down than up? The answer to that question lies in one word: productivity. Productivity is the child of creativity. The secret of modern industrial capitalism was to create more with less. To achieve more with less, science was applied to production, commerce was freed from government bureaucracy, the work ethic spread, and social institutions were stream-lined. In the twentieth century, a counter-thrust occurred. Late twentieth-century science was consumed by the art of grant-getting and rent-seeking. State capitalism rose to prominence. Hedonistic and remissive behaviors were widely sanctioned while increased regulation petrified flexible institutions.

The idea of social and geographical mobility driven by education, and culminating in 'going to university,' proved to be one of the most powerful post-second world

---

1   Google N-gram analysis of the terms 'university' and 'universities.'

war ideologies. Across the OECD, 30 percent or more of 19-year olds now attend tertiary institutions. Ready access to higher education prevails. The underlying assumption is that education-fuelled social and geographic mobility is ennobling. It emancipates human beings from a life of labor and enriches the mind. But does it? Students often acquire proficient professional knowledge in contemporary universities yet these same universities now also often bore the brightest students. At the same time, 25 percent of students drop out of university permanently without completing a degree.[2] Another 25 percent of students graduate but never work in a job requiring a degree. While the post-industrial universities redefined themselves as vehicles of social and spatial mobility, their ability to satisfy the most inquiring minds or produce path-breaking work diminished, as did their vocational salience.

This kind of unseemly roundabout was not peculiar to universities. It haunted much of the electronic age. A peculiar ambivalence beset the era. It saw out socialism and communism. Both were dead ducks by 1989. But the age could not let go of their asphyxiating legacy. So it turned from anti-capitalism to various kinds of faux capitalism. A legion of *fauxitalisms* mushroomed. These were encouraged by government subsidies, preternaturally-low interest rate policies and ideologically-inspired regulatory environments. The financial crisis of 2008 signaled the beginning of the end of the post-industrial age. We are starting to look back on it now. What we see in hindsight should inform the future. Times do pivot and behaviors do change. We cannot foretell the future but should the future turn out better than the past this will be because we have learnt something from experience. We do not know what the next economic wave will be. It is being invented right now. The open question isF whether, as a result, the creativity slump of the post-modern era will be overcome or not?

Post-modern sin was two-fold. First, it was not to go to university. Second it was not to invest large amounts of private and public money in the vain pursuit that everyone should attend a college or university. Accordingly, the higher education sector attracted untold billions in tax-payer funds and student fees. Yet what it delivered to millions of individuals and the larger society was paltry. Drop-out rates were intractably high. On a mass scale, these rates were socially and financially unsustainable.[3] A quarter to nearly a half of graduates ended up in

---

2   In 2011, the comparative figure for the United Kingdom (one of the world's better performers) was 21.6 percent. Paton 2012. The OECD, 2007, Table A3.4, calculated that 72 percent of Australian university students completed (28 percent didn't) by measuring graduates as a percent of entrants for the year. The OECD average, on this measure, was 69 percent completion. The United States had 56 percent completion and the United Kingdom 79 percent completion. The OECD, 2013a: 68, reported completion rates of 80 percent (Denmark), 74 percent (Germany), 66 percent (Israel), 64 percent (USA), 59 percent (Norway), and 47 percent (Hungary). Australia's rate in 2013 (81 percent) was arbitrarily high due to rapidly growing entry numbers.

3   In 2013, 37 million Americans (about one in 10) had some college credits but had not completed a degree.

jobs that did not require a degree.[4] Chronic grade inflation diluted the meaning of entry scores and performance results. After 1970, real research output per capita declined visibly and the rate of high-level creation diminished noticeably. Major breakthroughs in key areas from physics to medicine contracted.

When it comes to analyzing the universities, the current study draws principally on evidence and examples from Australia and the United States. The latter is a diverse higher education system with both public and private institutions; the former is a predominately state university system. The American system is large and leads the world; the Australian system is small but is strong academically and is a major exporter of higher education internationally. Yet both face serious systemic problems—as do university systems across the world. The problem lies not with this or that country but in the nature of the university and especially what became of it in the post-industrial era. The university was the signature institution of the post-industrial age. The age reaped what it sowed. As the last long economic wave unfolded between 1950 and 2010, universities expanded remorselessly. As they did, their intellectual productivity declined. They became massively bureaucratized. Their information technology proved dysfunctional. Central costs ballooned while governments mercilessly drove large numbers of young people who had no interest in and no aptitude for university curriculum into the universities. Today the clear evidence is that half of university entrants show no improvement in reasoning or understanding across their first and second year. In effect, they learn nothing. Half also either drop out of university or else are never employed in a job that requires a degree. What would we say of a factory that produced 50 percent unusable widgets? We would say it had a productivity problem. All the serious empirical indicators suggest that too many young people today go to university or degree-granting colleges not too few, and that the *raison d'etre* of universities has been lost amidst a fog of fake social pieties, insipid intellectual activity, and illusory promises of social advancement.

Governments funded the remorseless expansion of the universities.[5] In doing so, they created problems that they could not afford to fix. They raised expectations that more and more young people would go to university, far in excess of population growth. None of this was sustainable.[6] So governments did one of three things.

---

4   Forty-eight percent of US college graduates in 2012 were in jobs that did not require a degree. Vedder, Denhart and Robe 2013.

5   The breathlessness of government reports that hailed the expansion began early on. In 1964 Australia's Martin Committee reported that 'since the end of World War II, there has been a revolution in the interest in higher education in Australia' (volume 1: 12) inciting images of an implacable flow that all subsequent government inquiries would in turn summon up. The separation between fact and norm blurred. The Martin Committee was the second of Australia's major official inquiries into its universities in the post-war period.

6   In 1947 Australia spent 0.11 percent of its GDP on the universities; in 1962 this had risen to 0.67 percent (Martin Committee 1964 volume 1: 13). In 2011, the expenditure was 1 percent. In 1947 the outgoing was fiscally inconsequential. In 2011 it was fiscally noticeable and thus subject to political considerations.

They borrowed the money to fund university places, exacerbating long-term public debt problems. They introduced 'fees-and-loans' packages for students, creating unproductive private debt for the many students who would eventually drop out of university or never use their degree in a job. Finally, governments systematically underfunded student places. This careless system undermined the intellectual productivity of the university in the name of expanding the university. It financed millions of people to learn approximately nothing while those who were in a position to seriously benefit from a university education were habitually short-changed by the skimpy curricula and ballooning size of the mass university.

The post-industrial era stimulated a raging social appetite for higher education. In the wake of this, the word 'university' became a synonym for virtually any kind of tertiary education of any description. The university subsumed the college, the technological institute, the seminary, the gallery school, the conservatorium, and the sports team. In so doing it radically expanded the range and (more importantly) the type of discipline it offered. Management, media, and business 'studies' joined physics, economics and philosophy in the university. Yet it remained an open question whether the four-year undergraduate university degree was a suitable replacement for on-the-job training in the para-professions such as journalism or social work. Nevertheless, the status of the word 'university' is very seductive. As a consequence the institution of the university has continued to proliferate inexorably while the universities on average have become more and more trivial in their spirit and practice. A handful of universities escape this fate. Most do not.

Universities are defined by three great functions. One is to transmit knowledge in order to provide students with an understanding of the humanities, the sciences or the social sciences. The second function is to transmit knowledge in order to prepare students for a learned profession. The third and highest function of the university is to create knowledge. The university thus is defined by the advancement as well as the transmission of knowledge. A university that advances knowledge is different from a humanistic college or a vocational institute. The latter principally convey knowledge rather than create it. The discovery university (the type of university that advances knowledge) relies on high levels of self-education and intellectual modelling. A firmer or clearer distinction between the discovery university (on the one hand) and the humanistic college or the technological institute (on the other hand) might help to resolve some of the conundrums that we currently face as a consequence of the repeated inflation of the concept of the university. We cannot escape the simple reality, though, that a large portion of what today is called 'the university' is not a university at all.

The problem is not new. The modern idea and practice of the university took shape in the nineteenth century. What resulted from that was an institution (even then) whose self-understanding and practices were ambivalent and conflicted. The American university scene of the late-nineteenth century had all the features in miniature of what was to come. It was torn between vocational and scholarly study, undergraduate and graduate missions, professional schools and the liberal arts and sciences, the advancement of knowledge and the diffusion of knowledge, professional training and intellectual calling, pure and applied knowledge, wide curricula choice and narrow disciplinary specialization. It prepared students for the learned professions (originally divinity, law and medicine) while opening the university to vocations that aspired to professional status. Programs for musicians, dieticians, pharmacists, teachers, veterinarians, social workers and business administrators sprang up. Some of the new professions, like engineering, matched the intellectual demands of law and medicine; others struggled (and still struggle) for credibility. And the question of how the 'lower faculties' related to the 'higher faculties,' how philosophy related to law, or science to engineering, or the liberal arts to the professions was never resolved. Did a new discipline like that of business belong in a professional 'school' or in a 'college' of liberal arts and sciences? What in any event was the relation or separation between the words 'school,' 'college,' 'institute,' and 'university'?

Overall, 'the university' belies its name. It has evolved as a disjointed and jumbled institution, with a fractured identity, often united by one thing only: the desire to grow ever-larger. The post-industrial era exacerbated and compounded this tendency, often radically. Excess was its middle name. The consequence of the post-modern age was to blur still further the idea of the university. It did this on a very large, concerted scale. It accelerated and magnified a process that turned the university into the multiversity and then into the megaversity. The institution of the university became all things to all people. Distinctions between training providers, colleges, polytechnics, technological institutes and universities blurred. Intellectual goals vied with social goals and vocational goals and expansionary goals. This all gelled with the conceptual relativism of the age. Haziness, confusion, and muddle reigned.

The post-industrial age witnessed some counter tendencies. Between 1974 and 2004, across the world, the term 'research university' gained ground.[7] Self-described 'research universities' began to assert their identity. Since the creation of the University of Berlin in 1810, there had been a presumption that a university was a place where research happened and knowledge was advanced. Yet this idea of the university always sat uneasily with collegiate-style teaching universities and vocational-style technological universities along with the professional 'schools' and undergraduate 'colleges' of universities, and a myriad other half-way houses, suggesting that the idea of the university has been one of the most contested and confused ideas in modernity. Everyone one desires the status that research confers because only a relative handful of the members of a university routinely produce research. Not only that but also a tiny number of universities produce most of the world's academic research. The sudden emergence (in the mid-2000s) of global rankings of universities merely highlighted this. While at the other end of the spectrum new versions of the 'vocational university' proliferated (especially in East Asia) whose rationale was that graduates would get 'jobs.' In between these two poles sit most universities who are uncertain of their identity and who rely on

---

7   Google N-gram word analysis search.

vague notions of 'scholarship' to bridge what is for most purposes an unbridgeable gap between intellectual discovery and job training. Most of these institutions claim to do research but in practice produce little of it. All in all, that suggests the need for a more affirmative and systematic distinction between the discovery university, the humanistic arts-and-sciences college and the technological institute.

'Polytechnic,' 'technical college,' 'college of advanced education' and 'institute of technology' are still today much more accurate words to describe many of the institutions that are called 'universities,' no matter that these labels have fallen into disuse. The astute US Carnegie classification of research, doctoral, and comprehensive universities indicates the difficulty of answering the question: 'what is a university?' Research universities give priority to faculty carrying out research; doctoral universities have at least a number of major doctoral programs but without an emphasis on faculty research; comprehensive universities offer graduate research degrees to Masters' level. Is a university then defined by the conduct of research or can it be defined by the quasi-teaching function of supervising graduate research students?

The confusion of naming has been caused in no small measure by the social desire to expand universities. By the mid-2000s, this expansionary impulse had turned into a hubristic ambition that 30, 40 or 50 percent or more of 19 year-olds attend university. This was invariably tied to post-industrial claims about achieving 'equity' in higher education; claims that only ever produce ever-larger equity bureaucracies, never ever-greater equity. Post-industrial equations of degree-granting with the advancement of learning (in turn) with the advancement of knowledge (in turn) with economic advancement proved a chimera. The post-industrial era achieved little more than the proliferation and inflation of qualifications and the moral disenfranchisement of those without them. Post-industrial higher education promised social equality but more commonly produced unrepresentative, obsequious, and morally-smug meritocracies whose actual merit was difficult to determine. It acted as a model for the wider bureaucratization of social systems in general and the zealous over-extension of procedural rationality in society. The post-industrial university failed to deliver on any of its social equity talk. Its failures then became the justification for repeating more of the same. After 1970, universities promised to match the percentage of low socio-economic status (SES) student enrolments with the proportion of low SES individuals in the general population. Forty years on, the universities had failed to do this almost completely. All that equity policy did was to generate university equity bureaucracies in which university graduates were employed. This was a microcosm of a wider social phenomenon that saw the multiplication of public spending on procedure and process and the consequent proliferation of null offices with exorbitant titles occupied by graduates to no good social effect.

More compelling than the self-interested promises of equity bureaucracies is the auto-poietic model of educational attainment. Bureaucracies seek procedural and institutional solutions to problems that cannot be solved by organizational means. Advancement to university is a classic example of this. Institutional policy techniques such as lowering or manipulating entrance requirements, setting entrance quotas, multiplying the number of places in universities, offering special (aka non-meritocratic) scholarships and income support, and so on, make little or no difference to social outcomes. This is because advancing to university is not a generic social process but rather a socio-intellectual one. The single most powerful predictor that an individual will get to university is not parental status, income or occupation. It is the size of the home library that a child has access to. If one wants to attain equity of entry to higher education then the familial-bibliophilic model of educational attainment is a more realistic way of achieving this. This is comparable with the efficacious role that self-education plays in the lives and careers of creative individuals in the arts, sciences and the professions. Rather than bureaucratically-driven 'access' programs, bibliophilic programs that support reading at home (such as investing in public libraries) are more effective in achieving broad educational success. There is good reason as well for skepticism about bureaucratically-delivered schooling. Bibliophilic self-education combined with familial inculcation of time-management and other key behavioral and character traits is central to getting to and succeeding at universities. Post-industrial obsessions not only with schooling but also with social media have endangered this. There is a close correlation between the pervasive rise of social media and the critical collapse in hours spent reading at home in recent times. Just as institutionalized schooling is no guarantee of learning, equally questionable is the proposition that 'more places at universities' means 'more social opportunity' and 'greater life chances.' In reality, 'more places' in the post-industrial universities has simply meant less and less learning going on in those institutions. The post-industrial equation of ever-higher formal levels of education with better learning outcomes, better graduate incomes, and better economic performance or social prosperity is fallacious. For the present, the mythologies of the post-industrial society keep social demand for university places in OECD countries high. But myths are not forever and realistic questions keep being raised: How can demand, outcomes and the fact of shrinking government budgets be reconciled? How (then) are scarce public resources to be allocated?

If resources are scarce, to whom or what should those resources flow? This is a classic question of public policy. What criteria do we have to help us choose between what we spend money on and what we don't spend money on? There is reason to consider sympathetically the criterion of discovery. Discovery is a public good. Done in a serious way it produces tangible, long-term, collective social value. It represents the human capacity for initiating, preserving, inventing and finding what is significant. Discovery, though, is not a populist criterion. While the fruits of discovery are widely shared, the human talent for discovery is not broadly distributed in society. Psychological studies of creativity and intelligence persistently conclude the same: around 8 percent of the population has a clear and evident gift for intellectual discovery. Around 16 percent of the population will end up in the professions and the semi-professions (combined) and that cohort benefits from some kind of higher education (though it may not be a university education in the strict sense of the word university).[8] A similar percentage of 19 year olds are 'college-ready'—meaning that there is a high probability that they will successfully complete their tertiary studies. Discovery is not for everyone. The modest-sized discovery cohort is proficient at abstract thinking, reasoning, and speculation. It is comfortable with university-level curricula. It works with a substantial degree of intellectual autonomy and self-direction.

At the highest level, what results from informed self-direction—namely, invention, innovation, and initiative—is generated by a small number of researchers, writers, scientists, technologists, artists, political actors, policy makers, and leaders of the professions whose work, by its nature, is publicly communicated and widely diffused. There is an outward in-principle reason for society to support higher education especially of the 8 percent discovery cohort, and most especially its 2 percent high-performing core, because what that cohort creates has a general, transferable and durable social value. That said, though, post-industrial subsidies (as the current study shows) over time have only made higher education more expensive not more accessible. In other words, state subsidies in practice have been counter-productive and self-defeating. In the post-2008 era, scarce public finances can be best and most effectively used for limited, targeted, merit-defined support of higher education and principally of discovery universities.

The size of the discovery university sector is inherently small.[9] Historically the university sector as a whole was small as were universities as institutions. The

---

8   Australia's Martin Committee (1964 volume 1: 12) asked in passing the useful question: 'Should the nation make facilities available to all students wishing to become doctors or engineers or lawyers, if it is doubtful whether the community will need this number?'

9   This view may be contrasted with that of Australia's Martin Committee. In 1964, the Committee stated that: 'Some of [the] disadvantages of large institutions are inevitable and they should be set against the possible advantages of size. The truth is that there cannot be an optimum university size, for there are no agreed criteria against which to judge size' (volume 1: 54). However, if the extent of discovery, productivity, and efficiency are the agreed criteria, then a 'large' university is not optimum. It is notable that the Protestant universities that were the engines of the European Enlightenment were small institutions. A case in point is the Scottish Enlightenment. Its great universities, the University of Glasgow and the University of Edinburgh, in the eighteenth century had 400 and 600 students respectively, about 1 percent of their cities populations. These universities led the way in philosophy and medicine, harbouring figures like Hume and Hutchenson, Adam Smith and Adam Ferguson while the southern counterparts of these institutions, the much larger Oxford and Cambridge universities, were in the doldrums. (Instructively, Adam Smith cut short his stay at Oxford where he had gone to carry out private scholarship on a very generous post-graduate Scottish scholarship.) Size is not the only cause of university lethargy but it is a factor. A city or region with a population of 1 million warrants a university with a student population of 10,000 students. That is around the maximum size of a proficient university today. Six-to-eight thousand students is the optimal size for a contemporary university. Significantly larger growth engenders progressive entropy, beginning with disproportionate transaction and process costs. Structural factors like multiple campuses magnify entropic cost growth.

importance of this is unchanged. The future of the sector lies not with the megaversity or the multiversity but with the microversity. The demands of the microversity on the public purse are properly modest. It is defined by a visible and tangible commitment to intellectual discovery and by a distinctive style of autodidactic exploration-based learning. This mode of education supposes motivated self-learners who advance in their studies via a vast range of extra curricula intellectual activities and through the medium of exploratory research-based essays, artistic works, science experiments, and theses. The latter are supervised by a professoriate that provides both undergraduate students and graduate candidates with visible and credible models of imaginative research and inspired discovery. Competitive scholarships are the most effective means available to governments to support and fund discovery-based higher learning. A system of scholarships—awarded on the basis of scholastic and creative aptitude tests—can properly underwrite both full fellowships and subsidized university places. The rationale for the state and society doing this is that discovery is a clear and demonstrable public good from which all, including future generations, benefit.

The discovery sector is tiny. It is not for every student who might benefit from higher education. The technological institute and the humanistic college naturally complement the discovery university. Those who might benefit from some type of higher education are the college-ready 16 percent who have a good probability of completing a degree or working in a vocation that requires a degree. This applies to around half or less of the number of students today in higher education. Higher education is a mixed private and public good. For graduates, a higher education provides intellectual self-enrichment and leads to professional, skilled para-professional and office work as well as higher incomes on graduation and higher social status. For employers higher education sorts aspirant employees. The state's responsibility is limited in most cases. The exception is the exceptionally talented whose capacity for intellectual discovery and professional initiative provide a manifest long-term public and social benefit.

The public purse is not unlimited. It should not encourage over-education, as today, with millions of students enrolling in higher education with faint chance either of graduating or ever working in a job that requires a degree. Loans for tertiary study—repaid as a taxable percentage of graduate income—are an efficient way for able individuals to pay for a university place, allowing them to defer payment of fees and expenses until they are working. The over-expansion of the post-industrial university, though, created ballooning student debt. A large number of those who are indebted gain no rational private benefit from this debt. Student debt today has started to become a cause of marriage postponement, home loan unaffordability, and delay in the beginning of families. It also eats into the modest capital needed for garage-scale business start-ups. This suggests that not more but fewer university places per capita are needed. University places cannot replace jobs nor can they replace workplace apprenticeships, traineeships, cadetships, paid internships, and small business start-ups. The latter are more valuable now to those wanting to enter the workforce than the ever-decreasing marginal returns of ever-more university places, be these privately or publicly funded. The proper principal function of public policy is to aid in the creation of jobs, not university places. The chief economic illusion of the post-industrial age was that the latter could replace, stimulate, and generate the former.

The carrying-out of research defines a university. Yet most post-industrial universities produce meagre amounts of research. They are in reality teaching institutions, i.e. de facto colleges or institutes. They principally function to transmit knowledge, not to create knowledge. Even then their rates of retention of undergraduate students are often poor and their record of graduate employment placement is mediocre. In the post-industrial era, non-academic professional and administrative costs grew from 40 percent to 70 percent of university budget spending while university performance measured against key indictors remained static or declined. Most serious of all, the models of post-industrialism promised the vitalization of creative economies and societies. The converse occurred. Per capita rates of discovery in the arts and the sciences declined in the post-industrial era. Fewer major works of note were produced compared with earlier historical periods. Political concern with providing more and more university places had detrimental effects. It muddied the social goal of advancing knowledge. It moved focus away from high-level creation and discovery—even when (in doing so) it deployed the rhetoric of creation and discovery. OECD countries in 2008 were less creative and less proficient in the arts and sciences than they were in 1908. By way of illustration, the US rate per capita of patent registration peaked in 1914. Since the discovery of the DNA double helix by Crick and Watson in 1953, the per capita number of high-level science breakthroughs has diminished markedly. The half-life of contemporary scientific knowledge is short—meaning its obsolescence factor is high. Much of its experimental results are never verified and the failure rate of retested results is also high. While universities expanded massively during the post-industrial era, per capita research productivity inversely declined. No more than 20 percent of 'teaching and research' academics in OECD universities routinely produce research, even if most relish the kudos and social status of a discovery university.

A common theme highlighted by extant studies and biographical accounts of creative figures in the arts, sciences and the professions is self-education. High-level creators flourish when they have access to first-class libraries and laboratories and first-class intellectual models. Together, these provide a powerful context for the adventive mind. The twin imperatives of self-education and intellectual modelling animate the forms, structures, expectations and needs of the autodidactic discovery university. Its overarching goal is discovery. Its meaning and motion derive from this goal. A university of this kind provides its students with an apprenticeship in discovery. There are many techniques for achieving this. Large libraries, broad curricula, interdisciplinary freedom, one-on-one research-based tutorials, small seminars, public lecture series, project-based learning, research-based assessment, and student-staff societies are common examples. Most important though is a pervading ethos of inspired objectivation. The auto-poietic university is a place for learning how and witnessing how the act of creation takes place. That requires the direct observation of acts of discovery as they happen, as professors write books, conceive experiments, give papers, submit articles, posit artworks, and profess fresh ideas.

Discovery universities are small in size and number. They are devoted to vigorous intellectual discovery through self-directed pedagogy and research. The discovery university relies heavily on autodidactic learning. It is a place of self-direction. The institutions of the library and the laboratory are at the heart of it. Compared with this, most contemporary universities offer a form of 'higher schooling.' The discovery university is defined not by the transmission of knowledge but by the adventurous finding of knowledge. Its first task is creation. Its second task is to prepare those who one day will do the same. Classically this is achieved by self-education supported by the superlative modelling of creative action.[10] The auto-poietic archetype of learning is borne out by a century of studies of creative cohorts in the arts, sciences and the professions. Discovery is the apprehension of previously unobserved relations and forms. It manifests itself in learning, teaching, research, and innovation. While discovery is not identical to research, research typically accompanies discovery-based learning. The chief medium of both is the imagination. Research and discovery-based learning call upon similar capacities. Both require high levels of autonomy and both are marked by a strong propensity to objectivation, that is, the positing of intellectual and symbolic objects. These range from undergraduate research essays and reports through the graduate thesis to the book, artwork, model, exhibit, patent, and paper.

Through the post-industrial era, social engineering decimated the ecology and media of the imagination both in the universities and in the larger society. The

---

10   Albert Jay Nock, 1932: 73, observed: 'Let us speak of the university and the undergraduate college. Traditionally, the university was an association of scholars, grouped in four faculties Literature, Law, Theology and Medicine. When I say an association of scholars, I mean that it was not quite precisely what we understand by a teaching institution. The interest of the students was not the first interest of the institution. Putting it roughly, the scholars were busy about their own affairs, but because the Great Tradition had to be carried on from generation to generation, they allowed certain youngsters to hang about and pick up what they could; they lectured every now and then, and otherwise gave the students a lift when and as they thought fit. The point is that the whole burden of education lay on the student, not on the institution or on the individual scholar. Traditionally, also, the undergraduate college put the whole burden of education on the student. The curriculum was fixed, he might take it or leave it … Moreover, he had to complete it pretty well on his own, there was no pressure of any kind upon an instructor to get him through it, or to assume any responsibility whatever for his progress, or to supply any adventitious interest in his pursuits. The instructor usually did make himself reasonably helpful, especially in the case of those whom he regarded as promising, but it was no part of the institution's intention or purpose that he should transfer any of the actual burden of education from the student's shoulders to his own, or contribute anything from his own fund of interest in his subject by way of making up for any deficiency of interest on the part of the student.'

consequence of this is that the kinds of eccentric, wide-ranging, free-wheeling, difficult and demanding intellectual modes, milieu and means—necessary for the brightest of the bright from all backgrounds to flourish—have diminished. In all but a handful of universities, these often-astringent intellectual methods have been replaced by the pedestrian media of the textbook, the unread weekly reading, and the content-starved power-point-driven lecture course. The latter deliver on fiercely audited political goals to increase social mobility and promote status-climbing by increasing 'participation' in higher education but these also marginalize and trivialize high-level intellectual formation and bore senseless the most intellectually-gifted students. In the end, a paradox is created. Everyone wants to have the glittering prize but to achieve that goal the glittering prize has to be destroyed.

There are a number of practical ways by which nations and universities can reverse this situation. The intent of proposing these is to overcome the tyranny of tedium that has been unleashed on the gifted, to find ways of re-birthing the media of the imagination at the heart of the university and in the wider society and restore a congenial place for adventurous minds. Rather than post-modern 'participation,' 'access' and 'mobility,' which have become tiresome clichés (rolled out by glib political actors) or worse still meritocratic dystopias (promoted by over-professionalized ghouls), there is a need today to think about pathways and destinations for the modest numbers of bright or highly-curious individuals, many of whom (in their student days) will fail exams, drop out, write papers that are out of their depth but for whom intellectual excitement and audacity matters, and who we know (from the evidence of very good studies) in the end will form a small but socially-essential cohort who are highly creative and who deliver virtually all of the lasting and transmittable achievements across the arts and sciences, in business and the professions.

Chapter 1
The Creativity Deficit

The Sciences

The rate of creativity in OECD countries is in decline. It has been so for a long time. A pronounced downturn began in the 1970s. This fall closely tracked the rise of mass higher education. A noticeable sharp downward turning-point occurs around 1974. This is when the post-industrial, post-modern era began.[1] The rhetoric of the knowledge society supposed an age of intense creation. The actual record of the period was tepid. The mass university was the signature institution of the post-modern, post-industrial era. The singular failure of the era was the failure of that institution. It promised much but delivered little.

Universities relentlessly expanded after 1970—in number and size. They employed ever-more academic staff, which meant ever-more presumptive researchers. The same was true of large corporations with R&D departments and dedicated government scientific research institutions. In 1950, the number of scientists and engineers engaged in research and development in the United States was one quarter of a percent of the workforce. By 1993 that figure had risen three-fold—to more than three quarters of a percent.[2] Yet the rise in unique discovery in the period was not three-fold, far from it. The Stanford economist Charles I. Jones put it rather delicately when he said that 'if we double the number of researchers looking for ideas at a point in time, we may less than double the number of unique discoveries.'[3] Indeed so. After 1970, OECD countries spent a large amount of money on research and yet achieved only a minimal amount of advancement in the arts and sciences.[4] The Australian case is typical. From 1993 to 2010, the amount Australia spent on the external funding of university research rose from $751,300,000 to $3,070,703,000 (all amounts in 2010 dollars), a four-fold real increase.[5]

---

1 Daniel Bell wrote one of the great studies of the post-industrial era. Bell 1973: 263 credited Robert Lane with coining the phrase 'the knowledge society' in Lane, 1966.

2 Jones 2000: 220.

3 Jones 2000: 223.

4 In the post-modern era, employment in research and development per capita in OECD countries grew markedly. It tripled in West Germany and France and quadrupled in Japan between 1965 and 1989. From 1994–2008, GERD (gross domestic expenditure on R&D) as a percentage of GDP rose from 2.1 percent to 2.3 percent across the OECD, from 2.4 percent to 2.75 percent in the United States, and from 2.6 percent to 3.4 percent in Japan.

5 Data source: Australian Government Higher Education Research Data Collection (HERDC) 1992–2010 archived at Universities Australia: https://www.universitiesaustralia. edu.au/ArticleDocuments/410/HERDC1992–2011.xls.aspx In 2011, Australia's Department

In the same period, the output of research journal articles grew from 21,183 to 33,928, a 1.6-fold increase.[6] The size and return on investment in medical research is both revealing and typical of the dead-end of post-modern creation. In 1947 the United States government established the National Institutes of Health (NIH) funding body. In that year its budget was $8 million. In the 2009 fiscal year its budget was $29.5 *billion* dollars.[7] In real terms, accounting for population growth and inflation, American federal government spending on medical research had grown 237 times in the intervening period.[8] Did breakthrough discoveries multiply by a factor of 237? No. What about by a factor of just 23? No. Australia's National Health and Medical Research Council was established in 1937 with funding that year of £30,000 or $2.5 million in 2013 inflation-adjusted dollars. Two future Nobel Laureates, J.C. Eccles and F.M. Burnet, received funding in the first NHMRC funding round. The average grant size in 1937 was £728 or $61,440 in 2013 dollars.[9] In 2013, 825 projects were funded for $663.65 million, or $804,000 per project, 13 times the 1937 real cost. Australia in 1939 had 605 full-time academic staff (and an additional 30 percent FTE of part-time academic staff), around 800 FTE; compared with 48,000 in 2011. Between 1937 and 2013, the Australian population grew from 6.8 million to 22.3 million, 3 times; academia grew 60-fold; NHMRC funding grew 161 times over. Despite the massive increase in external funding, ironically the most important bio-medical research discovery to come from an Australian lab was

---

of Innovation, Industry, Science and Research attempted to measure the performance of Australia's research internationally. In Appendix A of the report, *Focusing Australia's Publicly Funded Research Review*, Graph 1.3.2 tracked the 1992–2008 increase in Australian publications per 1000 population from 0.8 to 1.6, a 2-fold increase. This calculation was based on the Thomson-Reuter database which while comprehensive is nevertheless selective in its range of journals (presently at around 12000). In contrast, based on the much more complete HERDC data (above), the calculation for Australian journal article publications per thousand population rises from 1.07 journal articles per capita in 1992 to 1.4 articles per capita in 2008, a 1.3-fold increase. *Focusing Australia's* Graph 1.3.3 showed that Australia's relative citation rate (the ratio of citations per Australian paper compared with the global average) went from 1 to 1.2 over the period 1992–2008. Broadly the same improvement was achieved by all the leading comparator nations in the same period. The 1.2-fold increase in citations relative to the global average also reflected almost exactly the modest 1.3-fold increase in absolute and relative Australian publication output over the period. That is, as Australia produced slightly more publications, so Australian research articles were slightly more cited.

6   In absolute terms, in 1995 Australia was the largest research producer after Japan. In 2009 it had fallen to fifth, behind China, Japan, South Korea and India (Marginson, forthcoming).

7   Cole 2009: 184.

8   $US135 spending in 1947 equated $US1000 in 2005 (Cole: 184); US population rose from 144 million in 1947 to 306 million.

9   In 1966, the Council awarded over $1 million, or $9.15 million in 2003 dollars, 3 percent of the actual 2003 expenditure.

not externally funded.[10] Barry Marshall and Robin Warren earned the 2005 Nobel Prize in Medicine for their 1984 work on the cause of peptic ulcers. The breakthrough research that they did during the period 1982 to 1984 was funded in-house by Fremantle Hospital not by an external funding agency.

Costs rise in the bio-technology sector not least because the cost of developing new drugs rises not least because research costs rise. Yet what results do we get for all of that investment? The answer is surprisingly little anymore. Charlton and Andras, and also Wurtman and Bettiker, observe that the big developments in bio-medical science took place between 1935 and 1965 with key advances occurring in antibiotics, glucocorticoid steroids, hormone replacement therapies, psychiatric drugs, surgical technique, anesthetics, and DNA.[11] Le Fanu identifies the period between 1940 and 1975 as the era of major clinical discovery.[12] The rate of major clinical advances since has declined. Developments in cancer therapies, psychiatric drugs, and new antibiotics have slowed to an incremental pace that is marked by a marginal benefit increase, often severe side-effects, and very expensive clinical trialing.

An auspicious mid-twentieth-century period of bio-medical science was followed by a marked increase in human life expectancy for those born between 1960 and 1980.[13] Female life expectancy (at birth) in Australia in 1901 was 58. In 1980 it was 78.

---

10 Martyr 2014.

11 Charlton and Andras, 2005; Wurtman and Bettiker, 1995. '[O]ver recent decades the rate of major clinical breakthroughs has probably declined, even as claims for the importance of medical research have grown more exaggerated. Perhaps the major deficiency of current therapy is the lack of significant progress in treating common solid cancers such as brain, lung, bowel, prostate, ovary and breast, which together make-up the main cause of mortality in developed countries. Available therapies typically offer only modest or marginal benefit, detectable only in very large clinical trials, and usually at the cost of severe side-effects. In psychiatry the major classes of useful drugs all date from before 1965, excepting the selective serotonin re-uptake inhibitors (SSRIs) which (like the neuroleptics and the tricyclic anti-depressants) were synthesized in the early 1970s by chemically modifying a 1940s anti-histamine (i.e. chlorpheniramine/Piriton). In other words the developmental strategy underpinning SSRIs was not new. The phenomenon of a declining frequency of breakthroughs seems common to many medical specialties. Furthermore, the output of effective new drugs for serious diseases, such as novel classes of antibiotics, seems to be drying-up.' Charlton and Andras, 2005.

12 Le Fanu, 2012. Wurtman and Bettiker, 1995, listed the following as conditions that were defeating medical research: multiple cancers, congestive heart failure, Alzheimer's disease, stroke, alcoholism, drug abuse, AIDS, motor neurone disease, emphysema, and autoimmune diseases. Since 1965 there have been new drugs developed but most of these represent incremental advances on previous treatments only. Another avenue of advance has been serendipitous off-label uses of drugs. The Australian finding that peptic ulcers could be treated with antibiotics is a case in point. Yet, as Wurtman and Bettiker also note, such findings do not attract research funding. Serendipitous discovery represents a very cost-effective form of inquiry.

13 http://www.aihw.gov.au/australian-trends-in-life-expectancy/.

Over an 80 year span, life expectancy increased 20 years. By 2006 life-expectancy had increased a further five years to 83. While in this later period life expectancy had increased, the rate of increase slowed from a one year increase every four years to a one year increase every five years. At the same time, real levels of funding for medical research had catapulted. By the 2000s funding in real terms vastly exceeded by many orders of magnitude that of the propitious 1930–1960 era of medical science, the era of Howard Florey and Frank Macfarlane Burnet. Yet scientific outcomes were visibly on the wane. In a more general sense, in the post-industrial era the measure of scientific success shifted from outcomes to inputs. The more money secured for research, the more successful research was. Excepting that it wasn't.[14]

Post-modern scientific achievement lagged both behind its promises and its predecessors (see Table 1.1). Big science endeavors like the International Space Station (ISS) promised breakthroughs in materials science ('smart materials') yet little came of it.[15] Small-scale science with tiny numbers of researchers meanwhile is starved even of miniscule funds. Small science is mocked. Today instead science is 'all about teams' and the 'age of the lone researcher in the Patent Office (Einstein) is over.' Fields like cosmology and particle physics still inspire yet in recent decades the discoveries they have produced have fallen short of the excitement they have generated. The ideas of supersymmetry, the multiverse and string theory (no matter how interesting these are in principle) have not led to cascading theoretical or practical applications. Conversely, bigger telescopes and more powerful particle accelerators and colliders do not, alas, mean better ideas. Quantum mechanics consolidated as a field in the 1920s. It laid the foundation 30 years later for the transistor (1947), the laser (1958) and the micro-chip (1958). It continues to generate ideas and applications and even social science metaphors. Meanwhile alternate-energy research and climate-change research produce far fewer compelling findings than advanced fundamental research does, yet they receive much higher levels of funding. In general in the post-modern age, the more money that has been spent the

---

14   The funding-trumps-all mentality of post-modern research is well illustrated by the response of the US National Institutes of Health to the serious outbreak of the ebola virus in West Africa in 2014. Responding to the crisis, the Director of the NIH commented: 'Frankly, if we had not gone through our 10-year slide in research support, we probably would have had a vaccine in time for this that would've gone through clinical trials and would have been ready.' Ebola was first discovered in 1976, in the Democratic Republic of Congo; a second major outbreak of the virus occurred in Africa in 1994. Between 1994 and 2013 the funding of the NIH increased in real terms (measured in 2003 constant dollars) from $14.6 billion to $21.1 billion (Johnson, 2013). It reached a peak in the Bush Administration years of $27 billion (in 2003). Funding for the National Institute of Allergy and Infectious Diseases, the primary infectious diseases research body, rose from $19 billion in 2000 to $24.6 billion in 2014 (in constant 2000 dollars). Declining income is a myth. It serves instead to cloak the declining performance of research institutions that look ever-more like lobbies for money rather than bodies for discovery.

15   The toughened glass used in the contemporary smartphone is an everyday example of such a material. Research on chemically-toughened glass began in the 1960s.

Table 1.1   Key Figures by Decade of First Major Work

	1900s	1910s	1920s	1930s	1940s	1950s	1960s	1970s	1980s	1990s
Photographers	3	3	8	20	8	21	17	21	18	12
Photographers per million capita	0.006	0.006	0.014	0.032	0.012	0.029	0.022	0.025	0.020	0.012
Film Directors	1	27	42	34	44	67	116	80	68	32
Film Directors per million capita	0.002	0.050	0.072	0.054	0.065	0.093	0.148	0.095	0.075	0.033
20th C Painters	6	7	6	4	1	5	1	0	0	0
20th C Painters per million capita	0.012	0.013	0.010	0.006	0.001	0.007	0.001	0.000	0.000	0.000
20th C Scientists	37	41	55	50	33	18	14	13	11	3
20th C Scientists per million capita	0.076	0.076	0.095	0.080	0.049	0.025	0.018	0.015	0.012	0.003
20th C Composers (Art Music)	4	6	1	6	5	7	3	1	3	4
20th C Composers per million capita	0.008	0.011	0.002	0.010	0.007	0.010	0.004	0.001	0.003	0.004
Key Works										
Top 100 literary novels	6	4	20	12	19	20	12	4	2	0
Novels per million capita	0.012	0.007	0.034	0.019	0.028	0.028	0.015	0.005	0.002	0.000
Combined European and North American Population (millions) per decade	490	536	582	627	673	719	782	846	909	973

Data Sources: Painters: C. Murray, *Human Accomplishment*, 2005; Google Ngram, 1950–2008; Composers: C. Murray, *Human Accomplishment*, 2005; The Guardian, *A Guide to Contemporary Classical Music*, 2012–2013; Google Ngram, 1950–2008; Film Directors: Schneider, *501 Movie Directors*, 2008; Photographers: R. Golden, *Masters of Photography*, 1999; C. Dickie, *Photography*, 1999; P. Stepan, *50 Photographers*, 2010; *Professional Photographer*, 100 Most Influential Photographers; *Digital Camera World*, 55 Best Photographers of All Time; Scientists: C. Murray, *Human Accomplishment*, 2005; Garwin and Lincoln, eds, *A Century of Nature*, 2003; Literary novels: *Le Monde's* 100 Books of the Century, 1999.

Note: Painters and composers in Murray with an index-ranking 8 or above are included. The index-rank is a quantitative measure of attention to figures in reference literature. Murray stops at 1950; figures after 1950 whose incidence of mentions in the Google book archive equal or exceed that of a 8-rank Murray figure are also included. Scientists in Murray with an index-ranking 8 or above are included; lists of science figures after 1950 are based on Garwin and Lincoln.

less significant have been the outcomes. Neither money nor technology produces the theories about the world whose applications create world-making technologies and economies. The logic of Big Science is upside down. What the logic of discovery of Big Science regards as effect is cause—and vice versa. The promises of Big Science consequently continue to disappoint.[16] There are advances, spin-offs and applications from its projects. The technology of particle accelerators (as an example) has contributed to MRI technology, medical linacs, security scanning, and synchrotron light sources. But not on the scale (for example) of the advances, spin-offs and applications that came out of the small-scale science of Bohr, Dirac, Fermi, Heisenberg, Planck, Schrödinger, and Pauli.[17] The argument is not that post-modern science did not produce work of significance but rather that it did so less often than its predecessors, especially once the comparative scale of funding and population is taken into account.

The post-modern era was an age of proxies. Every imaginable substitute for the real thing—from peer review to citations to research income—served as a meager replacement for actual discovery.[18] Instead of measuring discovery, the many bureaucracies of the mass university system measured anything-but-discovery in a futile attempt either to avert or ignore the underlying decline in breakthroughs, the nub of discovery.[19] Thus while cancer treatments continued to

---

16   The pioneer geneticist Sydney Brenner suggests why: namely, having different ideas is important: 'But today there is no way to do this without money. That's the difficulty. In order to do science you have to have it supported. The supporters now, the bureaucrats of science, do not wish to take any risks. So in order to get it supported, they want to know from the start that it will work. This means you have to have preliminary information, which means that you are bound to follow the straight and narrow. There's no exploration any more except in a very few places.' The discoveries of Brenner and his close colleagues were done against the grain. '[A]ll the others sort of thought that there was something wrong with us. They weren't willing to believe. Of course they just said, well, what you're trying to do is impossible. That's what they said about crystallography of large molecules. They just said it's hopeless. It's a hopeless task.' Dzeng 2014.

17   'To get a graphic appreciation for the growth in the research establishment, it is instructive to look at pictures of participants at any of the Solvay congresses held between the world wars. There are only a few dozen people in any one of these pictures, but they usually contain most of the creators of modern physics, scientists like Bohr, Einstein, and Heisenberg. Today, a typical physics conference has hundreds or thousands participants, and there are many more conferences than before.' Andrew Odlyzko, AT&T Bell Laboratories, 1995.

18   Arbesman and Christakis 2011 argue for focusing on discovery rather than on citations. As for peer review: '[Peter Higgs'] first paper was rejected by a journal, while other scientists accused him and his colleagues of failing to grasp the basic principles of physics.' Collins 2012.

19   What are provided instead are endless promissory notes, as in this all-too-typical headline: 'DNA map *offers hope* on cancer treatments. Cancer will become a manageable disease rather than a death sentence thanks to a revolutionary treatment which will be available within five years, British specialists predict'—from the UK *Daily Telegraph*, 28 January 2013. Two matters stand out from this report by medical correspondent Stephen

improve incrementally, definitive therapies or vaccines remained elusive as did a unified theory of the cause of cancer. The gene associated with the Huntington's degenerative neurological disorder was discovered in 1993. Yet a cure for the Huntington's malady remained stubbornly out of sight. William Rutter and colleagues at the University of California in San Francisco isolated the gene for insulin in 1977. This allowed the mass production of genetically-engineered insulin. Yet both the cause and cure of diabetes continued to elude researchers. The point is not that there is not good research but rather more simply that the rate of incidence of it has over time declined.[20] Retroviruses were connected to the HIV-AIDS condition in the early 1980s and life-extending antiviral suppressant therapies emerged quickly thereafter. And yet no vaccine for the condition has been discovered despite the large investment in research in the area. The 2.7 billion dollar Human Genome Project (1990–2003) mapped the sequence of chemical base pairs that make up the 25,000 or so genes in human DNA. The project promised clues to deciphering the causes of diseases. A decade on, some breakthroughs had been achieved but fewer than expected. The cystic fibrosis gene was discovered in 1989 after a $50 million search. Yet while median survival rates for the genetic mutation disorder improved markedly through improved treatments, currently there is still no effective gene therapy and no cure for the disease. Diseases, it appears, do not necessarily have 'linear' genetic causes but rather 'complex' multi-causal origins, suggesting conceptual problems that neither funding nor large-scale organization will solve.[21]

Adams, first is the announcement of promises rather than results; second is the admission that research is not heading for a cure, confounding medical science's ultimate promise. 'All patients will soon have their tumour's DNA, its genetic code, sequenced, enabling doctors to ensure they give exactly the right drugs to keep the disease at bay. Doctors *hope* it will be an important *step towards* transforming some types of cancer into a chronic rather than fatal disease. The technique *could* enable terminally ill patients, who can currently expect to live only months, to carry on for a decade or more in relatively good health, according to specialists at the Institute of Cancer Research in London. "We should be aspiring to cure cancer, but for people with advanced disease, it will be a question of managing them better so they survive for much longer—for many years," said Prof Alan Ashworth, chief executive of the institute' (emphasis added).

20   At the time of writing, two promising lines of inquiry for Type 1 and 2 diabetes were announced by Harvard scientist Douglas Melton and teams from Boston's Beth Israel Deaconess Medical Center and California's Salk Institute. Melton's experimental success in cell re-programming was the outcome of 23 years of research

21   As science writer Philip Ball 2009 observed: 'to judge from some of the hyperbole it elicited, you would think that it has provided us with a complete instruction manual for the human body. But it does not do that at all. The Human Genome Project has created a bank of genetic data that is sure to be of immense medical value, and which contains a great deal of information about how our cells work. But for biological questions that have a genetic component (and not all of them do), the respective genes are just the beginning of an answer. Most of these genes encode the chemical structures, and thus the chemical

It is important to point out that it is not only government investment in ideas that has been, to a significant degree, fruitless. The same has been true of industry. Consider journalist Michael Mandel's observation about the multitude of promises that were made in the late 1990s about the then-coming bio-medical and other 'revolutions.'[22] The world was assured of breakthrough cancer treatments, gene therapies, stem cell therapies, tissue engineering, high-speed satellite Internet, cars powered by fuel cells, micro-machines on chips, and so on. What happened to such products, Mandel asked? A decade on, he noted that no gene therapy had been approved for sale in the United States. Rural dwellers could get satellite Internet but the service was far slower than what had been promised. The terrible economics of alternative energy had not changed much in a decade. And while the bio-technology industry had produced some important drugs—such as the cancer drugs Avastin and Gleevec—Mandel reflected that the gains in health care had been disappointing compared with the sums invested in research.[23]

Indeed they have. Nightingale and Martin noted that between 1980 and 2003 there had been a seven-fold increase in patents but a 10-fold increase in R&D spending in the pharmaceutical industry.[24] The number of drugs approved by the US Food and Drug Administration in the same period increased through to the mid-1990s and then sharply decreased to 2003. The authors noted that this performance was even worse when we consider the 8-to-12 year time lag between research and product release and then compare that with the substantial increase in R&D expenditure between 1970 and 1993. Dorsey et al. in 2010 concluded the same. Private and public funding of drug research in the US doubled in real terms between 1994 and 2003 but the number of new drug approvals by the US Food and Drug Administration declined. The decline continued through to 2008. The more that was spent the less was produced. Despite huge investments, Nightingale and Martin observed that only 16 bio-pharmaceuticals evaluated between 1986 and 2004 showed more than 'minimal improvement' over existing treatments.[25] From

---

functions, of proteins. The issue is how the production (or absence) of a particular protein affects the network of biochemical processes in the cell, and how this gives rise to the particular physiological consequences that we are studying.' In effect: 'we know that the presence or lack of a gene in the genome is linked to a certain manifestation at the level of the whole organism, but we do not know why.'

22   Mandel 2009.

23   See also for example Horrobin 2000.

24   Nightingale and Martin 2004.

25   In a similar vein, Herper 2011 noted that broadly speaking the 'number of new drugs approved every year by the Food and Drug Administration has remained constant, even as scientists have learned a great deal more about biology ...' Pammolli, Magazzini and Riccaboni, 2011: 429 observe the 'accumulating evidence of a long-term decline in the productivity of research and development (R&D)'. Their own study, based on the large Pharmaceutical Industry Database (PhID), concluded that from 1998 to 2008, the number of NMEs approved per year mostly declined, while attrition rates (the project failure rate), development times and R&D expenditures increased. They attribute the research failure

the 1980s going forward, recombinant DNA techniques were widely touted yet as of 2003 they were responsible for only a handful of successful new drugs. The US Food and Drug Administration approved 2891 new drugs in the 1950s and 964 in the decade of the 2000s. The number of new molecular entities approved for drug use in the United States in the 2000s was barely more than in the 1950s.[26]

The *Economist* magazine in a 2005 report made an interesting point.[27] The modern pharmaceutical industry began with the re-discovery of penicillin by Alexander Fleming in 1928 and the development of its use as a medicine by the Australian Howard Florey, the German Ernst Chain and the Englishman Norman Heatley. What is notable is that between 1930 and 1970, drug research operated on the basis of serendipity and it was successful. Come 1970, the ethos changes. The biotechnology model of rational drug design, high-throughput screening and genetic engineering takes over. Big things were expected of this. The result though was that only little things happened. It seems after all that the serendipity of the individual investigator cannot be replaced. The word serendipity, in case you are

---

to market disincentives to focus on incremental innovation and to chase areas of high uncertainty and risk. But the latter is the point of research, even when it builds, at it almost always does, on the past. The contemporary problem is not the lack of increments but rather the lack of fundamental outcomes. Cockburn 2007 questions whether there is a research productivity crisis, arguing that nominal expenditure is not real expenditure (though that is widely understood even by non-economists); results lag expenditure by a decade (also generally understood) and the sheer numbers of approvals of New Molecular Entities are not everything: after all, not every new molecular entity approved will be a blockbuster. He argues rather for quality-weighting of drugs, suggesting, reasonably, that today's drugs, using rational drug design are 'better' than their predecessors: they have great efficacy, fewer side effects and easier dosing. Yet even Cockburn notes the basics: that 'no new broad spectrum antibiotics have been marketed in almost 40 years, and chronic diseases and disorders such as atherosclerosis, diabetes, obesity, Alzheimer's, Parkinson's, and schizophrenia still lack effective and well-tolerated treatments.' In short, refinement of drugs is not the same as the discovery of new classes of drugs. It is ironic that Cockburn says we don't account for the quality of incremental innovation while Pammolli, Magazzini and Riccaboni say we don't incrementally innovate. Scannell, Blanckley, Boldon and Warrington 2012 point out that the number of new US Food and Drug Administration (FDA)-approved drugs per billion US dollars of R&D spending in the drug industry has halved approximately every 9 years since 1950, in inflation-adjusted terms. That figure matters. They offer four explanations: the 'better than the Beatles' problem (existing successful drugs are a barrier to new drugs in the same field); the 'cautious regulator' problem (which increases research costs); the 'throw money at it' tendency (the obverse of the stochastic innovation process); and the 'basic research–brute force' bias (the move away from older methods of identifying drug candidates and the adoption of possibly false methodological assumptions such as that drugs have a single target, something that could explain why the old costly labour-intensive model of animal testing, well-adapted to modelling complex biological causation, produced more cost-effective research than the nominally-inexpensive molecular assays of today).

26   FDA 2013.
27   The Economist Intelligence Unit 2005: 18.

interested, was coined by the English man of letters and Whig politician Horace Walpole in 1754, writing to Horace Mann. Walpole devised the term after the heroes of the Persian fairy tale *The Three Princes of Serendip* who 'were always making discoveries, by accidents and sagacity, of things they were not in quest of.' Walpole's word points to the tangential, off-beat nature of discovery that no systemic or institutionalized process can replicate.[28]

The Arts

In decline along with the sciences are the arts. Economics, political thought and philosophically-inflected theory in the last century have been major sources of ideas in the social sciences and humanities. Since the 1970s their energies have clearly subsided. There is the odd exception, such as the newish discipline of International Relations, but mostly high-level work both in the humanities and the social sciences peaks in the 1970s, and diminishes thereafter (see Table 1.2). In part this can be explained by factors internal to the universities, where the larger portion of social science and humanities research takes place. There are matters that we shall look at presently, such as the bureaucratization of the mass university, that explain the flagging of the university mind. But the evident dissipation of the intellectual strengths of the university in the post-modern era is not peculiar to the university. That is a point that needs underlining throughout this entire discussion. While the university contributes to the broader culture, it is also a function of the broader culture. The depleting of the university reflects the depleting of the larger culture. The condition of the university is both a cause and a consequence of what has happened in the larger culture.

The larger culture is in trouble. The creative arts are a good example of this. The post-industrial university to an extent colonized the creative arts, as they did so many other areas of teaching and research, from journalism and social work to education. That said, though, the vast majority of creative art and design work still takes place outside of the universities, in a mix of private and corporate studios, labs and offices. What is striking is that the creative impulse outside the universities in the post-modern era proved to be as anemic as that inside the universities. This suggests that creative institutions generally did not fare well in the era. The era

---

28   The following is a classic example of serendipity in science: 'Huge advances in the treatment of high cholesterol and high blood pressure have led to a sharp decrease in the number of strokes in the past 16 years. The prescription of statins, drugs administered to lower cholesterol levels, has been credited with helping to dramatically lower rates of strokes amongst older people, the group most vulnerable to the condition. More than 8 million Britons take statins, whilst an additional 6 million take drugs to lower blood pressure. The incidence of strokes has fallen from 247 per 100,000 in 1995 to 149.5 in 2010, according to research from King's College London. Higher awareness of medical check campaigns and healthier lifestyle choices are also credited with helping to reduce rates.' Williams 2013.

Table 1.2   Key Works in the Humanities and Social Sciences by Decade in the Twentieth Century

	1900s	1910s	1920s	1930s	1940s	1950s	1960s	1970s	1980s	1990s*	2000s*
20th C Key Works in International Relations				1	7	30	62	79	130	170	50
Key IR works per million capita				0.002	0.010	0.042	0.079	0.093	0.143	0.175	0.048
20th C Key Works in Religious Thought	8	6	12	7	7	33	65	41	35	33	22
Key religious thought works per million capita	0.016	0.011	0.021	0.011	0.010	0.046	0.083	0.048	0.039	0.034	0.021
20th C Key Works in Historical Thought	4	5	11	20	21	23	40	71	46	43	37
Key works by historical thinkers per million capita	0.008	0.009	0.019	0.032	0.031	0.032	0.051	0.084	0.051	0.044	0.036
20th C Key Works in Economics	10	12	24	31	22	34	37	46	36	29	22
Key economic works per million capita	0.020	0.022	0.041	0.049	0.033	0.047	0.047	0.054	0.040	0.030	0.021
20th C Key Works in Political Thought	27	42	54	44	49	73	88	133	112	54	
Key works of political thought per million capita	0.055	0.078	0.093	0.070	0.073	0.102	0.113	0.157	0.123	0.055	
20th C Key Works in Theory	5	6	14	17	37	37	91	128	104	60	
Key theory works per million capita	0.010	0.011	0.024	0.027	0.055	0.051	0.116	0.151	0.114	0.062	
Combined European and North American Population (millions) per decade	490	536	582	627	673	719	782	846	909	973	1036

Data Sources: John Lechte, *Fifty Key Contemporary Thinkers: From Structuralism to Post-Humanism*, Routledge, 2007; Steven Pressman, *Fifty Major Economists*, Routledge, 2006; R. Benewick and P. Green, *The Routledge Dictionary of Twentieth-Century Political Thinkers*, 1998; Gary Kessler, *Fifty Key Thinkers on Religion*, Routledge, 2011; Martin Griffiths, Steven C. Roach, M. Scott Solomon, *Fifty Key Thinkers in International Relations*, 2nd edition, Routledge, 2008; Marnie Hughes-Warrington, *Fifty Key Thinkers on History*, 2nd edition, Routledge, 2007.

*1990s figures for works by political thinkers projected for the decade, based on part-decade, 1990–1996 list; 1990s figures for Theory works projected for the decade, based on part-decade, 1990–1995 list; 2000s figures for Economics works projected for the decade, based on part-decade, 2000–2005 list; 2000s figure for International Relations works projected for the decade, based on part-decade, 2000–2007 list.

excelled in messages about creativity yet its creative output relative to population was paltry. The post-modern age was a master of the rhetoric, signs, logos and emblems of innovation but was a poor practitioner of what it preached. Creativity, along with education and the environment, was part of the secular faith of the era. The rhetoric of secular faiths replaced religion. But hardly ever was the promise of those secular faiths realized.

What is at stake here are works that have long-lasting social effects and that have great social, existential and utilitarian significance. High-level creation is difficult to measure in the contemporary moment as opposed to the distant past. Contemporaries find it tough to distinguish between greatness and glibness in their own time. Special pleading ingratiates creative work that is specious. Power, influence, office and status magnify the importance of works that make no lasting contribution to the arts or the sciences. To make a plausible judgment of greatness (or not) in our own era, we have to step aside from the feeble rhetoric of the booster and look at some hard numbers. Consider then what has happened in the creative arts. In the visual arts, the period between 1890 and 1970, i.e. between Cezanne and Rothko, was outstanding. What followed was dismal. Too often the visual art of the post-modern era was forgettable. Exceptions—like Gerhard Richter or the late-period David Hockney—unfortunately only proved the rule, not least because they first produced artefacts in the 1950s. Contemporary post-2000 digital media art works were occasionally interesting but lacked the kind of stickiness (the durable claim on social memory) that great works in general secure. The media arts fused technology and the arts, moving them close to the STEM disciplines and away from the humanities. This intensified the wider tendency for social aesthetics to replace capital-A Art. This took aesthetics out of the galleries and into everyday life and industry.[29] Yet as their ambivalent name suggests, the media arts lacked the kind of strong conceptual identity that marked the modernist era in art. Since the end of the modernist period, art has been dominated either by kitsch concepts or weak concepts.[30] Correspondingly, the judgment of Time on

---

29   Murphy 2014; Murphy and Fuente 2014.

30   'About 100 art enthusiasts and professionals gathered at Traffic on Saturday, February 26 and Sunday, February 27 [2011] for a two-part lecture by Canadian economist Don Thompson. Professor Thompson is renowned for his bestselling book *The $12 million Stuffed Shark: the Curious Economics of Contemporary Art and Auction Houses*. Over the two lecture sessions, Thompson discussed the state of the global art market leading up to the 2008 financial crash. Throughout the 90's and into the new millennium art prices spiraled toward the stratosphere. Thompson's main observation is that branding had supplanted critical judgment, citing advertising magnate Charles Saatchi and his role in making Damien Hirst (creator of the stuffed shark) the most successful artist of all times. Thompson noted that the top selling artworks over the last three decades have all been conceptual pieces, have all been made in multiples, and have all been made by technicians, not the artists themselves. In addition to the stuffed shark installation, which is famously named 'The Physical Impossibility of Death in the Mind of Someone Living,' other examples included works by Jeff Koons, Andy Warhol and Takashi Murakami, among others.' Brown 2011.

post-modern art has been severe. The Canadian economist Don Thomson in 2008 calculated that, of the 1,000 artists with major gallery shows in London and New York in the 1980s, only 20 of those artists were offered in evening auctions in Christie's or Sotheby's in 2007. Art without traction, art that is not memorable, art without longevity, is not art.[31]

The contemporary creative deficit applies just as much to 'popular-marketed' artworks as it does to 'elite-gallery' artworks. *Rolling Stone* magazine's 2012 music industry poll of the top 500 music albums lists 11 works from the 1950s, 105 from the 1960s, 187 from the 1970s, 82 from the 1980s, 75 from the 1990s, 38 from the 2000s and two from the truncated 2010s.[32] This collective judgment, and the arc of creation it reveals, is an accurate one. More interesting still are the figures from the 1970s. Technically the creative output of the 1970s exceeds that of the 1960s, excepting that when one drills down into the figures, what is revealed is that 50 percent of the best 1970s albums came from the first four years of the decade (the years 1970–1973), and immediately after that point there is sharp drop-off in first-class output. The distinct downward shift after 1973 pin-points the general problem of creation in the last 40 years.

Writing in the *Wall Street Journal* in 2012 Camille Paglia asked *'Does art have a future?'* That was a very good question. She noted that, while some artistic genres have remained relatively speaking healthy—notably performance genres like opera, theater, music and dance—the visual arts have been in acute decline for four decades (see Table 1.3 below). What I find interesting about the decline of the visual arts is that it is *not* exceptional. Rather it is typical and not just of the arts but of the arts and sciences as a whole. As Tables 1.1, 1.2 and 1.3 indicate, the general state of the arts and sciences in the latter third of the twentieth century was one of atrophy. The key creative figures counted in the tables are figures with a broad, recognized and durable cultural impact. These are figures producing works of lasting significance.[33]

---

31 Don Thomson 2008: 26. Everything enters the world with ephemeral characteristics but some things defy their own rapid extinction. They last. Serious creation bequeaths new things that endure. These are the acts of modernity that survive into their own knowing antiquity. When art succeeds, fashion transmutes into tradition. As soon as art stops producing durable things, it stops creating. The paradox of art is that its passing fancies, trends, tastes, rages and vogues at most are ornamental entrées and appetizers for the creation of objects that are long-lasting. If art cannot do that, it fails. If it cannot create objects that are resilient in the face of Time and that provide human beings with a canopy of meaning that is stable and permanent, then the work of creation has failed.

32 The list was principally based on two industry surveys, one in 2003 of 271 industry experts and one in 2009 of 100 industry experts.

33 The lists of pre-1950 key figures are drawn from Murray (2003). These are 'major' figures; most of them have entered into public consciousness, especially figures from the arts and humanities. They are separate from Murray's more encyclopedic 'significant figures' that are recognizable principally by experts. Significant figures are 'important enough to the development of a field that a well-versed student of that field is likely to be familiar with them' while major figures are that readily recognized 'subset of people who

Table 1.3   Key and Significant Painters by Decade in the Twentieth Century

	1900s	1910s	1920s	1930s	1940s	1950s	1960s	1970s	1980s	1990s*
20th C Key Painters	7	5	5	10	2	2	5	1	1	1
20th C Key Painters per million capita	0.014	0.009	0.009	0.016	0.003	0.003	0.006	0.001	0.001	0.001
20th C Significant Painters	17	33	27	38	31	26	31	24	25	35
20th C Significant Painters per million capita	0.035	0.062	0.046	0.061	0.046	0.036	0.040	0.028	0.028	0.036
Combined European and North American Population (millions) per decade	490	536	582	627	673	719	782	846	909	973

Data Source: The Twentieth Century Art Book, Phaidon, 1996; C. Murray, *Human Accomplishment*, 2005; Google Ngram, 1950–2008.

Note: (*)1990s figures are projected for the decade, based on a part-decade 1990–1995 list. The Phaidon volume is the source of the significant figures; key figures are painters listed in Murray whose index-rank 8 or more. Murray stops at 1950; figures after 1950 whose incidence of mentions in the Google book archive equal or exceed that of a 8-rank Murray figure are also included.

They are the rare individuals that affect society's view of itself and of nature. In traditional fields—such as painting, art music and the core sciences—any post-1950 figure has to sit comfortably alongside an Einstein or a Dirac, a Stravinsky or a Picasso. That proved in practice difficult. In the less traditional fields, such as film and photography, matching a John Ford or a Man Ray was still possible in the 1960s and 1970s and (in film's case bolstered by world cinema) the 1980s—see Table 1.1. Yet, even then, as Tables 1.1 and 1.4 illustrate, genres like art-music, which appear to be comparatively vital in recent times, nevertheless show nothing like the vigor of their counter-parts in the nineteenth century or the Renaissance or the modernist decades of the first half of the twentieth century.

That is to say, a genre such as art music looks good only because the state of the traditional visual arts is terrible. Or as Paglia puts it: 'no major figure of profound influence has emerged in painting or sculpture since the waning of Pop Art and the birth of Minimalism in the early 1970s.' In the post-modern era, there were sizeable numbers of secondary and tertiary figures who produced significant works of interest now listed in the encyclopedias of twentieth-century art. Yet no painter of true first rank emerges after Johns, Warhol, Richter, Lichtenstein, and Hockney—all of whose first works were executed in the 1950s. And as goes the first tier, so goes the second and third tiers of art—and the broader culture as well. On the whole, as Table 1.2 illustrates, there was a general decline in cultural output after 1970. The commercial arts fared better in the second half of the twentieth century than did the fine arts. Again Paglia's judgment is accurate: we find recent work of originality and beauty in architecture, 'a frankly commercial field.' The examples that she cites of outstanding work—'Frank Gehry's Guggenheim Museum Bilbao in Spain, Rem Koolhaas's CCTV headquarters in Beijing and Zaha Hadid's London Aquatic Center for the 2012 Summer Olympics'—sit comfortably in the architectural

---

are crucial to understanding the development of a field' (Murray: 478). The significant and major figures listed in Murray's inventories of accomplishment are persons to whom scholarship devotes a large amount of column inches or numbers of pages or image plates. Murray's lists of 'major' figures concur with virtually any comparable lists, both expert and amateur. Murray's lists are based on the measurement of pages, columns and plates devoted to arts and science figures in multiple expert encyclopedia and reference-works. But there is also a deep social consensus about major pre-1950 figures. The judgments of experts, taste-makers and lay opinion-makers converge. Murray's lists stop in 1950. He was aware that contemporaries tend to disagree more about who is important in their own time. Notwithstanding that, N-gram google searches have been used to search for significant post-1950s figures. This allows the repeated mention of contemporary figures to be compared to the rate of mention of older figures in recently published books. A measure of significance is whether the mention of a contemporary figure in books published since 1950 matches or exceeds the recurring mention in those books of older figures of established importance. As to the permanence of the judgments that are made: lay, taste-maker, and expert judgments change with time, and new figures appear, and some older figures fade from memory but this does not mean that the incidence of figures per decade changes that much. Fertile periods remain fertile periods; arid periods remain arid.

pantheon of the last two centuries, no mean feat. And yet in all of the arts, even in the commercial arts like architecture and photography, where we have long-term points of comparison, we find that the rate of incidence of exceptional works and figures has declined: a tell-tale sign of what has happened in the broader culture.

Exceptional works and major figures play a particular role in life. Intellectual and artistic works play many roles. They charm, they inform, they clarify, they direct, they entertain—and so on. Exceptional works, and their authors, do something in addition. These works evoke worlds. It does not matter if they are artworks or works of social science, they are all works of imagination in that they inspire in the human imagination of readers, listeners and viewers a sense of a world that is more intense, more profound, and more illuminated than the everyday world of the immediate and the familiar. Such works, and there is only ever a relatively small number of them, are capable of shaping both individual souls and social structures. They communicate in an instant that they are capable of giving form, which is to say that they suggest that their forms can be lived in. We can imagine living in a Vermeer or Mondrian-like world just as we can imagine living in an Aristotelian or Cartesian world. We may not wish to do so or choose to do so—but that is not the point. The mind sees in these precipitate forms depth and wholeness and dimensionality that most works of the mind or hand, no matter how competent or proficient they are, do not summon up. These are the most profound works of the imagination and because they have such effects they become (as C.S. Lewis put it) 'indispensable.'[34] That is, they intimate worlds that you cannot anticipate before you encounter them, and then, once you have encountered them, you cannot forget them.

Most works of the mind and hand, while they might be useful or pleasant or informative, are not unforgettable. Most works do not shape either the soul or society even though they may have numerous other admirable qualities. They may even be significant works and find their way into expert catalogues and compilations but they are still not indispensable. They do not enter resolutely into the common wealth of the human imagination, teasing out its contours. Painting is a good example. You see the difference clearly across the twentieth century. The indispensable work is concentrated in the early decades of the twentieth century. Interesting but not indispensable work continues to be created in the latter decades of the century. And, tellingly, as the indispensable work shrinks, the rate of production of interesting works also declines. For indispensable work sets the tone for the culture as a whole. Marked by its absence, ours is a time of waning across all tiers.

Power Law of Research

So—what happened? Paglia is right to ask: what 'sapped artistic creativity and innovation in the arts?' She identifies two major causes of decline: one is the rule of ephemera; the other is the rule of ideology. She observes that, when painting

---

34   Lewis 2000: 485.

Table 1.4   Key Figures by Century of First Major Work

	15th C	16th C	17th C	18th C	19th C	20th C
Painters	20	19	12	14	23	28
Painters per million capita	**0.333**	0.224	0.100	0.085	0.076	0.039
Novelists	2	18	17	37	86	91
Novelists per million capita	0.033	0.212	0.142	0.224	**0.285**	0.127
Scientists	7	32	57	93	278	275
Scientists per million capita	0.117	0.376	0.475	0.564	**0.921**	0.382
Composers (Art Music)	3	7	7	17	42	40
Composers per million capita	0.050	0.082	0.058	**0.103**	**0.139**	0.056
Combined European and North American Population (millions) mid-century; 15–16 C Europe only.	60	85	120	165	302	719

Data Sources: C. Murray, *Human Accomplishment*, 2005; Google Ngram, 1950–2008; Le Monde's 100 Books of the Century, 1999; J.H. Tiner, *100 Scientists Who Shaped World History*, 2000; J. Balchin, *Science: 100 Scientists Who Changed the World*, 2003; L. Garwin and T. Lincoln, eds, *A Century of Nature*, 2003.

Note: Painters and composers in Murray with an index-ranking 8 or above are included. The index-rank is a quantitative measure of attention to figures in reference literature. Murray stops at 1950; figures after 1950 whose incidence of mentions in the Google book archive equal or exceed that of a 8-rank Murray figure are also included. Novelists in Murray with an index-ranking of 8 or above are included; the last listed is for 1938; figures after 1938 are drawn from Le Monde's 100 Books of the Century, 1999. Scientists in Murray with an index-ranking of 8 or above are included; supplemented by post-1950 figures listed in Garwin and Lincoln, eds, A Century of Nature, 2003.

was dethroned by the multimedia revolution of the 1960s and 1970s, 'permanence faded as a goal of art-making.' With permanence went significance. In its place rose up various kinds of fake significance—not least that generated by a relentlessly intellectual-oxygen-depriving left-liberal political orthodoxy. That is all true so far as it goes. However, the problems encountered by art are also only a sub-set of the problems encountered by discovery as a whole. At the end of the day, what we have experienced is a decline not just in the creative arts or the humanities or in the social sciences or the natural sciences. Rather the decline has occurred across the spectrum of the arts and the sciences. The over-arching problem is the decreasing ability of both the arts and the sciences to produce works of lasting significance—that is, works of permanent value.

At the moment when the multiple-decades-long post-modern creative recession began in the 1970s, the philosopher Cornelius Castoriadis observed that the social impetus to discovery had begun to wane radically.[35] At the time he was virtually alone in noting this. The post-modern decades were filled with creative boosters often of a very pretentious kind. Today Castoriadis' then-rather-lonely observation has been elegantly confirmed by Dean Keith Simonton. Simonton is Professor of Psychology at the University of California at Davis. He has spent four decades writing about creativity. In 2013 in the journal *Nature*, he bluntly stated that the kind of scientific originality that characterized the eras of Michelson and Morley or Einstein had abated.[36] Imaginative leaps today have become much rarer.[37] Domain-specific expertise now dominates science—and while scientific

---

35 ' ...Hegel thought that he understood the rise and fall of cultures. I do not think he really did. All he could say was that the spirit of a certain people (*Volksgeist*) had exhausted itself, which is, of course, a tautology. When we look at a culture on the rise, we see an amazing number of geniuses and great oeuvres, as well as the genius of the entire community. For instance, Pindar, Aeschylus, Sophocles, and many important philosophers existed within a short span of time, along with the buildings of the Acropolis and the Demos of the Athenians. This same sort of extraordinary string can be seen from Dante and Giotto through Shakespeare and Bach to Proust, Kafka, Joyce, and Picasso. And then, in the same places, with the same geography, under the same sun, the 'same' people, practically the 'same' society does not create anything new. For centuries it just goes on imitating, rather poorly, what has been done before—like the thousands of statues remaining from the third century B.C. to the victory of Christianity. Even if you know nothing about sculpture, it is impossible to confuse these with the products of the previous period. I think that the same phenomenon is starting to happen today. This is what has been called postmodernism: eclecticism and imitation. In fact, it is a rather cheap version of Alexandrianism. The only really significant contribution of postmodernism is that is has shown how great and creative modernism was.' Castoriadis 1979, which was the basis of the 1986 English-language paper published in Castoriadis 1991b.

36 Simonton 2013.

37 '... "Science at the margins, where great discoveries are made, is in a total mess," says Don Braben a physicist and honorary professor at UCL. He fears that even the established scientific nations, including the UK, have drastically undermined their ability to conduct blue-sky research, the kind of free-wheeling activity with the potential to make genuine scientific

knowledge still advances, it does so (on the whole) without expanding the deep-set foundations of our understanding of nature.

The problem, as Castoriadis saw it, was that we had entered an age of insignificancy.[38] The rule of insignificancy applies to the micro, meso-, and macro-levels of creation. Human beings—who are social beings—generate both significance and insignificancy in ways that range from the highly specific to the historically epic. In our time, insignificancy is produced by institutional mechanics at the micro level and by the social passion for big organization at the meso-level. On the epic scale of modern history there appears to operate a kind of long-term entropy. At the micro level we witness the hilariously-misconceived criteria of value—everything from vacuous creativity clichés to specious external grants criteria to extraneous impact measures. All of these are creatures of a social world that equates creation with organization and that has sought (rather unsuccessfully) to institutionalize and professionalize discovery. This institutionalization is a function of a meso-level phenomenon: the bureaucratization of the world. In turn, the bureaucratization of the world is both a consequence and an expression of a macro-level phenomenon: the long-term entropy of modern creation. That is to say, at the highest level the shrinkage of discovery is a socio-cultural problem that has long historical roots while at the most elementary level the micro-workings of our research institutions are filled with countless counter-productive traits of recent origin.

The Micro-level: Ephemeral Impact

In place of lasting significance, institutions at the micro-level devise all kinds of measures of ephemeral pseudo-significance. A common-place example is the habit of governments and universities to substitute for discovery misleading proxies

---

leaps, thanks to the introduction of peer-reviewed grant applications. "Many of the scientists like Einstein and Planck who made the major discoveries of the 20th century wouldn't have got funding under today's rules," he says. "Until 1970 good scientists were guaranteed some money just to think. Not anymore." The result, he says, will be countless missed opportunities to answer great mysteries on everything from human consciousness to the nature of gravity. A letter laying out this argument, prepared with four others scientists and signed by an international group of 50 researchers, including nine Nobel laureates, was sent to the science minister, David Willetts. "We've yet to get a reply," Prof Braben says' (Day, 2011). Braben's group objected to the use of impact statements in the assessment of grant applications. Braben provided the Minister with a list of 11 ground breaking but unpredicted discoveries that he believed would not have attracted funding if an impact assessment had been made at the project formulation stage. In response, Dr Graeme Reid, the deputy director of economic impact in science and research at the UK Department for Business, Innovation and Skill, said that the UK research councils' peer review system was regarded as an 'international benchmark of excellence,' suggesting to the observer that three words—'international,' 'benchmark' and 'excellence'—had become a perfect storm of bureaucratic meaningless (Jump 2010).

38   On post-modern culture as a culture of insignificance, see Castoriadis, *Postscript on Insignificance* 2011.

like citation counts and impact factors. These encourage researchers to research a popular topic not because the underlying concept is interesting but because the work will enhance a career—on the grounds that research in a popular area is more likely to get cited. And yet we know that the hotter a scientific field is the less likely research findings are to be true.[39] We know that in the hottest disciplines, the half-life of citations—the point at which 50 percent of articles in the field are no longer cited—is typically very short, the antithesis of enduring intellectual value.[40] We measure the 'impact' of journals similarly by measuring the average number of citations received per paper published in a journal normally during the two preceding years. Yet it is the lasting nature not the passing stir of research that matters. What 'impact factor' of a journal ends up measuring is the sensation of the moment. This reduces research to a tabloid phenomenon.

The Meso-level: The Power-Law of Research

What is most interesting at the meso-level of creation is the problem of scale over time—that is how big or small institutions of discovery are, how the evolution of their size over time has affected research, and what size (how big or small) they should be in principle. Simply put: the bigger that the arts, the sciences and the universities grow, the more they expand beyond an optimal size, the lower is the incidence of per capita creativity, and the more that the rate of unique discovery in the arts and sciences slows. A way of better understanding this is to revisit the instructive work of Derek Price. Price was a physicist and a historian of science. He was one of the founders, along with Alfred Lotka, of the field of bibliometrics. In 1963 Price identified a key statistical pattern of research publishing. This is Price's square root law of research. To fully understand the significance of Price's square root law, some additional background is first necessary.

The origin of Price's Law goes back to the pioneering 1926 paper by Alfred Lotka on the frequency distribution of scientific productivity. In that paper Lotka examined a large sample of scientific publication data. The bulk of Lotka's data came from the 1907–1916 series of *Chemical Abstracts*. This encompassed 6,981 contributors to the chemistry research literature who had produced 22,939 research records. Lotka's sample was the entries under letters A and B of the *Chemical Abstracts*.[41] The key thing that Lotka identified was the highly skewed distribution of research output. Simply put, a very large amount of

---

39   Ioannidis 2005: 698. Ioannidis was recruited by Stanford University to head up its Meta-Research Innovation Center, a center for the study of bad science (Diep, 2014). Part of the remit of the center is to look at the problem of studies that are poorly designed and that can't be reproduced by independent researchers, or that are based on poor statistical analysis or otherwise are invalid.

40   Abersman 2012.

41   A second sample was drawn from Auerbach's *Geschichtstafeln der Physik* for the years 1900–1910.

research is produced by a small number of researchers, while a large number of researchers produce a small amount of output each. If we revisit Lotka's original *Chemical Abstracts* data, what that reveals is an average output per person per annum of 0.33 items, a third of an item per year. In contrast, the average output for the top 10 percent most frequent contributors was 1.68 items per person per annum. The top 1 percent produced 5 items per person per annum. The top 2 percent produced four items per person per annum. The bottom 58 percent of authors contributed 1 item in a decade and 17 percent of the total output. The top 25 percent of the most frequent authors contributed 73 percent of the total.[42] Wayne Dennis confirmed this pattern of output. He found a similar skewed distribution in a 1955 study.[43]

Lotka noted other patterns in the data that he had collected. In particular he observed that the number of persons making two contributions to the research literature was about one-fourth ($=1/2^2$) of those making one contribution, those making three contributions was about one-ninth ($=1/3^2$) of those making one contribution, and so on. Those who made 100 contributions were about one-ten-thousandth ($=1/100^2$) as common as the single contributor. Lotka offered a law of research output in light of this observed pattern: the number making n contributions is $1/n^2$ those making one contribution. Derek Price subsequently re-formulated Lotka's Law. Price proposed that if there are n numbers of scholars in a field then the square root of n will produce 50 percent of papers in the field. Thus, for example, if there are 100 scholars in a field, then ten of them will produce 50 percent of the papers in the field. If there are 1000 then 31 will produce 50 percent of the papers.

Dean Keith Simonton later noted that Price's Law was a simpler yet cruder and thus less accurate measure of predicted output than Lotka's.[44] However Price's starting point was different from Lotka's. Price wanted to answer the leitmotif of Lotka's paper. 'It would be of interest,' Lotka had declared 'to determine, if possible, the part which men of different caliber contribute to the progress of science.' This is what Price pursued. The question of research productivity was important but secondary to the question of research caliber. That said, Price and others including Simonton concluded that productivity and caliber were nevertheless strongly correlated.[45] High caliber researchers tend to be very

---

42   Or in simpler terms, 20 percent of academics produce 80 percent of published output, which is a variant of the Pareto Principle named for the Italian economist Vilfredo Pareto by Joseph Juran, the engineer and quality management theorist. Pareto had observed that 80 percent of land in Italy was owned by 20 percent of Italians, an insight he formed after observing that 20 percent of the pea pods in his garden contained 80 percent of the peas—much like universities.

43   Dennis 1955; see also Simonton 1984: 78–80. The skew is even more pronounced for journal readership. Urquhart 1958: 293 calculated that less than 10 percent of serials satisfied more than 80 percent of reader demand.

44   Simonton 1984: 80.

45   Price 1963: 40–41. Price drew on Wayne Dennis' 1954 study of the US National Academy of Sciences *Biographical Memoirs* for 1943–1952. This showed that of the 41

productive even if the converse cannot be guaranteed, *viz.* that a highly productive researcher is of a high caliber.[46] Either way, the number of productive researchers and the number of eminent researchers is small. What Price defined was a law of caliber. Price proposed that the total number of scientists is the square of the number of good ones—or conversely, the number of stellar contributors to a field is the square root of the total number of contributors to the field.

Small Science

The implications of Price's Law are significant. It means that good science is *small* science. This is true as much for the arts as it is for the sciences. And for the creative arts it is doubly true. Even more so than the sciences, a very tiny number of highly productive creators dominate the visual and performing arts. Employing more researchers and creators cannot reverse the law of small numbers. If anything, it intensifies it.

In 1963, Price observed that the time it was taking for the number of scientists to double was three times faster than the time it was taking for the general population to double.[47] More than anything, this fostered the delusions of the post-modern age about its own cognitive capacity. The problem with this hyper-rate of growth of science personnel—impressive as it sounds—is that the number of eminent contributors to a field over time cannot grow faster than the rate of population growth. This means that if a field is growing faster for a long time than the general population is, then the larger the field gets, the poorer the field becomes. The same applies to the arts and sciences as a whole. Price made the imperishable point: increasing the number of researchers may increase the number of research papers but it will not increase the number of distinguished papers.[48] The number of persons who create work that is exceptional, accomplished or noteworthy remains

---

figures who had a full life and a full career, the average number of publications was more than 200—and only 15 figures had less than 100 publications to their name.

46   Derek Price tried to compensate for this problem by proposing that we can measure caliber by the number of citations of an authors' works (Price 1963: 78). This began the vogue for measuring the impact of scholarship. The difficulty though with this measure is two-fold. First, 80 percent of cited works are unread. That is, citation is a phenomenon of a celebrity culture in which works become well-known for being well-known. Simkin and Roychowdhury (2005, 2003) calculate that only 20 percent of cited work is read. The second problem relates to what Price dubbed the 'half-life' of citations (79–81). Citation falls off with the age of a publication. Many works are cited for short lengths of time and then afterwards are not cited. Many fields also have short citation periods. The half-life of a field is that point (X years) when half of all references in a field are made to papers less than X years old. Whether it is a whole field or an individual paper or book, it is not clear that the rapid obsolescence of knowledge, even highly-cited knowledge, is a good thing. Vogue knowledge, irrespective of the sensation that it causes, is not really knowledge in any durable sense.

47   Price 1963: 14.
48   Price 1963: 54.

a constant proportion of the larger population. Growing the number of scientists or artists faster than the growth of the general population does not change that fact.

This is because, as Price also observed, while every doubling of the population had produced at least three doublings of the number of scientists (as far back as the seventeenth century), the number of entries in dictionaries of national biography over time remained a constant proportion of the population. In 1874 Francis Galton calculated that 1-in-20,000 of the general population is an eminent person and 1-in-100,000 of the general population is an eminent scientist.[49] If we include the social sciences, humanities and creative arts, the latter figure becomes 1-in-75,000 persons.[50] Price noted that the starred names in J. McKeen Cattell's 1903–1960 biographical dictionary *American Men of Science* made up a portion of the population similar to that which Galton had calculated.[51] In the 50 years prior to 1963, the numbers of American scientists grew 16-fold, doubling about every 12.5 years. The American population in those 50 years grew two-fold (from 92 million to 179 million). The post-industrial era replicated this growth differential on a mass scale. For example, from 1989 to 2009 full-time faculty in American degree-granting institutions expanded from 524,000 to 728,000, a 0.4 increase while the general US population grew from 246 million to 307 million, a 0.2 increase, half of the rate of the faculty increase.[52]

This confounded the modus operandi of high-level creation. Until the appearance of big science, big arts and the big university, this work involved tiny numbers of practitioners operating in small milieus. We have reversed this. We have created large institutions and hired a large number of practitioners and we have ended up with comparatively miniscule results. This does not mean we get no significant results but we do get relatively far fewer of them. Straightforwardly put: big science does not work, big social science does not work, the big humanities and the big arts do not work. Above all big universities and big university sectors do not work. The big university works no more than big government does. Indeed the former is simply an extension of the latter. Even though numbers in the arts and science outstripped population growth from the 1450s onwards, the numbers of scientists and artists in the population still remained tiny relative to population until the twentieth century. Even if nineteenth-century bohemians had an exaggerated opinion of themselves, no one talked about a creative class in their time. There was no creative economy for officials and commissions to collect statistics about. The power of tiny numbers is a recurrent feature of outstanding culture and science.

---

49 Galton 1874: 6, 9–10; Price 1963: 36.

50 Galton 1874 calculated there were 300 eminent scientists in the United Kingdom out of a population of 28 million persons. An additional 60 (17 percent of the expanded total) would capture persons from the social sciences, humanities and creative arts, based on today's academia. In 2009, Australia had 45,000 academics, of which number 8,000 were from social, cultural and creative fields (Hugo 2011).

51 Price 1963: 36.

52 National Centre for Education Statistics 2011 Table 257.

But what exactly do we mean by big or small? How big is big and how small is small? As previously noted, Francis Galton calculated that the number of eminent scientists in the population was 1-in-100,000 persons. If we add social, cultural and creative fields, that scales to 1-in-75,000 persons. We can extrapolate from that. Universities have eminent, distinguished and talented faculty. Let us further assume that 1-in-75 faculty is eminent, 6-in-75 is distinguished, and the others (68-in-75) are talented. Now let us take the case of Australia. Its 2009 population was 21 million. That predicts 280 eminent academics and an academic population of 21,000. In actuality Australia had 45,000 full-time academic staff in 2009, about twice as many as the model would predict.[53] One can infer that the university sector in advanced countries should be half the size it is today.

The illusion of the post-industrial knowledge society was that we could multiply discoverers faster than the general population—and its constant fraction of inventive souls—grew. This is just not possible to do. In fact, at the level of disciplines, the obverse is true. That is to say, more is less. Consider the case of economics. In the 1930s and 1940s it was an intellectually powerful discipline. It was distinguished by figures like Schumpeter, Hayek and Keynes. One of them (Hayek) even predicted the onset of the Great Depression. He was almost alone among economists in doing so. Consider then the effects of time and size. The American Economic Association (AEA) had 572 members in 1893, 2621 members in 1936 and 16,944 members in 2009. Using Price's Law, that gross membership translates to 23, 51, and 130 outstanding contributors respectively.[54] It is little wonder then that, in 2008–2009, in response to the global financial crisis most of the American and international economics profession endorsed Keynesian pump-priming government-spending techniques that in the past had repeatedly failed.[55] These techniques had almost zero effect in reversing the world's economic downturn. The economic advisors to the Obama Administration predicted that,

---

53 Australian universities operate with 25 equivalent full-time students per academic staff member; the United States with 16. If Australia had 21,000 academics with 525,000 students (or 336,000 students using the American scale) spread among (say) 40 institutions, that would equate somewhere between 13,000 or 8,000 students per institution, depending on the staff: student ratio. Australia arguably last had a right-sized university sector, with one academic for every 1000 persons in the general population, in 1970. In 2009 in Australia, there was twice that number of academics per 1000 in the population.

54 Murray (2003: 92). Even though he cites studies (Moles 1958; Zhao and Jiang 1985) where Price's Law accurately predicts outcomes, Murray also speculates that the larger the group, the less accurate that Price's Law becomes. This is a charitable reading of the situation; in reality, the meagre intellectual fruits of large group dynamics suggests otherwise. Murray's own view (82) of the declining quality of the arts after 1950 is predicted by Price's Law.

55 The failures included the 10 stimulus packages the Japanese government employed to try and re-ignite the Japanese economy in the 1990s. It invested 100 trillion yen in the exercise to no effect, excepting the massive accumulation of public debt. It tried another 11.5 trillion yen stimulus in 2008, again to no effect.

as a result of its super-sized $831 billion stimulus spending package in 2009, the unemployment rate in the United States in the third quarter of 2013 would be 5 percent.[56] In the third quarter of 2013 it was still 7.2 percent.[57]

What is at issue here is not simply predictive failure, though the predictive failure is serious. What is also at issue is the near-unanimous support of economists for theories that spawn wrong predictions.[58] Unanimity points to intellectual conformity, hardly the animating spirit of discovery. Underlying this is the mono-culture of a discipline grown too large—and the accompanying failure of imagination. The discipline's mono-culture is reflected in the voting and political preferences of American economists. Klein and Stern surveyed AEA economists.[59] The researchers reported that very few (3 percent only) of 264 survey respondents held strong free-market views. Most either leant toward or supported government activism. The Democrat-to-Republican voting ratio of American economists is 2.5:1. There is nothing surprising in those figures. With the rise of the mass university came political homogeneity followed by intellectual homogeneity.[60] Even though one might have expected the growth in the size of the university sector to have increased intellectual diversity, the converse happened. The consequence is that when poor predictions occur, as they will, there are now very few faculty left proposing alternative theories that offer different predictions.

Declining predictive power is a sign of sciences that are in trouble. So also is the rapid obsolescence and outright invalidity of knowledge. It is well-established that the post-modern era had a problem with truth. Truth implies that knowledge is accurate, sound and reliable. Yet much of what presents as knowledge today is

---

56   Romer and Bernstein 2009: 6.

57   Due to the decline of labour market participation, the level of unemployment was in reality higher again than this.

58   Indicative of this is the very large number of economists (9,440) who signed Paul Krugman's 2012 ultra-Keynesian manifesto http://www.manifestoforeconomicsense.org/

59   Klein and Stern 2007.

60   Fosse and Gross 2012 report that 'voter registration records of faculty at the University of California, Berkeley and Stanford reveal that of the 67 percent for whom information could be obtained, almost 50 percent were registered Democrats and about 5 percent Republicans (Klein and Western 2004–5; but see Cohen-Cole and Durlauf 2005). A national survey of faculty in six social sciences and humanities showed ratios of Democratic to Republican voters somewhere between 7:1 and 9:1 (Klein and Stern 2004–5). A 1999 study of faculty in all fields reported that 72 percent identify to the left of center and 15 percent right of center; that 50 percent are registered Democrats, compared to 33 percent Independents and 11 percent Republicans; and that faculty attitudes display "an across the board commitment to positions that are typically identified with contemporary liberal ideals" (Rothman et al. 2005:8). Another faculty survey using a more articulated scale found that percentages of liberals, moderates, and conservatives fall around 48, 31, and 17, respectively; that in the 2004 elections 72 percent reported voting for John Kerry and 25 percent for George Bush; and that professors hold liberal views on business and the free market, support for international institutions, and separation of church and state (Tobin and Weinberg 2006).'

none of those things. In 2002, Thierry Poynard, his co-researchers, and the expert reviewers they called-in, looked at almost 500 articles on the liver diseases cirrhosis and hepatitis published between 1945 and 1999 in the journals *Gastroenterology* and the *Lancet*. What they found was that 285 of 474 conclusions (60 percent) were still considered to be true, 91 (19 percent) were obsolete, and 98 (21 percent) were false. Derek Price had observed that truth had a half-life. The half-life of truth is the point at which 50 percent of the published research on a subject is either out-of-date or wrong. Poynard and colleagues concluded that the half-life of the truth of the research that they examined was 45 years. That is not really very long. Following Price's lead, Samuel Arbesman nick-named this: the half-life of facts.[61] Obsolete knowledge is unavoidable to a point. But how much obsolescence, and what speed of obsolescence, and how much accumulated false knowledge, can be borne by science or social science before its credibility is shot? The advancement of knowledge ought not to be confused with the progress of knowledge. Knowledge *advances* when additional true knowledge is discovered and secured. In contrast, knowledge *progresses* by the belated discovery of falsehood and the consequent disposal of it. The latter gives us short discipline half-lives. This is a lot less compelling than the accumulation of durable knowledge.

Related to the fascination with falsification is the desire to dispense with truth as a skeptical check on claims to knowledge. Consequently today many fake facts and spurious explanations flourish.[62] One reason for this is that invalid findings of scientific studies are accepted as valid at the time they are produced because no one bothers to test, double-check, or even doubt them, especially results that serve the needs of lobbies and ideologies.[63] 'Science says' or the 'study reports' has become the effective pseudo-validation of knowledge (see Figure 1.1). Baseless

---

61   The half-life of the citation is shorter still than the half-life of truth: '[A] study of all the papers in the *Physical Review* journals, a cluster of periodicals that are of great importance to the physics community, found that the half-life in physics is about 10 years. Other researchers have even broken this down by subfield, finding a half-life of 5.1 years in nuclear physics, 6 years for solid-state physics, 5.4 years in plasma physics, and so forth. In medicine, a urology journal has a half-life of 7.1 years, while plastic and reconstructive surgery is a bit more long-lived, with a half-life of 9.3 years ... [Derek] Price himself examined journals from different fields and found that the literature turnover is far faster in computer science than psychiatry, which are both much faster than fields in the humanities, such as Civil War history.' Arbesman 2012.

62   'Dietary science' provides good examples: see the case of the purported link between saturated fat and heart disease. For five decades this link was retailed as fact based on what recently has been revealed to be a very shoddy, biased University of Minnesota study—the conclusions of which were subsequently taken up by one of the many powerful health science lobbies, the American Heart Association (Teicholz 2014).

63   Begley and Ellis' 2012 paper in *Nature* reported on the work of a team of researchers who over a period of 10 years had been able to reproduce the results of only 11 percent (six) out of 53 landmark papers in preclinical cancer research that they had reviewed. Another study from Germany could only reproduce the results of 25 percent of published papers reviewed. Many of these had appeared in 'high-impact' journals and they had high mean citation rates.

verification is often correlated with science that has turned itself into a public lobby or advocacy enterprise. Eventually its findings will be falsified but by other studies years later. In between time, billions in public spending can rest on specious science. This is especially so when the post-modern age increased the propensity of authors to make statements like 'science tells us' or 'the science is settled.' In doing so, the public posture of science moved from the skeptical to the authoritarian.

The past 40 years has seen a significant decline in the arts and sciences. This is, directly and indirectly, the predicted effect of the operation of Price's Law. In 1963, Price forecast the eventual entropy of all intellectual fields in the sciences due to the spiritual dominance of each field's periphery.[64] What he predicted for the natural sciences is equally true of the social sciences, the creative arts and the humanities. As a field grows rapidly or exponentially for a time, its long tail and its shallow margins eventually overshadow and dilate the strong yet always tiny core. Nominally knowledge may be produced in greater absolute quantities yet this occurs with diminishing intellectual returns. As a field grows, knowledge is stripped of imagination. Emphasis tacitly falls on dissemination in place of creation. Knowledge becomes characterized incrementally by ever-larger portions of tepidness, ineffectuality, and inhibition.[65] In such a context, fewer and fewer great works are incubated. The ecology of dissemination is different from the ecology of creation. The larger the field grows, the larger becomes the gap in numbers between core and peripheral contributors. Dissemination, interpretation, and spreading-the-word are crucial to inquiry. Researchers need readers. Yet there is a point at which dissemination feeds back into the discovery core and corrodes it. Intellectual fields are like super-nova stars. Beyond a certain point, their growth is the prelude to entropy and eventual extinction. These fields burn their creative fuel. They die out. This is what is happening to contemporary research.[66]

---

64   The post-structural theory of the margin then is the correct self-representation of the age of insignificance. Jacques Derrida's theory of infinite deferral captures the spirit of much of the research of the era. It was always coming but never actually arrived.

65   Carroll, 2008: 143–58.

66   Larsen and Ins 2010. Evidence is drawn from the major journal publication and citation indexes excepting the Arts and Humanities Citation Index but including Chemical Abstracts, Compendex (engineering), Cambridge Scientific Abstracts, Inspec (Computers/ Control Engineering, Electrical/Electronic Engineering, Manufacturing and Production Engineering and Physics), LNCS (Lecture Notes in Computer Science), MathSciNet (American Mathematical Society), Physics Abstracts, PubMed Medline (National Library of Medicine), Science Citation Index (Thomson Reuters), Social Science Citation Index (Thomson Reuters), Scopus (Life Sciences, Health Sciences, Physical Sciences, and Social Sciences and Humanities). Larsen and Ins estimate that around 24,000 serious journals exist. The citation databases cover a significant sample of these. In 2008 for example the Science Citation Information Expanded (SCIE) list covered 6,650 journals and the Social Sciences Citation Index (SSCI) covered 1,950 journals.

The Macro-level: Long-term Entropy

Derek Price (1963 and 1965) calculated that over the historical long run, between 1650 and 1950, the numbers of records in science journals (articles, reviews, notes, abstracts, etc.) had grown at an annual rate of 4.5 percent and had doubled every 10 to 15 years.[67] Examining the evidence for the period between 1907 and 2007, Larsen and Ins in 2010 calculated that in the aggregate the rate of doubling has been subsequently maintained. Yet beneath that headline number, a much bleaker picture emerges—with the rate of growth of core science disciplines declining sharply.[68] This is set out in Table 1.5 (below). The headline figure in fact is only secured by compensating growth in the applied science disciplines of medicine, computer and electronic engineering, and technology. And these we have already seen are displaying evident weaknesses in their capacity to generate derivative applications and products. At the same time, the core sciences (mathematics, physics and chemistry) have been sharply declining since 1974 with doubling times increasing to the 20- and 30-year scale.[69] If the core sciences look bad, then consider the state of the social sciences. The growth rate for the Social Science Citation Index for the period 1987–2006 was 1.6 percent per year for all records and 2.0 percent per year for journal articles. The corresponding doubling times were 44 and 37 years. By the standard measure of modern scientific growth, the social sciences are dying. Mathematics, chemistry and physics are not far behind.

Data from a Google N-gram word and phrase search of the Google Books database reveals a similar picture.[70] See Figure 1.1 (below). Use of the terms mathematics, physics and chemistry declines after 1964; biology after 2000; engineering after 1990; computer science after 1990. The incidence of bio-technology and information-technology words flat-lines in the decade of the 2000s. Biomedicine is a rare word-cluster that continues to grow. The terms social science, sociology and political science decline after 1970 and economics does

67   Price 1963, 1965.

68   A core science as well as a core social science is measurable by the half-life of the literature in the discipline (Arbesman, 2012). In a core science, published work is cited for much longer periods of time than in disciplines that are not core. The end-life of a paper or book is the time after which it is no longer cited. The half-life of a field of research is when half of the publications in the field are no longer cited. Redner 2005; Tonta and Ünal 2005; Price 1970; Tang 2008.

69   One of the ironies of the timing of this downward trend is that it follows soon after the introduction of one of the classic supposed guarantees of journal 'quality,' peer review, which appears as late as the 1960s and 1970s. The journal *Nature* introduced it in 1966. The bureaucratic category of 'quality' however can never do what it pretends to do. Process is not a substitute for intellectual judgment nor can it ensure it.

70   The results measure the incidence of the selected words or phrases in a given year, thereby normalizing for the varying number of books published in different years. The database contains 5.2 million books published between 1500 and 2008, containing 500 billion words.

so after 1990. Philosophy, history and literature as well as art and architecture sit on a two-century plateau that is broadly speaking static. The absence of growth in the humanities is reflected in publication output (see Table 1.6 below).[71] The rate of growth of publications per annum since 1975 has been substantially less than even the social sciences. After 1970, the humanities did not share in the post-modern knowledge industry boom. Relative to the rest of the universities sector, a major drop in humanities enrolment in universities occurred between 1971 and 1985. This was a distinctly post-industrial phenomenon. The humanities shrank in size relative to health and technology fields and the business sciences and public administration.[72] Peripheral fields of knowledge—typically under the rubric of

---

71   Between 1970 and 2003, the number of humanities majors in US universities and colleges dropped from 30 percent to less than 16 percent (Chace 2009). The big drop occurred between 1971 and 1975, at the beginning of the post-industrial era. The number of humanities students as a percentage of all degree completions dropped from 16 percent in 1971 to 7 percent in 2011 (AAAS 2013).

72   Between 1970 and 2011 in the United States, measured by undergraduate degrees completed, Science and Health disciplines grew from 26 percent to 36 percent of degrees conferred; Business and Law from 14 percent to 24 percent; Education fell from 21 percent to 6 percent; Humanities, Social Sciences and Creative Arts decreased from 39 percent to 34 percent. Humanities dropped from 12.4 percent to 8.1 percent. Humanities would have fallen further except for the growth of 'general studies', one-off subject electives taken by the general student population. Creative Arts, which was one of the few arts areas to adapt to STEM, grew from 3.6 percent to 5.3 percent. It is also notable that the drops in fields of study, when they occurred, did not occur incrementally but rather dramatically. Humanities conferrals plummeted in the period 1975–1980 as did the Humanities, Social Sciences and Creative Arts cluster collectively; Science and Health ballooned during the 1975–1985 period as did Business and Law. Education was the exception: its decline was incremental across 1970 to 2008. In short, a dramatic shift in student choice of fields of study occurred in the 1970s. That the relative sizes of discipline areas in the humanities and social sciences have typically fallen since 1980 is a further and separate phenomenon explicable in terms of the hyper-multiplication of disciplines. Humanities and social science cannibalized itself. Between 1970 and 2012 in the United States, the number of bachelor's degrees conferred per annum doubled (specifically the number rose by a factor of 2.13). Looking at the arts and social sciences alone, different degree types fell above or below this threshold. Those that did well (exceeding the 2.13 threshold) included creative arts (increasing 3.15-fold), theology (2.52), public administration (5.43), psychology (2.85), interdisciplinary studies (7.23), liberal arts and general studies (6.27), law (8.43), communications (8.11), business (3.18), and area studies (3.58). The losers in the great post-industrial readjustment in higher education were education (0.6), English language and literature (0.84), foreign languages, literatures and linguistics (1.04), library science (0.09), philosophy (1.55), and social sciences and history (1.15). In the decade between 2002 and 2012, the pattern was starting to change. Across that decade, degree conferral per annum increased 0.75. The disciplines that fell below that threshold were area studies (0.72), law (0.54), interdisciplinary studies (0.6), psychology (0.72), and public administration (0.67). The previous explosive growth of communications also plateaued out (0.81). Data source: US Department of Education, 2013, Table 322.10.

Table 1.5   Academic Publishing Growth Rates

Period	All records		Journal articles	
	Annual growth rate	Doubling time, years	Annual growth rate	Doubling time, years
Chemical Abstracts				
1907–2007	4.6	16	4.8	15
1907–1914	12	6.1	11	6.6
1920–1930	10.3	7	8.4	8.6
1930–1939	2.3	30	4.2	17
1945–1974	8.4	8.6	8.8	8.2
1974–1990	1.7	40	1.6	44
1990–2007	4.1	17	3.6	20
Compendex				
1907–2007	3.9	18		
MathSciNet				
1907–2007	5.9	12	5.9	12
1907–1960	6.1	12	6.3	11
1950–1984	6.2	11	6	12
1984–2007	2.5	28	3.3	22

Physics Abstracts				
1909–1960	3.9	18		
Inspec physics				
1974–2004	3	23	2.1	**33**
Chemical Abstracts	4.3	**16**	3.4	**21**
Compendex	13.5	5.5		
CSA, natural science. Only 1998–2004	4.7	15	5.3	13
CSA, technology	7.5	9.6	7.5	9.6
Inspec, all sources	5	14	7.3	9.8
Inspec computers/ control engineering	5.5	13	6.6	11
Inspec electrical/electronic engineering	6.2	12	9	8
Inspec physics	3.8	**18**	3.8	**18**
LNCS. Only 1997–2006	4.2	**17**		
MathSciNet	2.8	**25**	3.7	**19**
PubMed medline	5.6	13		
SCI	2.7	**26**	2.2	**31**

Adapted from: Peder Olesen Larsen and Markus von Ins, 2010

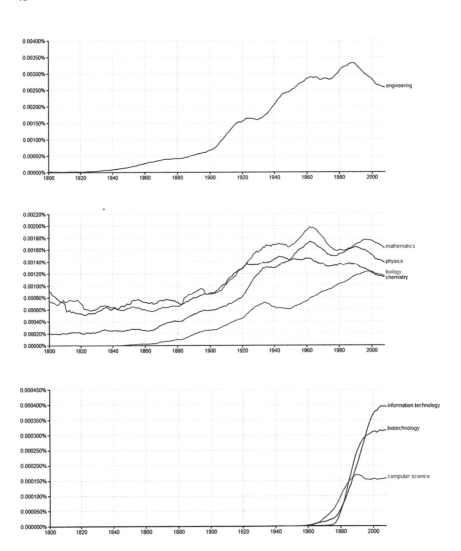

Figure 1.1   Science, Social Sciences, Humanities: N-Gram Analysis of the Annual Incidence of Key Words in the Google Book Database

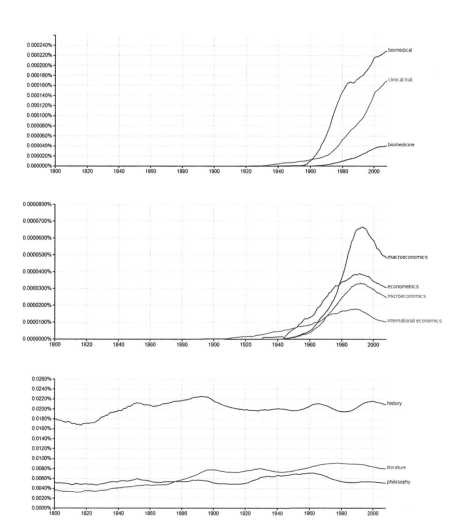

Figure 1.1   *continued ...*

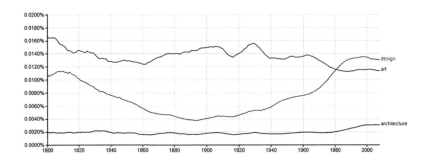

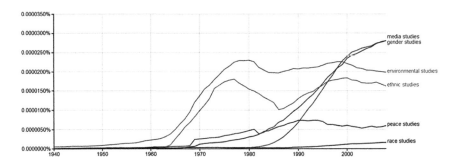

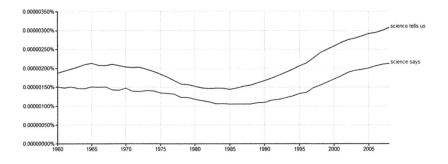

Figure 1.1   *concluded*

Table 1.6   Arts and Humanities Publication Output by Year

Year	Number of articles listed by year	Growth/Decline	Average Annual Growth by Decade
1975	65150		
1976	92373	1.42	
1977	88655	**0.96**	
1978	88300	1.00	
1979	96614	1.09	
1980	105708	1.09	
1981	107970	1.02	
1982	112773	1.04	
1983	116315	1.03	
1984	119725	1.03	
1985	120354	1.01	1.07
1986	125292	1.04	
1987	120718	**0.96**	
1988	121298	1.00	
1989	116517	**0.96**	
1990	116149	1.00	
1991	118453	1.02	
1992	126901	1.07	
1993	125443	**0.99**	
1994	134641	1.07	
1995	135516	1.01	1.01
1996	138765	1.02	
1997	134142	**0.97**	
1998	131964	**0.98**	
1999	131944	1.00	
2000	132710	1.01	
2001	129615	**0.98**	
2002	130184	1.00	
2003	121310	**0.93**	
2004	113866	**0.94**	
2005	124481	1.09	0.99
2006	128219	1.03	
2007	129855	1.01	
2008	139682	1.08	
2009	145443	1.04	
2010	140882	**0.97**	
2011	139770	**0.99**	
2012	130289	**0.93**	

Data Source: Arts & Humanities Citation Index (Thomson Reuters Web of Knowledge).

'studies'—flourished in post-industrial period, from the 1970s through the 1990s. Yet even these, by the decade of the 2000s, had flat-lined, were in decline, or else had a rate of growth that was decelerating.

In spite of all of the above, though, neither rapid growth nor short-term doubling rates are everything. Nor are they sustainable in perpetuity. In fact, the contrary—being small and staying small—can be a virtue in matters of discovery and invention—that is, in matters of creation, formation and conception. This is because of the paradox of growth that applies to the arts and sciences. In a normal sense, say in economic life, growth creates '*more*.' In the arts and sciences, however, beyond a certain point, growth creates '*less*,' not more—that is, each additional unit of artistic or scientific effort represents a diminishing return on the aggregate effort. Once they are generated, fields of inquiry and domains of creation grow and often grow rapidly. Yet beyond a certain point or degree, that growth switches from being a positive to a negative. Success becomes a kind of failure.[73]

A model for visualizing this is 'inception-contagion-saturation.' At its inception, a field is small and highly-charged. Beyond a certain threshold, as numbers of practitioners multiply, a contagion starts.[74] The more practitioners, the more contact between practitioners, the more the contagion spreads. The mark of contagion is rapid growth. The rapid growth though eventually slows. It ends in saturation. Derek Price proposed that, when graphed, the pattern of 'take-off-explosive growth-saturation' looks like a logistic curve, an 'S'-shaped symmetrical sigmoid curve. Price also estimated that explosive growth would occur for five to six periods of rapid doubling before slackening off.[75] Accordingly, how long does it take a major intellectual field to go from the first point of acceleration to saturation? If we assume an average of 5.8 periods of rapid doubling before

---

73   Institutional scientific success is a premonition of failure, and growth of decline, as Charlton and Andras observe: 'Physics was once the richest, most-self-confident and prestigious science; it attracted the brightest students and the bulk of funding. From the late-nineteenth century through the first half of the twentieth century was the golden age of fundamental breakthroughs. The subject was thronging with "geniuses": of whom Faraday, Maxwell, Curie, Thomson, Einstein, Rutherford, Bohr, Heisenberg and Dirac are only a sample. After a lag, this led to the massive post-WW II expansion in funding, with physics as the first "Big Science." For several decades, the continual growth of physics funding seemed inevitable and permanent; but expansion went too-far, the achievements of late-twentieth century physics did not live-up to the hype, and the last couple of decades have seen a collapse in physics support and the closure of many physics departments. Currently, fundamental physics research is pursued in only half a dozen UK universities. We suggest that medical research will follow a similar trajectory to physics—with revolutionary breakthroughs leading to over-expanded funding then collapse—but with the time-course of medical science delayed by several decades compared with physics.' Charlton and Andras 2005; see also Horrobin 2000; Wurtman and Bettiker 1995.

74   The term contagion derives from Richard Stone 1966. Daniel Bell 1973 took up Stone and Price in tandem (177–85) in an interesting discussion.

75   Price 1961: 115–16.

saturation and 12 years as the average time-span for rapid doubling to occur, then the average time-span of a discipline from acceleration to saturation is 70 years. The history of intellectual discovery looks a lot like a series of interlocking logistic curves, such that the inception of one adventive field coincides with the saturation of another one.

This by the way resembles the pattern of Kondratieff waves of economic growth in industrial societies since the late-eighteenth century. Both display overlapping curves of saturation and inception.[76] Underlying this is a powerful social fact: modernity is not progressive. It is cyclical.[77] It rises and falls, rises and falls. Being today at the bottom of a cycle should mean that things will get better. However the real longitudinal problem is the possibility that each up-swing of modernity is less powerful than the previous one. What if modernity is suffering from a subtle form of entropy?

Table 1.7   Major Science Discoveries by Century

	16th C	**17th C**	**18th C**	**19th C**	*20th C**
Major science discoveries	30	83	97	283	*386*
Discoveries per million capita	0.353	0.692	0.588	**0.937**	*0.537*
Combined European and North American Population (millions) mid-century; 15–16 C Europe only; mid-half-century for 1900–1950 period	85	120	165	302	*719*
Data Source: C. Murray, Human Accomplishment, 2005, 163–204.					
*Assuming the centennial average of 719 million combined European and American population and that the rate of discovery after 1950 was the same as before 1950 (193 major discoveries from 1900–1950), then the projected discoveries per million capita for the 20 C would be 0.537, the 18 C rate, though indicators are that the rate of discovery decreased after 1950.					

Table 1.7 and Table 1.4 suggest that this is happening. While discoveries in medical science and technology in the period 1935–1965 were notable, as was the physics, painting and art music of 1910s and 1920s, most of the landmark achievements in the arts and sciences occur before this—and long before the twentieth century. If we wish to be more specific and not look at whole centuries but rather at clusters of decades then the peak of creative work in the core natural sciences occurs at the end of the eighteenth century and in the early-nineteenth century; in mathematics it is the late-sixteenth and the seventeenth century; in medicine the nineteenth century;

---

76   Murphy 2012: 151–5.
77   Heller: 1992.

in technology the key period is from the mid-eighteenth to the mid-nineteenth century; in western philosophy the latter part of the seventeenth century and the latter part of the eighteenth century; in western art it is during the fifteenth, early-sixteenth and first half of the seventeenth centuries; western literature crests at the end of the sixteenth century and in the nineteenth century, and western art music in the late sixteenth and early-eighteenth century and the nineteenth century.[78]

What is crucial to understand though is that the story of modern creation cannot be imagined as a flat-line either up or down. The arts and the sciences, in our time, and in the larger time of modernity, are not progressive, nor are they regressive, rather they are cyclical. They cycle up and they cycle down. Western culture, which has been for the most part the mainstay of modern culture, has periods of intense creative impetus. Each of these is marked by a pervasive sense of paradox.[79] The eras of Luther and Shakespeare, and Hegel and Kierkegaard, are good examples. Yet each of these periods gives way to something less enigmatic, less paradoxical, something shallower and pettier. Today we inhabit one of the lesser periods. Our own malaise will be corrected in time. What has gone down will go up. As Agnes Heller observed, modernity is like a pendulum.[80] It swings backwards and forwards. The question though that I have then is whether the swing of the pendulum slows down with the long passage of time. Does entropy set in? Is each 70-year Kondratieff-wave-like arc of creation less vigorous than the preceding one?

Entropy in the Age of Organization

If inception-contagion-saturation is the pattern of discovery in modern times, then ours is a saturated age. This is so for a reason. The gap between the intractably small discovery core and the escalating dissemination tail has grown. If the cyclical model of modern creation is correct then this has happened before. Yet that begs the question: what is the specific mode of saturation of our own time? To which comes the answer: ours is an organizational age. We seek to discover, create and innovate through organization and professionalization. But this in effect enervates and exhausts inquiry. It has the opposite effect to what is intended. Organization allows us to disseminate and deliver what we discover; it is a poor mechanism though for discovering what we discover.[81] An undergraduate teaching program

---

78   Murray 2003: 309–29.

79   'Kierkegaard was the first to discover that modern thinking was paradoxical ... The modern world as Hegel sees it can survive not because it has a foundation but because it can be kept in balance.' Heller 1999: 18, 23. '[F]ocus on the paradox which cannot be thought ... at its core, great thought depends on paradox.' Carroll 2004: 190.

80   Heller 1992, 1999.

81   Dyer, Gregersen and Christenen 2011 make the same point about innovation businesses.

is organized. It delivers established knowledge, divided into neat pre-digested disciplines. The process of discovery looks quite unlike this.

Thus as fields professionalize, research moves from being a vocation to being a job. An apparatus of committees and conferences along with norms, procedures, expectations and criteria forms. When that happens, culture and science are transformed. In their tiny volcanic cores, both culture and science are highly productive. This is because both exhibit the characteristics of what Heller calls 'the objectivation for itself.'[82] Creation is a type of object producing.[83] This kind of production is distinctive. It is the production of objects with a massively integrated character by means of strongly assimilating imaginative processes. Intense integration is characteristic of creative work of all kinds—whether in philosophy, theology, art or science. Creation emphasizes systemic connection.[84]

---

82   Heller 1985: 105–19.

83   As Georg Simmel 1971: 230 observed 'culture exists only if man draws into his development something that is external to him. Cultivation is certainly a state of the soul but one that is reached only by means of the use of purposefully created objects.'

84   Henri Poincaré and Albert Einstein both gave descriptions of this adventive connective process. In a letter written to the mathematician Jacques Hadamard in 1945, Einstein observed that 'combinatory play seems to be the essential feature in productive thought.' Einstein had in mind combinations of physical images not words. Poincaré 1913: 392–3 talked about a process that moves from the semi-directed collision of ideas and thoughts to their systematic combination. He struggled to find a successful metaphor for this, as we can see: 'The conscious self is narrowly limited, and as for the subliminal self we know not its limitations, and this is why we are not too reluctant in supposing that it has been able in a short time to make more different combinations than the whole life of a conscious being could encompass. Yet these limitations exist. Is it likely that it is able to form all the possible combinations, whose number would frighten the imagination? Nevertheless that would seem necessary, because if it produces only a small part of these combinations, and if it makes them at random, there would be small chance that the good, the one we should choose, would be found among them. Perhaps we ought to seek the explanation in that preliminary period of conscious work which always precedes all fruitful unconscious labor. Permit me a rough comparison. Figure the future elements of our combinations as something like the hooked atoms of Epicurus. During the complete repose of the mind, these atoms are motionless, they are, so to speak, hooked to the wall; so this complete rest may be indefinitely prolonged without the atoms meeting, and consequently without any combination between them. On the other hand, during a period of apparent rest and unconscious work, certain of them are detached from the wall and put in motion. They flash in every direction through the space (I was about to say the room) where they are enclosed, as would, for example, a swarm of gnats or, if you prefer a more learned comparison, like the molecules of gas in the kinematic theory of gases. Then their mutual impacts may produce new combinations. What is the rôle of the preliminary conscious work? It is evidently to mobilize certain of these atoms, to unhook them from the wall and put them in swing. We think we have done no good, because we have moved these elements a thousand different ways in seeking to assemble them, and have found no satisfactory aggregate. But, after this shaking up imposed upon them by our will, these atoms do not

Those engaged in creative work constantly attend to the demanding work of making connections. For each part or element that they encounter or use, they try and figure out how to fit that with other parts or elements. This is one of the chief reasons why creative work typically takes multi-disciplinary, inter-disciplinary or trans-disciplinary forms.[85] This is a symptom of the restless weaving of things together in creation.[86] At its peak, this weaving involves the unlikely fusion or union of incongruent things. At the tip of its peak, creation trades in paradoxes and enigmas that bring together things that are normally thought to stand apart or be opposed.

Lotka, Dennis and Price all observed how a few researchers produce a lot of output and how a lot of researchers produce a tiny amount of output. No research

---

return to their primitive rest. They freely continue their dance. Now, our will did not choose them at random; it pursued a perfectly determined aim. The mobilized atoms are therefore not any atoms whatsoever; they are those from which we might reasonably expect the desired solution. Then the mobilized atoms undergo impacts which make them enter into combinations among themselves or with other atoms at rest which they struck against in their course. Again I beg pardon, my comparison is very rough, but I scarcely know how otherwise to make my thought understood.'

85   As an example, Charles Darwin's work required knowledge of geology, zoology, botany, ecology and psychology (Simonton 1999: 76). Sydney Brenner, professor of genetic medicine at the University of Cambridge, Nobel Laureate in Physiology or Medicine in 2002, and a pioneer of genetic research, observed in interview (Dzeng 2014) the importance of disparate intellectual influences: 'In most places in the world, you live your social life and your ordinary life in the lab. You don't know anybody else. Sometimes you don't even know other people in the same building, these things become so large. The wonderful thing about the college system is that it's broken up again into a whole different unit. And in these, you can meet and talk to, and be influenced by and influence people, not only from other scientific disciplines, but from other disciplines. So for me, and I think for many others as well, that was a really important part of intellectual life. That's why I think people in the college have to work to keep that going.' Brenner was a biochemist trained in medicine, and his colleague, double Nobel Prize winner Frederick Sanger, was a chemist who was more interested in chemistry than in biology. 'I'm not sure whether Fred was really interested in the biological problems, but I think the methods he developed, he was interested in achieving the possibility of finding out the chemistry of all these important molecules from the very earliest ... The thing is to have no discipline at all. Biology got its main success by the importation of physicists that came into the field not knowing any biology and I think today that's very important.'

86   Despite endless official rhetoric that proclaims the virtues of inter-disciplinary work, disciplines remain the bulwark of both the university as an organization and research management systems. Woelert and Millar 2013 note the resulting contradictions. In the Australian context they reflect on the programmatic discourse of interdisciplinarity in government reports and government policy and strategy documents, often tied to notions of innovation and applicability, that runs parallel with the persistence or even reinforcement of modes of governance that almost exclusively rely on rigid discipline-based classification systems to evaluate and fund research.

management policy in the world can change this law of intellectual productivity. It is as it is. Simonton and others (including more tacitly Lotka and Price) have also pointed to the correlation between caliber and productivity.[87] There is a statistical correlation between quantity of output and quality of output. It is not a causal law but it is a correlation. Thus we cannot say that if person Y produces *n* articles, the work will be of A-standard. Life is not so simple. Quantity is not a measure of quality in culture and science—or is it? This is a tricky matter. For consider what the vocation of creation involves. It involves making connections. Many of these are connections at a great stretch.[88] How does that happen? It happens in part through the sheer volume of trying things. It requires divergent thinking about a vast range of seemingly unrelated but nonetheless possibly related phenomena. It then requires convergent thinking to make plausible connections between what initially appears to be unconnected.[89] Overall this involves extensive and patient intellectual or artistic experiment, trial, failure, and success—to connect A to C,

---

87   The most creative individuals typically are very productive, as Simonton 1994: 139 demonstrates: 'Sigmund Freud's bibliography lists 330 articles and books. Thomas Edison obtained 1,093 patents, which remains the record at the US patent office. Balzac, by working over 15 hours a day for 20 years, wrote 85 novels. Picasso created approximately 20,000 works over the course of his career. And J.S. Bach composed enough music to keep a copyist, working only 40 hours per week, busy for a career.'

88   Derek Price observed that scientists of high achievement have a streak of *mavericity*: 'the property of making unusual associations in ideas, of doing the unexpected.' Price 1963: 107.

89   Divergent plus convergent thought gives us something like what Ernst Mach, 1896, described in his Inaugural Lecture (October 20, 1895) given on becoming Professor of the History and Theory of Inductive Science at the University of Vienna. 'A powerfully developed *mechanical* memory, which recalls vividly and faithfully old situations, is sufficient for avoiding definite particular dangers, or for taking advantage of definite particular opportunities. But more is required for the development of *inventions*. More extensive chains of images are necessary here, the excitation by mutual contact of widely different trains of ideas, a more powerful, more manifold, and richer connexion of the contents of memory, a more powerful and impressionable psychical life, heightened by use. A man stands on the bank of a mountain-torrent, which is a serious obstacle to him. He remembers that he has crossed just such a torrent before on the trunk of a fallen tree. Hard by trees are growing. He has often moved the trunks of fallen trees. He has also felled trees before, and then moved them. To fell trees he has used sharp stones. He goes in search of such a stone, and as the old situations that crowd into his memory and are held there in living reality by the definite powerful interest which he has in crossing just this torrent, as these impressions are made to pass before his mind in the *inverse order* in which they were here evoked, he invents the bridge. There can be no doubt but the higher vertebrates adapt their actions in some moderate degree to circumstances. The fact that they give no appreciable evidence of advance by the accumulation of inventions is satisfactorily explained by a difference of degree or intensity of intelligence as compared with man; the assumption of a difference of kind is not necessary.'

C to G, and G to A.[90] That already excludes 75 percent of contributors to Lotka's *Chemical Abstracts* who produced fewer than three papers in a decade.

Today the percentage of American academic economists with three or more publications in a career-spanning 'two decades plus' is 76 percent.[91] That is a bit better score rate than Lotka's chemists in the early-twentieth century. Yet it still contributes little to creativity. In order for research to be creative, it must constitute a 'research program'—not just a handful of papers.[92] In most cases, three or four or five journal articles do not constitute a research program. This is also one of the reasons why citation counts are not that helpful as a measure of caliber.[93] This is

---

90   Arguably this is why Sir Francis Galton in *Hereditary Genius* 1869 held that, in addition to intelligence, genius requires the traits of hard work or persistence and striving or drive. Without such characteristics, the long preparation and pains-taking trials of creation are inconceivable. Even if the amalgam of divergent ideas or precepts comes all of a sudden in a neurobiological flash, the labor to get to that point and the arduous work required to then elaborate it does not happen in a similar flash. Cf. 'Again, we have seen that a union of three separate qualities—intellect, zeal, and power of work—are necessary to raise men from the ranks,' 'intellectual ability, eagerness to work, and power of working,' 'Such men, biographies show to be haunted and driven by an incessant instinctive craving for intellectual work,' 'they do not work for the sake of eminence, but to satisfy a natural craving for brain work, just as athletes cannot endure repose on account of their muscular irritability.' Catherine Cox, 1926: 187, observed that 'high but not the highest intelligence, combined with the greatest degree of persistence, will achieve greater eminence than the highest degree of intelligence with somewhat less persistence.' See Simonton *Greatness* 1994: 231–2 for comments on Galton and Cox.

91   Hartley, Monks, and Robinson, 2001.

92   Imre Lakatos 1978.

93   Derek Price helped to get the career of the citation metric going as a response to the question of how the *quantity* of output can be a measure of the *quality* of work produced. In a strict causal sense, it is not. Given that then how does any statistic measure the value of a work (good, bad, indifferent)? It can only really establish a statistical correlation indicating at best the probability that some large number correlated to the work is a signal of quality. But we cannot be *certain* that a big number of publications per annum is a sign of high intellectual quality; any more than we can be certain that a small number of publications per year is the sign of a poor standard. Likewise a large number of citations or even a large number of citations in highly-cited journals or a big h-index number or a large i–10 index number cannot establish a conclusive indicator of eminence or excellence. Price suggested citation as a proxy for measuring the quality of work that is produced in varying quantities. The difficulty of any proxy measure is that the metrician is measuring not the thing-in-itself but something standing for the thing-in-itself. We know little about why researchers cite other researchers; is it a sign of value, and if it is, what is being valued? Do researchers cite because they are obliged to cite all recent papers in the relevant sub-field, or because the work cited has information-value, or status-value, or conceptual-value, or is original, or has reputational-value, or ideological-value, or is produced by an established leader in the field, or is an intriguing obscurity, or in order to fill-out a bibliography, or because the work cited has shaped the argument of the paper, or because the cited work includes a crucial fact to be relied on in evidence? Furthermore, what is the value of each of these acts of valuation?

because citations are a measure of the use or reception of individual items of work produced but not of a systemic program of inquiry. There is a difference. Good or great science and culture require a sustained program of investigation. Such a program of necessity is more than the representation or recording of interesting events, observations or experiences, even if these are well worth citing many times over. Such observations have information value and thus they have a value that is sometimes keenly sought. But information value is not creative value. Whether it is the arts or sciences, creation takes place in the realm of the 'objectivation for itself.' Here diverse elements are woven together into a pattern of connection.[94] Such patterns are difficult to establish. An example from contemporary science illustrates the point. In 1993 the *Huntingtin* gene was isolated. The gene 'causes' the toxic protein that 'causes' the neuro-degeneration experienced by those with the Huntington's condition. Yet, to date, these bio-chemical connections have proved to be more weak indices than strong causal mechanisms on which effective therapies, medications and preventative techniques can be built. Establishing connections is very difficult.

In light of all that then what does a research program involve in a quantitative sense?[95] Across a career it probably takes (on average) 60 papers or six-to-10 books—something of that magnitude—equivalent to the top 2 percent of Lotka's contributors scaled over two to three decades of output.[96] That's an informal rule

---

And what is the intensity of each citation? What is the relative value of a smaller number of intense citations of work that deeply affects subsequent work as opposed to the pro forma or obligatory citation of high-status, well-known, or recent work of relevance? How could we ever measure intensity? Many or most of these tricky matters can only be resolved over the long term. Work that is still cited after 50 years has a high probability of being good; the same applies to artworks. If people still relish viewing an artwork or listening to one 50 years after it was created, it is likely to be a work of genuine significance.

94 The philosopher William James 1880 described the process thus: '... turn to the highest order of minds, and what a change! Instead of thoughts of concrete things patiently following one another in a beaten track of habitual suggestion, we have the most abrupt cross-cuts and transitions from one idea to another, the most rarefied abstractions and discriminations, the most unheard-of combinations of elements, the subtlest associations of analogy; in a word, we seem suddenly introduced into a seething caldron of ideas, where everything is fizzling and bobbing about in a state of bewildering activity, where partnerships can be joined or loosened in an instant, treadmill routine is unknown, and the unexpected seems the only law.'

95 Simonton's stab at this is as follows: '... Terman's notable scientists produced about 29 publications by the time they had reached their mid-40s. In contrast, American Nobel laureates in the sciences averaged about 38 publications by the time they were 39 years old, and claimed about 59 publications by their mid-40s.' Simonton, *Greatness* 1994: 222.

96 This suggests a fractal structure of creativity, namely that if 2 percent of a population has the ability (if they choose) to become professional academics then 2 percent of the academic population is likely to contribute to high-level creative academic achievement of some kind. A measure of this might be work cited and influential 50 years after publication.

of thumb. It is not a bureaucratic 'metric.' It is not a 'key performance indicator.'[97] The latter, the KPI, is a delivery measure, not a discovery measure. Contemporary research, or rather contemporary research management, confuses the two. Organizational productivity and inventive productivity are not the same. For one thing, organization tends to confound the latter even when it tries to boost it. One of the reasons for this is that, paradoxically, the condition of big output is small ecologies. Creativity flourishes best in small scale not large scale environments. Here we see one of the fatal flaws of modern research. It grew too large for its own good. Out of success came failure.

As an example, in 2011 Australia had 48,000 continuing academic staff. Two percent of that total is 960 persons. To follow the fractal metaphor one step further, it is then plausible that 2 percent of that 2 percent (around 20 persons) will endure in an intellectual sense for 100 years or more.

97   The distinguished research geneticist Sydney Brenner explains what happens when bureaucratic indicators take hold: His colleague, and twice Nobel Prize winner, Frederick Sanger was a key in the discovery of DNA sequencing. 'A Fred Sanger would not survive today's world of science. With continuous reporting and appraisals, some committee would note that he published little of import between insulin in 1952 and his first paper on RNA sequencing in 1967 with another long gap until DNA sequencing in 1977. He would be labelled as unproductive, and his modest personal support would be denied. We no longer have a culture that allows individuals to embark on long-term—and what would be considered today extremely risky—projects' (Brenner, 2014). The key word is: *long term*. Bureaucratic time horizons rarely extend beyond one to three years. A research program is impossible under those conditions. Today: '[Sanger] wouldn't have survived. It is just the fact that he wouldn't get a grant today because somebody on the committee would say, oh those were very interesting experiments, but they've never been repeated. And then someone else would say, yes and he did it a long time ago, what's he done recently? And a third would say, to top it all, he published it all in an un-refereed journal.' That said, though, like almost all major figures, Sanger *was* productive. His selected papers (Sanger and Dowding 1996) include 48 papers published between 1945 and 1988.

Chapter 2
The Innovation Economy

Cyclical Creation

Growth is an unambiguous plus in modern economies, even though economic growth is a paradoxical phenomenon. Every expansion contains the seeds of contraction and each contraction presages future growth. Successful modern societies are not progressive nor are they regressive.[1] Rather they have a swinging, pendulum-like, undulating, and cyclical quality about them.[2] They grow but that growth also oscillates. It expands and contracts. To be successful, modern economies have to expand more than they contract over time. Growth is the net value of the great modern oscillations, the swaying, swinging, deeply contradictory manner in which modern societies develop.

In major modern economies in the past two centuries the economic growth that has been achieved has been on a scale that is unprecedented in human history. One of the reasons this happened is that the major growth economies were successful at translating science into industry technology, social science into industry organization, and political philosophy into elegant systems of property rights and contract law. However, in the post-industrial era, economic growth rates in the major established economies began to decelerate. Indicators hint that, as the underlying real rate of discovery and creativity has declined, so has long-term economic growth. The further irony of this is that economic growth has been likely stymied by the growth of science. This is because of a conundrum. While growth mostly is an unalloyed positive for economies, beyond an optimal point and possibly a very modest optimal point, growth is a negative for culture and science. This observation points to the paradox of intellectual productivity. The bigger science is, the less it creates. Beyond a modest threshold, the bigger a field gets, the fewer works of lasting importance are produced proportionate to scale. The more money we spend on research, the less we get in real terms for that expenditure.

The principal problem of big culture and big science is that it suffocates thought in its most fertile mode. Creation works by amalgamating hitherto unrelated insights—such as when Einstein merged Maxwell's electromagnetic theory with Newtonian mechanics.[3] Dean Keith Simonton put it beautifully

---

1 Despite this, since the time of John Dewey, most intellectuals have become progressives.

2 On the metaphor of the modern pendulum, see Heller 1992.

3 Simonton 1984: 74.

when he said that creative innovation depends on the ability to see relationships between hitherto unconnected ideas or methods and then to fuse them into a new synthesis. In large part we have lost, or we are losing, the capacity to do this.[4] Why is this so? In the near-run, this is a consequence of the professionalization of culture and science. That professionalization in its turn is an aspect of a larger phenomenon. This larger phenomenon is the bureaucratization of the world. Our problem is an excess of bureaucratic legal-rationality. Procedural rationality or legal rationalism—the essence of modern bureaucracy and modern procedural organization—is lethal to creation and innovation. The logic of creation is not procedural. It is not legal-rational. It is not a methodical logic of process, policy or procedure. It is analogical.[5]

Bureaucratization is the result of the large-scale administrative colonization of contemporary cultural and science institutions including the universities. The bureaucratization of these institutions is matched by the declining creative

---

4 'America today has many technical intellectuals—people like doctors, engineers, and others who are able to carry out complex tasks—and we are extraordinarily rich in specialist intellectuals who have a deep knowledge of a particular subject. Our educational and professional systems are set up to train and support the large numbers of people needed to fill these roles. We are much less effective at teaching and supporting people who are able to master the essentials of many complex subjects, integrate the insights from this kind of study into a coherent social or political vision, and communicate what they have learned to a broad general lay audience. The more complex a society and the more rapidly it is changing, the more need it has for multi-disciplinary, synthesizing intellectuals who are focused on communicating serious ideas to a large audience. Otherwise, a gap grows between the technical and specialist intellectuals and the values and ideas of society at large.' Walter Russell Mead 2010.

5 Aspects of the Scholastic Assessment Test scoring, which was introduced in the United States in 1901 to eliminate assessment biases, shine a light on attitudes to discovery. Historically the SAT tested for antonyms and analogies. In 2005, at the behest of the University of California, questions about analogies were eliminated from the verbal (critical reading) test on the ground that they were 'ambiguous.' Yet what else is an analogy supposed to be? Ambidexterity is what makes analogies the most powerful means of discovery and invention. The University of California system effectively got them ditched from the test. The university's rhetoric espouses discovery yet it does not want a test for the primary medium of discovery. In 1994 antonym questions were removed from the test. Double definitions were eliminated in 1946. Analogies had been dropped once before, between 1930 and 1936. 'UC President Richard Atkinson had railed against the analogies, which account for 19 of the SAT's 72 verbal questions, as a memory drill that measured little of a student's potential. He threatened to scrap the SAT as a UC requirement unless the test makers replaced the multiple-choice analogies with reading comprehension questions, added a writing exercise and expanded the math portion. The College Board, the New York-based firm that owns the SAT, gave Atkinson what he wanted. And no wonder: UC is to the board as General Motors is to US Steel—a huge customer. The analogies will disappear in 2005. "I'm extremely pleased," Atkinson said. "I always just hated the verbal analogies. There was just a trickiness to them."' Pringle 2003.

impetus of socialization. The young today are less creative. This is a wide-spread cultural trend. Contemporary measures of the level of youthful creativity show that it is declining. The most evident decline is among pre-school children. What this suggests is that the retreat in creativity in institutions like the university is part of a deeper shift in the general culture. Contemporary societies unconsciously socialize their young to live in a prosaic world. The standard contemporary test of human creativity is the Torrance Tests of Creative Thinking (TTCT). The battery was designed by University of Georgia Professor Ellis Paul Torrance in 1966 and multiple versions of it have been devised since then.[6] Its origins go back to Torrance's time at the University of Minnesota in the late 1950s. When administered to children, the test is three times more likely to predict adult creativity than IQ tests do.[7] In 2010, a professor at the College of William and Mary, Kyung Hee Kim, published a re-analysis of nearly 300,000 Torrance scores from five decades worth of tests on children and adults administered by the US-based Scholastic Testing Service.[8] The results of Kim's study were chastening.[9] Her research revealed that creativity scores, which previously had risen steadily, had stopped rising in 1990 and had experienced a statistically-significant decline after that turning-point. Twenty years into the post-modern era, creativity scores were generally falling-off and some of the subsidiary components of creativity tested for by the TTCT had begun to decline as early as 1984.[10]

---

6 Torrance took as his starting-point the work of J.P. Guilford.

7 Kim 2008.

8 The test today is administered across the world in 35 languages.

9 Kim 2011.

10 Analysing data from the TTCT-Figural test, Kim found declines across all the Torrance-defined elements of creativity including: Fluency, Originality, Elaboration, Abstractness of Titles, Resistance to Premature Closure and the 13 creative personality traits that comprise the *Creative Strengths* subscale of the test. *Fluency* scores decreased from 1966 to 1974, increased from 1974 to 1990, and decreased from 1990 to 2008. *Originality* scores increased from 1966 to 1974, decreased from 1990 to 1998, and remained static from 1998 to 2008. *Elaboration* scores increased from 1966 to 1974 and decreased from 1984 to 2008. *Abstractness of titles* scores increased until 1998 and decreased from 1998 to 2008. *Resistance to premature closure* scores decreased from 1984 to 1990, increased from 1990 to 1998, and decreased again from 1998 to 2008. *Creative strengths* scores decreased from 1990 to 2008. What the Torrance Tests assess for is:

Fluency: The total number of ideas generated in response to test stimuli.
Originality: The statistical rarity of test responses.
Elaboration: The amount of embellishment and development in test responses.
Abstractness: The ability to capture the abstract essence of test stimuli.
Resistance to premature closure: The ability to complete the test in an unexpected way.
Strengths: emotional expressiveness, story-telling articulateness, movement or actions, expressiveness of titles, syntheses of incomplete figures, synthesis of lines, synthesis of circles, unusual visualization, extending or breaking boundaries, humor, richness of imagery, colorfulness of imagery, and fantasy.

The fall-off was worst among the very young, those aged from kindergarten years to third grade. What does this mean? It indicates that the observed decline in creation and innovation, in universities and the innovation economy, extends deeply into the pores of the wider society. Kim found that the drop in creative thinking was steady and persistent from 1990 to 2008 and ranged across the various components tested by the TTCT. At the same time, IQ tests (on certain dimensions) trended in the opposite direction, upwards.[11] What this hints at is that a typical post-modern 'clever' country or 'smart' society (like the United States or Australia) might manage in certain ways to be measurably more intelligent and yet at the same time end up being disarmingly less creative. This is a paradox worth reflecting on. It suggests, among other things, that the post-modern identification of education with creation is misleading. More education does not make societies more creative. In fact over the decades that OECD countries have aggressively expanded higher education, social creativity has declined.

From young to old, this effect is now visible. The decline in Torrance test scores is echoed at the highest levels of social creation and innovation. Key works are produced by a small number of creators. Cultural creation is not a democracy. And neither is science. In modern life, we are good at disseminating the fruits of culture and science. In that aspect, we are democratic. We are masters of access and mistresses of distribution. The ages of mechanical and electronic reproduction brought the wonders of Cézanne and Shakespeare along with electro-magnetism into every home that wished it. While everyone wanted the electric light bulb, not everyone wanted to read by it. But even if everyone did wish to read voraciously, democratic distribution is still not creative production. We live in an age that confuses the two.

This confusion points to something deeper. There are two basic orientations to the world. One is production. The other is distribution or allocation. Contemporary societies prefer the latter to the former. Why produce something when a society can allocate, donate, award, gift, dispense, issue, allot or distribute it instead? Why aspire to be a J.S. Bach who produced 1100 works in his life-time? Much better if we bow to the ethos of dissemination. The post-modern view is that it is better to spread the wealth than to produce it. It is better to deal out, dole out, share out, and dish out wealth than to make, manufacture, establish, found, bring forth, give rise to, bring about, institute, engender or produce it. There is much less effort involved.

Almost no one bar a tiny handful of individuals can meaningfully aspire to be a Piet Mondrian, an Adam Smith, or a Michael Faraday. Yet the many

---

11   This reflected the 'Flynn effect' that more exposure to problem solving leads to better IQ results, an effect of living in ever-more complex modern societies. The upward trend of measured IQ in recent decades is mainly a result of a rise in the low IQ bands and is restricted to performance on visual tests not on logical or mathematical tests. It is an effect of post-modern visual intensity and visual-kinetic screen culture. The relation of this Flynn effect to the dumbing down of society is discussed in Bauerlin 2008.

also reflect the few. For even the most prosaic, the most demotic and the most incremental examples of human innovation have a structure that is shared with the most soaring instances of human ingenuity and creativity. There are not just exceptionally creative human beings. There are also exceptionally creative times and places. The social incidence of creation (measured in real per capita terms) varies in time and space. It varies with geography and history. Ours is not one of the intensely creative times. There has been a distinct downward trend in creativity since 1974. The arc of creative decline also appears to be a longer one than 40 years. In the longer term, it is as if we were dealing with some kind of fractal geometry of creation.

What then is it that dampens the collective imagination whether across the medium or long term? Ironically an over-expansion of the number of science and culture professionals per head of population is a factor. The expression of this in our own time has been the seemingly unstoppable spread of knowledge institutions followed by omnivorous knowledge bureaucracies. The spirit of 'objectivation for itself'—the spirit of inquiry—has been killed by the machinery of the 'objectivation in and for itself.'[12] Big science, big culture, and big art generate big bureaucracies. We see this in the massive post-1970 bureaucratization of university research and (even before that) the development of the arts-grant bureaucracy.[13] The last interesting art period, the Modernist era from 1890 to 1950, produced a series of durable artistic figures and works. In that era, most of the Modernists readily accepted that creation was done by a tiny handful of very gifted individuals. When the genuine momentum of Modern Art ran out of steam, what replaced it was the official modernism of the arts-grant bureaucracies. This was followed in swift succession by the rhetoric but rarely the durable works of post-modernism and most recently the media-arts.[14]

A list of the 50 greatest British inventions was compiled by BBC science experts in a 2013 Radio Times poll.[15] It is notable that the decade of the 1820s accounted for a tenth of the poll-nominated 'biggest breakthroughs' in 350 years of British innovation. The decade included Charles MacIntosh's waterproof material, Michael Faraday's electric motor, Joseph Aspdin's cement, George Stephenson's passenger railway, and Edwin Beard Budding's lawnmower.[16] The physicist

---

12 On the distinction between objectivation for itself and objectivation for and in itself, see Heller, 1985.

13 The model of the Arts Council was pioneered in the United Kingdom by John Maynard Keynes who was the first chair of the Arts Council of Great Britain. The Arts Council of Great Britain was established in 1946; the Canada Council for the Arts in 1957; the US National Endowment for the Arts in 1965; and the Australian Council for the Arts in 1968.

14 Scruton 1998.

15 Collins 2013.

16 Budding and Stephenson were both engineers, Aspdin was a bricklayer, Faraday was a self-taught scientist who ended up as Fullerian Professor of Chemistry at the Royal Institution of Great Britain, and MacIntosh was an amateur chemist.

Jonathan Huebner calculated that the peak of global technological innovation occurred in 1870. My calculation is that the peak of US patent registration per capita occurred in 1914 and the peak of US copyright registration per capita occurred in the 1890s.[17] Data of this kind points to a long-run time-line of ebbing cultural-creative energy. A long-run line of decline appears to begin around 1870. There is a more recent decline line that begins around 1970. What this points to is that the arts and the sciences of the last 40 years have been in aggregate distinctly inferior in quantity and quality to those of both the nineteenth century and the first half of the twentieth century.

How do we explain such creative peaks and troughs in time and space? Why do they appear and disappear? Peaks of collective creation are a function of times and places that are open to deep paradox. Paradox is the ultimate progenitor of culture and science. Take the case of the culture and science of Renaissance Europe in the fifteenth and early-sixteenth century. It was permeated to an extraordinary degree with paradoxical thinking. It yielded the most profound results. A classic example is the case of Johannes Gutenberg (1395–1468) who took the long-established technologies of printing and paper and fused these with the technology of the wine screw-press and his knowledge of the gold-smith trade to create the printing press with molded moveable type. The printing press provided one of the crucial pre-conditions for the next propitious era of creation, the Lutheran and Protestant Reformation. The Reformation triggered a marked upswing in culture and science in the late-sixteenth century. As with Gutenberg, and later on with Luther, creativity is the work of a mind that merges what others think of as unrelated.[18] Consider

---

17   *Patents*: In spite of its comparative global creative power in all areas of the arts and sciences in the last 100 years, the peak year for patents registered per capita in the United States was 1914. The registration rate trended downward till 1985 where it stood at 50 percent of the 1914 peak. It rose again, as might be expected, in step with the information technology boom after 1985. But even at its renewed highest in 2005 it was still only 95 percent of the 1914 per capita figure. *Copyright*: Again taking the case of the United States, we find that the registration of copyrights per capita increased in a nominal sense slightly between 1900 and today. But only because the number of kinds of copyrightable objects increased markedly in the same period—meaning that copyright registration per capita in real terms fell. The 1890s appears to be the peak time for per capita copyright creation in the United States once we take into account the increase in copyrightable objects during the last century and a half. Murphy 2010: 93.

18   The neurobiology of this is starting to be investigated. For example: 'Spearman (1931) suggested that creative ideas result from the combination of two or more ideas that have been previously isolated. Because the right and left hemispheres store different forms of knowledge and mediate different forms of cognitive activity, different neuronal architectures probably exist within the association cortices of each of the hemispheres. A possible method of resolving a previously unsolved problem is to see this problem "in a new light" and a means of seeing a problem in a new light is to use a different form of knowledge and a different cognitive strategy that might be mediated by the hemisphere that is opposite to the one previously used. The largest structure connecting independent

what it actually took in order to make a connection between the agricultural press and the process of printing or between the mold of the metal smith and the impress of the type-face. Consider likewise what was involved in Luther seeing in the volition of election, the absence of free will and the phenomena of predestination and necessity.[19] Upon that singular and extraordinary act of imagination not only was Protestantism founded but also eventually the idea of the United States.

Creators are the masters and mistresses of terrifying contradiction. Human creation starts in mythology. It begins with the merging of sea creatures and women—and it ends with Descartes merging arithmetic and geometry, Niels Bohr merging wave and particle, Einstein merging time and space, simultaneity and non-simultaneity, and Cezanne and Braque merging two dimensions and three dimensions, and motion and stillness. That is the imagination at work. It matters little whether its domain of application is art, science, industry or technology. The case of Edwin Beard Budding illustrates the logic or more exactly the analogic of the imagination perfectly. Mr. Budding observed a machine in a local cloth mill. The machine used a cutting cylinder (a bladed reel) to trim the irregular textile nap off the surface of woolen cloth in order to give it a regular even finish. Budding metaphorically, that is to say imaginatively, translated from shaggy cloth fiber to overgrown grass. In doing so, his lawn mower replaced the labor-intensive scythe and saved generations of gardeners from back-breaking work.

The analogic of creation repeats itself. Arthur Fry was an inventor and a chemical engineer. He worked for the great innovation company, 3M. One day he heard about a botched invention created by one of his company's research chemists, Spencer Silver. This was an adhesive that did not stick very well. What kind of adhesive was that? Well, obviously, it was a failed one. Arthur Fry, however, had a problem of his own. He was a member of a local choir. He was always folding the edges of his music sheets down in order to find his place. Could he do better than this? Well, he thought: what about attaching a bit of note paper to those sheets with an adhesive that didn't stick very well? Thus was born the 3M Post-It Note. A sticky note that does not stick very well does not tear the surfaces that it attaches to. This example illustrates perfectly how innovation and

---

modular systems is the corpus callosum. Lewis (1979) administered the Rorschach test to eight patients who had undergone a cerebral commissurotomy and noted that disconnection of the two cerebral hemispheres tended to destroy creativity as measured by this test. Bogen and Bogen (1988) noted that although the corpus callosum transfers high level information, normally this interhemispheric communication is incomplete. Bogen and Bogen posited that incomplete interhemispheric communication permits hemispheric independence and lateralized cognition, important in the incubation of ideas. These authors mention Frederic Bremer, who suggested that the corpus callosum subserves the highest and most elaborate activities of the brain, in a word, creativity. They also suggest that it is the momentary suspension of this partial independence that accounts for illumination. They did not say, however, what could account for this momentary suspension of partial independence.' Heilman, Nadeau and Beversdorf 2003.

19   Carroll 2004: 51–68.

imagination actually proceeds. The innovator is someone who looks at one thing and sees it as something else in order to solve a problem. Arthur Fry looked at a failed adhesive and saw (in it) a potentially successful sticky note paper.

Innovation thinking is the ability to see ends in beginnings and success in failure or vice versa. The key is not so much 'changing' what we do, but rather re-imagining it. Imagination requires us to 'switch' how we see what we do. If there is no cognitive 'flip' then there is no invention. There is no taking the 'fixed' phone sitting on your desk and re-imagining it as 'mobile' device or taking the portable audio cassette player and re-imagining it as a hand-held computer hard disk. Innovation is the re-imagining of the hospital in-patient as an out-patient. It is contrarian thinking that we can raise revenue by reducing taxes or tackle big crimes by focusing first on petty crimes. The same applies to research. It is well-established that the great innovations in ideas occur at the inter-section of disciplines and fields. And yet most people in universities resolutely stick to their fields. Why? They do so because it is safe, secure, comfortable, and reassuring. To cross disciplines means turning the inside of a field, department, or organization into an outside. That means psychologically having to cope with ambiguity, uncertainty, and role conflict. And yet any kind of creativity, big or small, typically happens when insiders also become outsiders.

Sometimes it is thought that multiplying functions and acquiring 'new' functions is being innovative. Mostly it is not. Rather innovation and creation primarily refine and make more effective what exists. In 1988, Northwest Airlines pilot Robert Plath took the traditional luggage bag and added wheels to it. He fused the bag and the wheeled vehicle. That action transformed, for the good, the experience of travel. Robert Plath didn't try and replace luggage. Rather he put wheels on it and a chassis that flipped the orientation of luggage from horizontal to vertical. In so doing, he made the carriage of airport baggage much easier. In short, what creation and innovation does is to reframe, sometimes dramatically, what we are familiar with in ways that save time and energy. Innovation and creation in everyday life and social organizations makes life simpler and more efficient. That is different from the appetite for 'new' programs and 'new' functions.

Take the case of the invention of the Internet. It was created bit-by-bit using existing technology in ingenious ways. It was built on old-fashioned copper-wire telephony not on fiber-optics. It combined existing computer networks and harnessed established mark-up languages and so on. It innovated on the basis of the tried-and-true. Compare this real innovation with contemporary information technology. Fifty to 70 percent of *all* contemporary IT projects fail.[20] Government and university use of office IT is worse than the average. One of the least successful domestic policy initiatives in United States history, the 'Obamacare' health insurance scheme, began with the massive dysfunction of its information technology platform. Innovation and creation is not a function of 'change' but rather of the balancing of change *and* continuity. Change is a pervasive part of

---

20   Ellis 2008.

human experience but so is continuity. Successful innovation and creation adapts and improves but also simultaneously preserves and builds on what works. We don't get rid of the luggage bag but rather we add wheels and a chassis to it. The fusion of 'bag and vehicle' and the analogical leap 'from textile fiber to lawn grass' are typical of the path of creation. Procedural rationality (even of a 'smart' kind) is the antithesis of these strange imaginative fusions. In relative historical terms, we today are not that imaginative. The contemporary preference is to use linear procedural logics—rather than analogical thinking that encourages us to see one thing as another thing.

Contemporaries talk a lot about creativity, innovation and imagination. Yet that does not necessarily make our age as imaginative as Edwin Beard Budding's age. Indicative of the problem is the obsession that our own time has with procedural rationality. The spread of procedural rationality in the past half century has been massive. The increase (relative to population) of regulation is a clear symptom of this. The habitual response, not just of organizations but of citizens as well, is that if we are confronted with a problem we want immediately to know what 'system' or 'process' will fix the problem. In fact, often we don't fix the actual problem at all. Rather we institute a method to deal with problems 'of its type.' This is a habit that leads to a deeper problem, which is the relative decline over time of creativity. The more that contemporary culture is dominated by procedural rationality and the more that we load up universities and firms and institutions with professional logics, bureaucratic modes of organization and administrative rationalities, the less creative in practice we are.

Creation is an act of consilience. It is an act of the coalescence, concurrence and accordance of insights and meanings drawn from widely differing observations and groupings of phenomena. Procedural reason obviates consilience. It turns each field of inquiry from an 'objectivation for itself' into an 'objectivation in and for itself.'[21] In this way, the nucleus of a field becomes an institution. This leads to the growth of numbers, personnel, prestige, offices, power, and influence. It also leads to a loss of intellectual vigor as the intense work of analogical fusion abates. Institutions are analytical rather than analogical or topological in nature.[22] They operate via procedures and methods that require the carving up, dissection and vivisection of the world into elements, items, steps, sections, divisions, stages, phases and periods. Institutionalized fields of inquiry sub-divide and partition themselves. The topology of creation in contrast continuously transforms one thing (the bag) into some other thing (the wheeled transporter). As analytic vivisection gains the upper-hand, the integrated (that is to say topological) nature of creation weakens. Professionalization encourages inward-looking, demarcating

---

21   Heller 1985: 120–50.

22   Topology represents a kind of continuous transformation in which 0 becomes 1 or 1 becomes 0 and yet there is no breach, break, fissure, rupture, cut, crack or gap between the state of 0 and the state of 1. This means that for certain purposes there is a latent identity between 0 and 1, or a super-positioning of 1 and 0.

expertise. Highly specialized knowledge is at odds with the simultaneous divergent-convergent thinking of creation.[23] As fields are disciplined and normalized, incongruous unions and paradoxical mergers are tacitly forbidden. The discipline grows. On the surface of things, this looks like a plus. Conferences get larger, the number of journals multiplies, and citation numbers swell. But this growth comes at a cost. The ordinary contributor (the disseminator) begins to over-shadow and out-number the gifted core of creators. Contemporary societies are addicted to procedural rationality. Steps, plans, methods, routes, pathways, courses, techniques, systems, and schemes abound. These are helpful in many ways. Indeed these are indispensable in some ways. But they also have a habit of crowding out the metaphors, similes, allegories, comparisons, resemblances, semblances and strange affinities by which we couple together what normally stands apart. The latter is the kind of act that creates what does not exist from what does exist.

Creation is translated into economic life through innovation. Innovation is an analogue of creation. It is the spirit that animates wealth generation and exercises the prosperity levers of modern economies. It is a complex chain that extends from metaphorical insight to growth industries. Moving along the chain takes time, just as it took time for Mr. Budding's machine to be turned into the motor-mower and the ride-on mover, and much more. But complex or not, if the insight-innovation impulse weakens, so do its consequences and effects. This is the underlying story of post-1970 and post-2008 economies. It is not the whole story. A story of that kind is inevitably multi-faceted. Part of it has to do with the great repeating cycles of expansion and contraction that characterize modern economies. The story of the cyclical behavior of credit, debt, production, and consumption is fascinating its own right. But if we ask ourselves (just to give one simple example) why it was that central banks in the decade after 2000 locked in low interest rates that fueled speculative investments in real estate that subsequently collapsed in 2008, then one answer is 'lack of innovation.'

Take the case of the personal computer. It was a mass market innovation in the 1990s. A decade or so later, what did a personal computer's operating system and key software applications offer that these did not offer in 1996 or 2000? The answer is: not much and in fact often very little. And therein is the core of a problem. In the years just before and after 2000, the word 'creativity' became a standard economic trope. It was a rhetorical go-to word for governments and policy-makers. Yet the troubling irony of this was that 2000 was a moment in which productivity visibly slumped across advanced economies, driving national and global economies downwards. This irony of rhetoric and reality suggested in its turn a couple of

---

23   Consequently, innovation in disciplines ends up being triggered by persons who are not normalized and who oftentimes are outsiders. These are individuals who have wandered into a field that is not theirs. Simonton calls them trespassers and interlopers. 'Great innovations often come from those who were self-taught or else switched fields.' Simonton, *Greatness*, 1994: 172.

possibilities. Perhaps creativity and productivity were not closely connected. Yet the history of industrial modernity strongly suggests otherwise. Perhaps then post-industrial theories of economic creativity were wrong. If so, then it is not the case that we should be disinterested in the economic consequences of social creation but rather that we should return to the drawing-board and reconsider what it is that produces the creativity that produces the innovation that expands social and economic productivity.

Questioning Human Capital Theory

There is nothing simple about the chain of creative causation and consequence. Modeling creation is difficult. Even modeling its consequences is difficult. There is much that we do not know (even at an elementary level) about social creation and its economic applications. It is riddled with enigmas, conundrums and paradoxes. If these fuel creative behaviors they also confound analytic models of those behaviors. In some basic way, the topological character of economic and social creation is the antithesis of analytical modelling. One tends not to square with the other. Yet creativity still plays a central role in economic behavior. So theories of creativity remain crucial—if we are to better understand the deep sources of economic growth and social prosperity.

Yet such theories at times function like sleights-of-hand. The human capital school of economics is a case in point. It says that ideas generate growth. Knowledge creates economic value. Such propositions are not per se wrong. And yet, as with so much in life, the devil is in the detail. Or in this case the devil is in the definition of what is an idea. In 2000, the Stanford University economist Charles I. Jones estimated that 80 percent of economic growth in the United States during the period 1950–1993 had come from the application of ideas.[24] At first glance the analysis appears persuasive. On closer examination things start to look less convincing. Jones calculated that GDP growth was principally generated by increases in the level of education in society and in the percentage of the workforce engaged in research-related activity.

It is true that the unrivalled economic growth of the past 200 years could not have happened without the science of electricity or the idea of the factory. In this sense, ideas *do* generate growth. But neither the expansion of education nor the growth of a R&D workforce are effective proxies for powerful ideas. The first (education) confuses the dissemination of ideas with the creation of ideas. The second (R&D) assumes that greater spending on research generates more ideas. Neither is true. Yet both are commonplace. Both represent the standard outlook of post-industrial knowledge-society elites. Education plus R&D is today a cliché of public policy. The logic of the cliché is that if you spend more on universities

---

24   C.I. Jones 2000, 2005.

and schools and on research and development then economic growth will either increase or else be sustained at a virtuous plateau over the long term.[25]

This view, I suggest, is wrong. The successive waves of industrialization since the 1870s demonstrate clearly that it is neither re-cycled old ideas transmitted through education nor transient vogue new ideas produced by expensive research that has a short shelf-life that generate economic growth. Rather it is surprising, distinctive, mostly modestly-funded ideas with durability and lasting power that matter. In other words, it is unusual ideas that are born prematurely old that make a difference. In 1940, 5 percent of the American population aged 25 and older possessed a bachelor's degree or higher. By 2009, this percentage had increased more than five-fold to 30 percent.[26] Yet growth in real GDP per capita in the United States trended in the opposite direction.[27] In the 1950s and 1960s, the average

---

25   Lee, Lin, Chuang and Lee 2011 conclude that there is not a strong positive correlation between academic research output and economic output. Attempts by external academic research funders to estimate contribution to national wealth strain credulity. The Allen Consulting Group report, 2003, for the Australian Research Council (ARC), one of Australia's major external grant funders, is a case in point. Allen Consulting builds assumption upon assumption. The first assumption is that technological progress contributes 50 percent of economic growth in advanced economies. Skills and economic efficiencies and organizational innovation add to that. No overall figure is concluded. Then it is asserted that R&D contributes 10 to 15 percent of the uncalculated and presumptive 50 plus percent that innovation contributes to economic growth; then it is further asserted, in the case of Australia, that innovation contributed 40 percent of Australia's economic growth in the 1990s and that R&D was responsible for half of that (36–7). As a small nation, Australia benefits in a large way from foreign R&D whilst the major part of Australian R&D is publicly-funded. Taking those two factors into account, the report additionally asserts that publicly funded R&D contributed 25 percent of innovation's 40 percent presumptive share of Australian economic growth in the 1990s—that is, it contributed 12.5 percent of total economic growth. On the basis of this tendentious chain of 'it would be reasonable to attribute,' the report concludes that, as Australian Research Council funding was 5.2 percent of the total of publicly-funded R&D consequently the ARC generated 0.65 percent of innovation-driven growth. Aside from multiple asserted-but-unexplained assumptions, the report ignores that the salaries of ARC Chief Investigators on research projects are not paid by the ARC but by the universities: meaning that the major substantive funding source for ARC researchers (namely, the universities) is not accounted for in these calculations, even if all of the assumptions about R&D's contribution to Australian economic growth through innovation were true. Two additional general observations follow from this: one is the generally dismal nature of the 'social science' used in official and semi-official reports on universities and research. This social science functions as advocacy not as any kind of science. The second is how little we still know about the relation between knowledge generation and economic behavior.

26   US Department of Commerce, Economics and Statistics Administration, US Census Bureau, *Educational Attainment in the United States: 2009* February 2012.

27   Average Growth Rate 1931–1940: 1.54%; 1941–1950: 3.87%; 1951–1960: 1.75%; 1961–1970: 2.88%; 1971–1980: 2.16%; 1981–1990: 2.26%; 1991–2000: 1.94%.

growth rate of American GDP was 2.3 percent. This compared with 1.46 percent in 2001–2005 and 0.07 percent in 2006–2010. The years 1971–75 and 1991–95 were equally forlorn.[28] The big-picture outlook for the United States is not promising. The annual average growth rate for US real GDP per capita from 1870 to 2010 was 1.96 percent per annum.[29] Compared with this long-term multi-decade historical norm of around 2 percent real growth per year, the mean of expert predictions is that the US through to 2027 will grow at 1.4 per annum on average.[30] Predictions can prove wrong, but the evidence to date indicates that the contribution of innovation factors to growth have been winding down.

The major impact of 'total factor' or 'multi factor' productivity drivers (education, technology and efficiency factors) occurred between 1950 and 1972.[31] A second much weaker wave occurred between 1996 and 2004, the only post-industrial high spot, directly attributable to the information technology boom. The years 1972–1996 and 2005–2012 offer little in the way of 'total factor' growth in the United States. Yet the ideology of the period said the opposite. In short, post-industrial claims about the economic value of mass higher education were false. Overall the higher the level of post-1970 education attainment the poorer was the rate of real GDP growth in the United States. Human capital theory assumed the subtle equation that the more places in universities and schools and the greater spending on research personnel, then the greater a society's economic performance will be. This is not so. It is wrong for two reasons. First, increasing the levels of education qualification and research personnel in a society does not correlate with greater inventiveness or ingenuity or creative insight, the most auspicious driver of economic growth. Second, increasing numbers of qualified persons beyond an optimal point in fact *reduces* the rate of intellectual discovery and multi-disciplinary creation in society.

From 1995 onwards globally there was an explosion of talk about the role of 'creative economies.' In one sense this was a continuation of an older discussion that originated in the economic theory of Joseph Schumpeter in the first half of the twentieth century and extends back as far as the remarkable Jean-Baptiste Say. In another sense, it tapped into the self-justifications of post-modern, post-industrial elites. There can be little doubt that creativity thereby became a social talking point. The irony of this turn-of-the-century preoccupation was that the more that creativity was talked about, the less demonstrably creative contemporary

---

Angus Maddison, *The World Economy: Historical Statistics* 2003; see also summary tables of this data at: http://socialdemocracy21stcentury.blogspot.com.au/2012/09/us-real-per-capita-gdp-from-18702001.html

28   World Bank data.

29   Lindsey 2013: 15–16, based on Maddison's data.

30   Lindsey 2013: 17, based on predictions by Dale Jorgenson, Dale W. Jorgenson, Mun S. Ho, and Jon D. Samuels; Robert Gordon; John Fernald; Federal Open Market Committee; and the US Congressional Budget Office.

31   Lindsey 2013:13–14.

economies proved to be.[32] This is demonstrated in the case of productivity. The simplest measure of human creativity is economic productivity. Productivity is institutionalized ingenuity. The rate of productivity increase or decrease is an expression of the success or failure of innovation and its applications. It is innovation manifest at a very practical, concrete social level. Productivity is a measure of the human capacity to do more with less. It is innovation underpinned by fundamental human creation that allows us to do this.

In the post-modern era, employment in research and development per capita in OECD countries grew markedly. It tripled in West Germany and France and quadrupled in Japan between 1965 and 1989.[33] From 1994–2008, GERD (gross domestic expenditure on R&D) as a percentage of GDP rose from 2.1 percent to 2.3 percent across the OECD, from 2.4 percent to 2.75 percent in the United States, and from 2.6 percent to 3.4 percent in Japan. Yet globally, amongst wealthy countries, productivity has trended down since the 1970s. See Table 2.1. Australia is a typical example. In the 1960s, its annual average rate of growth of labor productivity was 3.1 percent. After 1970, this falls sharply. In the 1970s the rate was 1.8 percent. In the 1980s it was 1.1 percent. This improved a bit in the 1990s, mainly in the second half of that decade, averaging 2.3 percent. Then it fell away again to 1.7 percent in the 2000s. In the United States, STEM (Science, Technology, Engineering and Mathematics) workers were 1.5 percent of workforce in 1950 and just shy of 6 percent in 2000; yet the growth of 'total factor' productivity (the measure of productivity factors excluding labor and capital, namely technology) trended down over the same period, from 3 percent to 1 percent.[34]

---

32   The demonstration of this economic irony proceeds mainly via a historio-metrical examination of the relation between creative outputs and economic productivity and the larger cycles of expansion and contraction of creative output that have characterized leading economies and societies in the past 40 years and in the past 250 years. The methodological spirit of this draws on the historically-framed empirical analyses of creativity pioneered by Dean Keith Simonton (2013; 1984: 74–5) and the historically-sensitive business cycle analyses of Joseph Schumpeter. Lying at the intersection of these approaches is the promise of a temporally-based analysis of modern cycles of creativity and the way in which these cycles interact with, shape, and ultimately coalesce with the productivity of firms and organizations.

33   Cowen 2011: 205–6. This is confirmed by the 2010–2011 Australian Bureau of Statistics analysis of Australia's multi-factor productivity performance (i.e. productivity driven by technology and efficiency). This performance grew from 1998–1999 till 2003–2004 and then fell off sharply through to the 2010 reporting period end. 'For the growth cycle of 1998–99 to 2003–2004, real output growth (3.6%) exceeded growth in inputs (2.7%) resulting in positive growth in multifactor productivity (0.7%). In the most recent productivity growth cycle, 2003–2004 to 2007–2008, growth in inputs (4.5%) exceeded growth in outputs (3.7%) and multifactor productivity therefore experienced negative growth (−0.8%).' http://www.abs.gov.au/ausstats/abs@.nsf/Lookup/by%20 Subject/1370.0.55.001~2012~Main%20Features~Productivity~20.

34   Lindsey 2013: 15.

Table 2.1   Labor Productivity Annual Average Growth Rate (%)

	Australia	OECD*	EU15^	United States	Canada	New Zealand
1960–1970	3.1	4.6	5.4	2.6	2.8	1.9
1970–1980	1.8	2.9	3.8	1.6	1.4	0.8
1980–1990	1.1	2	2.1	1.4	1	2.1
1990–2000	2.4	1.9	1.9	1.6	1.7	1.2
2000–2007	1.7	1.2	1.2	2	1.2	1.3

* OECD is an aggregate of the 24 longest-standing member countries

^EU15 is an aggregate of Austria, Belgium, Denmark, Finland, Germany, Greece, Ireland, Italy, Luxembourg, Netherlands, Portugal, Spain, Sweden and the United Kingdom.

Data Source: Australian Government Productivity Commission, International productivity comparisons. Calculations are based on The Conference Board and Groningen Growth and Development Centre, Total Economy Database, September 2008.

While after 1970 investment in higher education and in research increased dramatically, economic productivity declined visibly. This is the converse of what the endogenous growth-human capital argument (of Gary Becker, Paul Romer and others) would lead us to believe. Not only that but also the research yield per real research dollar declined. In respect of the latter, the Australian figures are revealing. In 1993, Australian academics produced 1.6 unweighted publications per head.[35] This metric tumbled as low as 0.6 in 1997. It was an anemic 1.08 per capita between 2004 and 2010. During the period Australia increased its real external funding of research. Total university research income (in 2011 dollar terms) rose from $720 million in 1992 to $3,070 million in 2010. Yet the number of research publications per $100,000 income fell from 5.2 in 1992 to 1.6 in 2010.[36] In real terms, accounting for the growth of the academic population, weighted publication output per fulltime equivalent academic in Australia rose minutely from 0.95 per head in 1960 to 1.1 per head in 2010, yet spending on research and research administration multiplied in real terms across those decades.[37] In the

---

35   The weighted measure counts a book as 5 units compared to one unit for an article, paper or book chapter.

36   Research by the statistician Adrian Barnett concluded that 'Australian scientists spent more than 500 years' worth of time preparing research funding applications for the country's largest grant scheme in 2012 … And as only one-fifth of proposals to the federal government's National Health and Medical Research Council were successful, scientists wasted the equivalent of four centuries diverted from their research.' Phillips 2013.

37   The Social Science Research Council of Australia, 1966, undertook a detailed survey of humanities and social science publications in Australia for the years 1960–1963 inclusive. This provides the basis for a long-term comparison of research output. In 1960, there were 4,909 academics in Australia. In 2010, there were 46,969 academics in Australia. The humanities and social sciences in Australia produced 107 books, 826 articles, 20 papers and 35 book chapters in 1960. Weighting books at 5 and other outputs at 1, the

years 1992–2010 alone, external research funding per FTE academic in Australia in 2011 real dollar terms increased from $27,565 to $67,535. This is a problem reflected across the board. In the United States, external research funding for universities grew from $646 million in 1960 to $16 billion in 1990.[38] Adjusting for population growth and inflation, the real value per capita of direct government investment in US research rose 4.3 times.[39] Did research output per capita or the measurable scale of research impact (e.g. citation volume per article) rise by anything like that? No.[40]

One of the key propositions of human capital theory is that the creative ideas that drive economic growth are non-rivalrous. In other words, such ideas are essentially a type of public good, such that one persons' use of an idea does not exclude another persons' use of the same idea. This is meant as a kind of intellectual socialism. The problem with this theory is that the best ideas in fact are rivalrous. The whole architecture of modern free speech and intellectual inquiry assumes this to be so. Good science requires debate as do just laws and intelligent policies. The better, the tougher, and the more intense the debate—that is the greater and deeper the conflict of frameworks and paradigms—then the richer and more resonant will be the resulting science and social policy. It may well be that one of the underlying problems of the post-industrial era is that the necessary intellectual rivalry of ideas declined during the period and with that decline went the impetus to creation and

---

total Arts output in 1960 was 1,416. Projecting on the basis of relative Arts Faculty output, that represents 4,672 for the total output for Australian academia. In 1960, Arts Faculties made up 30 percent of the academic population (Martin Report, 59, Table 49). In 2010 terms (adjusting for relative academic population size, which was 9.5 times larger in 2010) that represents 44,384 weighted outputs. In contrast, Australian academics in 2010 actually produced 54,042 weighted outputs, a marginally higher output. Output rose from 0.95 weighted publications per head in 1960 to 1.1 weighted publications per head in 2010.

38   Cole 2009: 185.

39   US population rose from 180 million in 1960 to 249 million in 1990. The purchasing power of $US100 in 1960 was $441 in 1990.

40   The Australian Research Council (ARC) measures 'relative citation rate' which is calculated by dividing the average number of citations per publication linked to ARC public funding in a given subfield by the average number of citations for all publications in that subfield, i.e. the world citation rate for that subfield. (ARC 2009). Overall for ISI Thompson publications for the period 2001–2005, ARC-funded publications produced a rate of 1.19 compared to the world citation rate of 1, a negligible difference (2009: 14). In constant 2000 dollars, the competitive research grants and infrastructure funding administered by the ARC cost $239 million in 2001 and $238 million in 2002 (Allen Consulting 2003: 13). That represents a major investment for an inconsequential comparative performance outcome. Note in addition that the proportion of humanities and social sciences research output linked to ARC external funding is minimal (2009: 14) yet the relative citation impact of these fields is either as high or else higher than the major externally-funded fields (2009: 16–17). The more that is spent on external funding, the less that is achieved. Martyr (2014) raises similar questions about the Access Economics 2003 and updated 2008 report (*Exceptional Returns*) on Australian medical research.

innovation even if the rhetoric about such matters intensified at the same time. A related problem is apparent with human capital theory. It assumes that ideas do not wear out whereas traditional economic inputs (including land, labor and capital) do wear out. This also is questionable. While it is evident that a small amount of science and philosophy pretty much never wears out, such high-durability ideas represent a very small fraction of the totality of human ideas—even of the most successful ones. Most ideas have a short life. The power of ideas typically expires or diminishes with time. This means that ideas-driven growth has to replenish not only growth but also the ideas themselves.

The classic supposition was that ideas replenished themselves through competition, intellectual debate and political conflict. Human capital theories proposed instead that, by investing in higher education and correlated research infrastructure, research would thereby expand, ideas would multiply, the numbers of knowledge-driven jobs would swell, and economies would grow. The human capital literature is large. Convincing evidence, though, that spending on education results in economic growth is slim.[41] In fact the more that has been spent on research in the past 40 years, the slower advanced economies have grown. Not only that but also the flood of symbol-wielding jobs predicted by post-industrial prophets after 1970 did not eventuate. In fact, the largest job categories in the United States today are retail, cashier, clerical, food preparation, nursing, waiting, customer service, janitor, stock and freight, secretarial and administrative assistant jobs.[42] Most of the occupations that the US Bureau of Labor Statistics today projects to grow in the decade following 2010 are jobs for nurses, sales assistants, health aides, office clerks, food preparers, customer service reps, truck drivers, nursing aides, child care workers, book keepers, cashiers, receptionists, janitors, ground-keepers, medical secretaries, carpenters, waiters, and security guards.

---

41 Wolf, 2002; Vedder and Denhart, 2007; Hohman, 2010. Alison Wolf puts it succinctly: 'the simple one-way relationship—education spending in, economic growth out—simply does not exist.' Regarding the United States, Vedder and Denhart conclude: 'The statistical correlation between state and local governmental expenditures on higher education and the rate of economic growth (growth in real income per capita) is typically negative—higher spending for universities is associated with lower growth in a state, other things being equal.' Examining US states, Hohman observes: 'between 2000 and 2008, Georgia experienced substantial growth in the number of residents with college degrees, increasing its proportion of graduates by 13 percent. But it fell 11 places in state per capita personal income rankings, from 26th to 37th place. Indiana's graduate population grew more than all but two other states, but that didn't prevent its income ranking from dropping eight places, from 32nd to 41st. North Dakota led the country in increasing its graduate population, and it also enjoyed the second best performance among the states in per capita personal income growth. In contrast, the similar economy of Wyoming had the best performance by this measure, but was near the bottom (48th) in growing its graduate base. Large amounts of oil and natural gas exploration were responsible for much of that economic growth in this western state.'

42 Vedder, Denhart, and Robe 2013 Figure 4: 14 and Table 3: 18.

What happened? In the simplest terms, the knowledge society was a fake. Post-industrial knowledge economies produced extravagant promises of knowledge jobs. Yet knowledge in the post-1970s era proved more often than not to be a euphemism for bureaucracy. What the knowledge society generated were larger bureaucracies and ever-more regulation. Bureaucracies measure success by inputs (resources obtained) not by outputs or outcomes. The contemporary mass bureaucratic universities are typical of this. Philosophically they find it easier to make counts of research income and expenditure than research outputs and outcomes. Bureaucracies do not really know what to do with creation in any of its forms. Administrations exist to implement standardized courses of action—not to create things. Organizations typically deliver; atypically they discover.[43] Discovery nonetheless is the propelling force of both modern inquiry and modern economic life. The conundrum of the modern university is that, as it has grown, it has developed a mass apparatus of delivery that overshadows its mechanisms of discovery.[44]

Human capital theory says that economic growth is ideas-driven and that ideas are driven by education. Half of that theorem is true—the first half. The second half of the theorem is doubtful. It is discovery and the related generation of distinctive ideas—not education per se—that creates the concepts and frames that drive the science and social science, the art and technology that generate the economies and elegancies that spur the productivity gains that underlie real increases in human wealth and social prosperity. It is simply not true that if we build a university we will cure the economic problems of a region. A more plausible supposition is that firms and organizations employ persons with ingenuity and inventiveness to solve problems and create products that consumers want to buy and citizens benefit from.[45]

---

43   Dyer, Gregersen and Christensen 2011.
44   Murphy forthcoming 2015.
45   People copy ideas. Human beings are mimetic creatures. In that sense, ideas are non-rivalrous. But each time an idea is copied, it becomes less powerful. Peter Theil (2014) observes that what matters in modern wealth creation is to find new ways of creating wealth that also create long-term value. Compare the typewriter and the word processor. Every time a better typewriter was made, the ur-model of the typewriter was copied and finessed. Such cases involve modestly adapting what we already know how to do. They take the world from 1 to n. They add more of something familiar. This drives competition. Firms that compete introduce new variations of the same in order to defend or expand the share of an existing market. When the word processor was invented, it created a durable new market for a durable new product by creating a template of something new-to-the-world. This kind of creation goes from 0 to 1 rather than from 1 to n. Far from being non-rivalrous, the replication of ideas is the basis of competition. Take the case of the contemporary universities. They innovate by replicating ideas. When their enrolments shrink, they observe their competition and copy their courses. The idea of a discipline cannot be subject to copyright; it is not anyone's property; anyone can use the idea. That is what rivals do.

Modern economics, which is to say that the period of economic life that begins with Industrial Revolution of the late-eighteenth century, relies on creation. I don't mean simply that societies have increased their wealth because machines and devices made them more productive, though that is true. More specifically I mean that modern economics is governed by Say's Law: *supply creates demand.*[46] That summation of Jean-Baptiste Say's Law was coined by John Maynard Keynes who took the opposite view to Say. Keynes thought that demand governed supply. But Say was right. It is not just any kind of supply that creates demand. It is the supply of interesting, economical, superior, and ingenious objects that stimulates modern economic demand and sets it running. When economies turn downwards, and periods of recession or tepid growth begin, demand has waned. It is not that individuals and firms do not have money to spend but rather they have stopped spending it. When American and European economies after 2001 were threatened with recession, many governments encouraged consumers to buy houses with low interest rates. But in an advanced economy most people have a house. So the houses they purchased were bought with cheap credit to sell again quickly for a speculative return, a practice that has an inherently limited life. When the speculative housing bubble eventually burst in 2007, a financial crisis ensued. The financial crisis was the creature of a bubble that was a pseudo-solution to a periodic problem in modern economies. This is the problem of a lack of supply of objects that people want to buy. It is interesting to see this apply also in the case of China. When the Global Financial Crisis hit in 2008, the Chinese government responded with massive infrastructure spending. Chinese banks financed buildings, networks, apartment blocks and cities. But by 2012 the efficacy of the technique had faded. How many empty cities and buildings does any one country need? Again the problem was the lack of supply of objects that people wanted.[47]

They compete on the terrain of the same, each believing that what they are doing is different whilst having appropriated the idea from their competitor and modified it ever so mildly.

46   This view was re-stated by George Gilder in *Wealth and Poverty* 1981. Karlgaard notes that '[it] became the book most frequently cited by President Ronald Reagan and turned systems analysis, as applied to economics, on its head. Any systems-analysis view of a struggling economy, at any given time and under all circumstances, will show the chief problem to be lack of demand. In a closed system this would be true. If capital and inventory were plentiful while consumer income stagnated, then the fix would surely be obvious: Get more money in the hands of consumers! Print more money! Redistribute more income! Whatever it takes. But in *Wealth and Poverty* Gilder showed that the problem has always been a lack of supply. And here's the key: not a lack of the same supply; rather, a lack of a new, inventive and entrepreneurial supply that meets consumers where they live and takes them to new heights. Focus on the supply-side entrepreneurs, who will deliver these goods, not the demand side, said Gilder. (Steve Jobs said the same thing when explaining why he eschewed market research: "People don't know what they want until you show it to them.")' Karlgaard 2013.

47   As opposed to government-mandated wants typical of bureaucratic capitalism and state capitalism, and also of totalitarian states which are built on a dictatorship over needs.

How is such a problem overcome? It is not simply that firms and organizations identify people's wants and satisfy them. That is what an economy in equilibrium does. In such an economy it is a matter of supplying known wants with known objects. The problem arises when normal demand diminishes because it is satisfied. Then supply has to create new demand. But the problem then arises: the supply of what? What the question hints at is the paradoxical supply of objects that do not (yet) exist.[48] The object-to-be supplied has still to come into existence. Consumers do not know yet that they want this object. Producers are not yet geared up to furnish supply chains with the objects of future demand. Till this happens, consumers, firms, organizations and banks sit on their money. They husband it. They pay down debt. They accept a lower return on investments. They behave in a waiting mode. They wait for the next-big-thing, the next-wave, whatever that might be.

It might come in the form of the electric light bulb, the telephone, the motor car, the fridge, the air-conditioner, the television. It may be the hospital bed, the university place, the concert seat, the paved road. What private or public good or service will come into existence that consumers and citizens in the future will want? What is it tomorrow that we will wish for, hope for, and pay for? Modern economies accelerate when such propitious goods appear for the first time at an affordable price or at an acceptable level of taxation. Supply creates demand. Yet it is difficult to create a supply of objects that do not yet-exist. They will come into existence but the act of creation is arduous. These good or services have to be—invented. And that invention then has to be turned into an innovation so that it can be finally turned into an act of production or distribution, i.e. into routine economic acts of making and allocating, purchasing and acquiring, trading and handling, storing and accounting. Invention and innovation are far removed from the economic routine. Yet they are indispensable. Modern economies cannot grow without inventiveness, ingenuity and creativity. These are rare yet crucial. Without them—and the adventive supply they generate—economies become slack. An advanced economy was once mostly agriculture. Now agriculture is only a few

---

48   To supply a demand that does not yet exist, is the problem that haunts China's economic model: 'The death of Apple founder Steve Jobs ... triggered rounds of soul-searching over why [China] lacks technology entrepreneurs as successful as Mr Jobs or Mark Zuckerberg of Facebook, who came up with products that changed the world. "Chinese companies can be expected to have market valuations and business models like Apple's within 10 years but it is difficult to expect any type of Apple-like innovation," says Lee Kaifu, the former head of Google China who, with his incubator Innovation Works, has become a guru for internet start-ups in China. Although the number of Chinese internet users—now at 500m—has overtaken the population of the European Union and that growth keeps hatching new internet ventures every day, most of these copy ideas from the US. To name the best-known examples, Baidu, China's largest search engine by revenue, is a copy of Google, while RenRen, China's largest real-name social network, was modelled on Facebook. China is estimated to have as many as 5,000 clones of Groupon, the US daily deals site.' Hille 2011.

percent of total economic activity. That is because secondary, tertiary, quaternary and quinary sectors have been created and each in their turn superseded. Nothing disappears. Indeed the oldest sectors, to continue in a viable and vibrant way, have to continue to be creative, inventive and ingenious. No one and no sector is exempt from the pressure to innovate even the most venerable and traditional. And sometimes the most traditional sectors are the most innovative.

Innovation is Objectivation

The core of innovation is objectivation. That is what made the difference with modern economies. The era of the modern economy begins around 1780. An important watershed is crossed in the late eighteenth and early-nineteenth century. This is the era when high-level creation starts to have a broad measurable social and economic impact. The phenomenon of cyclical ideas-driven growth begins. The modern economy is as Jean-Baptiste Say (1767–1832) described it. His description is better than that of his great intellectual precursor Adam Smith (1720–1790). Say in simple terms and G.W.F. Hegel (1770–1831) in metaphysical terms both described something essential to the spirit of the modern economy. This is the act of objectivation. This is the notion that the act of creating objects is the animating spirit of the highly productive force of modern capitalism. We can describe this very successful variant of capitalism in temporal terms (as 'modern'), in technological terms (as 'industrial'), in temporal *and* technological terms (as 'post-industrial'), and so on. But in truth it is better described as 'creative capitalism,' as an economic mode that is animated by productive creation and creative objectivation, in short by a drive to create objects.

The era of creative capitalism has not been the only highly creative period in human history or even in the larger sweep of modernity. There are exceptionally fertile periods for mathematics, physics, art, and philosophy from the fifteenth century onwards. Creative capitalism begins in the late-eighteenth century with the onset of the industrial revolution. From 1780 until the post-industrial turning-point (which occurred between 1968 and 1974) creative capitalism excelled at translating creative accomplishment into social and economic productivity.[49] It had fierce—and sometimes vicious—external competitors in socialism, communism and state capitalism. It also had more subtle competition in the form of the philosophies and practices of bureaucratic capitalism. The latter flourished during the post-industrial era. Bureaucratic capitalism borrowed various signifiers from creative capitalism. Its sponsors translated the language of creation into the language of knowledge. The preliminary step in doing this occurred in the 1930s in the United States when progressive 'think tanks' helped hatch the New Deal version of capitalism. The New Deal was the first draft of bureaucratic capitalism. The Keynesian revolution in economics ran parallel to this. The British and

---

49   Gordon 2012.

Continental welfare states and the American Great Society elaborated the theme while the post-industrial economic model consummated the theme. The key aspect of bureaucratic capitalism was a shift in the dominant social signifiers: from output to input, production to distribution, and creation to knowledge. This shift subtly but powerfully had the effect of (partially) reconfiguring capitalist economies. It did not eliminate them as socialism or communism once hoped. It did not subject them to authoritarian political direction as state capitalism promised. Rather bureaucratic capitalism aimed at changing the ethos of modern capitalism by 'socializing' it from within.

To understand the paradigm of post-industrial bureaucratic capitalism, it is important to understand what it fought with and what it sought to replace. Creative capitalism is founded on a distinct view of the world. This is the view that the core of economic behavior is the act of creative production. J.B. Say gave a scintillating description of this. In Book 1, Chapter XV, 'The Demand or Market for Products' in his *A Treatise on Political Economy* (1803), Say says '[it] is common to hear adventurers in the different channels of industry assert, that their difficulty lies not in the production, but in the disposal of commodities; that products would always be abundant, if there were but a ready demand, or market for them.' This was the basis of Keynesian economics in the twentieth century. Say begged to disagree. In his view, it was not a lack of consumer demand or a lack of money on the part of consumers to buy goods and services that was the problem. Rather it was the lack of valuable products or objects for sale. He acknowledged from the outset that his conclusion might 'at first sight appear paradoxical, namely, that it is production which opens a demand for products.' But nonetheless that was the essence of a modern economy: supply creates demand. Say understood in the clearest possible way that this paradox was the basis of good public policy. He put it bluntly: 'the encouragement of mere consumption is no benefit to commerce; for the difficulty lies in supplying the means, not in stimulating the desire of consumption; and we have seen that production alone, furnishes those means. Thus, it is the aim of good government to stimulate production, of bad government to encourage consumption.' The observation of Say points to why Keynesian economic policies of demand management have proved to be a failure including in Europe and the United States following the global economic down-turn of 2008. This is because creative products create their own markets. Or more precisely entrepreneurs ('economic adventurers') devise the creative products that generate their own markets. This is the real stimulus for economic demand when demand has shrunk. Government spending, bank loans, and cheap money (and so on) are all fake stimuli in the absence of adventive products that lead people to consummate their latent desire. As Say made perfectly clear, in poor economic times consumers have the desire, and they even have the money, they just don't have the objects (the means) to realize their desire. The creation of such products and their production requires a social context that is friendly to acts of creative production. That was the line that was crossed sometime around 1870. At that point in time in north-western Europe and in the European settler societies in North America and elsewhere, a revolution in social outlook occurred such that Say's paradox of political economy was tacitly translated into social common sense. People began to think that it was a good thing to be productive in a creative sense and creative in a productive sense. The alliance of creativity and productivity came into being.

The German philosopher G.W.F. Hegel put into metaphysical terms what Say had summarized in practical terms. This is the idea that human development is a kind of objectivation. Human beings individually and socially create by objectivating themselves. They externalize their thoughts and sentiments. They posit objects around themselves. They create a world for themselves composed of those objects. In markets, such objects are for sale. And as Say held, those who create interesting objects create expansive markets. Supply creates demand. And that in a nut-shell is the history of modern capitalism. It sums up its strength and its weakness. When interesting objects come into being (a difficult process) they stimulate in their wake demand. Demand translates into sales and sales into thriving businesses. What about the public goods that government supplies? J.B. Say thought these should be kept to an absolute minimum, and he had a point. A market tells you instantly if an interesting object is for sale. The signal of a vote is much slower to give effect than the signal of a price. What governments supply tends to create not demand for adventive objects but rather a supply of things for which there is no demand (such as more process and paperwork). The model of a citizen shopping with a voucher for a public good comes closer to replicating the modern object-orientated market.

There is much opposition to Say's Law. After all, Say posited his law in contradiction to the common-place mercantilist economic policies of his own age. Object-orientated markets and object-orientated supply are not universally applauded. They suppose the primacy of production over consumption and inventive and adventurous supply over that which is timid and routine. Thus in competition with object-orientated markets and creative capitalism in the twentieth century emerged a rather determined species of capitalism: bureaucratic capitalism. The axiomatic value of bureaucratic capitalism is distribution. The axiomatic value of creative capitalism is production. While each mode of capitalism of necessity entails both production and distribution, in each case the leading value is different.

Like most modern institutions, the mass university is caught between these two orientations to the world. Buoyant productivity is the necessary accoutrement of any successful modern social arrangement. However the allocation and dissemination imperative is a powerful counter to this. Societies disseminate in two ways. One is by bosses to clients; the other is according to impersonal rules and processes. One method is patrimonial; the other is procedural. The latter (with odd ghostly residues of the former) dominates the contemporary mass university. Because university bureaucracies exploded in the post-1970 post-modern era, they (like all the bureaucracies of that era) combine method with moralizing and process with preaching. That is to say, the post-modern era saw the rise of redemptive bureaucracies. These were devoted to all manner of scolding improvement. In each case, the operational result was the same. Absurd pieties were amalgamated with mind-numbing procedure in pursuit of the spurious fulfillment of fanciful policies.

The work of policy-process-and-piety is now at least 60 percent of what universities do and what they spend their resources on. This shapes the nature of contemporary research. More than conduct research, the contemporary university likes to codify, proselytize and supervise it. The ambition, in some sense the primary ambition, of the post-industrial university is to administer, control, fund, run and direct research rather than undertake it. Consequently universities classify, regulate, categorize, moralize, prioritize, and strategize research. They rank, class, group, and arrange it. They preach, advocate and urge it. Although contemporary universities don't care much for its substance, they happily brand, badge, tag, type, label, market, and advocate it. What they do is turn research into a lobby. The university knowledge lobby claims to redeem society by producing big ideas. These nonetheless never seem to materialize. This sets up an unconscious anxiety for governments and university administrations. They feel obliged to prove the unprovable, that contemporary universities produce great works, when on the whole they do not. They bridge the gap between fiction and reality by various kinds of measurements.

Contemporary governments and universities claim to measure something called the 'quality' or 'impact' of research. No-one can convincingly define what those words mean. They are typical empty post-modern pabulum, i.e. thin, trite, bland and generally unsatisfying. They are so because they are for the most part measures of dissemination not of production. They are measures of citations, requests, down-loads, and so on. Please do not misunderstand me. It is a perfectly normal human curiosity to want to know the size of the readership or the audience of works. These may range from the miniscule to the mammoth. It is interesting to note the different patterns of citation in different fields and disciplines (see Table 2.2). Yet what really matters for culture and science is a tiny portion of society's total research output—1 or 2 percent of it. If 10 percent of creators produce 50 percent of works, then 10 percent of that 10 percent produce significant or important works that have an enduring readership, audience, reception and consequence. It does matter that Google Scholar in 2014 records that John Rawls' *A Theory of Justice* has been cited 47830 times in the scholarly literature or that Cornelius Castoriadis' *The Imaginary Institution of Society* is cited 1423 times. These are serious works by serious intellectuals. But it matters even more that the production of works of this kind is rare and that the incidence of the creation of such works varies according to place and time.

Conversely, most culture and science, in the judgment of Time, is redundant. It has no staying power. Ninety-nine percent of it effectively disappears. That is just the way it is. Everything but a tiny portion of culture and science fades to nothing. Most culture and most science cannot survive the passing of its own time. It withers and dies. No honor, no title, no office, and no citation or down-load-count matters in 50 years or so. Most human works are ephemeral. But a few, the crucial few, endure. Culture and science are ultimately conservative. They may begin in

Table 2.2   Citation Rates by Field

Fields	Average Citation Rates for papers published by field, 2000–2010
All fields	10.41
Agricultural Sciences	6.74
Biology and Biochemistry	16.67
Chemistry	10.74
Clinical Medicine	12.46
Computer Science	3.53
Economics and Business	5.82
Engineering	4.52
Environment/Ecology	10.8
Geosciences	9.26
Immunology	21.13
Materials Science	6.65
Mathematics	3.32
Microbiology	15.3
Molecular Biology and Genetics	24.89
Multidisciplinary	4.98
Neuroscience and Behavior	18.75
Pharmacology and Toxicology	11.79
Physics	8.74
Plant and Animal Science	7.41
Psychiatry/Psychology	10.67
Social Sciences	4.45
Space Science	13.78
Data: Thomson Corporation, 2010.	

innovation but they end in preservation. What abides is what is great. The effect of big science and big culture is to disempower the tiny minorities that create durable culture and science.[50] This disenfranchisement helps produce a half-hearted world in which everyone talks in wretched anodyne tones about 'quality' rather than excellence—just as they talk about being 'appropriate' or 'inappropriate' rather than being right or wrong. This is a world of procedural rationalism.

The spread of procedural-legal rationalism asphyxiates the act of creation. It denies it oxygen. It diverts attention to policy, process and procedure instead of the production of output. Objectivation lies at the heart of innovation and creation.[51]

---

50   Einstein used cost-free thought experiments to test his theories.

51   The theory of objectivation derives from the philosophical tradition of G.W.F. Hegel. It enters the sociology and economics of knowledge notably through the work of Peter Berger.

Under bureaucratic conditions, the act of objectivation is subsumed by norm and regulation. Research is over-determined by research management bureaucracies that value procedure in place of productivity. This is both a symptom of—and metaphor for—the larger decline of social and economic productivity.

On Becoming Less Creative

In short today, the more that we research, the less productive we are. As noted, this is the opposite of knowledge-society and human-capital theory predictions. It is also a reversal of a historical trend that had the most far-reaching consequences for human well-being. In a series of industrial revolutions, from approximately 1770 to 1970, the ingenious application of the arts and sciences utterly transformed human standards of living. The economist Deirdre McCloskey put it this way: two centuries ago the world's economy stood at the present level of Bangladesh.[52] In 1800 (in our dollar terms) the average human being lived on $3 a day; a person today in France or Japan lives on $100 a day. In Norway, the average person earns 45 times more than their predecessor did in 1800, a remarkable $145 a day. The Chinese have now got to an average of $13 a day—four times the 1800 level—and that average figure continues to rise. Today only 1.1 billion of the world's 6.7 billion people still live on $3 a day. If anything is progress, then that is progress. So what made it possible? It was not any of the usual suspects. It was not education nor was it trade per se. It was innovation. It was the institutionalization of inventions from automobiles to elections, constitutional states to antibiotics that made the difference.

Today, however, we are *less* inventive than we were 200 years ago. We are less fundamentally imaginative in the arts and the sciences (including the social sciences) than we were in the nineteenth century. We have also fallen significantly behind the distinctive short burst of technological creativity in the mid-twentieth century. We see the symptoms of this in declining real economic performance. The chain of 'creation, innovation and productivity' is the driver of real GDP growth and real income growth. When the former declines so (with lags) does the latter. In addition, real GDP and real income growth drive relative income equality. This is because higher real wages are the most effective vehicle of income proportionality.[53] Not only that, it is innovation-generated growth alone that can lift the poorest up out of the misery of living on $3 a day.

---

52   McCloskey 2010: 1–2; see also Fogel 2004 for the human consequences of this.

53   Not equality which is a social mirage but proportionality, which means not the making of small, medium and large incomes equal (which is a spurious goal) but rather making them proportional so that none is out of proportion with the other. There is a long history of the theory of just proportions (Murphy 2001).

Data collated by Northwestern University economist Robert Gordon indicates that growth in real GDP per capita from 1300 to 1700 was 0.2 percent per annum.[54] Between the first Industrial Revolution and the beginning of the twentieth century, Britain increased that to just over 1 percent per annum. In the 1940s and 1950s, the United States achieved a remarkable 2.5 percent growth in real GDP per capita. After that heroic peak, US growth begins to ratchet downwards. It does this in a series of steep step-like movements in 1964, 1972, 1987 and 2008 to today's level of around 1.3 percent growth in real GDP per capita. This long historical development is reflected in average real per capita income. In the UK in the 1300s average real income was $1,150 per person in 2010 prices. By 1800 average income was $3,450 per annum. It almost doubled a century later, reaching $6,350 in 1906. In the United States in the 28 years between 1929 and 1959, real income doubled again rising from $8,000 in 1929 to $16,000 in 1959. But then the pace starts to slow. US per capita income doubles again, this time in the 31 years to 1988. Then the pace slows once more. George Mason University economist Tyler Cowen suggests that a key moment is the early 1970s. He points out that 1947 US median family income (calculated in 2004 real dollar terms) was $21,771. By 1973 (that is 26 years later) it had more than doubled to $44,381. In the following 31 years, from 1973 to 2004, median family income rose only to $54,061, which was less than a 22 percent increase. Cowen points out that with a growth rate of 2 percent a year, real income doubles in size about every 35 years. At a 3 percent rate of growth, living standards double about every 23 years.[55] The US grew an average 1.5 percent per annum over 2005–2013. Median household income is treading water.[56] Calculated in constant 2012 dollars, median US household income in 1975 was $45,788. In 2012 it was $51,017. It had virtually flat-lined across the period.

How and why did this happen? Was it the case that, in the 200 years between 1770 and 1970, humankind plucked the 'low-hanging fruit' of the tree of technology creation?[57] Was it that paradigm-shifts like the mass transition from country to city are 'once-ever' achievements? Are there are no more of these to be had? But how can we know this? 'Once ever' statements are like all knowledge of the future: there is no such thing. Knowledge of the future is a myth of progressive epistemologies and philosophies of history.[58] In any case, at exactly the same moment, in 1970, when there is the start of the down-turn in technology innovation and science, there is also a down-turn in high-level culture, including the social sciences, humanities and creative arts. Culture cannot be conceivably subject to the constraints of 'once-ever' achievement. It is not plausible to say that 'once'

---

54   Gordon 2012.

55   Cowen 2011.

56   US Bureau of Census, http://www.census.gov/hhes/www/income/data/historical/household/.

57   Tyler Cowen and Robert Gordon both offer a version of this hypothesis.

58   Heller 1982.

there was the philosophy of Aristotle or the philosophy of Descartes—and that was then the *end* of philosophy. It may be true that there is relatively little work of the quality of Max Weber or Joseph Schumpeter produced today. That does not mean though that the classic works of sociology or economics were a 'once-ever' achievement. Exactly the same applies to technology advances. These are not 'one-off' but rather an on-going series of achievements that appear with greater and lesser frequency across time and space. In the second half of the twentieth century and the beginning of the twenty-first century the frequency of work of the quality of Thomas Edison measurably declined. Ours is not a creative epoch nearly to the degree that was true of the period between 1770 and 1930, even though it is ironically in the era between 1950 and today and especially between 1970 and today that social talk about creativity escalated. The more we talk about it, it seems, the less good we are at it.

The question then is: why? To put it another way: what caused the downturn in the creative impulse after 1970? To begin to answer this question, let us turn attention back to 1970. Unless the reader lived through that year, it is difficult to understand its atmosphere. It was a time when not just the youthful 'anything is possible' dominated but rather a sense that the coming generation, the young, the baby-boomers coming-of-age, would *revolutionize everything*, including human knowledge. One of the canonical texts of the era was Thomas Kuhn's *The Structure of Scientific Revolutions*. Its key concept—paradigm-shifts in knowledge—was inescapable. It was the cliché of its time. The irony was that the baby-boom generation and the subsequent advertising-industry-dubbed X and Y generations produced mostly anything but revolutionary ideas. Their art, science and social science in the main were ordinary and frequently less-than-ordinary. If any historical generation failed, it was the generation of 1968. The '68 generation and those they influenced in their wake did not produce revolution but rather tedium. If we can explain why this was, we can begin to understand the serious deterioration in the quality of the arts and the sciences in the past 40 years.

The '68 generation promised to 'change the world.' It wanted to de-institutionalize and de-school the world. There was a libertarian, liberationist streak in its rhetoric but one which swiftly turned into its authoritarian opposite, and without the virtue of any compensating sense of irony. The liberation generation quickly became the regulation generation. De-institutionalization set in train a ferocious, even compulsive, program of bureaucratization. Every putative innovation nation in due course became a regulation nation par excellence. The impulse of the '68 generation was romantic and anti-social. But note how quickly it spawned anti-romantic theories of creation. I have no great liking of romanticism in any of its guises but I do observe how the anti-romantic romantics of the post-68, post-modern, post-structural, post-post era managed to combine both a rejection of institutions with a vast appetite to expand them. In doing so they combined a moralizing dismissal of tradition with the ferocious spread of every kind of bureaucratic process imaginable.

Nowhere was this contradictory development more apparent than in the universities. Universities began as medieval institutions for training doctors, lawyers and clerics. They retained that role but added to it in the nineteenth century with the rise of the research university. They increasingly assumed a role in discovery such that the advancement of knowledge, and not simply its transmission, became key to defining a university. Universities expanded rapidly in the era between 1880 and 1920 and again after 1970. In fact they expanded so much after 1970 they began to squeeze out most other institutions of discovery. They became the central institution of creation. Yet, at the same time, the pulse of collective creation weakened. These events were obviously related in some way, but how? The primary thread of connection between the two was the phenomenon of bureaucratization. The post-1970 period didn't invent bureaucratization. It did intensify it, though. One sign of this intensification was the massive growth in the university sector. What followed from that was that, as bureaucratization grew, the creative impulse declined.

I am not suggesting that creation is an 'individual' phenomenon asphyxiated by 'collective' forces. Rather I am suggesting that creation has a dual collective and idiolectic aspect. It is a Janus-like function of individual action *and* coordinated action, unique personality *and* impersonal pattern. However bureaucracy is entirely the wrong model of organization for creative action. Creation is stimulated by association, informal organization, parallel coordination, collaboration, boundary crossing; indeed almost any kind of coordination excepting that of patrimonial and procedural-rational bureaucracy. In most OECD countries in the post-1970, post-modern era, procedural-rational bureaucracies boomed. In a few countries, patrimonial bureaucracies held sway. Neither was conducive to creation. The dominant procedural-rational bureaucracies grew rapidly. As they did, the creative impulse weakened. As it did, bureaucracies offered 'more bureaucracy' as the solution to problems caused by the proliferation of bureaucracies.

The driving force of modern industrial capitalist societies is the imagination. It produces high levels of innovation and invention. The national income of many societies is as much as 20 times higher in real terms than it was 200 years ago. There is no precedent for this in human history. Life expectancy, housing, education, disposable income, transport and comfort levels have risen multiple times in modern industrial capitalist societies. To achieve this, these societies set in train a still little understood avalanche of creation. They also set in place a horizon of expectation of perpetual innovation. Time and again, they raised productivity and increased efficiency. Sometimes this was done by rationalization but the greatest developments happened through the medium of acts of imagination. These created not just intriguing products and processes, ingenious technologies, and fascinating aesthetics but most importantly ones that lasted and that became the building-blocks of further generations of ingenuity.

Ingenuity translates into productivity. Productivity is the practical effect of innovation. When we innovate with consequence, we improve the measurable rate of productivity. This matters a lot. This is because productivity, the fruit of nitty-gritty innovation, is the driver of wealth creation and social prosperity. There is a golden chain of causation that extends from creation to innovation to productivity to growth to wealth creation to social prosperity. In the course of the industrial age human beings learnt to do more with less on a mass social scale. Yet it is an odd thing about human beings that what we learn, we can unlearn.

A crucial turning point happened around 1970.[59] Sociologists refer to the period after 1970 as the 'post-modern' or the 'post-industrial' era. That simply means something fundamental changed around the start of the 1970s. What happened was that institutions started to crowd-out core with peripheral functions and to expand procedure and process at the expense of productive outcomes and objectivations. Today advanced countries are addicted to auditing, reporting, testing, evaluating, certifying, documenting and data collecting. The 500-bed Waid City Hospital in Zurich generates 100,000 pages of documentation each day which is 200 pages

---

59   Peter Theil Comments, Wall Street Journal/Uncommon Knowledge. Peter Theil, Co-founder of Pay Pal. Interviewer Peter Robinson/Uncommon Knowledge, Hoover Institute, Stanford University, September 13, 2013:

Peter Robinson: 'Peter Theil, in remarks to the International Students for Liberty, I quote you: 'How much technological progress is actually happening? Is it getting faster and faster or is it actually decelerating and in some ways slowing down a great deal? The basic conclusion that I've reached is that outside a few areas we've had very little innovation in 40 years.' Peter, 40 years has taken us from the Ford Pinto to the Google Driverless vehicle, explain yourself.

Peter Theil: 'Well, if you look at the last 40 years we have had tremendous progress in computers and very little progress just about everywhere else … The most straightforward way to measure how fast we are moving is literally how fast are we moving? And travel speed has gotten faster century after century, decade after decade; we had faster sail boats in the nineteenth century, faster trains, then faster cars, faster airplanes. It culminated with the Concorde which was decommissioned in 2003 and today if you include low-tech airport security systems we are back to travel speeds circa 1960. In energy, there has been a massive failure of innovation which is reflected by the fact that oil prices and energy costs still have not recovered from the oil shocks of the 1970s. In inflation-adjusted dollars it costs as much as it did at the end of the Carter years today.

Peter Robinson: Despite fracking …

Peter Theil: Despite fracking. Without fracking it would be even worse. But despite fracking we are basically in a Carter-age energy crisis. You look at bio-technology. We probably have about as third as many drugs being approved by the FDA per year as were being approved 20 years ago. You can go through sector after sector and say the technology has not lived up to its hopes. We can certainly hope that it is going to accelerate and we are on the cusp of a new golden age which is what we are constantly being promised but I think after 40 years of hype and failed expectations, the burden of proof has shifted very much towards those who claim that we are about to see a lot more happen. And I think that this slow-down of course is reflected in the economic data. We have had generally stagnant wages since 1973. Median wages have been stagnant and mean wages are up maybe 22 percent, and it is reflected in the sense that things are not getting better for a lot of people.

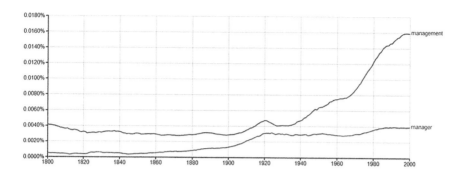

Figure 2.1   The Rise of Management: N-Gram Analysis of the Annual Incidence of Key Words in the Google Book Database

per bed.[60] As the rhetoric of accountability, risk reduction, and quality control has escalated to shrill levels, the prudential baby is being drowned in the procedural bath-water. The spread of process and procedure in the past half century has been massive. The increase in the volume of regulation relative to population is a clear symptom of this. Confronted with a problem, the habitual response now, of organizations and citizens equally, is to demand a 'system' or a 'process' to fix the problem. Often the problem is not fixed at all. Rather we institute a 'method' to deal with problems 'of its type.' Moreover, when we could have flexible general principles, instead we institute a plethora of cumbersome policies, rules and steps. Plans, routes, pathways, courses, techniques, programs, and schemes abound. Some of these are helpful. Some are even indispensable. Many though have a habit of crowding out the creative moments that make life better, more efficient, and more enjoyable.

---

60   Beglinger 2012.

Chapter 3
The Bureaucratic University

Bureaucratic Capitalism

One of the most influential visions of capitalism in the twentieth century was derived from the theory of rationalization. The theory was coined by the sociologist Max Weber early in the century. Weber was sensitive to the changing historical dynamic of capitalism. Modern societies, he understood, had come to equate reason with rationalization, rationalization with development, and development with growth. Weber observed that this complex equation had buried within it an ethic. This ethic was a re-statement of the Protestant ethic. It rested on a paradox: that less is more. By being austere, trimming waste, cutting slack, reducing expenditure, a company and an economy could grow. Accordingly, austere or ascetic behavior led to riches. The Weberian capitalist in other words was an ascetic in order (paradoxically) to produce wealth, a contrary non-ascetic condition. Many critics of rationalization today criticize riches in the name of an equally austere view of the world. They respond to Protestant asceticism with their own brand of authoritarian and moralizing asceticism. Romantic anti-capitalists criticize the wealth produced by industrial development and capitalist growth on the basis that it offends their ascetic sensibility, an outlook they impute to society as a whole. Less, in their eyes, ought to produce not more but less. Only the ascetic elite should enjoy more, in virtue of their virtue.

In this way rationalization has proved to be not only a driver of industrial capitalism but also (in certain hands) a negation of it. It is easy to understand, in no small measure thanks to Max Weber, how the relatively austere nature of Protestantism explains the mountainous riches of modern capitalist economies, especially when the Protestant ethic was translated and refigured in the American context. Even if double-entry book-keeping was an invention of the Renaissance, Protestant religious budgeting amplified and elucidated capitalist economic budgeting. It subtly encouraged individuals and companies to do more with less. Christianity is a religion of paradox. The paradox of religious budgeting lent the modern economic concept of productivity a considerable part of its essence and its power. Productivity is a function of the paradox that less is more. This paradox, applied subtly, is a potent animator of modern economies. At the same time, every improvement in productivity in a modern economy eventually exhausts itself. What is today's innovation is tomorrow's norm. So that the 'less' that produces 'more' (eventually) produces 'less' again. And so the cycle goes, on and on. Significantly though, rationalization also produces another kind of capitalism. This kind—bureaucratic capitalism—far from driving the cycle of growth-shrinkage-growth instead leads to the slow asphyxiation and self-cannibalization of capitalism as a productive system and the emergence of multiple parasitic classes and parasitic offices and processes within modern societies.

James Burnham speculated in his 1941 book *The Managerial Revolution* that managers were becoming a new ruling class. This extrapolated from what Adolf Berle and Gardiner Means observed in their 1932 study *The Modern Corporation and Private Property*, namely that the ownership and the control of companies were separating. What Berle and Means, and later Burnham, noted was the consequence of the forces of rationalization that Weber had observed in the first decades of the twentieth century. Weber looked back to a heroic era of modern capitalism but in the twentieth century the methodical nature of the mainstream Protestant ethic had begun to produce not a productive paradox but rather the kind of suffocating step-by-step processes that everyone would soon start to recognize as bureaucratization in the modern sense of the word. As bureaucracy spread in modern organizations, or rather came to define what a modern organization was, control was substituted for command. Rule was replaced by rules; obedience by compliance; direction by method; and initiative by system. This was the source of the ubiquitous world of 'paperwork,' a world in which information could become a technology, a system and a science.[1] In this world, form was replaced by paperwork forms.

Burnham intuited that the supposedly impersonal procedures of managers actually represented a very personal claim on power.[2] They wished to rule in place of others while insisting that they were doing no such thing. In other words, they used rules to rule. The Burnham thesis influenced the neo-conservative theory of the new class.[3] Neo-conservative writers in the 1960s observed the rapid expansion of an imperious new class of tertiary-educated graduates who had begun to stream out of the universities that were beginning to expand rapidly. The heads of these students were filled with all sorts of romantic ideologies. This new class began to capture the state, enlarge it, and drive the expansion of unsustainable entitlement and spending programs and all manner of bureaucratic law (i.e. regulations). They too wished to rule by rules. They proceeded forthwith to make up rules which others were supposed to live by. Whereas the traditional theory of democratic government had supposed that government was accountable to the people (the voters) the new graduate class assumed that the people were accountable to government.

---

1   A Google Ngram analysis of the term 'paperwork' shows that the use of the word takes-off in the 1940s and sharply increases after 1970.

2   'Fusion of the economy with the state, expansion of the state functions to comprise also control of the economy, offers, whether or not the managers individually recognize it, the only available means, on the one hand for making the economic structure workable again after its capitalist breakdown, on the other for putting the managers in the position of the ruling class.' Burnham, *The Managerial Revolution* 1960 [1941]: 127. Burnham's notion that managerial control could reverse the business cycle or replace the profit motive proved not to be true, but the vision of a class set upon shifting the locus of sovereignty from parliamentary assemblies to the administrative bureaus of an expanded state was spot on, as was the prediction of managerial hostility to entrepreneurial capitalism, freedom and initiative.

3   Kristol 1979: 24.

Bureaucratization can be understood in a conventional sense as the control of human activity by hierarchical apparatuses. All but the most elementary societies have bureaucracies in this sense. Modern bureaucracy though turns personal authority into procedural control. By the mid-twentieth century such control had become commonplace—in production, in the state, in consumption, leisure and scientific research. Bureaucratization proved to be more than the expansion of hierarchies. Universities, for example, were already systemically hierarchical institutions before the onset of bureaucratization. Rather what characterized bureaucratization in the modern sense was semanticide: the systemic loss of meaning through the pervasive spread of procedure. Bureaucratization was more than simply the generation of hierarchical apparatuses or the separation of corporate direction and execution or the cleavage of ownership and direction. In fact, truth told, all of those things came before the twentieth-century bureaucratization of the world. Bureaucratization in the post-industrial sense was connected with those older things. But it was also distinct from them. For at its core bureaucratization was the evacuation of meaning. All societies require the production of meaning. Bureaucratization in the twentieth-century sense can be best understood as the inversion of this: it represented the production of non-sense. Classic hierarchies were all capable (to a degree) of producing nonsense. But neither did they nor their effects explain the pervasive way in which all aspects of society became subject in the twentieth century to bureaucratic logic or more precisely to bureaucratic illogic and its meaning-destroying capability.

The pseudo-logic of the bureaucratic society empties out meaning. It produces vacuity. It is a kind of logic or reason that, as it unfolds, becomes illogical and unreasonable. If logic or reason is supposed to explain something, then bureaucratic logic makes things, while logical, inexplicable. An explanation is one of the key things by which human beings create meaning. If something does not make sense, then a basic response of all human beings is to ask for an explanation. In a bureaucratized society or institution, you will get an explanation—however that explanation will not make sense. Those who offer the explanation, often members of an apparatus, speak and yet manage to say nothing at all—or else not anything that other human beings regard as intrinsically meaningful. Twentieth-century societies developed a rich language to describe this impoverished manner of speaking. They called it spin, verbiage, waffle, gobbledygook, flimflam, guff, blather, drivel, gibberish, and so on. They learnt to recognize that most people in offices, not least of all those in high offices, spoke this language. They found that some people managed not to speak in bureaucratic riddles and evasions but that these were the exception not the rule. The tradition of plain-speaking, directness and forthrightness progressively disappeared as the world became bureaucratized.[4]

---

4   Against this, Cornelius Castoriadis often referred to the classical Greek tradition of direct speaking, aka *parrhesia*. See for example Castoriadis, 'The Greek *Polis* and the Creation of Democracy' 1991a: 107, 113.

Bureaucratic language tells us a lot about bureaucratic modernity. It suggests that bureaucratization was more than a function of rationalization, even if in part it was also that. As procedural rationality spread through the course of the twentieth century, the response of organizational actors to problems changed. Rather than fix a problem directly, they opted for the indirect approach. They began to prefer to create a new procedure whenever a new problem occurred. Procedural rationality pointed human beings away from the personal to the impersonal. No longer did any person stuff up. Instead any fault and any correction of a fault was the result of rules, methods, and procedures. This had a crushing effect on individual responsibility and on the substantive outcomes of organized human action. Organizations henceforth thought of improvement as procedural change. Every act of problem-solving generated new procedures. The shift from corporate 'ownership' to 'management,' or later on in the universities from 'collegiality' to 'management,' was a symptom of the dominance of procedural rationality. Its rise generated additional offices and multiplied functions. The creation, transmission and implementation of procedures required endless additional staff, resources and time. The resulting bureaus swamped organizations and the larger society with a tsunami of rules, handbooks, processes, plans, steps, guidelines, and policies. These were universally written in an awkward language that was pseudo-juridical and empty.

Mock Subjects and Management Lobbies

While bureaucracies have a long history, their impact on everyday life notably intensifies after 1970. Before that, they were mainly instruments of the state. Industrial bureaucracies appear in the 1920s as the modern firm starts to be bureaucratized. What happens after 1970 though is the general bureaucratization of society. This period, the post-industrial era, began as an age of liberation but swiftly turned into a time of expanding social regulation. The *Federal Registry* is a record of all US Federal government rules. It has grown from 2,620 pages in 1936 to 78,961 pages in 2012, 30 times the size.[5] The US population in the same period grew from 128 million to 312 million, 2.4 times. US federal regulation expanded 11 percent in five years alone (2008–2013) of Barack Obama's Presidency.[6] In the turning-point period between 1970 and 1975, the *Federal Registry* tripled in size, from 20,036 to 60,221 pages. What followed was an aggressive smothering of society in rules. This in turn was followed by spiraling regulatory costs. These have been estimated at 11.6 percent of US GDP in 2012.

Across civil society, the demands on time of process and procedure swelled as institutions succumbed to the well-spring of bureaucratization and the accompanying insistence that human activity of all kinds be subjected to plans,

---

5   Crews 2013: 48–9.

6   When President George W. Bush's second term ended, the US Code of Federal Regulations was 157,974 pages. It had grown to 175,496 pages by the close of 2013.

procedures, and processes. If the ideal state of the late-nineteenth century was a legal-rational one subject to precise, orderly, and regular laws, the ideal society of the late-twentieth century was one subject to ubiquitous methodical rules and regulations. The latter implied a notion of time that was meticulous, painstaking, systematic, and logical. The flip-side of this was a pervasive sense of time that was dispirited, desiccated, discouraging, and demoralized. The historical irony was that the administrated society was the by-product of nineteenth-century ideals of British liberalism and American progressivism. These movements promised improvement. Better education, better health, better roads and cleaner rivers were touted. Yet in almost every case the promise of improvement ended not in a more propitious world but rather in the spread of decrees, instructions, directives, norms, and guidelines. The older language of the state (laws, commands and directives) declined. Universities, long-time heralds of progress, were always precocious advocates of more regulation.[7] They applied this not just to society but also to themselves, with alacrity. So the all-administrative university came into being, though the word 'administration' does not quite represent the problem that was to emerge. Virtually any kind of organized human activity has an element of administration. Administration is a normal aspect of a university. However the 'compulsively-administered university' is another matter entirely. It came into existence not because of the need for organized activity but rather because universities multiplied their functions and activities so much that the demand for organization spiraled up beyond any normal call on administration.

The rise of the administratively-fixated university was slow but steady, until 1970 when, as across the wider society, the passion for rules exploded. The rhythms of university time before 1800 were dominated by rituals of entry and exit. Universities marked such moments with organized ceremonies of enrolment and graduation. A modest administration grew up around these points of entry and exit. The tenor of universities was collegial. Universities were run mostly by academics themselves. Two turning points occurred. One was 1920. The second was 1970. The first marked the age of industrial organization. The second marked the age of post-industrial organization. Industrial-age organization stream-lined, formalized and departmentalized some of the ways of universities. The information technologies of the industrial-era firm (the gestetner, the type-writer, and the filing-cabinet) made themselves felt. The idea of management began to appear. Pioneered by Henry Towne, Frederick Taylor, Henri Fayol, Henry Gantt, Alexander Hamilton Church, and others, the idea of management was to subject time and resources to cost-control, quality-control, standardization, and planning. This was achieved through schedules, rules, rosters, plans, procedures, policies, and obligatory staff 'participation.' The presumptive 'science' of management supposed that the marketing, finance, and personnel of an organization could all be controlled by strategies, projects, processes, implementation plans, measurement and reporting. This would lead to a more efficient and effective operation of the

---

7   On American progressivism and the universities, see Rudolph: 355–72.

organization. That at least was the theory. The practice though was the relentless expansion of the central offices of organizations. 'Management' was an ideology of ceaseless growth of central offices whose justification for existence was the claim to be able market, budget and staff an organization more effectively by deploying techniques of time-control and resource-control.

The irony of management is that the offices that seek to control time and resources routinely cause time and resources to blow-out. The apparatus of efficiency is the most common cause of organizational inefficiency. Partly this is a result of the phenomenon of bureaucratization and the related phenomenon of pseudo-rationality.[8] Bureaucratization occurs when central offices, notionally designed to rationally control organizational time and budgets, grow in an uncontrolled pattern. The paradox of this is that organizations bent on the control of time and resources lose control of their time and resources. They become bloated, inefficient, and deprived of clear purpose and direction. Management becomes a lobby fixated on expanding administration. Administrations lobby to expand their numbers. Organizations are turned into conglomerates of interests and lobbies. This has been a common problem of organizations across the last century. The problem is evident in the case of universities. The university proper is a small academic institution. Its animating purpose is to discover things. This is organized as a quest for truth. Only a tiny portion of the human population is interested in such a thing or able to engage in it. It requires staff and students who are independent and armed with initiative, resourcefulness, curiosity, ingenuity, creativity, and self-reliance. Original personalities create original knowledge. These are quite rare characters. The scarcity of such characters stands in contrast to the ambition of the typical university in the past century. The ambition was to get big.

Universities wanted to get big not least because of a social outlook that originates in British liberalism and American progressivism in the nineteenth century. This view suggested that one day everyone would go to university.[9] It has certainly long been the desire of university administrations to admit everyone as students.[10] Abraham Flexner did a detailed case study of Columbia University in 1930. What is notable about the university was its size, even then. In 1928–1929, Columbia enrolled 48,722 students.[11] In 2102 it had 28,824 students (8,274 undergraduates

---

8   Pseudo-rationality is the term introduced by the philosopher Cornelius Castoriadis to describe the failures of a lot of modern bureaucratic rationalization that offers outwardly the illusion of control over things but the accompanying reality of an actual loss of control. See, for example, Castoriadis 1997 [1992].

9   See e.g. Rudolph: 279 on the University of Michigan's James Burrill Angell in the 1870s.

10   Rudolph: 278 quotes a member of the University of California board of regents saying in 1872: 'The University is founded primarily on that essential principle of free Republican government which affirms that the state is bound to furnish the citizen the means of discharging the duties it imposes on him: if the state imposes duties that require intelligence, it is the office of the state to furnish the means of intelligence.'

11   Flexner: 175.

and 18,220 postgraduates). In the 1920s, its student number included 32,599 summer session, extension, and home study students, leaving it with 3,730 undergraduates and 12,393 postgraduates. Columbia has both grown and shrunk over the years, but the key point is that in 1929 the university had 32,599 extra-mural students that university administrations today would call 'unmet demand' for regular university places. Universities have lobbied aggressively across the past century for the fiscal resources (public and private) to meet this 'unmet demand' in the name of expanding 'access' and 'participation.' That could be said to be the self-defined highest purpose of the university in the twentieth century. It eclipsed learning and discovery.

The university moved from an institution in which supply (truth) created demand (student interest) to one in which demand (student aspiration) created supply (student places). But in turn universities believed that the demand itself could magically be created by universities. They could do this by creating central marketing offices to manage demand by stimulating it. In truth, universities more often than not have 'created demand' simply by lowering admission standards or else by eliminating admission requirements altogether—and then offering, in conjunction with this, pseudo-courses of no obvious intellectual merit.[12] The role of marketing is to sugar-coat the fakes. Flexner describes at length the antics of the Columbia University marketers in the 1920s which are identical to the antics of university marketers today.[13] The marketers' 1920s pitch to off-campus ('home study') students almost precisely replicates today's pitch to sign-up 'online' students.[14] There is nothing new a century later about students who are delivered courses away from the physical campus.[15] The aim then as now is to find 'new markets' to fuel further growth. The supply and demand is for simulations of university study. Accordingly the marketers at Columbia University in the 1920s happily spruiked home study subjects that ranged from the serious (philosophy

---

12   Some hair-raising examples of the race-to-the-bottom represented by low and no admission requirements in the United States in the nineteenth century are outlined by Rudolph: 260. Late-twentieth century mass higher education simply replicated the same—just on a larger scale.

13   Flexner: 127–38.

14   Massive open online course courses are the latest in a long line of home study options.

15   Australia historically had a large external student population. The Murray Committee on the universities in 1957 reported (33) that the 'Universities of Queensland and of New England have even established large special departments of external studies. In fact 64 percent of the students enrolled in the University of New England are enrolled in the department of external studies and in the University of Queensland the corresponding figure is 36 percent.' An early national peak was reached between 1956 and 1966, with 10 percent of the student body studying externally. That figure dropped away, picking up again in 1980; in 1980 the figure was 10 percent again, reaching almost 13 percent in pre-internet 1986; the internet made only a marginal difference. External study in 2000 was almost 14 percent as it was in 2011. Source: Australian Federal education department statistics.

and economics) to the silly, including Typewriting, the Slide Rule, Magazine Article Writing, Community Organization and Boy Scouting.[16]

Eighty years later the same kinds of mock subjects are still widely offered in universities as they were 80 years before. No form of spurious learning has been excluded from the modern university. This includes fake sciences like chiropractic, homeopathy, naturopathy, acupuncture, and other so-called 'complementary medicine'; pandering science courses on the physics of *Star Trek* or the science of superheroes; indulgent pop culture studies of Harry Potter, Lady Gaga or the *Simpsons* and philosophy; and pretend degree courses filled with certificate-level technology training, updating Typewriting for the computer age.[17] Universities inhabit a dilemma. They want to be mass institutions, allowing everyone to attend. Yet only a small fraction of any society has the appetite or aptitude for serious university learning. Higher learning is naturally stimulated by human curiosity. Many societies curtail curiosity.[18] Conversely, since the Renaissance a number of societies have encouraged curiosity. Liberal-democratic societies have been prominent among these. Discoveries in the arts and sciences expanded in the wake of this. A university is an institution that satisfies intense curiosity. It is a habitus for very curious people, in both senses. These are people who are driven to find out—and who, as a consequence of that drive, are often curious in the sense of being odd. The persistence required to discover anything interesting, often in the face of social resistance, alone guarantees a certain oddness in the personality of persons of high curiosity. Such personalities are a tiny minority in any society. Yet the administrations of twentieth-century universities and much of the political class of the second half of the twentieth century in OECD countries thought of the university as an institution not for a social minority but for the social majority.

In the 1920s Columbia marketed its wares as universities today do. It deployed the same mix of broadcast advertising and targeted mail-outs, the same combination of puerile badgering and ingratiating, inane messages, and the same relentless following-up of leads. The question that Flexner asked is the same question that generations of academics subsequently have asked: what has this to do with a university? The answer is 'nothing.' What Flexner recognized in 1930 was that a large number of the functions that universities had acquired in the preceding century were not university functions at all. Universities had become a mix of university, secondary, technical, occupational, vocational and popular education. Universities assimilated university-grade functions along with college, polytechnic, occupational and adult education activities. Each of these is a legitimate social function. The issue is not the existence of these functions but rather their absorption into the university. In the 1920s Columbia University at

---

16   Flexner: 130.

17   As of 2011, 15 Australian universities offered 29 certificates, diplomas and degrees in 'complementary medicine' as well as clinics and research programs. Mendham 2011: 20–25.

18   Ball 2012.

least still separated its core university study from its extra-mural margins and from the path-way colleges that it acquired and half-integrated into its operations. Post-war trends in higher education would break down these precarious demarcations. The destiny of Anglo-American-European universities was to become a blob of proliferating functions serving every conceivable type of education from high school level upwards.

Turning Higher Education into Administration

In the post-industrial era, government subsidy of student tuition ballooned.[19] Those who had accessed universities previously via summer schools and home study programs were now offered state subsidies to go to university. Loan schemes covered the rest of their costs. Access to higher education exploded. Government report after government report noted this, only then to say that the expansion was not enough. The participation rate in higher education was never enough. University administrations agreed. Report after report, study after study, recorded less-than-average participation by low socio-economic status (SES) groups, minorities, and (for a time) women.[20] By implication there was a moral imperative to expand university places. This imperative often proved tantamount to a moral panic. Without 'more' university places, the argument went, society would be morally tarnished. To this progressive moral trope was added a post-industrial economic trope. An elaborate equation developed. 'More places' meant more 'higher educated' meant greater 'human capital' meant a more 'knowledgeable workforce' meant higher 'economic growth.' Accordingly, governments that failed to fund more student places were the cause of both moral and economic grief in one hit. Governments duly did what was expected of them.

The number of places in higher education ballooned. Some of these were college places, some were in institutes of technology, and some were in universities. In Australia and the United Kingdom, and to an extent in Europe, governments collapsed the distinction between college, institute and university. In North America, such distinctions tended to survive. But everywhere across the OECD, higher education expanded at a much faster rate than population growth.

---

19   Or else as in the case of Australia, subsidy was redirected from state payment for bonded vocational study, such as teacher training, into 'support' for generic university study that was not bonded to any particular para-profession.

20   In the United States, the proportion of women in higher education grew from 21 percent in 1869 to 36 percent in 1899 and then to 47 percent in the 1920s; it dropped back to 44 percent in 1929 and then 30 percent in 1949. The figure was 31 percent in 1969. It then escalated rapidly; a decade later, in 1979, women were a majority of the student population. (US Department of Education, National Center for Education Statistics, 1993: 64–6) In Australia, women constituted a fifth of bachelor degree students in 1949, 30 percent in 1969, 44 percent in 1980, a majority in 1987, and 55 percent in 1991. DEET, 1993: 212.

Democratic 'access' to universities was widely extolled. Yet what did this 'access' mean exactly? One thing that it often did not mean was 'success.' After 40 years of mass higher education, routinely across the OECD 25 percent of university students dropped out of studies permanently; and more than 25 percent of those who graduated never worked in a job that required a degree.[21] A study in 2013 found that 45 percent of those graduating from Australian universities were over-educated and working in jobs for which they were over-qualified.[22] Notably, 'access' also means something different from active engagement in study, learning and discovery. A university place in itself is not an education. Rather it provides an opportunity for self-education: an opportunity for a person to educate their own self in a stimulating environment. This was a point that Flexner made very well. The university professor, he observed, has an entirely objective responsibility. This is a responsibility to learning and to the subject-matter of learning. This is not a psychological or parental responsibility for students.[23] Flexner argued that the best thing a university can do is make a student help himself.[24] The post-industrial university did exactly the opposite of this. It massively expanded student services.[25] The function of these services was to 'help' students. Universities created huge service bureaucracies. The self-reliance necessary for university inquiry was sapped accordingly. Every dollar spent on 'help' is a dollar that detracts from the self-help ethos crucial to university study and discovery.

From 1970 onwards, a massive expansion of centralized bureaucratic administration and service-delivery began. From 1993 to 2009 universities in the United States increased the number of administrators by 60 percent. That was 10 times the rate of growth of tenured academic faculty. This impacted deeply on universities. It transformed their character. In 2010, the University

---

21   Stille 2014 reports that 38 percent of American students who are enrolled fulltime in 4-year institutions will never graduate after 10 years. He estimates that this costs $11.7 billion annually in the misallocation of faculty, staff, administration and facilities.

22   Li and Miller 2013. After 40 years of expansion, the authors commented: 'It is not clear that the labor market can cope with such growth in the higher education sector' (14). Mismatching of education and job varies from university group to group. Fifty-one percent of graduates from the top-tier Group of Eight Australian universities were mismatched; 34 percent from the technology universities group and 49 percent from the innovation universities group (18). The study's data was drawn from the 1999–2009 Graduate Destination Survey that surveys all Australian university graduates four months after graduation. Li and Miller's conclusions are virtually identical to Kler's 2005 Australian study based on 1996 Census of Population and Housing data. Likewise in 1999, Battu, Belfield and Sloane 1999 found that a year after graduation, 37–46 percent of graduates in the United Kingdom were not in jobs that required a degree.

23   Flexner: 23.

24   Flexner: 85.

25   We see the beginnings of this in Australia with the landmark Murray Committee report of 1957 which recommended (40–41) to the federal government that the Australian universities begin to provide health services and guidance services to students.

of California at Berkeley reported that it had 11 layers of administration.[26] In 2009, American public research universities spending per full time equivalent (FTE) student on teaching and research was $15,785 while spending on student services, public service, academic support, institutional support and operations and maintenance was $11,930. That is, of the total spending per student FTE, 43 percent was on non-instructional and non-research functions.[27] And that does not even account for the fact that on this measure expenditure on teaching and research functions also included the administration of academic departments and research centers—whilst conversely a significant slice of the university research dollar is consumed by central research divisions managing the large pools of graduate research scholarship grant money that contemporary research universities dispense. The University of Berkeley's student services division in 2009 included more than 50 different student services.[28] Between 1993 and 2007 in the United States spending on university administration increased almost twice as fast as expenditure on research and teaching at 198 of the leading US universities.[29]

The same happened in Australia. The effects started to become visible in the late 1980s and early 1990s as a 'unified national system' of bureaucratic centralism and aggressive legal-rational proceduralism was instituted across the university sector

---

26   University of California, Berkeley & Bain and Company 2010: 17. Kiley 2011 reports that Berkeley removed 300 administrators and saved $20 million at $67,000 a head; this compared with a 2008–2009 operating budget of around $1.8 billion (http://www.berkeley.edu/news/budget/primer/sources.shtml). That is 'savings' of 0.01 percent. Berkeley would return to mid-1960s levels of administrative expenditure, if it removed $720 million from its budget. None of the core business of a university—its departmental research and teaching—is any different today from what it was in 1965.

27   Desrochers and Wellman 2011: 52–3.

28   University of California, Berkeley and Bain and Company 2010: 20.

29   'Enrollment at America's leading universities has been increasing dramatically, rising nearly 15 percent between 1993 and 2007. But unlike almost every other growing industry, higher education has not become more efficient. Instead, universities now have more administrative employees and spend more on administration to educate each student. In short, universities are suffering from "administrative bloat," expanding the resources devoted to administration significantly faster than spending on instruction, research and service. Between 1993 and 2007, the number of full-time administrators per 100 students at America's leading universities grew by 39 percent, while the number of employees engaged in teaching, research or service only grew by 18 percent. Inflation-adjusted spending per student on administration increased by 61 percent during the same period while instructional spending per student rose 39 percent. Arizona State University, for example, increased the number of administrators per 100 students by 94 percent during this period while actually reducing the number of employees engaged in instruction, research and service by 2 percent. Nearly half of all full-time employees at Arizona State University are administrators.' Greene 2010.

in that country.[30] The bureaucratic push had its origins in the late 1970s and early 1980s. It began with the creation of a federal Tertiary Education Commission in 1977 that immediately caused more layers of administration to be added to higher education institutions—a story which was to be repeated with every successive higher education 'reform' in the following 30 years.[31] The 'unified national system' introduced in 1989 promised quality, efficiency, and effectiveness. It achieved procedure, process, and portentous planning. The outward goal of this was an expansion of higher education that purported to serve two goals: 'participation and equity' and 'higher economic growth.' It achieved neither. Rather what it achieved was the aggressive bureaucratization of the universities. This amounted to the take-over of the university sector by the new class of university graduates that expanded after 1970. The universities produced the people who would go on to colonize it. 'Professional' and 'experience' and 'management' jobs in universities ballooned. The post-industrial social and economic rationale for this was window-dressing.

In the course of the large-scale bureaucratization of the university, the symbolic atmosphere of universities changed. The signifiers of the institution of the university radically shifted. The Murray Committee, Australia's official report on universities in 1957, talked about graduates with a wide general education, befitting 'the free man and the citizen,' a fully-rounded education producing rounded human beings, with the knowledge of human values matching those of technical matters. It imagined a world of free inquiry and intellectual curiosity, the pursuit of enlightenment for its own sake and the preservation of human integrity in facing truth and the demands of justice. By the 1993, and the *National Report on Australia's Higher Education Sector*, the integral pursuit of truth had been replaced with an obsequious language that invited procedural toadying and deference to vacuous performance indicators, compliance demands and participation rates. A phalanx of buzz words was unleashed on the sector. Everything was to be 'flexible' and 'strategic.' There was to be use of new technologies and more intensive utilization of existing institutional resources. In addition to technical expertise, students would now get highly developed 'generic skills.' These included 'communication skills,' 'interpersonal skills' and 'decision-making and problem-solving abilities.'

---

30   One of the many symptoms of the bureaucratization of the Australian university was the demolition of academic power. In 1957, the Murray Committee (25) could describe the administration of the Australian university succinctly thus: 'The administrative head of each university is a fulltime Vice-Chancellor except in Queensland where this is at present an honorary office. In each university the Professorial Board or its equivalent usually debates academic matters and makes recommendations on them.' In time, the professoriate would be stripped of power, vice-chancellery power professionalized and magnified, and internal debate within universities silenced, replaced by 'consultation.' In the same spirit, excellence was replaced by the imperatives of 'quality,' law by policy, and research by 'research management.' In place of discussion now is the silence of the lambs.

31   DEET 1993:14.

System-wide, 'diversity,' 'equity,' and 'quality' were going to be achieved. STEM (science, technology, engineering and mathematics) subjects and management and Asian studies were favored. Big was better. In 1978, two of Australia's 19 universities and 50 of its 75 colleges had enrolments of less than 2000, and 14 colleges had enrolments of less than 500. All institutions going forward would be consolidated and transformed into big universities. Small institutions were educationally ineffective and financially inefficient—so the rhetoric went. They couldn't support 'comprehensive' teaching programs or undertake research across a 'broad' range of academic fields. At the same time, each institution was expected to have its own particular areas of strength and specialization, while selectivity, concentration, and priority areas were demanded in research. The new order was for breadth and narrowness, comprehensiveness and prioritization. 'Excellence' in research 'disciplines' and 'fields' was demanded but so was 'the greater need for interdisciplinary research.' In this new world, it was thought that some universities might become known as research institutions that do some teaching while others would be teaching institutions where some research was also done. The clear distinction between a (research) university and a (teaching) college was being systematically dismantled. This was a putative world of 'closer links with employers,' improved credit transfer between institutions, 'state of the art' equipment and 'improved research performance.' Intellectual property and the commercialization of research were stipulated. Economic performance would be improved by 'raising the knowledge and skills base' of the workforce. Places in universities would be determined by 'demand' from industry and students along with fiscal and system constraints. Universities would be encouraged to seek 'non-government sources' of funds. Twenty years later the same banalities were being endlessly repeated by the sector.

The material counterpart of this inane discourse was the shift of Australian universities from collegial self-government to a centralist 'managerial' style of administration. The managerial style shifted the emphasis of the university from substance to process. It introduced its own symbolic universe of performance management, research management, student ratings, peer evaluations, research plans, teaching plans, strategic plans, performance indicators, and often-contrived measures of teaching and research output. Administrative, managerial, and professional staff numbers escalated with the explosion of elaborate procedures and planning processes. By 1996, the ratio of administrative to academic staff in Australia had reached 1.3:1 where it remained steadfastly for the following decade. This story is a familiar one across much or most of the OECD. Everyone experiences local variants of it but the grand narrative is the same. The modern university is a mix of welfare state, hotel and leisure center, centralized regulator, and academic institution. The seeds of this go back at least to the 1930s but the peculiar model of the bureaucratic-hotel-welfare-university takes-off in 1970s. It inflates rapidly in the 1990s and 2000s. By 2008, though, with the onset of the Global Financial Crisis and developing government debt crises, this inflation starts to arrest. The public and private money fuelling it begins to dry up.

The Fake City of Pointless Functions

The appetite for multiple functions drove universities on average from modest-scaled institutions to massive-sized leviathans. The more functions there were, the more coordination was required. The more demand for coordination, the more the bureaucratic component grew. A university in principle is a simple institution. To coordinate its basic functions—those of teaching and research—is not complicated. It needs no more than 20 cents in the dollar to administer a university. But when we try and turn the university into a city (a metaphor loved by Clark Kerr), its functions multiply. It has roads, car-parks, industrial parks, hotels, centers, sports venues, museums, hospitals, and much more to consider.[32] This is why senior university managers often feel more comfortable in the company of mayors and regents and developers than they do with academics. Their enterprise is not really an academic one, though it is not a business one either. The modern university is a multi-function polis. It is consumed by the complexity of that entity. The coordination of core departmental teaching and research involves a handful of interactions and variables. The university-polis—the *'unipolis'*—on the other hand has tens of thousands of points of intersection and yet it is not a city. It has none of the self-regulating attributes of a city. Cities and markets are the only two social-scale self-regulating institutions. Markets achieve that through the medium of prices; cities through the medium of patterns.

The failure of the modern university is its failure to live up to the metaphor of the city. It may pretend it is a city. It may take on the functions of a city. But it is not an actual city. It is an organization. Organizations, as they grow in size, become ciphers of procedures, plans and processes. They begin as semi-associations or quasi-partnerships but end up as bureaucracies. That is their Achilles heel. Organizations, in contrast to both cities and markets, are not self-organizing. They are not auto-poietic. This means that cities and markets get more efficient the bigger they get but organizations get less efficient the bigger they get. West and Bettencourt (and their colleagues) calculate that cities are 1.15 more efficient each time they double in size. Companies are 0.8 times more efficient.[33] Markets get

---

32   'Many colleges, [Vedder] notes, are using federal largess to finance Hilton-like dorms and Club Med amenities. Stanford offers more classes in yoga than Shakespeare. A warning to parents whose kids sign up for "Core Training": The course isn't a rigorous study of the classics, but rather involves rigorous exercise to strengthen the gluts and abs. Or consider Princeton, which recently built a resplendent $136 million student residence with leaded glass windows and a cavernous oak dining hall (paid for in part with a $30 million tax-deductible donation by Hewlett-Packard CEO Meg Whitman). The dorm's cost approached $300,000 per bed. Universities, [economist Richard] Vedder says, "are in the housing business, the entertainment business; they're in the lodging business; they're in the food business. Hell, my university runs a travel agency which ordinary people off the street can use."' Finley 2013.

33   Bettencourt, Lobo, Helbing, Kuhnert, and West 2007; Bettencourt, Lobo, Strumsky and West 2010. 'After buying data on more than 23,000 publicly traded companies,

increasingly efficient with size because they operate through the medium of prices. Large modern markets composed of large numbers of strangers make endless constant micro-adjustments through the impersonal price mechanism, generally with great rapidity and ease. Cities self-organize through patterns, principally through 'aesthetic' patterns of 'ideal' ratios, symmetry, hierarchy, proportion, and the like.[34] The university, as an institution, lacks forms of self-organization. It is constituted through departments, faculties, councils, policies, protocols and rules. Informal relationships between academic actors are important but these serve as much to remind us that the primary medium of modern (or for that matter medieval and ancient) creativity is the city. The campus has proved to be a fake substitute for the city.

The American social scientist Charles Murray carried out an interesting statistical exercise. He constructed lists of the outstanding creative figures in the arts and sciences. He then looked at rates of creative accomplishment relative to population in Europe and the United States between 1400 and 1950. Then he asked the question: what is it that can *explain* accomplishments in the arts and sciences? Explanation is the key word. For statistics cannot explain phenomena, they can only point to potentially significant correlations that still require explanation. Murray asked whether creative accomplishment was statistically correlated with war or peace, with wealth, with particular political forms, with the presence of universities or with particular kinds of city. He showed in fact that there is a significant correlation of high-level creative accomplishment with wealth (GDP

Bettencourt and West discovered that corporate productivity, unlike urban productivity, was entirely sublinear.' The reason for this is that the 'efficiencies of scale are almost always outweighed by the burdens of bureaucracy' (Leher 2010). 'Are corporations more like animals or more like cities? They want to be like cities, with ever increasing productivity as they grow and potentially unbounded lifespans. Unfortunately, West et al.'s research on 22,000 companies shows that as they increase in size from 100 to 1,000,000 employees, their net income and assets (and 23 other metrics) per person increase only at a 4/5 ratio. Like animals and cities they do grow more efficient with size, but unlike cities, their innovation cannot keep pace as their systems gradually decay, requiring ever more costly repair until a fluctuation sinks them. Like animals, companies are sublinear and doomed to die.' Brand 2011. http://longnow.org/seminars/02011/jul/25/why-cities-keep-growing-corporations-always-die-and-life-gets-faster/ See also: http://www.edge.org/conversation/geoffrey-west. http://www.ted.com/talks/geoffrey_west_the_surprising_math_of_cities_and_corporations.html.

This is why large, successful, established, mature companies are poor innovators (see for example Christensen 2003; Dyer, Gregersen and Christensen 2011) and why smaller newer companies not only are the crucible of innovation but also consequently of job growth in a contemporary economy. The key to economic futures are not the Goliaths but the Davids (see Reynolds 2006). Likewise university futures lie with lean start-ups—small academic universities focusing on departmental research and teaching, and stripped of multiple *unipolis* functions.

34   Murphy 2001.

per capita), with cities that are 'political and financial centres' and with elite universities.[35] In terms of statistical correlation, Murray hit the nail on the head. But correlation is not causation. A correlation is evidence of a relationship between two entities. It is not though a statement that one entity causes another. Is wealth the cause of ideas or are ideas the cause of wealth? Do growth-driven ideas exist or ideas-driven growth or a bit of both? It is a stretch to go immediately from ideas to economic growth. A mediating element is required. In causal terms, the city is an excellent candidate for this mediating element.

Murray identified a series of European cities across 1400–1950 from which originate large numbers of creators relative to population size. These are not destination cities where the creators end up working but the origin cities that nurtured their drive. The cities included (in descending order of magnitude of significant creative figures per million of population) Geneva, Stuttgart, Konigsburg, Paris, Edinburgh, Bristol, Oslo, Dublin, Hamburg, Prague, Vienna, and Copenhagen.[36] What did these cities have in common? Murray calls them 'centres of finance and politics' but that description also applies to many other European cities of the period including Moscow, Warsaw, Berlin, Liverpool and London that did not incubate major or significant figures on nearly the same scale. Shakespeare, remember, did not come from London. We need to be more precise in identifying what it is about some cities that make them creator-incubators. One thing that Murray shows that did make a clear difference was whether a city had an elite university. Just having a university was not important but having an elite university correlated significantly with whether a city generated a mass of creative figures relative to population size. Few educational institutions matter in the formation of highly creative talents but elite universities do matter. But again the problem of causation arises: was the elite university the cause of the creativity of the city, or was the city the cause of the elite university? And here the answer seems clear: the city is the root of creativity. This is because cities are not organizations. Rather they are self-organizing, autopoietic, aesthetic, patterned entities. Some cities are very good at incubating creative figures and (as a by-product of that) are good at generating university organizations. Arguably both prodigious wealth and elite universities are the by-products of something much more fundamental: the creative energy of the city.

Universities are like companies. They coordinate their many employees through rules and policies, altogether less efficient media than prices and patterns.[37]

---

35   Murray 2003: 331–81.
36   Murray 2003: 356.
37   Work health and safety provides a simple example of the inherent inefficiency of the university-polis. A university modelled on 'the professor and the classroom' has to comply with many health and safety laws. To do so, it must meet the demands of hundreds of clauses of legislation. The university-polis has many more functions. Accordingly it must meet the demands of thousands of clauses of legislation. The tacit cost of this in time and resources makes the university-polis manifestly inefficient. It must constantly divert funds

As the demands on coordination are magnified, not simply 'administration' but bureaucratic administration grows. Bureaucracy is a short-hand term for arrangements that asphyxiate productivity. Bureaucracy promises it can master complexity through process and procedure. It cannot. Its growth shrinks productive action. As the bureaucratic component of the *unipolis* has expanded, the creative capacity of the university has declined. It has ended up in varying degrees of ruination, often deeply dysfunctional, barely able to operate beyond an uninteresting level, consumed by large drop-out rates, poor rates of graduate employment in jobs requiring a degree, and declining per capita levels of research and innovation. An air of ennui now surrounds the university.

The Soft Despotism of Insignificancy

Time is the most precious resource of a university. The spread of bureaucratic demands on time has changed the rhythms of the university fundamentally and not for the good. University research and teaching has been systematically transformed by omnivorous calls on academic time by centralized administrations and their distinctive bureaucratic language and empty imperatives.[38] The cost of this, and its impact on the serious creative endeavor of the university, has been marked. Universities have been plunged into a miasma of insignificance. Their scale of values—what they consider important—has changed as the bland language game of officialdom has become increasingly prominent on campuses. So that where individuals once talked about concepts, they now talk about careers. Instead of ideas, policies have come to the fore. Instead of hypotheses, universities are now galvanized by plans. This did not happen overnight. It took 40 years after 1970 for the full extent of the bureaucratic take-over to become apparent. There were plenty of critics along the way. There were lots of objections to something called the 'corporatization' of the university in the 1990s. Both the critics and protagonists of the corporate university though mistook what was going on. Universities were not mimicking firms. They were much more closely mimicking the behaviors of the civil service. They were becoming extensions of the state—and yet crucially without becoming *part* of the state. Instead they were inhaling its ethos. They became spiritual replicas of the machinery of the

---

from its notionally core business of research and teaching into its many polis functions. Yet it is not a city in reality and it does not have the taxing powers of a city. It is not designed to deliver roads and parks and parking spaces and security and galleries and sports arenas and residences and so much else—yet it is preoccupied with doing so, so much so that the world of 'the professor and the classroom' shrinks ever further into the distance, vaguely admired, good for reputation, but understood incrementally less and less.

38   See Murphy, forthcoming 2015, for a discussion of the impact of the bureaucratic university on academic time.

state without relinquishing their nominal autonomy.[39] Universities could not aspire to the grandeur of the state. But they engaged with growing glee in the pseudo-legislation of a cornucopia of rules and requirements. Universities came to resemble in the end 'municipal corporations' concerned more with parking spaces than with class rooms and obsessed with codes, protocols, guidelines, rubrics, directions, documentation, supervision, and management.

The all-administrative university was a product of modern liberalism as it steadily evolved from a philosophy of individualism to a philosophy of regulation.[40] The great French liberal-conservative thinker, Alexis de Tocqueville, foresaw this. He warned that modern democracies would end up in a state of democratic despotism. Democratic despotism is not like traditional tyranny. It does not mean the rule of a dictator. Rather it means that creative freedom is suffocated by petty rules. This is a world of nations where not just the state but also the larger society is consumed by multitudinous regulations. Few if any of these rules have any significance. Their point rather is to trivialize everything in sight. From the heights of audacity, society is cast into a penumbra of insignificancy. This is a world in which the surface of society is covered—as Tocqueville put it—by 'a network of small complicated rules, minute and uniform, through which the most original minds and the most energetic characters cannot penetrate, to rise above the crowd.'[41] That aptly describes the contemporary university. The key attribute of democratic despotism is that it is *not* tyrannical. Its 'despotism' is bland and harmful in a harmless way. It is mild such that the 'will of man is not shattered, but softened, bent, and guided.' Such a power then 'does not destroy, but it prevents existence; it does not tyrannize, but it compresses, enervates, extinguishes, and stupefies a people, till each nation is reduced to nothing better than a flock of timid and industrious animals, of which the government is the shepherd.' No one in a university dictates to anyone. Power is exercised only in the mildest and softest ways. The contemporary university is pristinely liberal. It eschews violence at every possible turn. It does not command. It has policy, rules and procedures. It is liberal in a managerial way and managerial in an exemplary manner. Soft despotism rules by rules. It expands everywhere and yet it is not totalitarian. Rather its power is mimetic. It rules by being imitated. If one looks at the figures on the number

---

39   Australia produced a series of official reports on its universities after 1945. The first of these, the Murray Committee in 1957, opened with a ringing declaration of the autonomy and self-determination of the universities (7). This was entirely sincere but then the Committee members could not possibly foresee how the recommendations of the Martin Committee (1964), the Dawkins' ministerial Green and White Papers (1987 and 1988), the government post-mortem of the Dawkins' changes (DEET 1993), and the Bradley Report (2008) would hollow out this autonomy to the point of evisceration whilst upholding it in principle.

40   On the intersection of progressivism, the call for regulation and the American university in the late nineteenth century, see Rudolph: 355–72.

41   Tocqueville, *Democracy in America*, Volume II Book 4 Chapter 6.

of federal government employees in the United States since 1970, these have not risen as a percentage of the population. Observers sometimes then conclude that government has not expanded since 1970. But it has. It has done so, first, by adding contractors instead of employees to the federal budget. Government contractors have been the fastest growing component of US federal discretionary spending.[42] Yet contractors do not officially count as employees. Second, government has expanded by *not* expanding. Rather what has expanded is the *modus operandi* of modern government. Civil society has been governmentalized. In democracies the institutions of civil society have been encouraged to mimic the mode of operation of government. That mode is rule-governed. It spreads tiny rules everywhere. It turns all activity into an extension of procedure and process. Since the 1970s, the institutions of civil society have become enamored of these tiny rules. The cultural explosion of the late 1960s promised emancipation, creativity, and release. Very quickly the participants in that explosion decided they preferred the opposite of that. Promptly they began to impose formulae, steps, methods, schemes, and plans everywhere. Soon these were specified to the nth-degree of minuteness and detail. The motive for this was morality. The rule-makers constantly promised that they would make things 'better.' That justified infinite interference in social life in the name of vague abstractions like 'education,' 'health' and 'the environment.'[43] Nowhere was the spread of soft democratic despotism more pervasive than in the universities. Empty moral slogans like 'sustainability' and 'diversity' allowed the mavens of policy and procedure to exert control with what amounted to a strange flaccid intensity.[44] Plans that were invariably vacuous were prosecuted

---

42   Schuck: 325.

43   The writer C.S. Lewis (1972: 202) made an observation in much the same spirit as Tocqueville: 'Of all tyrannies, a tyranny sincerely exercised for the good of its victims may be the most oppressive. It would be better to live under robber barons than under omnipotent moral busybodies. The robber baron's cruelty may sometimes sleep, his cupidity may at some point be satiated; but those who torment us for our own good will torment us without end for they do so with the approval of their own conscience.'

44   Many of the left-liberal slogans popular on American campuses also have a totalitarian feel about them. The language of therapeutic pedagogy, ableism, affirmative consent, fat-shaming, safe spaces, trigger warnings, and sensitivity training is a creepy, Orwellian-style of talk that is imperious, moralizing, euphemistic, censorious, awkward, bureaucratic, puerile and aggrandizing. It encourages the codification of everyday life. Instead of being able to talk in normal terms about what is right or wrong, legal and illegal, this talk resorts to language about what is inappropriate or unwelcome, offensive or hurtful. It avoids both law and ethics for an infantile jargon-laced talk that is simultaneously banal and insidious. This is what you get if you cross teen totalitarians with policy mandarins. It is what happens when the juvenilia of the contemporary campus intersects with its administrative over-drive. The effect is to discourage dissent and opposition. It turns claims of 'diversity' into a claustrophobic monolith of left-liberal orthodoxy. Certain favored words—diversity, inclusion, social justice, and sustainability notable among them—are endlessly repeated like a childish magical credo. This credo permeates everything from

often with a rage for control. The cultural effect of this was debilitating. The controlling impulse combined with the banality of policy elevated things that were unimportant, irrelevant, inconsequential, trivial and petty. The promise of the procedural phalanx was 'more education.' What actually occurred was more administration.

Classroom Versus Campus: The Rise of the Omniversity

For much of the history of the modern university, universities spent 20 cents in the dollar on administration. Expenditure was still only 40 cents in the dollar in 1931 and 50 cents in 1970. Today it is 70 cents in the dollar. The reason this happened in part was rooted in the past. This was astutely observed by Clark Kerr in 1963.[45] He noted that there was a historical difference between the German and English (Oxbridge) models of the university. The German model provided students with a professor and a classroom. The Oxbridge model offered residence halls, student unions, and playing fields. American universities borrowed from the Oxbridge model. Abraham Flexner understood very clearly the significance of this. Flexner's 1930 book *Universities: American, English, German* describes how the modern university evolved as both a university and as something else altogether. Flexner's work is one of the greatest studies ever of the university.[46] He relates how so much of the activity and resources of even the most distinguished universities of his time had nothing to do with the core idea of an academic university. Universities, he observed, were over-determined by a vast range of extraneous endeavors. These marginalized serious academic teaching and research. The problem was not the idea of the university but how unlike a university universities had become.

The expansion of the mass bureaucratic university after the 1970s magnified the traits of the non-university university. These traits were already deeply etched into the character of the early-twentieth-century university. They can be traced back a long way into the nineteenth century. They point to an enduring deep confusion about what a university is. The modern university is an enigma. No-one has ever been able to say with any assuredness what it is. Lip-service is often paid

---

ritual protests to official documents in a thoughtless deluge of prattle. The atmosphere created encourages the conversion of juvenile insecurities into reasons for banning acts. Many American universities, notionally places of adult, free, robust inquiry, have become institutions where immature individuals routinely claim to have their feelings 'offended' by speech acts or claim that they 'feel unsafe' because of something that someone has said. Institutions often now consider the 'upset caused to feelings' or student displays of emotional insecurity sufficient to have speech acts banned, sanctioned, or in other ways debarred. Under these conditions, universities are turned into kindergartens.

45   Kerr: 17.

46   From the same period comes the less well-known but equally interesting book by Albert Jay Nock, *The Theory of Education in the United States* (1932) that shares Flexner's skepticism about what universities had become.

to the notion that a university undertakes 'research.' This is a nod to the prestige and intellectual power of the modern research university. The idea of the research university begins with the creation of the University of Berlin in 1810. Yet many, and in all probability most, universities are teaching universities. Research is marginal occupation in them. Even then, as Flexner was quick to point out, research can range from the serious to the silly. But the ambiguous character of universities hardly stops there. For even the teaching function of a university is uncertain. Teaching in a university can range from programs in the liberal arts and programs for the learned professions through to courses of study that are by turns pseudo-professional, crassly vocational, overly technical, extra-mural, or edutainment-driven. Most universities do not have a definitive function. Rather they have a multiplicity of functions. They are indiscriminately part-university, part-college, part-polytechnic, part-adult-educator, part-vocational-trainer, and part-entertainer.

The modern university has an identity that is not an identity. This is long standing. Take the case of the United States. Until the latter part of the nineteenth century most American institutions of higher education were denominational colleges. The university movement that began in the United States in the 1860s naturally had to justify why an institution should be a university and not just a college.[47] The university typically was an institution that had a graduate school of arts and sciences (which produced PhDs, nascent researchers) and graduate professional schools. The university was notionally defined in post-collegiate terms.[48] However this legitimating core was always surrounded with a welter of other institutional components. Graduate education was not financially self-sustaining.[49] More than that, the idea of the university became a peg or hook to which all manner of things were appended. There were college-like undergraduate programs; upper-division undergraduate programs that aspired to discovery; vocational education; industrial and technological programs; high schools; institutes; extension courses; and then the panoply of add-ons that included sports and civics, extracurricular theatres and academic presses along with large residential and campus developments that

---

47   Rudolph: 329–54.

48   Albert Jay Nock (1932) in the Page-Barbour Lectures he gave at the University of Virginia in 1931 noted the historic logic of American education. A student went from primary to secondary school then to an undergraduate college and then either to a university for professional school or to an institute of science or a technological school (47–8). He noted though that often the orderly consecutive progress through these grades didn't quite work in the conceptual fashion intended. Nonetheless that was the underlying schema. Universities would eventually compound the professional school, science institute and technology school into one institution.

49   Consequently it became one of the major sources of unsustainable university costs: as a proportion of population, graduate education became as large as undergraduate education had been in the 1960s; the graduate degree became the legitimating device for the salary-claims and moral-superiority of the managerial new class. Graduate classes were an oasis of relief for harassed academics pressed into teaching undergraduates who were disinterested in learning.

transformed universities into mini-towns.[50] Clark Kerr summarized the multiple roles of the American university as collegiate, academic, vocational, and non-conformist (bohemian).[51]

Flexner in contrast saw the university proper as a small *academic* institution with a limited number of well-defined functions. Its heart was its doctoral programs and professional graduate schools serving the learned professions along with a small self-sufficient undergraduate population devoted to serious university-grade study.[52] He pointed to the early years of Johns Hopkins University as an example of a great university.[53] Following this line of thought then a university is an institution of discovery. It is not that most universities of Flexner's time lacked the capacity for discovery. Rather this capacity was diluted, watered-down by the activities of the helping-counselling-sporting-public-service-work-integrated university. The serious and substantive thread of the university—its curiosity function—was not eliminated. Rather it was over-determined by a vast array of other imperatives and activities. This continues: research, one of the ultimate embodiments of human curiosity, was re-shaped by the servitude of a gentle kind—as universities turned their attention away from the conduct of research to the management of research. A key factor in this since the 1970s has been the shift of the funding of research from internal university schemes to external (national

---

50   Opening Vanderbilt University in 1875, Andrew Lipscomb stated that: 'The University is bound to recognize every department of true thought, every branch of human knowledge, every mode of thorough culture ... What is best in the University is the catholicity of its views ... It must have an open-minded hospitality to all truth and must draw men together in the unity of a scholarly temper.' Rudolph: 344–5.

51   Kerr: 42.

52   A learned profession is one where the failure of the professional to learn what is needed is potentially catastrophic. A failure of a learned profession may mean for others the loss of life (doctors), the loss of wealth (accountants) or the loss of liberty (lawyers). It can mean the calamitous failure of structures that we depend on (engineers). A learned profession is different from a para-profession like journalism or teaching or administration, whose failures though common enough are rarely if ever ruinous. We do not often die from bad journalism. A learned professional is also different from a legal officer or a scientific officer or a finance officer, each of whom may be required to know something of the law, science or budgets, but they never sign-off for anything and are not responsible agents. The proliferation of such officers has meant the accompanying trait of hand-balling action to others, because of the chronic incapacity of such 'agents' to take responsibility, which ultimately is the responsibility for avoiding catastrophic failure.

53   The closest Australia came to this model was the Australian National University (ANU) in its early days which was created (unlike most Australian universities) under federal law rather than state law in 1946 and solely financed by Australia's federal government. At the time it was 'concerned only with research and post-graduate studies in the special fields of its four divisions: Medical Sciences, Physical Sciences, Social Sciences and Pacific Studies' (Murray 1957: 26). The ANU was not involved in under-graduate teaching. This was later undermined by the Australian government. In 1960, the ANU established an undergraduate teaching division when it absorbed the Canberra University College.

competitive or federally-funded) schemes. Such schemes attempt to translate (not very successfully) curiosity-driven inquiry into bureaucratic procedures. They entail elaborate steps of application, with standardized criteria, application forms, instructions, and a large apparatus of peer review, reporting and auditing. Starting in the early-nineteenth century, 'research' began to be talked about as the defining character of a university. Research was a function of a curious society. It required the initiative to explore and the freedom to discover. Today instead universities see themselves providing a 'safe-and-secure environment' for their students to 'explore responsibly.' That sounds like a third-rate kindergarten.

The university has become the new surrogate parent in everything but the regulation of sex which it generally indulges in a manner designed to impart a knowing tone of superior left-liberalism.[54] Universities routinely declare in a tired and mechanical fashion their support for the freedom of expression but equally routinely squash it not by dictatorial acts or even by censorial acts but rather by the power of enervation. They make everything they say so colorless and tedious that it is sleep-inducing. At every turn the contemporary university declares itself soporifically in favor of diversity in the sure understanding that anything that defies its own norms of correctness and petty rightness will be codified out of existence; corralled into submission by repeated acts of nullity, banality, triviality, tediousness, monotony and lifelessness. The principal tools of the contemporary university—to get its own way—are the tactics of blandness, flatness, and unimaginativeness. It bores everyone into submission. In all behavioral matters, it avoids the law. It relies instead of its own self-assumed executive authority. It promulgates codes and policies that have no standing in law and surrounds these with the pedantry, pomposity and pseudo-legalities of unchecked executive power.

From the second half of the nineteenth century onwards, a great social appetite for higher learning opened up. It was what university administrators today like to call 'demand.' But demand for what? It was not a demand to discover the nature of things. It was not a social desire to become a Columbus of knowledge. It is true that universities are status institutions and that, since the Romantic Age, status and sometimes glamour attaches to the idea of research. Many students today choose a university on the basis of its research ranking or reputation, even though they are not the slightest bit interested in discovery and have no idea what it might entail.

---

54   The exception to this is the use by American universities of amateur pseudo-juridical ideologically-loaded discipline panels and codes to deal with alleged serious sex crimes rather than turning matters over to the proper authorities, the police and the courts. Official campus liberalism defends and promotes sexual license. So when confronted with the miserable alcohol-and-sex culture of the contemporary American campus, the fruit of liberation, it can't invoke the precepts of classical moral character (restraint, etc.) nor does it demand that students study rather than cavort (MacDonald, 2012); instead it creates sex bureaucracies that set about defining bizarre policies intended to administratively regulate the pathos of drug-fuelled semi-anonymous sexual encounters and the resulting explosive emotions of embarrassment and regret.

In Flexner's time just as in ours incoming students typically saw the university as a continuation of high school. Their 'demand' was that universities shepherd them. They would have been horrified by the thought that students at the University of Berlin in the 1830s enrolled for four years, audited lectures that interested them, and submitted a thesis at the end of the four years that they might pass or fail. Since those audacious days, universities have taken to creating an ever-more complicated and stringent apparatus of majors, minors, credit points, grades, exams and assessments. This was followed by the machinery of student policy, appeals, reviews, and monitoring. Flexner observed that the consequence of this was that the first two years of university functioned at a secondary school grade rather than at a university grade. The university, in other words, infantilized itself. This was true even of its leading institutions.

Compounding the general difficulty of the self-imposed regime of child-minding were the expectations of students. Increasing numbers wanted to go to university. In 1928–1929, 900,000 out of a population of 120,000,000 in the United States did so. That was one in 125 of the population. When the US federal Office of Education first started to collect education statistics in 1869–1870, 1 percent of the 18–24 year-old population in the United States attended some kind of higher education including 2 year colleges.[55] By 1899–1900, the figure had risen to 2 percent and by 1929–1930 the figure was 7 percent. In the 1950s, the figure rose from 15 percent to 24 percent and by 1969 it had reached 35 percent of the 18 to 24 year old population. The size of higher education institutions rose accordingly from an average of 112 students in 1869 to 781 in 1929 to 3,830 in 1989.

But what did these students want from a higher education? Exactly the same as students 'want' from a university today: they wanted anything that ranged from an academic education to a technical education to a vocational education to a professional education to edutainment to a social experience. Everything that students in the eighteenth and nineteenth centuries wanted from universities, colleges, technical institutes, and adult education became compounded in the offerings of twentieth-century universities. This was not a late-arriving development. Modern universities early on acquired an omnivorous appetite. They had a chameleon-like desire to be anything-to-anyone. They should have been titled omniversities. Clark Kerr nicknamed their mid-twentieth century progeny multiversities.[56] They compulsively engage in the most astonishing range of activities in which serious departmental teaching and research often play little or no role.

Over the long historical term the combined effect of the universities' omnivorous appetites and the large social appetite for universities was to massively inflate spending per student measured in constant dollar terms. In 2009, 3.7 million staff members were employed in American colleges and universities including 2-year colleges. There were 2.8 million professional staff, 0.9 million nonprofessional staff, and 1.4 million academics made up of 0.7 million full-time

55   US Department of Education, National Center for Education Statistics 1993: 64–6.
56   Kerr: 1–45.

faculty and 0.7 million part-time faculty.[57] In 1976, in public 4-year institutions in the United States, 33.8 percent of employees were faculty; 9.6 percent were graduate assistants; 56.7 percent were executive (4.6 percent), professional (10 percent) and non-professional (42.1 percent) staff members. In 2011, the comparable numbers were 37.4 percent faculty; 11.3 percent graduate assistants; 51.3 percent other, including 4.6 percent executives, 20.6 percent professionals and 26.1 percent non-professional staff members. This data mixes full-time, part-time, teaching staff together, so it is not very illuminating except to clearly illustrate the rise of the professional staff category, the major shock-troops of university post-industrialization. The rising power of professionals in universities and colleges—and the decline of both academic faculty and non-professional (technical, clerical, secretarial, craft, service and maintenance) staff—is striking. The institutional power shift is evident in the contrast of full time equivalent (FTE) students per FTE staff in each staff category across time. When we compare the years 1976 to 2009, we find that faculty load is static over time (17.7 v. 17.3 students per faculty member), graduate assistant load has dropped slightly (100.1 v. 95.7), professional load has dropped dramatically (52.4 v. 23.1), non-professional load has gone up substantially (12.9 v. 19.2), and executive load has dropped mildly (106.6 v. 98.1).[58] This shows every sign of a sector being colonized by the managerial-administrative class on the road to class power.

Academic salary increases in inflation-adjusted terms in the post-industrial era were negligible. Public 4-year doctoral universities in the United States illustrate the case.[59] In the 1980s tuition and other fees rose 55.9 percent while faculty salaries rose 19 percent; in the 1990s tuition and fees rose 37.1 percent and faculty salaries 9.6 percent; in the 2000s, tuition and fees rose 72 percent in contrast to the academic salary rise of 0.7 percent. The average salary increase for all ranks of academics (including continuing and casual staff) in the years 1971–2012 measured in real inflation-adjusted terms was 0 percent.[60] For continuing professors, it was 1.1 percent.[61] Academic salaries treaded water over the period, unlike tuition fees and professional salaries. At American research universities net fees per FTE student (in constant 2009 dollars) rose from $5300 in 1999 to $8000 in 2009.[62] Over the recession-wracked 2007–2011 period, inflation-adjusted academic salaries at doctoral universities grew by 1.4 percent while presidential

---

57 National Center for Education Statistics 2011.

58 National Center for Education Statistics 2011 Table 258.

59 Thornton and Curtis 7: Table B.

60 Thornton and Curtis 6: Table A.

61 The average salary of a full professor at a US doctoral university in 2010–2011 ranged from $116,000 to $152,000 depending on whether they were in a public or private institution (Thornton and Curtis Table C, 12). The average salary of all ranks combined ranged from $85,000 to $110,000.

62 Thornton and Curtis 9: Figure 2 based on Desrochers and Wellman 2011 48: Figure A1.

(CEO) salaries in US colleges and universities grew 9.8 percent. Professional staff salaries in 2013–2014 rose by 2.1 percent compared to the 1.5 percent rate of inflation.[63]

The big winners in the higher education sector in the post-modern era were professional staff. The big losers were skilled blue-collar workers. The rise of the professional class in colleges and universities is reflected in the changing cost structure of US institutions over the last century. The biggest change was the dramatic reduction in the portion of spending by universities and colleges at all levels on 'instruction and departmental research' (including the administration of those departments).[64] Department-level instruction and research was the historic core of higher education. Spending on it was 60 percent of higher education expenditure in 1931. This dropped to 50 percent in 1970;[65] 41 percent in 1980; 37 percent in 2000;[66] and 31 percent in 2011.[67] It halved in 80 years. Accordingly, the knowledge core of the university shrank as the knowledge age became ever more self-conscious. As staple departmental expenditures contracted, generic university-wide commitments rose. These included academic support, student support, general administration, administered research and scholarships. Universities and colleges channelled an increasing portion of their total income into a panoply of services including galleries, audio-visual support, academic computing support, libraries, academic administration, personnel development, course and curriculum development units; social work, guidance, health, psychological services, speech pathology, audiology, and other support for students; general administrative services, executive direction and planning, legal and fiscal operations, and community relations; grants, stipends, tuition and fee remissions; residence halls, food services, college stores, and intercollegiate athletics; hospitals; and the maintenance of plant. Not all of these services increased as a percentage of total expenditure over time. Looking at the period 1977 to 2011, maintenance of plant dropped noticeably from 8.7 to 5.9 percent of spending. Academic support, institutional support, public service, and student services dropped slightly from 24.4 percent to 22 percent. Rising sharply as a percentage of total spending was administered research and scholarships: external ('separately organized') research rose from 8.4 percent to 12.1 percent; scholarships rose from 2.7 percent to 4.1 percent.[68] The knowledge society lived up to its self-image in a particular way:

---

63   Mueller 2014.

64   'Organized activities related to instructional departments'.

65   US Department of Education, 1990, Table 303 and Table 304. This is calculated as a percentage of the general and educational expenditures of higher education institutions. This total excludes expenditure on hospitals, independent operations and auxiliary enterprises.

66   US Department of Education, 2006, Table 348.

67   US Department of Education, 2012, Table 412.

68   Looking at hospitals and auxiliary enterprises, the increase in expenditure on hospitals over the period was cancelled out by a corresponding fall in spending on auxiliary

it spent more on centralized research administration, organization, knowledge support and grant allocation as it reduced its commitment to core departmental instruction and research.

The post-industrial university bulges with offices for careers counselling, chaplaincy, disability, well-being, corporate relations, ethics, estates, external relations, finances, governance, health and safety, human resources, information technology, legal and compliance, planning and statistics, research management, residential services, security, teaching and learning development, and training along with hospital administrators, quality assurance staff and auditors. In sharp contrast, the historic core of an academic university is 'a professor and a classroom.' This core has been marginalized. Or perhaps more accurately the core marginalized itself. The professoriate was the source of the post-industrial ideologies that turned universities and colleges into a sanctimonious sanatorium for every imaginable kind of student grievance, anxiety, hobby, sports-fixation, neurosis, media-obsession, and pop-cultural campaign. It was the professoriate, enamored by a century of progressive ideologies, who waxed lyrical *ad nauseam* about a planned entitlement society run by omniscient qualified professionals super-charged with the miracles of information technology, databases and left-liberal regulation. What resulted was the university over-run by a condescending class of managers and professionals. This class is besotted with a vacuous snobbish rhetoric that is in equal measure mawkish, unctuous, patronizing, and hackneyed. It is an update of the pre-enlightenment language of tutelage, an infantilizing language for perpetual adolescents that manages to turn words like 'dialogue' and 'civility' into ciphers of obsequious moralizing. This is not just an ideological class, though. Much more it is a class on the road to institutional power. As such it is smitten by baroque goals, clinical measures and vaulting ambitions whose point of reference is completely removed from the very simple and straightforward tasks of departmental teaching and research. Today most of what universities spend their money on is neither professors nor classrooms. In 1930 Flexner observed the beginnings of the same. What universities prefer to spend their money on are codes, policies, committees, audits, strategies, special projects, and student services that are ever-expanding. Teaching is the least important student amenity in the modern university of pervasive student amenities. There are residences, sports facilities, counsellors, trip organizers, legal officers, academic helpers, career advisors, educational designers, student welfare officers, auditors, academic staff mentors, sustainability and diversity coordinators, statisticians, learning advisors, communications officers, student mentors, peer advisors, equity and diversity officers, student advocates, student engagement officers, among many others. All of these in their turn require a voluminous central administration to coordinate and regulate them. Each of these functions is subject to directions, guidelines,

---

enterprises. Auxiliary enterprises include dorms, dining halls, cafeterias, union buildings, college bookstores, university presses, student hospitals, faculty housing, intercollegiate, athletic programs, concerts, and other enterprises.

reporting requirements, evaluation measures, budgets, strategies, and performance indicators. With multiple activities come uniform policies. With policies come rules and instructions. Enormous sums, Flexner noted, were spent on the complex administrative organization required to keep this unwieldy machine going.[69] Already by the 1930s, universities were not as they imagined themselves to be: organisms governed by a high aim. They had in fact become administrative aggregations—'so varied, so manifold and so complex that administration is reduced to budgeting, student accounting, advertising, etc.'[70] Looking at the case of American universities between 1975 and 2005, Benjamin Ginsberg observed that even as higher education spending had continued to sharply increase, the faculty-to-student ratio had remained constant over 30 years at approximately 15 or 16 students per instructor. As fees rose precipitously in real terms, no further resources were added to college instruction. What changed dramatically though, as Ginsberg notes, were the ratios of administrators and professionals to students.[71]

The Administered Experience Hospitality Service University

The laying claim to the university by administrators and professionals is a significant part of the explanation of why the modern university is the way it is. The contemporary university in many respects is no longer a university. It is, as Flexner concluded, simply an administrative aggregation. This aggregation serves to coordinate an inordinate number of functions, few of which have anything to do with the ostensible central role of a university to teach and research substantive matters in a serious post-collegiate manner.[72] The 'professor in a classroom' model of a university is economical in terms of time and resources because it is simple. The omniversity in contrast is a study in self-defeating complexity. Complexity wastes time and money. Rather than having three or four clear-cut functions to coordinate, the modern university coordinates hundreds of functions, many of which are elusive. The resulting number of permutations of functions is outlandish. Coordination time expands while teaching and research time shrivels. One of the great devourers of academic time has been the remorseless rise of 'experience'

---

69   Flexner: 185.

70   Flexner: 166.

71   'In 1975, colleges employed one administrator for every 84 students and one professional staffer for every 50 students. By 2005, the administrator to student ratio had dropped to 1 administrator for every 58 students while the professional staffer to student ratio had dropped to 1 for every 21 students.' Ginsberg 2011.

72   Reflecting on a scandal at the University of North Carolina, where college athletes had passed fake courses, Kevin Carney at the New America Foundation observed that what happened was only possible because 'UNC Chapel Hill is not a coherent undergraduate institution. It's a holding company that provides shared marketing, finance and physical plant services for a group of autonomous departments, which are in turn holding companies for autonomous scholars who teach as they please.' Quoted in Reynolds January 14 2014.

time. While the omniversity spends ever less time and resources on academics, it spends ever more time and resources on administered experiences. This is the higher education version of the post-industrial experience economy. It translates the nineteenth-century coming-of-age syndrome and the rituals of the transition to adulthood and attendant apparatuses of sororities and fraternities and residential colleges into an ever-more encompassing constellation of administered rites of organized sports, social activity, travel, alumni networks, pathways to university, mentoring, volunteering, orientation, recreation, graduation, student employment, career planning, health and medical services, extra-mural activity, community engagement, public safety, commencement, admissions, historical tours, visitor guides, and museum and gallery events. Immanuel Kant defined enlightenment as the release of humankind from tutelage. The contemporary university seeks to restore that tutelage through a multitude of helping bureaucracies.

As Google's N-gram analysis indicates, from the 1920s onwards the cluster of terms 'student experience,' 'student services' and 'university experience' takes off.[73] The incidence of these terms accelerates after 1966. By the 1970s elaborate student services had become a standard pattern for the contemporary university. By the 2000s, the regulatory-welfare-hotel-leisure model had begun to definitively eclipse the classic idea of the university. This was a very expensive model. No consumer good has increased in cost more than universities in the past 30 years. Between 1978 and 2008 in the United States, cost of living rose 3.5 fold, medical costs 6 fold, and the costs of private 4-year colleges 10 fold.[74] This cost inflation had almost nothing to do with academics. Universities cast themselves as a cross between the welfare state and the hospitality industry. The only difference being that to pay their price or enjoy their subsidies, a student had to pass the occasional exam and attend the occasional class. To provide their peculiar mix of residential-leisure, advisory-support, and pseudo-juridical-assessment-complaint-and-grievance services required an ever-expanding body of administrators and policy-makers. This is why private American universities, lush with residential and athletic services of all kinds, also registered the largest increases in administrators in a sector that was drowning in them.[75]

As noted, the 'student experience' university is not strictly new. Nineteenth-century universities and colleges often had been a mix of finishing school and coming-of-age pageants. The temporality of personal ritual haunts the university. It is an institution filled with young people who are in a stage of transition between

---

73 The Murray Committee report on Australian universities in 1957 gave expression to this idea of the university stating that 'when the student enters the university he should be entering a community with an intellectual and social climate of its own, and this experience for three or five or seven years of a unique manner of life will give to him one of the most valuable parts of his education. He should in later life remember common-rooms and playing-fields as well as classrooms and libraries.'

74 Eubersax 2009.

75 Ginsberg 2011 Table 5.

home and work. The post-modern era professionalized this transition. A large workforce developed in universities catering to this passage. In the United States employment of university administrators increased 60 percent between 1993 and 2009.[76] This was 10 times the rate of growth of tenured academic faculty. The difficulty with this accelerating administrative growth, as with much about the contemporary university, is that it had little or nothing to do with learning, research or academics as this is traditionally understood. The majority of money that goes into universities today is spent on activities that are far removed from the notionally core academic business of a university, namely its teaching and research. In fact if anything characterizes the post-70s university, it is that traditional academic activities have become marginal to the university. The center of gravity has moved to the housing, socializing, play-time and part-time jobs of students. Academics, study and inquiry are peripheral matters. We have moved a long way from the model of 'a professor and a classroom.'

Too few students today go to university to learn. Probably no more than 40 percent of the total does so. In Australia, 61 percent of full-time first-year students work an average 13 hours a week. They put in a meagre 10 hours a week studying for class and 15 notional hours in class.[77] Governments heavily subsidize tuition fees. What they really do is subsidize students to stack shelves and game online. University of California Berkeley students spend 12 hours a week socializing with friends, 11 hours using computers for fun, 6 hours watching television, 6 hours exercising, 5 hours on hobbies, and 13 hours a week studying.[78] In research universities with 'very high research activity,' 55 percent of senior students in the United States spend an unassuming 15 hours a week studying for class, many in courses that have minimal reading or writing requirements.[79] Only 15 percent of seniors spend more than 25 hours a week preparing for class. Yet 25-to-30 hours of out-of-class preparation is requisite for any kind of serious study.[80] Similarly in the course of a year's senior study, a student in a serious program might be expected to write around 40,000 words.[81] Yet only 10 percent of seniors in the 'very high research activity' universities do so. At the same time, 30 percent of seniors get assigned only between one and four books or book-length sets of readings to study in their courses. (The baccalaureate colleges are a bit better than this but not much.) This is the 'student experience.' It is not surprising then that students in higher education often learn very little. America's Collegiate Learning

76 Hechinger 2012.

77 James, Krause and Jennings 2010: 1–3.

78 Arum and Roksa 2011: 98.

79 National Survey of Student Engagement (NSSE) 2012: 34.

80 American colleges typically advise spending two hours out of class studying for every hour spent in class (30 hours altogether), that is a total of 45 hours a week in and out of class studying. Very few contemporary students ever do that, only 11 percent. National Survey of Student Engagement 2004: 13.

81 At least 11 papers or reports that are 5–19 pages long (double-spaced).

Assessment exercise in 2005–2007 provided Richard Arum and Josipa Roksa with a sample of 2,000 plus tertiary students.[82] The students had been asked in their first semester and again at the end of their second year to read a set of documents about a fictional business or political problem and then write a memorandum to a notional official advising on what to do about the problem. This is an exercise completely appropriate for a university course. If university students can't do this, there is no point in them being at university. What the Learning Assessment data indicated was that 45 percent of students made no progress whatsoever in critical thinking, complex reasoning or writing between first and second year.[83] Any higher education that does not improve thinking, reasoning and writing markedly across the first two years of an undergraduate education has failed massively.

The typical academic at a typical university today knows perfectly well from their own professional experience of the classroom that a third to a half of their students learns little or nothing. There was a time when academic teachers would point this out to their institutions in a vain attempt to stop those institutions enrolling students who lacked the capacity to undertake a university-level course of studies. Universities responded by expanding teaching and learning administrations. They appointed associate deans of teaching and learning. They established teaching and learning development units. They hired project officers. They built databases. They initiated student feedback on teaching, as a way of disarming academic teachers and displacing responsibility for learning from the learner to the teacher. The administration of learning transferred the onus for the wide-spread failure of contemporary university students to acquire knowledge or expand their cognitive capacities. It shifted the onus for this from the student to the teacher—in an institution where self-learning is crucial. Student satisfaction with teachers became the focus of learning bureaucracies rather than student learning. Thus it became de facto okay for students not to learn anything—as long as no-one was insensitive enough to draw attention to the fact that was happening. What mattered was that students were satisfied with their vegetative state.

And so the less that students learnt, the more that learning bureaucracies expanded. This was process heaven. The less learning that happened the more that learning became administered. Subject guides became populated with pseudo-juridical policies, rules, instructions and grievance procedures. The size of these guides ballooned. The content of guides became swamped with legal-rational process advice and directives. In Chinese classical education, the budding imperial

---

82   Arum and Roksa's results echo the self-reporting of students. Astin (1993 223: Table 7.3) tabulates data on student assessments of their own cognitive and skill development after four years of higher education (1985 to 1989). The results were pretty grim, with 60 percent only of students reporting that their knowledge of a field was much stronger; only 27 percent thought their writing skills were much stronger and only 24 percent thought the same of their public speaking skills. A meagre 38 percent thought their ability to think critically was a lot stronger.

83   Arum and Roksa: 36.

bureaucrat first had to learn the works of the humanistic sages. The contemporary university concertinaed this. It placed modern bureaucratic procedure right up front. This was to be a subliminal education in what really matters. Forget the sages. What is important is the step-by-step process of modern bureaucracies. Meaning, insight, reflection, and understanding are all peripheral to process. In the same way, learning and teaching are peripheral to the administration of learning and teaching.

A new bureaucratic sub-culture and apparatus of learning and teaching development grew up in the late 1980s and early 1990s. Google's N-gram analysis shows the use of the phrase 'learning and teaching development' is almost non-existent before 1985. It takes off explosively in 1992. The world of 'learning and teaching development' has its own language, conferences, imperatives, and resource demands. Arcane impenetrable methodologies of learning objectives, learning outcomes, student engagement, flipped classrooms, small group discovery experiences, graduate attributes, e-learning, student portals, innovative assessment practices, teaching awards, program refreshes, 'state-of-the-art' lecture theatres and labs, academic learning development, pre-enrolment programs, bridging, training, counselling, information services and careers advice proliferated. A system of grants and awards and pseudo-scholarship accompanied this. Learning became a division of modern university administration. It was corralled safely away from academic teachers. Teaching and learning bureaucracies promise fixes that fix nothing.[84] When they fail, as they do and must do, they simply ask for more resources and demand new policies. The failure of all modern bureaucracies invariably is attributed by those bureaucracies to a lack of resources and not enough policy.

On the policy-front, the fix always is more rules: more small, complicated rules, minute and uniform. De Tocqueville's social theory perfectly describes how central administrations in contemporary universities think they can fix the failure of many students to learn anything. They believe that if the university makes rules that require academics to list the learning objectives of their subjects or provide three assessments in their course, and ensure that the first assessment is completed by the end of week three, then the failure of students to learn will be corrected. But it can't and it won't be. Forty years ago a subject hand-out was three pages in length. It set out class times and locations and weekly topics and readings. That sufficed for generations of students. Today these items have grown 10-fold or more. They are subject to the panoply of bureaucratic formatting rules and

---

84   For example the administered student rating of university teachers: as Ginsburg and Miles 2014 point out, one can use ratings as an indicator of teaching quality but are they really that or are they a measure of something different, *viz.* the popularity of teachers or some other dimension? 'Ideally one would have indicators of long-term absorption of subject matter as an indicator of teaching success, but such measures do not exist.' That is true—and that is an indictment of the measures of learning in a university. They don't actually measure learning.

filled with fake-legalistic advice to students on university policy and permeated by vacuous curriculum formulas like threshold learning outcomes. Today, as noted, 45 percent of students on average learn nothing in a university class across first and second year. Typically across OECD countries more than 25 percent of students drop out of university and another 25 percent graduate but never work in jobs that require a degree. As teaching and learning bureaucracies have grown, so have the numbers of students at university learning nothing. Not only do the bureaucracies have zero effect on this, but also the bureaucratic power of enervation makes it worse. If student excitement and engagement is part of successful learning and teaching, then the relentless exposure of students to the pseudo-legalities of university policy concerning submission, marking, plagiarism, appeal, and all the rest, reduces student performance. It communicates an underlying message that the university is a place of rules, procedures, instructions and policies. The point of the power of enervation is to weaken the mental and moral vitality of human subjects. Faced with a mountain of tiny rules, of the kind that now proliferates in subject guides, the response of any self-respecting human being is to slink away, discouraged.

In addition, the promulgation, implementation and endless revision of university policy rules are a systemic drain on academic time—with further bad consequences for teaching and research. Time is scarce.[85] There is never enough time in the day. Human beings have to apportion their time carefully, or else they will fail to achieve anything. University bureaucracy has malign effects

---

85   Time allocation studies of universities and colleges are bedeviled by definitional issues of what is included in the categories of teaching, research and service. The US Department of Education National Center for Education Statistics 2011: Table 265 reports that in 2003, in research universities, of the 48 hour paid week, 43 percent of time (20 hours) was spent on teaching, 33 percent (16 hours) on research, and 23 percent (11 hours) on administrative and professional activity. In private liberal arts colleges, the distribution of time (45 hours paid) was 65 percent (29 hours), 12 percent (5 hours) and 21 percent (10 hours) on research, teaching and administration respectively. Link, Swann and Bozeman's study of science and engineering faculty at top US research universities (2008: Table 1) calculates that academic time for this cohort approximately divides into thirds: one-third research, one-third teaching, one-third service and grant writing. Teaching includes meetings outside of class but not student advising. These academics work on average 54 hours a week. Allgood and Walstad 2007 undertook a study of US research university faculty. Faculty members reported working 56 hours a week on average. Almost half of their time was spent teaching (28.3 hours) including 16 hours a week undergraduate teaching and 12 hours graduate teaching. Teaching time allocation included a significant volume of email responses to students. Faculty reported teaching an average of 2.3 classes with an average of 58 students per course and having email exchanges with about a third of those students. The remaining time was split between research (14.4 hours) and other activities (13.3 hours). Allgood and Walstad divided other activities into four tasks: administrative duties (6.2 hours); service (3.7 hours); professional growth activities (1.7 hours); and working outside the university on consulting projects (1.6 hours).

on the academic economy of time. It steals time from teaching and research. It commissions committees to create and revise rules. That time-consuming task is then matched by imperious demands on academic time to ensure that policy is effectively implemented. As policy is generally filled with unintended consequences, reversing the pit-falls of ill-advised rules is a further drain on time. The primary casualty of this has been informal advising time; that is, the time that academics once spent informally inter-acting with, mentoring and advising students outside classes. Milem, Burger and Day in their study on faculty time allocation in 2000 noted that between 1971 and 1989/1992 the time that American academics across the board spent teaching and researching had increased while the time they spent advising and counseling students had decreased.[86] The authors observed the systemic nature of the decline and speculated that the decline could only be explained by institutional factors. It is not too difficult to identify what those institutional factors might be. The scarce time that academics once spent interacting with students outside class, and students with them, has been gradually consumed over decades by bureaucratic time. Bureaucratic time continuously eats away at the traditional time and vocation of the academic university.

The mass university has shrunk the academic university into a pitiable state. Along with this, and as a consequence of it, a convergence has occurred. Teachers have no time. Bureaucratic routines command their attention. At the same time, a large and growing proportion of the student body is disinterested in study. Casual work, entertainment, friends, and social media absorb the majority of their time. All parties have agreed an unspoken social contract not to interfere with each other. Outside of the traditional face-to-face class-room, academic time in the past 20 years has gradually been devoured by email. A significant portion of that email is student queries. But much of it also originates directly and indirectly with university bureaucracy demanding that academics undertake tasks that the administrative and service organs create or else provide the central administration with information that it has decided to collect. In fact a large share of bureaucratic work entails getting other people to perform tasks and furnish information. This is a natural expression of both the conceits of bureaucracy and its centralized nature. Its centralized structure means that it is removed from the point of delivery. The consequence of this is that it must find someone else to do what it wishes to be done. Being removed from the point of delivery means that it has no information about local conditions and so it must find someone who knows. This means that the collection of information is repeated twice, once at the central point and once at the local (departmental) point. The cost of this is crippling. Universities routinely claim that by centralizing professional services they save money. The opposite is true. Centralized delivery doubles costs. If the classic definition of bureaucracy is a system of expert knowledge, the reality on the ground is systemic ignorance.

Bureaucracies operate in a university yet have little or nothing to do with academic staff. Most bureaucratic personnel rarely meet academics and have little

---

86   Milem, Burger and Day: 9.

or no idea what they do. Yet central administrators make extensive demands on academics. This means that they issue requests for information and action without any comprehension of the effect of this on the economy of time of those whom they pressure. Pressure is the correct word. The warrant of university bureaucracies is policy. Policy is treated in universities as if it had a legal status. It doesn't in reality but that does not stop bureaucracies from assuming or even insisting that it does. 'It's the rules' and 'it's the policy' translate very quickly into imperatives. These imperatives are as Tocqueville assumed. They are the corollary of a 'regular, quiet, and gentle kind' of servitude. This is bondage not to the fleeting moods of a portentous despot but rather to the impersonal ambiance of a vacuous culture of insignificance.[87] This servitude does not oppress so much as put its subjects to sleep.

That this should have happened to universities is surprising. Their spirit of free inquiry should have protected them from this. But that free spirit was trumped by them being all-things-to-all-people. The modern university from the start was eclectic. It lacked a clear identity. Its only real identity now is its administrative center. Without that, it is just a collection of disparate entities and purposes. It is comprehensive but incoherent. It is united by its own innate disunity.[88] The modern university carries out so many functions that is unclear what purpose it serves except 'many' purposes, which is not a purpose. To which the reply goes: it is an institution built on 'diversity.' But that is a pious cloak for the fact that the university exists not in and through its academic function or for that matter in and through any of its other functions. Thus all that defines the contemporary university is its administrative center. It is what sticks the disparate functions of the *unipolis* together. But the binding agent only sticks insofar as the university can raise enough revenue and allocate enough resources for its multiple undertakings. Once the university experiences fiscal crises, which means once its organizing center becomes larger than what it organizes, then the question of its identity looms large once again and the question of the future of the university is posed in no uncertain terms.

---

87   On post-modern culture as a culture of insignificance, see Castoriadis, *Postscript on Insignificance* 2011.

88   In response to the fact that the contemporary university is an incoherent bundle, models are beginning to emerge that recommend the de-bundling of the institution. Dhar 2014 is one example. Influenced by Clay Christensen's disruptive innovation business model, Dhar notes how expensive the 'complex bundle' has become. He predicts that an un-bundling process will occur with other kinds of tertiary providers taking from universities the provision of introductory and vocational courses. These new entrants in the higher education market place won't replace the university degree but likely they will cause a substantial recalibration of the degree—resulting in a greater focus, or rather re-focus, on upper division, graduate and research courses, which were the inspiration (though not always the reality) of the nineteenth-century American 'university movement.' This was a model of the university in which 'college' (represented by two years of lower-division undergraduate study) was followed by the university domains of discovery-driven upper division study, the professional graduate school, or enrolment in research degrees.

The Production of Fake Meaning

Questions about identity ('who am I?') are questions about meaning. If the post-industrial university was a self, it would be one very confused self. *E pluribus unum* 'one out of many,' the tag on the seal of the United States, sums up neatly the problem of meaning. If there is no unity in a soul or an institution, there is no identity, and consequently no meaning. The problem of the contemporary university is that it is impossible to sum up in a brief sentence what it does. It does everything and so it does nothing that endows it with a clear meaning. It proclaims that it is many things but so frequently these assertions sound like nonsense. They end up by turns sounding awkward, spurious, sanctimonious, self-serving, pandering, vacuous, manipulative, pompous, smug, self-satisfied, or stupid. They lack the directness and frankness of the kind of speech that endows human action with clear significance. How can one love a state of meaninglessness? The problem of the university is the problem of post-modern societies. They are hollow. How can it be that a society that requires, like all societies, a core of meaning is able to live off the endless production of nonsense? Well it can to a point—but it cannot do so forever. It has been recently reported that baby boomers, the generation who came of age in 1960s and 1970s, are killing themselves at an alarming rate, raising the question: why? One clear answer is a lack of meaning. If you live in a society that is stripping itself of substantive meaning, and if your generation has led the way in doing that, then consequences follow.[89] The sociologist Emile Durkheim's great insight was that a lack of meaning leads to anomie that leads to suicidal behavior. What the post-industrial age offered its denizens was a simulation of meaning. Such simulation has a short shelf life.

The simulation of meaning is to life as kitsch is to art. Kitsch has the superficial appearance of art, but it is not art. Likewise bureaucratic language appears to convey meaning but in reality it does not.[90] Fake meaning is generated by authentic meaning. That is the cunning of bureaucratic reason. Fake meaning is created by identifying some non-contentious good—for example clean rivers, health or in this case education. One then attaches to such goods a machinery of

---

89   Bahrampour 2013.

90   A formulation such as the following appears to be meaningful, but on closer inspection is completely hollow: 'Translating the value of the research university in serving society, contributing to local and regional economies as well as promoting national innovation and security, needs to be a story well told. University faculty, students, staff, and administrators as well as external supporters need to provide clear, consistent, and focused messages to local and national opinion leaders and decision makers. Highly credible accountability and performance-based data from neutral sources need to drive the conversations.' This is how 25 American research universities head-line 'the value of research.' Along with the inevitable 'tsunamis of change,' the 'stories,' 'conversations' and 'messages' of this message point to the numb recursion of statements about statements, the dead end of a world that has been emptied of meaning. For the document in its banal entirety, see Research Universities Future Consortium June 2012.

process, procedure and policy. The apparatus so generated then defends itself. It lobbies for itself, often at taxpayer expense and often using a pseudo-religious language of redemption and righteousness. In the wake of this follows ever-expanding bureaus. Who can argue against these bureaus and their rules? They are for 'the good'. So they expand relentlessly. One of the most effective statements of post-industrial inauthentic authenticity was the proposition that 'everyone should go to university.' The idea that everyone could, would or should go into higher education gained wide social traction in the late 1960s and early 1970s. Vocational diplomas and certificates started to fall out of favor. The tastes of the qualified upper middle class took over.[91] Henceforth, the university would serve as a human universal. Everyone would become a university student and humanity would be united by the moralizing ethos of the higher educated. All work would be turned into professional-managerial work.

Universities originally were created to train the learned professions: doctors, lawyers and priests. In the post-industrial age, the image of the professional was over-determined by the image of the manager.[92] The manager became the ideal occupation of the age. All work aspired to management. Organizations were entranced by the idea of the universal manager who was generically qualified to administer anything. Society began to imagine that it was possible for everyone to become a manager. In the 1920s, the progressive-era American economist and sociologist Thorstein Veblen warned of the coming struggle between the price system and the engineers.[93] The engineers who created modern industry would be undermined by markets. Professional judgment would be overwhelmed by price signals. What happened in fact was that the professions were over-ruled by managers. The learned professions were dominated by serious minds. Managers were recruited from low-scoring university cohorts.[94] So began a class war with serious implications for the broader society. Take for instance the case of the British National Health Service (NHS). As of 2010, it had 1.43 million employees. The number of consultant doctors in 2009 rose by 5.8 percent, the last year of the Brown Labour Government in the United Kingdom. The number of managers in comparison rose by 11.9 percent. Strikingly, between 1999 and 2009, the number of managers in the NHS rose by 84 percent. An expert report in 2013 revealed that 14 NHS Trusts in England were responsible for up to 13,000 'excess deaths'

---

91   In the binary higher education system created in Australia following the Martin Committee report in 1964 it was intended that the technical and teachers colleges offer sub-degree diplomas. They were encouraged by the minister of the day to 'resist the temptation to copy the educational processes and curricula of universities' (DEET 1993: 12) an admonition they ignored. In a short time, they were offering degrees and higher degrees.

92   The moral consequence of the rise of the manager was astutely portrayed by Alasdair Macintyre 1981: 24–34.

93   Veblen 1921.

94   Motl 2006.

between 2005 and 2010. These deaths were caused by preventable factors such as infections, neglect and surgical blunder.[95]

The British doctor Max Gammon identified the larger affliction of the NHS. He called it bureaucratic displacement.[96] He summed up the syndrome in this way: When the NHS was established in 1948 the service had 480,000 hospital beds. By the year 2000 that number had fallen to 186,000. This represents a decline from 10 beds per 1000 of the population in 1948 to 3.7 in 2000. Gammon observed that meant insufficient hospital capacity for prompt investigation and treatment even of first-class emergencies. It left no adequate margin for handling epidemics or elective surgery. On the other hand, the number of staff employed by the NHS more than doubled from 350,000 in 1948 to 882,000 in 2002. The greatest percentage increase was among administrative staff. Between 1997 and 2002 Senior Managers and Managers increased by no less than 47.6 percent compared to an overall increase in the workforce of 16 percent (nurses increased by 1.8 percent) But, Gammon noted, the figures reveal only the tip of the bureaucratic iceberg. For example large numbers of nurses are now wholly engaged in management but are still counted as nurses. Of even greater significance, he reflected, was the proliferation of bureaucratic procedures involving all staff members. These procedures progressively consumed the productive activity of staff. The latter, Gammon concluded, was the heart of the matter.

In the 1970s, in a study of the NHS, Gammon observed that in a bureaucratic system increases in expenditure lead to a fall in production.[97] He discovered that there was a close correlation between the increase in the numbers of NHS administrative staff and the fall in the number of NHS hospital beds that had occurred over the preceding nine years. His linear regression analysis showed a correlation coefficient of -0.99. This had an important explanatory value if (as was the case) the number of NHS administrators was proportional to the bureaucratic activity of the NHS workforce as a whole. The correlation of the growth in numbers of administrators with the fall in the number of beds would then follow, Gammon observed, from a progressive displacement of productive activity of all NHS staff by the proliferation of useless and often counterproductive bureaucratic activities throughout the whole organization.[98] Paradoxically, an expanding workforce and

---

95   The report was undertaken by Professor Sir Bruce Keogh. Donnelly and Sawer 2013.

96   Gammon 2005.

97   Gammon 1975, 1988, 1993. Gammon's ideas became widely known when they were picked up by Milton Friedman 1977, 1991.

98   The most recent example to date of this phenomenon was the Veterans Administration (VA) scandal in the United States in 2014. Despite years of public warnings and large real increases in budget allocations by Congress, the Obama Administration's Veterans Administration oversaw massive increases in waiting times for hospital appointments and benefits approvals, leading to a large number of cases of documented avoidable patient death. The bureaucratic model of single-payer health services delivery

increased spending would thus be matched by a fall in production; the more that was put into the system, the less that came out of it. This process he likened to the implosion of a black hole.

The case of the NHS is typical of all modern bureaucratic organizations. It parallels very well what happened in higher education after 1970. The same story repeats itself endlessly through the whole of the post-industrial era. First there is a demand to expand a universally-recognized good like health. Public money is allocated to expand health services. That means in principle increasing the number of health professionals, para-professionals and workers per capita. What it means in practice is increasing the number of health administrators per capita. It is not the front-line professions and their allied staff that grow in real terms but the quantity of processes, procedures and policies followed by the relentlessly expanding volume of administrators and managers. The procedures promise 'quality.' The reality is that these rule-based systems undermine professional judgment and sap institutions of energy and commitment. They are in short the cause of the problems they seek to cure. The language of 'reform,' 'bench-marking,' 'quality,' 'alignment,' and 'validation' sets the tone for the institutionalization of lower expectations and less demanding practices.

There is no clearer case of this than the universities. From their medieval inception to the mid-twentieth century, the institution of the university was dominated by the scholarly academic who was devoted to the education of those who would graduate to work in the law, science, engineering, medicine, and the civil service. Beginning around 1970, this began to change sharply. As previously noted, from the mid-eighteenth century until the 1940s, universities spent between 20 cents and 40 cents in every dollar on administration; today the figure is 70 cents in the dollar.[99] That is to say, 70 cents in every dollar paid by an enrolling student goes to central bureaucracies in universities. Only 30 cents in the dollar is allocated to front-line departmental teaching and research, notionally the core functions of a university. Each year the amount devoted to the front line reduces. The principal driver of the increase of university central administration has been the post-industrial new class produced by universities and hungry for employment. One of the prime places of employment for this class (as it turned

---

results in queuing, delay, and resources re-routed to administrative process rather than clinical service. Much the same, with less catastrophic consequences, occurs in universities.

99   The 2013 Commonwealth of Virginia JLARC Joint Legislative Audit and Review Commission reported that at Virginia's 15 public higher education institutions, spending on 'instruction' (including departmental research) counted for one third only of institution spending on average; two thirds of spending went to other categories including separately-budgeted research, academic and institutional support functions, and physical plant operations and maintenance. One third of Virginia's higher education staff members were employed in instruction, research and service roles. Administrative, managerial, and professional and nonprofessional support staff made up the other two thirds.

out) were the universities themselves, not so much in the academic profession but in administration and professional services.[100]

Australia is a typical case of the administrative capture that happened across the OECD. From 1972 to 2012 the number of students in Australian universities (compared to the total Australian population) grew four-fold, while the number of non-casual academic staff grew two-fold and the non-academic administrative workforce grew nearly six-fold.[101] There was a proliferation of academic managers as well. When-ever academic professionals are asked what the academic management class does, the usual reply is: 'I am not sure.' Core academic work in a university has not changed much in 150 years. Departmental teaching and research are essentially the same. Enrolling and graduating students is the same. Supervising PhDs is unchanged. Even the basics of departmental administration are more or less constant. So what explains this proliferation of academic managers, administrators and professional office-holders? What do they do?

They produce fake meaning. Another way of saying this is that they produce prolific numbers of documents, reports and audits, they sit in endless meetings, and they oversee extravagant processes with multiple steps, all of which have no point. This is not just a problem of the universities. Post-industrial era organizations in general are addicted to meeting, conferring, auditing, reporting, testing, evaluating, certifying, documenting and data collecting. The post-industrial university compulsively documents itself. The documentation is meaningless. It serves no functional purpose except the reproduction of the apparatus that produces the documentation. The new class of post-industrial managers championed quality audits, registration and accreditation systems, and the setting, monitoring and maintaining of performance standards. The sociologist Max Weber was a skeptic of programs of social justice. He complained that they treated procedural questions of justice substantively. In fact, though, with the passage of time, the opposite proved true. Post-industrial society turned substance into procedure, and procedure into ideology. In its wake, an audit culture boomed. Regulatory norms proliferated. Post-industrial management furiously reported against these norms. The reports mimicked, often poorly, social science research. The ideology of post-industrialism married a low-level research culture with indicative institutional surveillance legitimated by claims to be improving social equity and mediated by information technology. Social science metrics coalesced with institutional target setting via systems of reporting fixated on chimerical social improvement. The

---

100   In the United States, in 1931–1932, in the American higher education sector *including two year colleges*, there was 88,172 instructional staff to 100,789 professional staff, a 0.8:1 ratio. Almost the same ratio had applied in the years 1919–1922. In 1989–1990, in contrast, there was 987,518 instructional staff to 1,531,071 professional staff, a 0.6:1 ratio. National Center for Education Statistics 1993: 80, Table 26.

101   Data sources: Australian Government, Higher Education Statistics Collection 1992–2014; Australian Bureau of Statistics, Australian Demographic Statistics; Hugo 2008, 2005.

new class of post-industrial managers and professionals drew on the prestige of research and the moral allure of fixing social problems in order to press claims for its own expansion. While this managerial and professional class was supposed to improve institutional performance, measured against its own indicators the performance of institutions routinely stagnated or declined. In its own terms of 'assessing, maintaining and improving quality,' this class was a failure.

Bureaucratic Growth and Knowledge Decline

The failure of the university was a function of its success. Its success can be measured by its propulsive growth. Such growth is not new. In the period between 1890 and 1925 in the United States enrolment in institutions of higher education expanded at a rate 4.7 times faster than the population as a whole. The appetite for university credentials again boomed after the end of the 1960s.[102] Through the 1970s and until the shock of the 2008–2010 Global Financial Crisis, universities across the OECD took in ever-greater percentages of the 19 year-old age cohort. Toward the end of the period, political fantasists were promising that 40 percent or even eventually 50 percent of young adults in wealthy societies would attend universities. In the United States in 2012, a third of 27 year-olds had a bachelor's degree or higher and 84 percent had participated in some form of higher education. Ten percent had an undergraduate certificate, 8.7 percent had an associate degree, and just over 32 percent had done some college subjects without completing a degree.[103]

Australia is typical of the larger OECD pattern. In 2007 24 percent of Australians aged 25–64 had a university degree; by 2011 that had grown to 28 percent. Another 10 percent had a vocational-type post-secondary qualification.[104] In 2011, 37 percent of Australians had some kind of tertiary qualification compared with the OECD average of 32 percent. That had risen from 34 and 27 percent respectively in 4 years. In 2007, 31 percent of Australians aged 25 to 34 had completed a university qualification; in 2011, the figure had grown to 35 percent. A further 10 percent had finished a vocational-type post-secondary qualification. Thus in 2011, a total of 45 percent of the 25–34 age cohort had attained a tertiary

---

102   Australia's Martin Committee (1964 volume 1: 11) commented that for a 'variety of reasons, individual members of society are increasingly demanding opportunities leading to higher education ... the propensity to attend universities is a reflection of the aspirations of young people and their parents towards higher education ... "qualifications" have become both a symbol of status and the *sine qua non* of a well-paid and interesting career.' This appetite for higher education was as much created by committees of government as it was felt by growing numbers of the population. The demand was generated in large measure by repeated official assertions that linked education and economic success.

103   Lauff, Ingels and Christopher 2014.

104   OECD 2013: 37, Table A1.3a; OECD 2009: 39, Table A1.3a.

qualification of some kind. In the same year, across the OECD 39 percent of 25–34 year olds had achieved the same.[105] As a striking point of comparison, in 1997 the OECD figure for the equivalent was 20 percent. Participation rates in higher education across advanced industrial economies exploded in the late 1990s and the 2000s. This reflected snow-balling demands generated by the knowledge society expectations and new class ideologies.

The knowledge society ideology crystallized in the late 1960s. In 1965, 1 percent of the Australian population—110,000 students—were at university. By 1991, that number had grown to over half a million, or 3 percent of the population. In 2012 it was 1.2 million and 5.3 percent of the population—a five-fold real increase over 50 years.[106] Not just in Australia, but across the OECD, governments created a huge demand for places in higher education which they part-funded. They offered the universities a devil's bargain: systemic bureaucratization of the university in exchange for public money for seemingly unlimited growth. Universities accepted the money with alacrity. For this they paid an enormous price.

Eventually a large proportion of every dollar that flowed to the universities was consumed in a miasma of policy, process and procedure. This crippled them. Universities grew rapidly but the cost of this growth was deep dysfunction. Less and less time was spent on the core functions of the university: teaching and research. More and more time was spent on auditing, reporting, administering, regulating, and codifying. The transaction costs of the university exploded. Nations are ranked according to the criterion of 'the ease of doing business.' After the 1970s the university became a place where it was no longer easy to do business. Extraneous offices, functions, meetings, procedures, steps and documents proliferated as universities adopted methods of behaving that parodied the very parody of management.

Bureaucratization accompanied expansion, and universities congratulated themselves on the growth of student places. Universities thought of themselves as providing a public good: access for all to higher education. Bureaucratic centralization, everyone was told, was cheaper and more efficient than older, more minimal, more informal, and more decentralized methods of university administration. The management of knowledge, academic staff members were assured, would expand knowledge. The university was portrayed as an icon of the knowledge society. This was one of the many clichés of the post-industrial and post-modern era. The period saw the frenetic and often splenetic rise of the bureaucratic university. Yet the growth of the universities proved to be as much a public pestilence as a public good. This is because bureaucratic centralism proved to be more expensive and more time consuming than old-fashioned administrative minimalism. Knowledge in the knowledge society declined rather than expanded.

---

105   OECD 2009: 39.

106   Data sources: Australian Government, Higher Education Statistics Collection, 1992–2014; Australian Bureau of Statistics, Australian Demographic Statistics.

The two decades following 1990 saw the aggressive rise of research management in Australian universities and a correlated decline of research output. In 1993, at the beginning of Australia's 'unified national system,' the spear-head of a concerted government-led bureaucratization of the universities, Australian academics produced 1.5 publications per head. This metric tumbled as low as 0.6 in 1997. After 2004 it was an anemic 1.0 per capita.[107] In contrast, the major American research universities produce 2 to 5 publications per head per annum.[108] The best Australia could manage once the bureaucratization process was complete was the Australian National University's 1.6 per capita. The University of Melbourne output fell from 2 per capita in 1992 to 1.1 per capita in 2011. This is a serious matter when we consider that high quality research strongly correlates with high quantities of output. The best researchers produce great work *and* lots of work. Quality and quantity are mutually implicated in serious creative work.

Australia increased its external funding of research as the bureaucratization process unfolded.[109] Starting in the 1980s, funds were directed away from support for traditional 'departmental research' to external grants provided through competitive funding mechanisms. The principal Australian funding bodies included the Australian Research Council (ARC) and the National Health and Medical Research Council (NHMRC). The shift from internal to external funding reflected a broader OECD-wide focus on external competitive research funding, a focus that had increased after 1970. This approach failed to correct the long-term problem of the diminishing rate of discovery and arguably made the problem worse. Jacob and Lefgren's 2011 study of US National Institutes of Health (NIH) grants between 1980 and 2000 show that external funding has only a miniscule positive effect on researcher publication rates and citation rates.[110] Baird looked at factors impacting publication productivity in research-focused departments in US universities.[111] The study encompassed the broad spectrum of science and social science disciplines. It showed that external funding had only a weak correlation

---

107   Data sources: Australian Government, Higher Education Statistics Collection 1992–2014 and Higher Education Research Data Collection.

108   The Carnegie-classified RU/VH—very high research activity Research Universities of which there are 108 in the United States, out of a total of 297 doctoral-granting universities. There are in addition 737 Masters' degree granting universities and colleges; 809 Baccalaureate colleges; 1920 Associate colleges; 850 Special Focus institutions; and 32 Tribal colleges.

109   The relation between the direct (external) allocation of research funds and the indirect allocation of funds to higher education institutions was transformed in Australia beginning in the 1980s. In 1987, 17 percent of research funds were directly allocated. By 1991, this had increased to 29 percent, with a shift of emphasis to national competitive grant schemes. DEET 1993: 253.

110   Jacob and Lefgren 2011.

111   Baird 1991.

with publication productivity. The major predictor of publication output was the amounts of *internal* university funding along with the (larger) size of departments.[112]

---

112   Despite this universities over time have massively re-allocated resources away from departments and departmental research. The way that this re-allocation has occurred has been completely non-transparent in the typical manner of university budgeting, a manner that makes the CIA look like a model of openness. In practice, even an insider finds it very difficult to track what universities, public or private, spend their money on. With the rise of the professional class to power in the universities, the classic distinctions between spending on teaching, research and administration have become blurred. The following example, though technical, illustrates the point. In a 2011 report to the Australian government, DeLoitte Access Economics concluded that teaching costs per equivalent full-time student load (eftsl) matched the combined income from the government contribution to student places together with student fees. This slice of income, sometimes called 'base funding,' made up 37 percent of total public university revenue in Australia—a mix of 21 percent government revenue and 16 percent student fee revenue. Cf. Deloitte Access Economics 2011: 8. Kemp and Norton (2014) point to Deloitte's 2011 conclusion that teaching is fully funded yet they slide over Deloitte's further conclusion that research is not fully-funded. This state of affairs points once again to a fundamental ambivalence: where legislators think of universities as research institutions, which they are, and yet conceive of their base funding as ear-marked for 'instruction'. In the United States what in 1930s was called 'instruction and departmental research' has been short-handed today to 'instruction'. So when Deloitte undiplomatically added research costs to teaching costs, income per eftsl fell short by 22 percent (34–7). One response to this is to say that Australian universities receive other government income, such as that for nationally-administrated research. The Deloitte report though subtlety pointed to the baroque evasions involved in this reasoning: for example, the Australian Research Council funds university research but under the terms of its grants, universities are obliged to pay the salaries of chief investigators on externally-funded research projects (9). As well, departmental research is a core duty of most teaching academics in Australian universities, who are employed as 'teaching and research academics'. Deloitte (21) calculated the mean cost of an equivalent full-time student unit (eftsu) in Australia to be $15,500, of which 21 percent of that cost was tacitly assigned to departmental research. (The traditional formula was 40 percent but causally and almost imperceptibly this has been eviscerated over time.) On the basis of Lomax-Smith (2011) and Deloitte (2011), Kemp and Norton (2014) speculated about the creation in Australia of teaching-only universities (that is, rebadged technical colleges). The government contribution to these would be 10 percent less than research universities. What this is oblivious to is that by the standards of the Deloitte report, departmental research in Australian universities is already effectively un-funded. Lomax-Smith's 'base funding' figure for an Australian undergraduate was $10,314; Deloitte's was $15,500. The difference of $5,186 is a ghostly amount, mainly representing departmental research costs that have a habit of appearing and disappearing in different accountings of university finances. In truth, departmental research is 'funded' by the free hours (about 15 hours a week) that academics give to research over and above paid working hours. The bureaucratic university codifies standard hours in industrial relations agreements yet relies on the ancient ethos of academia as a liberal profession to generate research which it has nonetheless convinced itself comes

As previously noted, in Australia university research income (in 2011 dollar terms) rose from $720 million in 1992 to $3,070 million in 2010. Yet the number of research publications per $100,000 income fell from 5.2 in 1992 to 1.6 in 2010. This strongly suggests an investment of research income in process rather than in the production of output. In 2012 Australian research scientists spent more than 500 years' worth of time preparing funding applications for the country's largest grant scheme—the National Health and Medical Research Council's Project Grants.[113] Only 20 percent of NHMRC proposals succeed. Scientists therefore wasted the equivalent of four centuries of time submitting failed applications. That represents $66 million in salary. The NHMRC distributed $457 million in grants. Thus for every seven dollars the Council granted, one dollar of applicant time was squandered. In 1937 Australia's National Health and Medical Research Council funding and application form was four pages long; two Nobel Prize winners that year were among the applicants. Today's documentation includes 20 pages of funding rules; the scheme's prefatory information form runs to 16 pages alone without even getting to applicants' publications lists or project descriptions.[114]

Paperwork adds zero to the act of discovery. The procedural constraints of the external application process drains energy from the curiosities of researchers. A process that asks researchers to define what they will discover before they discover it is intrinsically flawed. Typically no such distortion applies in the case of internal funding of research by universities. External funding schemes promise something called 'quality.' This is a bureaucratic category. Its results are designed to be achieved by process. High-achieving research is not a process-driven activity. It is a curiosity-driven activity. The best formal predictor of research outcomes is track record, which is a function of a person not a process. Research funding bodies do consider track record. But they also seek to evaluate project ideas. But discovery is simply not calculable or foreseeable in this manner. Discovery emerges tangentially and spontaneously or serendipitously when serious researchers go about their work. Yes, they prepare for it, but even then the outcomes are not predictable, and so they cannot be documented in advance, which is what the typical external grant application process of necessity requires. The key instead is to invest in good people, with demonstrable capacities, not in nebulous project descriptions subject

---

from external funding. It is well-known in Australia that the actual output of externally-funded 'research-only' staff is meagre. The whole enterprise is built on fiction upon fiction.

113   Phillips 2013.

114   According to the NHMRC, the 208 available reports for grants that ended in 2003, 2004 and 2005 generated 10,000 journal publications and 5,000 conference papers. Across those same three years the Council spent $1.06 billion on recurrent grants. That equates $70,666 per article or paper. Martyr (2014) notes that the NHMRC counts as "results": collaborations that leverage additional funding, funding leveraged from overseas and other bodies, commercial activity, publications, higher degree completions, and media attention. Yet it does not count actual discoveries as "results". See: http://www.nhmrc.gov. au/grants/research-funding-statistics-and-data/nhmrc-research-results.

to improbable evaluations of the 'quality' of what are promissory notes. Research varies enormously in its significance but that significance can only be established after-the-fact, retrospectively. Promise is worthless. We cannot know the future (what will be discovered); we can only know the past (what was discovered and who discovered it).

External peer-reviewed funding applications waste researcher time in tortuous processes of submission preparation, reporting and auditing. They waste money as universities install ever-larger research management bureaucracies to better communicate with national research bureaucracies so as to better compete for funds with other universities. The process of single-blind peer review used by external funding agencies is also fraught with flaws. Many peer-reviewers barely rise above venting in their reviews of applications. Willing peer reviewers are too few; reviews are often rushed and scrappy. Reviewers cannot but use their knowledge of applicants and applicant-affiliations in making judgments. The 'quality' control process itself is haunted by 'quality' issues. But, as serious as these can be, such problems are not the major affliction of the system. The ultimate problem of the process is similar to the problem of picking 'industry winners' in innovation funding. Simply put, 'winners' cannot be reliably predicted because neither innovation nor discovery can be anticipated. By their nature, the outcomes of discovery and innovation are 'surprise' outcomes that no process or procedure can divine.

Bureaucratic Pedagogy

In Australia there was one significant exception to the elevation of process over production in the era of the bureaucratic university. Australian universities massively increased teaching productivity. It doubled between 1965 and 2011 rising from 12 'full time equivalent student units' per academic in 1965 to 18 in 1991 to 25 in 2011.[115] It had averaged around 9 in the 1950s, see Table 3.1.[116] That meant a rise in the number of students an academic taught from 96 to 144 to 200. Few industries, especially labor intensive ones, could boast that kind of rise.[117] It was achieved in a number of ways, from larger classes to the

---

115   Data source: Australian Government, Higher Education Statistics Collection, 1992–2014.

116   The Murray Committee in 1957 reported (40) that the student:staff ratio in Australian universities varied quite a deal. The contrasting UK ratio was 1:7. Table 3.1 is based on the Murray Committee data.

117   And given its scale it is unlikely to be repeated again. Some think that online classes will deliver further productivity gains. But these will occur likely only in the case of the relative hand-full of MOOC super star classes. Production and preparation costs of online delivery inhibit its productivity potential unless these can be offset by large-than-normal class sizes. Conversely large lecture classes of up to 600 have long been common

extensive use of casual contract teachers.[118] Casual (sessional) and defined-term contract teachers today do about half the teaching in universities for around 50 percent of the cost of employing a continuing (tenured) academic staff member.[119] In Australia, causal staff rose from 12.7 percent of the academic workforce in 1990 to 22 percent in 2007, broadly at the expense of limited tenure ('3 year contract') positions rather than tenured positions.[120] It is striking that as student numbers in Australian universities increased relative to population size, the number of continuing academic staff grew at a much slower pace while the number of administrators increased at a much more rapid rate. As previously noted, between 1972 and 2012 the number of students in Australian universities (compared to the total Australian population) grew four-fold, the number of non-casual academic staff grew two-fold and the non-academic university workforce grew nearly six-fold.

Students at university today pay a significant portion of their tuition fees not for tuition but for a bureaucratic welfare state that escalates constantly and lobbies incessantly in order to expand. In the United States, university tuition has vastly exceeded the price rises of almost any other commodity. The reason is not the

---

on physical campuses. The major efficiency gain of online lectures is cutting travelling time to and from class, which can be very wasteful; and great flexibility for students as to when lectures can be viewed. The social appetite for lectures-on-demand (indeed all media-on-demand) has grown. The downside of online education is not lectures; these are probably on average better delivered online as long as they are professionally produced. Rather the downside is the loss of intimacy of tutorial classes and seminars. Threaded discussion online cannot match the pedagogic power derived from the familiarity and closeness of the traditional tutorial-style classroom. Online delivery also has a stickiness problem. Only 4 percent of students complete any sequence of MOOC subjects. Westervelt 2013. The model of blended classes, on campus and online, addresses these pedagogic issues but offers few productivity gains for institutions.

118   It is notable though that while the student: staff ratio in Australian universities in the 1950s and 1960s was low by contrast with the 2000s, class sizes were not. The Murray Committee noted (37, 39) the limited use of the tutorial system in Australia at that time (it was introduced as a norm later on, by the 1960s, in part of the behest of the Committee) and the consequent reliance for teaching on large lecture courses with 250–600 students in them.

119   The major cost saving is eliminating payment for the research component of the tenured university teacher. The sessional is exclusively a teacher. This arrangement is not just about cost. It also points to the stark fact that most tenured academics do not produce much research, certainly not over a full career, and certainly not such that would fill 40 or 50 percent of their employment time. Employing more nominal research-teachers only exaggerates the problem, itself a function of the radical mismatch between a large university and the enduringly tiny number of active researchers in the universities.

120   Coates, Dobson, Edwards, Friedman, Goedegebuure and Meek 2009: 7. The percent of the international academic workforce on permanent contracts: Australia (61.2 percent), Japan (86.8 percent), UK (81.9 percent), USA (67.5 percent), Canada (67.1 percent), Korea (61.5 percent), Norway (56.0 percent), Finland (54.4 percent), Germany (42.2 percent) and Hong Kong (34.4 percent). The average is 68 percent (24).

Table 3.1   Staff–Student Ratios 1957

University of Melbourne	01:12.6
University of Sydney	01:11.6
University of Adelaide	01:11.3
University of Western Australia	01:10.5
University of Queensland	01:09.0
University of Tasmania	01:07.9
N.S.W. University of Technology	01:07.9
University of New England	01:04.9
Canberra University College	01:03.7
Data Source: Murray Committee.	

cost of departmental research or teaching but the cost of professional services and administration. The university welfare state is extremely costly. Its expansion is unrelenting. The university welfare state functions as an anesthetic that protects students from the pain of learning. The majority come to university with no appetite for higher learning or taste for studying. Accordingly, universities today are filled with unhappy students. In Australia each year 18 percent of commencing students drop out (some return). The attrition rate varies between institutions, from 8 percent in the best case to 33 percent in the worst case.[121] This is not surprising. Many nominal students at university have no aptitude for higher education. Yet governments and universities pressure them to enrol. Large numbers are disengaged from classes and study. As previously noted, in Australia 61 percent of full-time first-year students work an average 13 hours a week and put in a meagre 10 hours a week studying for class and 15 nominal hours in class.

Ducking lectures is not the issue. Peter Cook and Christopher Hitchens spent little time in class at university. In fact the most powerful predictor of high-level professional and creative success is not undergraduate grades but extracurricular productivity.[122] It is equally true though that the extracurricular world of the inventive student is usually sparked by a strong connection with a decisive handful of academic tutors or mentors. The problem of the contemporary university is that extracurricular time is now mostly unproductive. It is spent in soporific idling or vacuous part-time work. As noted, a tacit disengagement pact has grown up between students and teachers. They agree not to bother each other. Students engage in passive leisure activities. Teachers spend more and more time emailing their colleagues in attempts to satisfy bureaucratic demands. Administrative auditing of teaching provides little useful information. Student 'feedback on teaching' surveys and surveys of 'student experience' are simply indexes of student unhappiness.

---

121   Data source: Australian Government, Higher Education Statistics Collection 1992–2014.

122   Simonton 1984: 73–4.

They do not measure whether or what students have learnt. They do not measure rates of student reading or writing. They do not track extracurricular creation. They tell us what we already know: a third or more of students are unhappy at university. What the surveys cannot tell us is that those students should not be at university. They should do a technical certificate or learn how to create their own small business. The older model of traineeship, apprenticeship and cadetship (TAC) entry to the workforce needs to return.[123] University attempts at 'work-integrated learning' are vain substitutes for this.[124]

Today's universities lurch between bureaucratic fatigue and enervated entertainment. They are devitalized, exhausted and debilitated. Signs of the debilitation of the university are everywhere. It has reached the point where bureaucracies think that they can teach students better than academic staff can. We saw this with some of the peculiar initiatives of Graduate Research Schools in Australia. These are bureaucratic offices that administer higher degree research candidates. In the 2000s these bureaucracies tried to refashion PhD research degrees in their own image. As often is the case with bureaucracies, they sought to expand their reach by offering solutions to non-problems. One of these non-problems is non-completion by PhD students. Many candidates who start PhDs do not complete the degree. They discover that it is too difficult or it is not for them. Often the PhD student who stops has been unable to find the right supervisor or a good supervisor. As long as there have been statistics on PhD programs, going back in North America to the turn of the twentieth century, somewhere in the range

---

123   'BMW's plant in Greer, S.C., is its only one in the United States. The company offers a program called BMW Scholars that allows young workers to study at technical colleges and work. "It seemed like we had sucked up everybody who knew about diesel engines," said Mr. Klisch, vice president for North American operations of Tognum America. "It wasn't working as we had planned." So Mr. Klisch did what he would have done back home in Germany: He set out to train them himself. Working with five local high schools and a career center in Aiken County, S.C.—and a curriculum nearly identical to the one at the company's headquarters in Friedrichshafen—Tognum now has nine juniors and seniors enrolled in its apprenticeship program. Inspired by a partnership between schools and industry that is seen as a key to Germany's advanced industrial capability and relatively low unemployment rate, projects like the one at Tognum are practically unheard-of in the United States. But experts in government and academia, along with those inside companies like BMW, which has its only American factory in South Carolina, say apprenticeships are a desperately needed option for younger workers who want decent-paying jobs, or increasingly, any job at all. And without more programs like the one at Tognum, they maintain, the nascent recovery in American manufacturing will run out of steam for lack of qualified workers.' Schwartz 2013.

124   Between the ages of 25 and 46, Americans on average change jobs 5.8 times (US Bureau of Labor Statistics 2012). The notion that a degree can be vocational, or that it can prepare a person for working life, is a fiction when persons change jobs so much. The working life is learnt at work, on the job. Education prepares the supple mind that can work at many different things.

of 50–55 percent of PhD candidates fail to complete. In the 2000s, centralized PhD administrations in Australia proliferated. To expand, they required a rationale. One such rationale was to save academics from non-completions, so graduate administrations came up with all kinds of worthless subjects and workshops for PhD candidates to do—not understanding that class learning and research have almost nothing in common.

There are two basic reasons PhDs do not perform well. One is that undergraduate scores are bad at predicting who will be a good researcher. This is because research and in-class competencies are very different. The second reason is that the relation of student and supervisor fails. In neither case will getting a PhD candidate to do a bureaucratically-invented coursework subject make an iota of difference. No amount of bureaucratic pedagogy can make the slightest difference to the natural fact of attrition. In Australia between 1991 and 2010 the median ratio of PhD completions to commencements three years prior expressed in percentage terms was 50 percent in the 1990s and 55 percent in the 2000s. This is consistent with the historic norm of PhD programs everywhere. This norm does not change.[125] Yet this did not stop a faux-solution to a fictional problem being promised. This is typical of administrative creep. In spite of obvious reasons to leave well alone, bureaucratic offices persist and prevail. They hoover up resources, they expand, they move into areas that are none of their business, and they reshape what the university is in their own image.

The ideology of the knowledge society has been a key way of justifying this behaviour. During the knowledge society push, Australia increased its higher degree research candidate population from 8,300 in 1989 to 40,000 in 2006.[126] Around 50 percent of these candidates completed their PhDs.[127] Forty-five to 50 percent is the rate of PhD attrition in comparable countries. This rate is long-standing. Tinto

---

125   Consider the sub-group of research-award holding PhD candidates in Australia, who are on a grant to study. Of those who began in 1979, by 1988 70 percent of award-holding science PhDs had completed the degree and just under 50 percent of arts PhDs had done so. In short about 65 percent of the total sub-group had completed after a decade; 35 percent had not completed. Average candidature was 4.5 years. Higher Education Council, 1989: 43. Predictably, the HEC complained that the completion of higher degrees was 'undesirably low' even though it was actually perfectly normal and entirely natural. Incompletion is the to-be-expected cost of difficult work that has no defined end-point. The real waste is not uncompleted research but reports that mandate spending to fix something that is not a problem.

126   The total Australian post-graduate population grew from 132,444 in 1996 to 278,257 in 2007—a growth from 20 percent to 27 percent of the higher education population, Bradley 2008: 70.

127   Bills 2003; Martin, Maclachlan and Karmel 2001. In Australia in 2008, the ratio of completing to commencing candidates was 72 percent for domestic doctoral candidates and 42 percent for international doctoral candidates. In 2004, the respective percentages were 59 percent and 53 percent for domestic and international PhDs. Access Economics 2010: 22.

noted that after 80 years of attrition research in higher education in the United States, and billions of dollars spent trying to improve completion rates, the rate remained constant—at around 45 percent.[128] The attrition rate in arts disciplines is 45–50 percent, in the sciences 30–40 percent.[129] When Australia went down the path of the rapid expansion of PhD programs in the 1990s, the response to the universal constant was ever-more administrative auditing. An analysis was done of the paperwork required for doctoral students to move from pre-admission to graduation at an Australian university. The analysis discovered that the university asked academics to provide 270 unique items of data, on average 2.7 times, in order to complete 14 different forms required by the university.[130] This amounted to 580 minutes of academic form-filling per PhD candidate. For a major PhD supervisor, with 10 PhDs, that is 25 hours of form-filling a year, or about $4500 in 2013 gross salary costs. The story is reminiscent of the case of the professor of epidemiology at the University of Minnesota who discovered that when he submitted a claim for re-imbursement of a $12 parking bill, his university spent $75 processing the claim. He stopped submitting such claims.[131]

In a classic attempt to provide a bureaucratic stick and carrot, in the late 1990s, the Liberal-National Coalition government of the day in Australia tied funding for PhD places to PhD completions.[132] This outwardly was not a foolish step, and yet, despite the incentives, there was no subsequent significant or visible improvement in national completion rates. This is because monetary incentives cannot solve intellectual problems. Yet the more that these problems persist, the more money is spent by governments on auditing and by universities on the creation of research welfare states.

---

128 Tinto, 1982. Lovitts and Nelson 2000 report as long-standing an attrition rate of 50 percent in the United States.

129 Jiraneck 2010: 2. The United States graduated its first PhDs in the 1870s. PhD programs and research universities expanded rapidly thereafter. By 1900, the American Progressive Age was in full flight. From it emerged advocacy social science, public interest research, think tanks, and ideological sciences like Social Darwinism (in 1900, a remarkably high proportion of American professors were Social Darwinists). Despite the enormous social reputation of progressive knowledge, an equally high attrition in PhD programs, one of the flag ships of Progressivism, set in.

130 Clarke and Graves 2010.

131 'Several years ago, Russell Luepker, a professor of epidemiology at the school of public health, sought reimbursement for a $12 parking bill. The form went from a secretary to the head of his department to an accountant who entered it in a computer to a senior accountant responsible for approving it. Richard Portnoy, chief administrative officer in the epidemiology department, estimates it cost $75 to move the paperwork. When Dr Luepker heard of it, he stopped filing for parking reimbursements.' Joyner 2012.

132 Kemp 1999. The Research Training Scheme (RTS) was subsequently introduced in mid-2001.

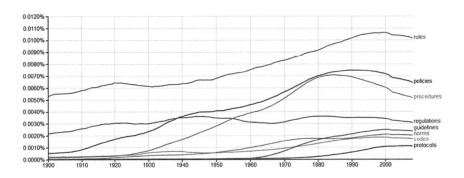

Figure 3.1   The Language of Bureaucracy: N-Gram Analysis of the Annual Incidence of Key Words in the Google Book Database

For example, most graduate programs have a large number of drop outs. But not all of all them do.[133] What is the difference? In essence one thing: a mutual disposition for intellectual inquiry on the part of candidate and supervisor. This nexus is a kind of master-apprentice relationship. Lovitts and Nelson found that the single most important factor in the decisions of graduate students to continue or withdraw was the relationship with a faculty adviser. 'Students who complete their degrees are fully twice as likely to express satisfaction with their faculty advisers as are students who leave.' What underlies such satisfaction is a mysterious relationship. It is not one that can be encapsulated in supervisor training or certification or other feeble bureaucratic devices. It is a relationship that involves initiation, revelation and an enigmatic bond. It evades procedural definitions. When it works, what it permits is the paradox of a student's self-education and self-formation in a collective setting. This paradox is a micro-cosmos of the successful university at large.

---

133   Lovitts and Nelson 2000 found in the United States higher degree attrition rates differing between 33 percent and 68 percent depending on the university. Different departments, likewise, have varying attrition rates.

Chapter 4

The Discovery University

What is a University?

The universities of the late-nineteenth and early-twentieth century were afflicted by conundrums. Were they status institutions devoted to producing persons of estimable character or research institutions dedicated to creating original knowledge—or alternatively were they diploma mills whose business was to certify people for jobs? The omni-functional post-industrial university amplified such identity problems. It made it more and more difficult to answer a simple question: 'what is a university?' The classification of American higher education institutions includes research, doctoral and comprehensive universities alongside liberal arts colleges, associate institutions (community colleges), masters and baccalaureate colleges and universities, and special focus institutions.[1] The research universities are further sub-divided into very high research activity and high research activity institutions. The folksier British schema of Oxbridge (ancient universities), red brick (nineteenth-century civic universities), plate glass (1960s universities) and the inevitable 'new' universities (the 1990s ex-polytechnics) indicate a similar incommensurable range of institutions.[2] To answer the question 'what is a university (or alternatively what is a college)?' is rendered difficult. Humpty Dumpty said: 'When I use a word, it means just what I choose it to mean—neither more nor less.' This would seem also to be the case with the 'universities'. Maybe this is a word we should always put in inverted commas. Nobody knows what it means except that it means whatever university presidents and vice-chancellors say it means. When the higher education sector expanded after 1970, the identity problem was exacerbated. The architect of the University of California's golden era of expansion, Clark Kerr, thought this was a virtue. He called the resulting institution the 'multiversity'. But what did that possibly mean? That a university was all things to all people?

The most influential universities in the world ('the top 200'), most of them American, routinely insist that their core business is research. They are 'research universities'. Indeed they are 'very high research activity' research universities. They draw immense status from this. They dominate national and world rankings because of it. Other universities lower down the totem pole cannot match their per capita research. Yet what those at the top produced at the beginning of the

---

1   Since 1973 the Carnegie Foundation has regularly published a classificatory scheme for American higher education, see http://classifications.carnegiefoundation.org/.

2   Australia has its nineteenth and early twentieth-century sandstone universities (its redbrick equivalent), along with its own plate glass and gum tree universities.

twenty-first century is less impressive than what the highest-ranked institutions produced 100 years before. No universities in the past could match in real terms the income or the resources of today's top echelon. The University of Chicago illustrates the point. Today it has an endowment of $6.57 billion for 2168 faculty, which is $3,000,000 per faculty member.[3] When it was founded in the 1890s, its endowment by the standards of the day was huge: $1 million then or $26 million in today's inflation-adjusted terms for 120 faculty members, an endowment in 2013 equivalent to $216,000 per faculty member. There is no doubt of the very high caliber of the contemporary University of Chicago faculty but equally so that caliber is not thirteen times as great as it was in the 1890s when the university was already of exceptional stature. In short, as great or greater natural science and social science was done in the past with considerably less resources. Today the intellectual output of prestigious big science and the high-status humanities cannot match what their institutions command in income.

What is apparent is that the chickens have come home to roost. So many uplift agencies and business centers—along with the growth of a huge university welfare state and the mission creep of universities as they sought to provide an eclectic myriad of vocational, professional, scholarly, and intellectual education along with social outreach, social justice, and every kind of upper-middle class moral cause and fad imaginable—meant that not only was the intellectually-inclined academic lost in the mix but the intellectual modelling of future researchers and intellectuals also shrank. Even in the most selective universities with the most competitive entry scores, the first two years of undergraduate education now edges toward little more than an extension of high school. It does not matter if the enrollees are gifted. Gifts by themselves, in the absence of a demanding ecology that stretches those gifts, are a waste of time. It takes hard work to turn gifts into efficacious talent. One thing is clear about the creation of serious new knowledge. It occurs in ways that are profoundly un-school like. There is no equating the model of learning required for research and creation with the model of school teaching or collegial transmission. Einstein avoided classes. Actually he hated classes. He only passed his exams because of the excellent notes his friend Marcel Grossman took. Conversely when Nietzsche and Newton taught classes, they taught to empty rooms. Students didn't understand them. They talked a babble language that would take a couple of generations to be translated into common sense terms. The logic of creation is not the school-like or collegial logic of transmission. The nineteenth-century notion of the research university, as it passed from the University of Berlin to Johns Hopkins University, and beyond, forged a style to accommodate the logic of creation. This style is captured perfectly by what the generation of Karl Marx was expected to do: students would spend four years at university, attend lectures

---

3   Original endowment: $1 million: http://president.uchicago.edu/directory/william-rainey-harper Worth in real terms today: $26 million for 120 faculty = $216,666 endowment per faculty member.

or not as they chose and then would have to produce a thesis, upon which they would either pass or fail at university. That was a very good system.

A University is not a School or a College

Fifteen thousand or more institutions around the world title themselves universities. Most of these operate on the principle of schooling. Schooling is concerned with the transmission and reception of knowledge. The principle of schooling has long played a significant and important role in tertiary education. Historically, tertiary-level colleges and institutes provided what was in effect advanced schooling in a range of arts, sciences and technologies. Professional schools and institutes elevated the model to the graduate level. The institution of the university however was meant (at least to a significant degree) to do something different. The United States has maintained the technology institute/college/university distinction, to a point. Elsewhere it has often fallen into abeyance. University is a high status word, and status trumps almost anything else. Even in the United States, where tertiary colleges are popular, the number and kind of universities have proliferated. In many respects, the word 'university' has become meaningless. In turn, many have adapted to the inflation of language by using qualifying words. So we talk about 'research universities' or 'research universities with very high research activity'. It now takes a prolonged mouth-full to hint at a fundamental distinction. Self-appointed institutional clusters, such as Australia's Group of Eight universities or the United Kingdom's Russell Group and the G5, have emerged to sally home the point.[4] These groupings allude to something, namely the substantive idea of the university that they themselves have great difficulty articulating beyond the somewhat prosaic fact that these institutions produce most of the measurable research in their respective societies. Bar one or two of their number, contemporary universities can barely say what it takes to produce that research because, under the impress of public policy, they have been turned inside out, and have lost sight of the animating spirit and constitutive idea of the university.

Universities know that this core means research combined with teaching. They say so. But most universities in reality do little (and sometimes very little) per capita research. The difference between the top and the bottom of the top

---

4   The Russell Group: University of Birmingham, University of Bristol, University of Cambridge, Cardiff University, University of Edinburgh, University of Glasgow, Imperial College London, King's College London (University of London), University College London (University of London), University of Leeds, University of Liverpool, London School of Economics (University of London), University of Manchester, University of Newcastle, University of Nottingham, Queen's University Belfast, University of Oxford, University of Sheffield, University of Southampton, University of Warwick. The G5: University of Oxford, University of Cambridge, University College London (University of London), London School of Economics (University of London) and Imperial College London.

200 universities in the world, all of them self-declared research universities, is striking (see Table 4.1)—let alone the gap between number 50 and number 500. It is well established that 10 percent of creators produce 50 percent of the research in any field. The productive, as well, tend to co-locate. The resulting gap between the creative minority of individuals and institutions and the rest is papered-over with euphemistic words like 'scholarship' that have their origins in the genteel collegiate teaching world. In most post-industrial universities, what academic faculty call 'research' is actually a kind of scholarship in the genteel sense of that word. In the most charitable sense, scholarship is keeping abreast of new research rather than the conduct of actual research. No artefacts come out of this scholarship. It produces no articles or books, no patents, artworks or designs, no papers for volumes of proceedings, or anything really.

In 1989, the Australian Government turned teaching colleges and technological institutes into universities on the grounds that some of the former were producing as much research as the traditional universities were. This argument was fallacious. The sandstone universities founded in the nineteenth and early twentieth century in Australia dominate research.[5] The Group of Eight universities, the majority of them sandstone universities, produce most of Australian university research output.[6] Tradition, it seems, matters. For the 2 percent or 1 percent or less of national research produced by most of the other universities, each Group of Eight university produces 5 to 10 per cent or more of the total university output. This is despite the fact that research and the advancement of knowledge is the defining symbol of the modern university.

Australia's Bradley Review of Higher Education in 2008 tiptoed around this issue.[7] It freely admitted that the production of new knowledge defined the nature

---

5   The universities of Sydney, Melbourne, Adelaide, Tasmania, Queensland and Western Australia.

6   Gallagher 2009; Valadkhani and Worthington 2006; Bourke and Butler 1998. Bourke and Butler calculated that 56 percent of research (represented by higher degree research candidates, publications, citations, research income and expenditure) was carried out by the Group of Eight universities—8 out of the 36 universities surveyed. Gallagher estimates that the Group of Eight undertake 72 percent of higher education basic research and 41 percent of Australia's total basic research. Valadkhani and Worthington, who exclude the Australian National University from their review because of the lack of comparable research data, conclude neatly that 'in total research performance terms ... the Go8 universities [rank] highest. However, when research performance is expressed in per academic staff terms, Monash is no longer among the top seven Australian universities and is replaced by the University of Tasmania. Regardless of specification, the University of Melbourne is always ranked highest, followed by the Universities of Sydney, Queensland, New South Wales, and Monash University in total research performance and by the Universities of Adelaide, Western Australia, New South Wales, and Sydney in per academic staff research performance.' The per capita figures illustrate the continuing power of the sandstone university in Australia. The University of Tasmania was established in 1890, and Monash University in 1958.

7   Bradley 2008: 123.

Table 4.1　　Publications per FTE University Academic Staff Member, 2003–2007

University	Publication Output 2003–2007	Continuing Academic Staff FTE	Publication Output per head per annum
Harvard University	57124	2107	5.4
Tokyo University	35622	2429	2.9
University of California at Los Angeles (UCLA)	29524	2035	2.9
Stanford University	25098	1910	2.6
University of Toronto	31780	2551	2.5
University of Cambridge	24748	2825	1.8
University of Chicago	13368	2168	1.2
Adelaide University	6612	1388	1
Sydney University	15419	3278	0.9
University of Western Australia	8194	1768	0.9
Queensland University	13268	2864	0.9
University of Melbourne	14757	3682	0.8
University of New South Wales	11164	2985	0.7
Australian National University	9237	2657	0.7
Monash University	9796	3552	0.6

Data Sources: Australian Government Higher Education Research Data Collection (HERDC) 1992–2010; DEEWR FTE Staff Statistics 2007; Harvard University; Tokyo University; University of Toronto; UCLA; Stanford University; University of Cambridge; University of Chicago.

of university. But while it accepted that research was the primary characteristic of a university, it was silent on the status of universities that produced little or virtually no research. In 2006, the production of weighted research publications per staff member across all Australian universities ranged from 0.34 to 1.64, and averaged 1 output (= 1 article) per staff member per annum across the sector. Contrast this with the fact that most eminent creators across a working life average the equivalent of between two and five articles per year.[8] An institution then that produced less than 1.5 items per head is hardly credible. Such metrics

---

8　Simonton 1984: 78–90.

in themselves are not important, except for what they point to. Research is not an artefact of accountancy. What does matter, though, is the nature of creation. To create is to produce. Accomplished creators produce a lot. Some of it is very good, a lot of it is middling, and some of it can be awful. But good, bad, or indifferent, creation is the out putting of the spirit, its materialization. Knowledge can only be advanced through objectivation, and new researchers can only learn how to create knowledge by observing experienced researchers in the act of creation, literally in the act of putting out. No putting out, no university.

Thus a lack of research invariably produces a legitimacy problem. How can an institution be called a 'university' if it does not create knowledge? If it doesn't do that, then its inward nature is properly that of a teaching college or technological institute. Invariably, legitimacy problems call forth validating procedures. Confronted with the fact that most of the post-industrial universities produce little research, what happened in Australia and elsewhere was the development of a large administrative apparatus to audit this inactivity. Failure justified the further expansion of the university. The context for this was pie-in-the-sky ideas about the knowledge society. Post-industrial pieties about knowledge encouraged an over-estimation of whom and what can create knowledge. In fact very few people can do research in any meaningful sense—just as there is only a tiny number of interesting works ever created. That's just the way it is. That is the rationality of the real.

Universities have three functions. One is the *preparation* of students for the learned professions; the second is the *transmission* of inherited knowledge; the third is *exploration* leading to the discovery of new knowledge. In short, universities prepare, teach and research. Research is the most difficult function of the university, because productive researchers who add to the society's knowledge are relatively rare. A tertiary college can prepare and can teach. But a university has a third function: to advance knowledge by creating knowledge. Because of the relative rarity of great classic research, universities have a high status. That status gives the name 'university' a cachet. The status of the name has caused many new 'universities' to be founded, and colleges and institutes to be re-named 'universities'. But these 'universities' often are universities in name only. This is because exploration leading to the discovery of new knowledge is beyond them. They are status institutions not adventive institutions. The highest purpose of a university is the creation of knowledge. This is not its only purpose but it is its most demanding purpose, one that is often allusive. In a great university all of the functions of the institution—not just research but also preparation, teaching, administration and service as well—are geared to the end of creation. The university is not just a place of transmission and preparation, or even of research. Fundamentally it is a site of creation. The creation of knowledge is its most arduous task.

The creation, leading to the advancement, of knowledge occurs through imagination, reason, objectivation, and self-formation. Knowledge, at its source, has first to be imagined or conceptualized. Abstraction, pattern and form—in short, ideas—are the principal media of the imagination. Having been imagined or conceived, an idea then has to be explained. Explanation is a function of reason.

Words are the primary medium of reason. Knowledge also has to be objectivated. It has to enter the world as an artefact, joining together with the other artefacts (some intellectual and some functional, some abstract and some concrete) that make up the world that we inhabit. The artefactual character of knowledge is essential in order that knowledge can be easily validated, replicated, transmitted and distributed—the latter so that others can be schooled in it. There are various media of intellectual objectivation: articles, books, papers, and science reports supplemented by lectures, patents, artworks and designs, together with the apprentice media of the undergraduate essay and project and the graduate thesis. Finally, the creation of knowledge is the product of a process of self-formation. The apparatus of formal instruction, which is principally a function of the transmission of knowledge, plays a relatively small role in preparing someone to create knowledge. A university is an institution that takes that into account. Most of all, it is a place where intellectual self-formation is possible.

Intellectual self-formation that begins in self-learning at university is the basis of the system of discovery. It is the foundation of curiosity-driven research. It is not only in the undergraduate university that self-learning has shriveled. It has also contracted in the graduate research science laboratory and in industry research science. Odlyzko 1995 observed the decline of unfettered research and the concomitant shift from person-centered to project-centered discovery. The former, driven by curiosity and serendipity, was incubated in laboratories where students had free reign to explore, including undergraduate students. The post-modern incubus of proliferating regulation, reporting, grant-seeking plans and deliverables have asphyxiated the traditional freedom of exploration that is essential to serious science. One of the phenomena related to this is the ageing of discovery; once young researchers made major science discoveries. Jones and Weinberg's 2011 study of Nobel winners from 1901 to 2008 showed that before 1905 about two-thirds of Nobel winners in chemistry, physics and medicine did their prize work before the age of 40. Around 20 percent did it before the age of 30. By 2000, no one any longer achieved a Nobel breakthrough before the age of 30; and only 19 percent of physics prize work was achieved before the age of 40; no one in chemistry managed this any longer. After 1985, the mean age for Nobel achievement was 48. Rather than simply doing research inspired by curiosity, the post-modern researcher must first get money, apply for grants, secure track record, and only then have a plausible shot at breaking ground; all the while the process of discovery has pushed up the age of peak discovery by a decade (from 37 to 48), not only delaying discovery but also arguably reducing its incidence. Over a century, the mean age of Nobel-winning work had increased by 7.4 years in medicine, 10.2 years in chemistry and 13.4 years in physics.

In the post-industrial era, the distinction between the transmission of knowledge and the advancement of knowledge was blurred. This blurring was driven by governments eager to prove their social policy credentials. Terms varied between countries but the same logic underlay post-industrial education across the OECD. Many segments of vocational education were given degree status. A one-year or two-year collegiate education (resulting in a diploma or associate degree) was turned into a four-year degree. The difference between the four-year 'college' degree and the four-year 'university' degree diminished. At the same time, the 6-month-to-one-year tertiary certificate level of education stagnated. Amounts of funding for it were effectively frozen. Workplace-based education, such as the training of nurses, was transferred to campuses. On-the-job apprenticeship training stagnated or shrank radically. What resulted was an intense bureaucratization of the semi-professions.[9] In the case of nursing, this led to a decline in on-the-job skills, a rise in preoccupation with paperwork and procedures, and an atrophying of sympathetic and caring attitudes.[10]

9   The UK experience is typical: 'Project 2000 was an initiative to professionalise nursing, which moved training out of hospital-based nursing schools and into universities. This initiative is widely applauded within the NHS for giving nurses degree status, enabling them to take over some tasks from doctors, and giving them more of a career ladder. But it has had two pernicious effects. First, the new training has left some nurses more confident in theory than in practice. They are underprepared to deal with patients when they graduate, because they have spent too little time on the wards. Under the old system, student nurses were paid as part of the ward team and valuable to that team, so got good supervised experience. Under Project 2000, nurses are "supernumerary" and their practical experience is more variable. At the excellent Queen Elizabeth Hospital Birmingham, a matron explained to me how she encourages new nurses to go up to each bed, make eye contact and ask patients if they need anything. That is after three to four years' training. Second, the removal of student nurses from ward teams created a hole in the workforce that was filled by a new cohort of people called healthcare assistants. These are lower-paid auxiliaries who are supposed to be supervised by a registered nurse but at chaotic times are not. They have almost no training. They do non-medical tasks such as feeding and washing. In other words, we have delegated the hands-on care that patients value to the lowest-paid, untrained people, some of whom find it hard to communicate well in English. It would be surprising if a new generation of nurses did not conclude that such tasks are low-skilled and low-status. It is a highly skilled task to give someone a bed bath with dignity, to stop them getting bed sores, to persuade them to eat. This kind of care can be as important to recovery as medicine. Yet we increasingly delegate it to 300,000 healthcare assistants who are not only untrained but also unregulated. The National Midwifery Council, the regulator that investigates complaints about nurses, can do nothing about healthcare assistants of which hospitals such as Stafford, with its scenes of appalling patient neglect, had a disproportionate number. Nurses and healthcare assistants dress in similar clothes: patients can't tell the difference. How could anyone have thought this was a good idea, either for patients or for the reputation of nursing?' Cavendish 2011.

10   'Some years ago I worked in a small hospital just outside London. The quality of the nursing on one particular ward was outstanding. I returned a few years later to find the ward in chaos. When I asked for the Sister who had previously run the ward so superbly I was told that she had been moved into administration. I found her in an office and she wept as she told me that she had been forced to leave her ward and become an administrator since her salary would have been reduced and fixed at a low level if she had remained in her clinical post. The focus of nursing had been changed from the ward and the patient to the office and the seminar room. The intimate care of patients had come to be regarded and

The concern moved from patient care to patient care plans. Every attempt to reverse this seems only to make it worse.[11]

The worst offenders in the post-industrial era were social democratic and left-liberal governments whose leaderships ignored post-school training, apprenticeships and cadetships. They made a fetish of university places instead. In the post-industrial moment, all of higher education began to aspire to a fake commonality. Terms like 'university', 'collegiate', 'community', 'further', 'advanced', 'degree', 'diploma' and 'certificate' began to fade into each other as if one elongated educational mash-up. University education began to be thought of as training for a job; while training providers aspired to be educators. In part this was a function of status-climbing. In part it was a function of the larger mythology of post-industrial societies. A potent myth grew up. This myth said that everyone should go to university and that everyone could go to university. Governments attempted to engineer this myth into reality. In doing so, they used public financing to re-fashion the character of the university. Note, though, that public financing was the means, not the end, of this action. It is wrong to assume that the transformation of the universities was a form of economic rationalization. In fact, the obverse is true. Governments transformed what had been historically a very tiny call on the public purse into an orgy of spending—much of which was systematically wasted. In short, in the post-industrial era, the universities became a pliant tool of social policy. To the extent that this happened, the ability of the universities to satisfy the most inquiring minds and creative wills diminished accordingly.

Social engineering progressively decimated the ecology of the imagination and reason in the traditional university. The kinds of eccentric, wide-ranging, free-wheeling, difficult, and demanding intellectual modes, milieu and media necessary for gifted students from all backgrounds to flourish struggled to survive.[12] The most

---

rewarded as a menial task, a preliminary stage in a nursing career which was now seen to be essentially that of management' Gammon 2005.

11 'Bureaucracy's most destructive effects are due to its permeation and impairment of the activities of non-administrative staff. An example is the progressive transformation of nurses from patient-centered carers to administroids whose requirement to produce detailed patient care plans and participate in workshops and seminars leaves them little time to attend to patients' basic dietary needs or prevent them developing pressure ulcers ... I am sure that almost every procedure in any bureaucracy can be convincingly defended as "essential to the working of the system". Moreover, experience shows that any attempt to modify or eliminate a procedure will add to the overall bureaucratic weight of the organization. As with the Hydra, if you cut off one head, two will grow in its place.' Gammon 2005.

12 This now has seeped into graduate research. As the pioneering geneticist Sydney Brenner notes (Dzeng 2014): 'Today the Americans have developed a new culture in science based on the slavery of graduate students. Now graduate students of American institutions are afraid. He just performs. He's got to perform. The post-doc is an indentured labourer. We now have labs that don't work in the same way as the early labs where people were independent, where they could have their own ideas and could pursue them. The most important thing today is for young people to take responsibility, to actually know how to

productive—which in many cases meant the most astringent—intellectual forms shrank into oblivion. Many of these modes and media were informal. They ranged from meticulous commentary on the work of top students to serious student-staff intellectual, scientific, aesthetic and political societies. These were subsumed, in a Borg-like manner, by the deathly dull, exquisitely pedestrian media of textbooks, unread weekly readings for mass tutorials, and lowest common denominator lecture courses.[13] Student interest in study fell dramatically. The most important single factor that improves the effect of university teaching—the closeness of faculty and students—was eviscerated.

The virtual eclipse of substantive relations between students and faculty has taken place in steps. Formal media of instruction has increasingly squeezed out the informal media of the imagination. But even the nature of formal instruction has changed—as the art of the lecture has become progressively bureaucratized.[14] A symptom of this has been the rise to ubiquity of the intellectually-anesthetizing power-point slide. It eliminated student note-taking in any real sense. Traditional note-taking in lectures was an apprenticeship in intellectual creation. It taught—by example—generations of students how to compose an argument or explanation simply by having them discover, for themselves on the run, the skeletal structure of an argument or explanation. This was an essential part of intellectual self-formation. Some of the greatest works of the mind of the last two centuries have been compiled from student notes—including Hegel's lectures on religion, history, and aesthetics. The rich milieu of the University of Sydney in the mid twentieth century, dominated by the ferocious intellect of John Anderson, yielded up Anderson's lectures on metaphysics reconstructed from the notes of his students.[15]

Borg pedagogy became the default setting of university education—simply because it was the only way that universities could deliver on the political goals that emerged in the 1970s and that solidified in the late 1980s. These goals were fiercely audited by governments. Political actors of all stripes made extravagant promises to enhance social mobility and status climbing by increasing participation in higher education. Around 1985–1988, an invisible limit was passed in most OECD countries. After that point, greater participation in the universities principally served to marginalize and frustrate high-level intellectual formation.

---

formulate an idea and how to work on it. Not to buy into the so-called apprenticeship. I think you can only foster that by having sort of deviant studies. That is, you go on and do something really different. Then I think you will be able to foster it.'

13   The Borg is a fictional species in the Star Trek science fiction series, a collective hive-like cybernetic organism that assimilates the members of other species. The Borg character was devised by writer and producer Maurice Hurley.

14   Even the subject guide became bureaucratized. A subject guide that was once a two or three page mimeographed document became a 20 or 30 page bureaucratic monster filled with institutional templates, rules, codes and warnings.

15   Peter Coleman 2010 launched the volume, *Space, Time and the Categories*, at Sydney University in 2007.

Despite commonplace assumptions, the larger social utility of this has been either minimal or non-existent. A contemporary undergraduate will tell you that study is easy for the intellectually gifted. Yet it is also soporific. Today's B+ student back in 1966 or 1972 was a C- student.[16] Apply the standard distribution bell curve to the work of 8 percent of the population, and thence to 24 percent of the population, and that is what you get. You can do everything seemingly correctly to advance knowledge, and still find that it moves backwards. In the end, a paradox is created. Everyone wants the glittering prize, but in order to achieve it, the glittering prize has to be destroyed.

The Status Trap

This is not to say that universities always value intelligence. Before the post-industrial age, the larger society and the university were in agreement. The university was a small place. But it also played a double game that it has never ceased playing. The university has always seen itself as a place for those who are gifted in the verbal, written and mathematical arts and to a significantly lesser extent in the performing and visual arts. But universities have also always regarded smallness as a function of social status. In the nineteenth century, the university was torn between being a status institution and a scholarly institution. The tension between the two has never been resolved. If anything it has been compounded. Universities and their faculty members delight in high status. In democratic societies this status for the most part is no longer modelled on patrician or aristocratic forms, as it once was, but on the prestige of the original knowledge and research that a small portion of the academic staff of universities create. About 3 per cent of total academic staff—and about 25 percent of faculty in the leading research universities—are proficient creators of research. The high status of research, in its turn, attracts vast numbers of enrolling students to universities, many of whom wish to maintain or advance their status in society. This leads to a paradox. The most competitive undergraduate teaching programs internationally are in the major research universities. These, as a result, are left in a double bind. Their status is dependent on original knowledge production, created by a minority of their staff, with tiny audiences in mind, who simultaneously teach or manage student populations many of whom are principally interested in winning formulas. It is not that the gulf between the two cannot be bridged. It is, on a daily basis. Rather what is noticeable is the latent cost of bridging it. The cost is the slow, almost imperceptible, but real erosion of the intellectual power of the university, as it has been compelled to revise its notion of knowledge in order to acquit itself in the post-industrial age. For the most part it has become in spirit a school or college or an institute.

---

16   Rojstaczer and Healy 2010. In a 2012 study, the researchers reported that in 2009 'A's represented 43% of all letter grades, an increase of 28 percentage points since 1960 and 12 percentage points since 1988.'

The distinction between a college, a university and an institute is important. Each has its rightful place in higher education. A college introduces students to various works of the mind. Its rationale is 'scholarship', literally an advanced form of schooling. Know-what is transmitted. An institute of technology or an art school has faculty who can model the creation of material artefacts. Know-how is transmitted. A university, in contrast, exposes students to faculty who are the creators of symbolic objects. Symbolic objects may be material, cultural, virtual, or functional. The production of such objects incorporates know-what and know-how, but goes beyond both into the realm of discovery. Know-what and know-how are transformed into know-what-and-how-to-create. What is created is a model that is subsequently transmitted. Creation in turn has its own models. That makes it a kind of discovery. But what sets it apart is that creation, in following models, also produces its own original models. These models then are replicated and transmitted through various kinds of scholarship and artefaction both inside and outside the university. This is the difference that makes the difference. At the dawn of the age of the modern university, William Rainey Harper—the Baptist lay preacher, Hebrew scholar and founding spirit of the University of Chicago—imagined an institution that would 'make the work of investigation primary, the work of giving instruction secondary'.[17] Discovery may be of immanent character (and thus of transient value) or it may be transcendental in nature (and thus of lasting value). Either way, the investigations that end in the act of creation—no matter how modest in nature—must attain some measure of the mastery of form. We discover in and through gestalts. We connect the hitherto unconnected through architectonic processes, both cognitive and intuitive. These cannot be taught but they can be learnt. They can be learnt in part through self-reflection and in part through an apprenticeship in discovery.

The apprentice in discovery watches and learns. The apprentice observes a master discoverer at work. Through observation the pattern of discovery is elucidated. It becomes an external prod and measure for the apprentice's own self-reflection about how discovery works. The apprentice has to learn how to give form to a medium. The medium may be words or mathematical symbols, paint pigment or photographic pixels. Whatever the medium is, the difficult matter is to impart form to it. Wittgenstein observed that—no matter whether it is in a primary school or in the philosopher's seminar room—the most interesting things are learnt by the process of them being shown.[18] The master of discovery shows others—by carrying out the act of creation.[19] In this way of working, we learn how to go from a blank sheet to a sheet inscribed with meaning. It does not matter whether the inscription is a depiction of (say) the DNA double helix or a typology of legitimate government or a way of designing a skyscraper. The university as the

---

17   Rudolph 1990 [1962]: 352.

18   Murphy and Roberts 2004: 133–4.

19   As Wittgenstein did: he would sit for hours at a time in seminars, painfully drawing out the ideas that would fill up *The Blue and Brown Books*, 1958, and other works.

laboratory of investigation and discovery gives those who are intellectually gifted insight into the laborious business of creation.

The English philosopher Michael Oakeshott drew a canny distinction between modes of thinking and texts.[20] Modes of thinking are productive. They create texts. A school or college teaches texts whereas a university teaches modes of thinking (in short: the ability to create). What is taught in a university is what Oakeshott called the 'living language' of thought. It is deployed with a view to bringing others to speak it and to say new things in it. The language of a college education in contrast is a 'dead language'. In other words, it is un-creative. Its function is not to create texts but rather to explain their meaning.[21] The role of the university, then, is to encourage and show students how to engage in high levels of creative objectivation. It is perfectly true that most works created are not first class or even second class. But, then, most eminent creators only produce great works occasionally. Much of what they create, which is typically a very large amount, is only average or less than average in quality, and on occasions it can be atrocious. Creation is a difficult business, even for the preternaturally gifted. All that is required of a great university is that those who attend gain some insight into how creation works. That includes an insight into how laborious it is, and how often it misfires.

The reason that the policies of the all-administrative university invariably fail and that they do so at a high cost is that tertiary study is not for everyone. While this is a very simple proposition, it runs against a vein of thinking that goes back at least to the middle of the nineteenth century. The University of Michigan's President James B. Angell in the 1870s thought that the institution of the university was not a luxury for the few but a necessity that should be made available to all.[22] The luxury-necessity rhetoric was misleading. Angell's view rested on an assumption that all persons should have the opportunity to develop their talent and character to the full.[23] That assumption in itself was sound. But the extrapolation from it was not. Angell's extrapolation incorrectly supposed that everyone has a talent for university study. That is not so. The very strange disciplines of university study are at best a minority taste.[24] Two things follow from this. Either it is the case that the university—in the very specific sense of a community of self-motivated investigators—is an inherently tiny institution with a small call on the public purse or else it inflates itself by assuming endless non-university functions, until

---

20   Oakeshott 1962: 301.

21   Oakeshott 1962: 309.

22   Rudolph: 279.

23   The character test, though, was on the way out. This was signaled in 1869 when Harvard decided to rank students on academic grades alone, dropping the behavioral standard (grades for attending chapel and turning up for class). Schneider and Hutt 2013: 4, 7.

24   Charles Murray 2008: 84 put it succinctly: 'Not many people enjoy reading for hour after hour, day after day, no matter what the material may be. To enjoy reading On Liberty and its ilk—and if you're going to absorb such material, you must in some sense enjoy the process—is downright peculiar.'

its core functions start to deplete and the bloated institution becomes a nightmare to properly finance.[25] It is evident from the middle of the nineteenth century that universities could not resist the temptation of inflating themselves. Andrew B. White, the first president of Cornell University, described Cornell as a place where 'any person can find instruction in any study'.[26] By 1931 the University of Nebraska subject catalogue fulfilled this promise to a tee. It offered courses in 'early Irish, creative thinking, American English, first aid, advanced clothing, ice cream and ices, third-year Czechoslovakian, football, sewerage, and a man's problems in the modern home'.[27]

A curious double bind emerged. In America, in the period between 1870 and 1890, an understanding was established that the spirit of a modern university was anchored in the post-collegiate graduate faculty of arts and sciences or else in the upper-division of undergraduate arts and sciences programs. The ever-astute William Rainey Harper identified a model for the budding University of Chicago whereby the traditional four academic years would be divided into two parts: 'the first to be known as the junior college or academic college, where the spirit would be collegiate or preparatory, and the second to be known as the senior college or the university college, where the spirit would be advanced and scholarly'.[28] That said though, most university leaders could not resist the temptation of indiscriminate growth. So that by the end of the nineteenth century in the United States, the core intellectual disciplines of the natural sciences and the social sciences were squeezed by an avalanche of newly-minted practical disciplines, some of dubious merit. The long-standing professional schools of divinity, law and medicine were joined by schools of business, journalism, agriculture, forestry, veterinary science, engineering, pharmacy, teaching and social work. The degree to which these new professions equated the old professions in seriousness and substance varied. Universities began to mix, but hardly match, the scientific and the vocational, the cultural and the practical, the moral and the useful. To do so, they often lowered admission standards. Into the university came home

---

25   It does not matter whether we are talking about private or public spending on universities. By the turning point of 2008–2010, both were under massive pressure all across the OECD.

26   Rudolph: 266.

27   Rudolph: 442. Today subject proliferation is matched by the proliferation of major sequences of study. In the United States in 2010 1500 different academic majors were offered in higher education, 350 more than a decade before. Simon 2012. This trend was underpinned by the post-modern multiplication of disciplines and sub-disciplines, driven in no small measure by the explosion of 'studies' fields that occurred after 1960. This eruption of fields had a political tone bent on replacing fact with norm. The result, as Victor Davis Hanson notes, 'was advocacy, not disinterested empiricism. Nationwide, thousands of traditional classes in history, philosophy, literature, and the social sciences gave way to ethnic studies, women's studies, leisure studies, gender studies, peace studies, environmental studies, etc.' Hanson 2014.

28   Rudolph: 351.

economics and domestic science, upper middle class moral outreach to the poor, summer sessions, extension courses, engineering English, library science, trade schools, teaching training, agricultural services, how-to courses, diet counselling, and thinks tanks aimed at propagating state regulation. The perennial favorites of the social engineers—those of regulating eating habits, the railroads and the forests—were there from the start. But a lot of this was back-to-front and not a little unhelpful. Recognizing that science was the driver of industrial innovation, universities perversely devised a thing called 'applied science' that was the exact opposite of what animated industrialization. Modern technology innovation was the application of pure mathematics by industry. What universities did well was pure discovery which others then found applications for. Long before Clark Kerr, the multiversity had arrived and its collection of disparate agencies as much obfuscated rather than clarified what the university was.

Universities in the restricted sense—let us say in the true sense of the word—are places for small numbers. No social policy can engineer it otherwise. The only effective way of reducing attrition and non-completion rates is to make sure that those who are entering university, at whatever level, are intellectually suited to it and it also to them.[29] This is a mysterious nexus and one that resists a pat policy translation. The nexus is partially conditioned by the intellect and motivation of the aspiring student. It is also partly conditioned by the capacity of the university to provide a suitable environment for those who have a gift for working with symbols and abstractions, and objectivating them.

A university is a place for higher-order thinking—that is, for sustained, rigorous abstract cognition, reasoning and speculation, and creative objectivation. Interestingly, the latter (creative objectivation) is the best predictor of high-level performance. Those who do best at university, and who will go on to successful post-graduate study and high performing careers, have a predilection for producing works. The best predictor of success in post-graduate research is not success in undergraduate studies but rather a record of having produced youthful work.[30] To have excelled in producing artefacts—whether it is articles for newspapers or

---

29 Standard predictors (tests, grades) of performance are not accurate. For example, good honors grades do not predict success at a doctoral level (Simonton 1984: 74). Still, universities use these poor predictors because tests and grades can be bureaucratically formalized. They match the liberal-procedural image of justice, which is pervasive both in contemporary society and in the university. It is unfortunate then that thinking is propelled by substantive characteristics such as wide-ranging intellectual interests, the capacity for sustained reflection and a strong impulse to produce intellectual artefacts.

30 Laurance, Useche, Laurance and Bradshaw (2013) in a study of 182 academic biologists on four continents evaluated the effects of gender, native language, prestige of the institution at which they received their PhD, the date of the biologists' first publication (relative to the year of PhD completion), and their pre-PhD publication record as potential indicators of long-term publication success (10 years post-PhD). The study concluded that pre-PhD publication success was the strongest correlate of long-term success.

entries in student art competitions or science competitions—is a good predictor of later success. Each of these requires the creative drive to compose and objectivate.

Everyone has a capacity for speculation, abstraction, and objectivation. Yet only about 16 percent of the population has some gift for it—meaning that they enjoy it and pursue it with a degree of frequency.[31] About 8 percent of the population (roughly the percentage of those who today undertake some kind of post-graduate study in Australia) have an elevated gift for it. They can sustain it day-in, day-out without being bored by it. About 1-in-20000 (0.00005 percent) of the population will make an eminent contribution to the arts, sciences and professions.[32] And two percent of those will make a durable contribution to human creation. The gift for higher-order objectivation and thinking, like all gifts, is not universal, just as in the same way the gift for courage or kindness, manual dexterity or technical adeptness is not universal.[33] As a teenager, I learnt piano and wood-working. I thoroughly enjoyed both, and have benefited all my life from having done so. I always look at the joinery on cabinetry with special affection. But I would have been horrified if someone had suggested to me that I had the making of a concert pianist or a cabinet maker. One of the most important things in life is to know one's limits. That we are good at some things and not good at others is what makes us who we are. An illusion common in modern social philosophy is the belief that everything is possible. It is not. If I was recruiting an

---

31   Murray 2008: 70 calculates that about 9 to 12 percent of seventeen year olds are college ready. This would give them 65 percent probability or higher getting a B- grade point average in their first year. Murray also observes (69) that for many years the consensus intellectual benchmark in the United States 'for dealing with college-level material was an IQ of around 115, which demarcates the top 16 percent of the distribution. That was in fact the mean IQ of college graduates during the 1950s.' Simonton 1994: 219, Table 8.1 notes a similar percentage. The data of the College Board, the body that administers the SAT, also suggests that 16 percent of high school graduates are college ready.

32   Clark Kerr in contrast developed the model of Californian tertiary education on the assumption that the research universities like Berkeley and UCLA would take 12.5 percent of the state's high school graduates, while another 33 percent of high school graduates would enter the state college system, while a further third would attend two-year community colleges (Cole 2009: 135). In short, around 78 percent of young Californians would stream into some form of tertiary study.

33   And like all gifts it has to be worked on in order to develop it into a talent. Creative people are not simply intelligent. That is only a part of the story. They also labor very hard and they have an intense drive to do what they do. As Simonton observes, often a full decade of arduous labor is required before a mature intellectual or artistic style crystallizes, and the hard work continues. Outstanding researchers in the physical and social sciences typically work 60 or 70 hours a week, virtually all year, and publish in large quantities (Simonton, 1994:139). Drive and hard work are personality traits that are not the same as intelligence. The drive to create is a drive to objectivate, to add objects to the external world. The irony of creative personalities is that though they are thought of as inward-looking and reflective, and this is a part of who they are, they are also driven to create objects in the world around them.

army I would not look first to my colleagues, nor if I was running a charity. While everyone is capable of courage and charity, not everyone has a gift for such things. So societies at a certain point have to be selective. Thus we place a certain portion of the population in universities. To others who apply, we say no.

But what portion? If it is not 100 percent, then is it 50 percent, 25 percent, 15 percent? Sometimes it is argued that human beings can be educated in anything. This is not true. The human persona is not infinitely plastic. For those who deal systematically in symbolic relations and abstractions, the direct testing of those capacities, IQ tests notably, give us some pretty useful empirical rules of thumb.[34] The core of the university professoriate, for example, is recruited from the ranks of those with the highest 2 percent IQ scores.[35] The traditional professions, like law, engineering and medicine, recruit heavily from the top 8 percent. The lesser professions, like accountants, pharmacists, nurses, and managers, recruit extensively from the top 15 percent. No-one mandates this. It is an empirical pattern, not a social norm. This is Hegel's rationality of the real.[36] It is the 'is' that matters, not the 'ought'. What counts are facts, not norms. We can inflate grades, we can create as many places as we want at university, we can automatically pass all but a nominal 5 per cent of students enrolled at university irrespective of how they actually perform, but we cannot change academic or intellectual abilities.[37] We cannot give higher intelligence to persons who are not born with it and no amount of teaching can alter that fact. A society can help turn the gifts of an individual into talents but society cannot change the nature of a human being's gifts. The romantic view which insists that we can is wrong.

The 'is' in this case was measured statistically for the first time by the US Army during the Second World War. The Army undertook the large-scale recording of IQ

---

34   Hauser 2002.

35   This is less significant than it may first appear. Broadly 1 percent of the population today in major economies gets a research degree (a Masters or PhD by research). Assume that 40 percent of those end up today in academia, and 10 percent of that 40 percent end up as full professors. That is 0.4 percent and 0.04 percent of the population, which plausibly places full professors in the top 2 percent of intelligence. But it is important to keep in mind that intelligence is a necessary condition but it is not a sufficient condition for intellectual achievement (or indeed for achievement in the professions or in politics or in the military). Three other things are needed as well: character, drive, and creativity. Without those, intelligence ends up being arid and unproductive.

36   Hegel's idea, 'the rationality of the real', refers to the rationality of the totality, the larger pattern, of empirical things. While many empirical things change, the larger pattern of things remains remarkably constant. In its constancy, and our capacity to adapt to it, lies its rationality and ours as well. In simple terms, there are some things that social policy can change and other things it cannot.

37   'The A is now the most common grade on college campuses nationwide; it accounts for roughly 43 percent of all grades given.' Romeo 2013. In 1991, the average student at a private college in the United States earned a Grade Point Average (GPA) of 3.09. In 2006, that had inflated to 3.30. American Council of Trustees and Alumni 2014.

scores of service personnel. The results were able to be mapped against records of prior civilian occupation. The landmark Harrell and Harrell study (1945) reported the resulting correlations of IQ and occupation. The correlation of measurable intelligence and occupation has been regularly confirmed in subsequent studies by Vernon (1947), Jencks (1972), McCall (1997), Brody (1992), and Hernstein and Murray (1994). It is important to understand that the empirical pattern of IQ and occupation that is observed is not something socially prescribed or politically legislated. Rather it is the informal outcome of innumerable micro affordances and constraints. The pattern that emerges does so ad hoc from an infinite range of social acts of grading, awarding, honoring, streaming, interviewing, and so on. This empirical pattern is resistant to social engineering. The rationality of the real is very powerful. Consequently, it makes sense if the intake into the universities broadly aligns with this. Not to do so is simply self-defeating and wasteful. No social policy can meaningfully change the empirical pattern any more than there is going to be a social future in which everyone ends up as a manager or a professional. Such a future, in any event, would be hideous. Like all modern utopias, it is simply a function of the projection by elites of their own desires, anxieties and fantasies onto the general population.

People often make an erroneous assumption when it is suggested that smaller not larger numbers belong at university. They assume that the claim being made is that *all* social goods should go to 'smart people' (aka 'smart people like us'), i.e. those who deal fluently in symbols and abstractions. If true, this would also be a meritocratic dystopia. But it is not true. The reality is that there are many powerful criteria for distributing the social rewards of income, status, location, power, honour, and office. These include everything from athletic ability, capacious memory, manual stamina, purposefulness, diligence, motivation and genetic inheritance to moral virtue, charisma, beauty, skill, general intelligence, academic achievement, and even good luck.[38] 'Which social good should be allocated on what basis?' is a matter of enduring dispute. The general question of justice cannot be resolved here. It is difficult enough to answer the question of who should get publicly-funded university places? What is clear is that intelligence is only one among many factors that determine 'who gets what when'. For many purposes, there is no way that intelligence can compete, for example, with charisma or star quality. It is also true that intelligent people who are not motivated, purposeful or persistent go so far but no further in life. The converse, though, of this is that

---

38   In short, cognitive testing and cognition itself, while important, is also of limited value. Since the late 1960s, elites in America defined themselves as cognitive elites. These elites go to the best schools on the basis of the top grades (Murray, 1994, 2012). Yet the performance (both economic and intellectual) of these elites since the late 1960s has been less than stellar. This is the paradoxical and unintended consequence of the ideology of the knowledge society. The pseudo-cognitive ideology of the age ironically produced less cognition of a useful kind. The 'clever class' in fact turned out to be fairly stupid

intelligence has its own justified claims. It is a proper basis for distributing the good of higher education places.

Belonging to the 8 percent of the population with an IQ of 120 or more is an entry-level requirement for high levels of creative achievement of all kinds.[39] Ever higher IQs do not equate with ever-greater achievement. On the other hand, the 120+ base level of high intelligence is a prerequisite for significant attainment in the professions and creative work. There are few exceptions to this empirical pattern. While it is true that intelligence without perspiration or inspiration is void, the converse is also true. Intelligence may not be the sufficient condition but it is a necessary condition of high creative achievement in most cases. The rationality of the real is unbending. Intelligence is required for creative achievement even if beyond that measure lie the unmeasurable qualities of dedication, hard work, perseverance, contrariness, and so on.[40] It is widely reported that a lot of the most successful creative people in the world possess an anti-social streak.[41] Some studies have suggested that many highly gifted scientists, like Einstein for instance, display traits that colloquially might be compared with Asperger's syndrome.[42] We would certainly not want to put such people in charge of the social committee organizing the Christmas party. We are not going make them Parent of the Year. But we do want them at university, and we do want them doing serious scientific research.

---

39   Simonton 1994: 216–37. The following, reported by the Czech physicist Motl, 2006, is a calculation of the average IQ scores for participants in American PhD programs, based on GRE (Graduate Record Examination) scores: 130.0 Physics, 129.0 Mathematics, 128.5 Computer Science, 128.0 Economics, 127.5 Chemical engineering, 127.0 Material science, 126.0 Electrical engineering, 125.5 Mechanical engineering, 125.0 Philosophy, 124.0 Chemistry, 123.0 Earth sciences, 122.0 Industrial engineering, 122.0 Civil engineering, 121.5 Biology, 120.1 English/literature, 120.0 Religion/theology, 119.8 Political science, 119.7 History, 118.0 Art history, 117.7 Anthropology/archaeology, 116.5 Architecture, 116.0 Business, 115.0 Sociology, 114.0 Psychology, 114.0 Medicine, 112.0 Communication, 109.0 Education, 106.0 Public administration. http://motls.blogspot.com/2006/03/iq-in-different-fields.html Lindsey Harmon, 1961, tabulated AGCT IQ scores for 1958 American PhDs: Physics 140.3 Mathematics 138.2 Engineering 134.8 Geology 133.3 Arts and humanities 132.1 Social sciences 132.0 Natural sciences 131.7 Biology 126.1 Education 123.3.

40   Harris and Kaine 1994 pointed out the importance of work drive. They established that research performance is related to work motivation rather than resource support. Highly active researchers worked longer hours (65 hours per week on average) than less active colleagues (53 and 55 hours per week). The highly active devoted a larger proportion of time to research (65 percent versus 53 and 52 percent). Highly productive researchers were also boundary-crossing. They interacted with academics outside their own departments and were active in several research-related areas.

41   See, for example, Feist 1999: 273–96; Storr 1972: 50–73; Cattell and Butcher 1970: 312–26; Ludwig 1995: 46–7, 63–7; Henle 1962: 45.

42   For a short literature survey of arguments for and against whether this is literally Asperger's syndrome, see Autistic Spectrum Disorders (N.D.). Literal or not, there is a strong correlation of asocial traits and high creative achievement. http://www.autism-help. org/points-%20aspergers-einstein-newton.htm.

We want them there creating works of art and philosophy. In the university, their anti-social traits turn into productive persistence. They spend decades working on ideas that everyone else dismisses, until they make a break-through. They have un-ending, un-extinguishable curiosity.[43]

We are talking about a tiny number of people.[44] Using data from the ISI citation indexes (which include a lot but not all academic publications), Toutkoushian, Porter, Danielson, and Hollis calculated in 2003 that the output of the top 50 US universities—ranked by output per capita—ranged from 1.6 articles per capita (New York University) to 7.63 (California Institute of Technology). What is equally interesting is the very long tail of minimal or non-existence output. The researchers investigated 1,309 four-year tertiary institutions in the United States (see Table 4.2).[45] A fraction of university faculty members produce most of the research of a university, and a fraction of that fraction produces the highly-accomplished research of lasting value or significance. The American biochemist and Nobel Prize winner Julius Axelrod put it thus: 'ninety-nine percent of the discoveries are made by one percent of the scientists'.[46] That is a good starting point for understanding the university proper. It is best understood as a place of small numbers, not large numbers. This runs against the idea popularized by post-industrial romanticism that everyone should to go to university.

Intelligence is a gift for abstraction—for understanding things in an abstract, that is to say in a swift, short-hand way. Charles Spearman defined intelligence as the ability to see relationships between objects, events and ideas, and to be able to draw inferences from those relationships.[47] It is a combination of pattern recognition and reasoning. Intelligence involves the ability to think quickly and persistently in abstract terms. In their survey of expert opinion, Snyderman and Rothman found that 99 percent of respondents identified 'abstract thinking or reasoning' as a key aspect of intelligence. Intelligence recognizes and manipulates underlying patterns or relationships quickly.[48] Whether overtly displayed in the verbal, mathematical, spatial, visual, or musical domains, the underlying gift for

---

43   The Murray Committee on Australian universities in 1957 put it rather well (9) when it said 'they are simply "knowledge intoxicated" men who love the life of intellectual effort and inquiry for its own sake, and will devote their lives to it if they possibly can. Though this pure pursuit of truth seems to many to be a rather inhuman, and to some a rather super-human, kind of life, there are fortunately far more of them about than most people would have thought possible'.

44   Toutkoushian, Porter, Danielson and Hollis 2003.

45   Self-reporting by American academics for a 1998 US Department of Education survey (of 819 responding institutions and 17,600 responding faculty members) shows (predictably) a larger per capita output reported and a similarly long tail of output. Zimbler 2001: 44, Table 28. Self-reporting is not a reliable methodology for collecting information about research output.

46   Synder 2005.

47   Spearman 1927.

48   Snyderman and Rothman 1988.

Table 4.2   Institution Type and Research Output

US Institution Type	Number of Institutions	Ratio of Publications to Full-Time Faculty
Research I	83	2.04
Research II	36	0.91
Doctoral I	48	0.35
Doctoral II	54	0.56
Master's I	398	0.1
Master's II	88	0.04
Baccalaureate I	158	0.14
Baccalaureate II	404	0.03
Data Source: Toutkoushian, Porter, Danielson and Hollis, 2003.		

abstraction is much the same. Some people are endowed with a greater gift for abstraction than others, in the same way that some people are more sociable than others, some are more courageous, and some are more physically attractive.

For a person to benefit from university they have to be good at pattern recognition and reasoning. Everyone understands what an election is—in an election, we choose our leaders. That is a classic theme of universal civic education. Yet pattern thinking does not stop there. It escalates in difficulty. Of necessity, a first year political science course at university must introduce concepts like democratic legitimacy. This will stump many contemporary university students. They have to understand not only the pattern of the election ('we choose') but the fact that governments may have moral legitimacy or not, and that elections (a set of procedures) carried out fairly may endow a state with legitimacy. A citizen does not need to understand that in order to be a citizen or form the expectation of fair elections or cast a ballot competently. A scholar on the other hand does need to be able to understand that, yet many contemporary political science students struggle to do so.[49] Add to that the number of individuals who end up today at university who are bright, whose pattern recognition and reasoning capacities are sound and yet who have no patience with book learning, an art that requires a mix of patience, concentration, and stillness that most human beings feel distinctly uncomfortable with.[50]

Whenever the pointlessness of much of contemporary university education is pointed out, a common response is to trumpet the moral pabulum of 'educational opportunity' and a 'place for everyone' at college. Rhetorical appeals to social inclusion are deployed in ethically manipulative ways to justify increasing the

---

49   Murray 2008: 70–75 offers an astute assessment of the difficulties that even the simplest entry-level university textbook presents students with.

50   Murray 2008: 84 notes that '[not] many people enjoy reading for hour after hour, day after day, no matter what the material may be.'

global participation rate in universities. That this policy consistently ends in self-defeating attrition and in the awarding of vocationally-useless degrees to individuals who pay a lot for them—in fees, loans and in income foregone—is blithely ignored. Yet today half of students learn little or nothing at university. So why are these students there?

After a century of adding tertiary places, societies are no better educated in real terms than when they began this process. As Nie, Golde and Butler note, despite the massive expansion of education in America in the twentieth century, there was no accompanying increase in the verbal abilities and skills of Americans.[51] The level of educational attainment in America rose from an average of 10 years in 1910 to 14 years in 1974. When researchers compared this with the scores for verbal abilities of people born between 1910 and 1974, it was found that, in spite of the much higher levels of formal education, verbal ability and skill over time had remained constant. In short, all of the additional spending on education had produced no better communicative competencies in the population across six decades. Simple observation suggests the same. Consider the newspaper. I have been reading newspapers for over 40 years. When I first started reading them they were written by journalists who had a high school education. Today, journalists have university degrees. Have newspapers improved? No. They are less well-written, less accurate, less factual, more superficial and more naively ideological. That is not an improvement.

The larger culture has stopped encouraging architectonic abilities in the young. The culture prefers to moralize. Education in form has been replaced by moral gimmickry. Yet serious creation relies on architectonic capacity. This begins with the polished paragraph and command of the periodic table and ends with peak creation in the natural and social sciences and in the wider social world. This requires dexterity in verbal patterns and semantic shapes. At its highest pitch the ability to intuit forms and relations (whether these are mathematical, spatial, musical or linguistic relations) is the precursor of human creation. Creation relies on the capacity to form connections and imagine shapes and patterns that hitherto have not been observed. That is what discovery is—whether in the fine arts or in physics. One sees, hears or says what has been there all along yet what has not been seen, heard or said before. 'It is so obvious, if only I had thought of that', we all say.

Apprenticeship for Discovery

What happened to journalism happened to the rest of the para-professions. They all wanted the status nominally bequeathed by degrees. Nurses wanted to get out from under the thumb of doctors. Managers wanted to be able to override the authority of engineers. So what was proficiently learnt on the job in the 1950s, 1960s and 1970s in Australia and the United Kingdom was migrated to colleges

---

51   Nie, Golde and Butler 2007.

and polytechnics in the 1980s and 1990s. With the flick of the ministerial pen associate degree-granting colleges and polytechnics were miraculously turned into full degree-granting universities. Even if the battle for the name 'university' was lost, the question of 'what a university is' remained stubbornly alive. To put it simply: what is a 'university-university' as opposed to a 'college-university' or an 'institute-university' or an 'ice cream making-diet counselling university'? All the semantic equivocation and public policy hum-bug in the world will not make this question go away. You can try, as Clark Kerr and others did, to fudge the question by creating a 'multiversity' that combines university, college and institute in one. But the appetite for an unambiguous university remains.

There are four dimensions of a great university. One is homogenization—the making of connections between disparate things. That is the work of intelligence. Its medium is the imagination. The second dimension is reason. In the imagination, we identify relationships between objects, events and ideas, and then we draw inferences from those relationships. The third dimension of the great university is objectivation. This is the 'putting out' of the intellect. That is the work of creation. The fourth, and final, dimension of the great university is the work of self-education. It is true that classes and instruction at school and university aid learning, but the most decisive aspect of learning is self-formation. The modern personality is self-determining. We make ourselves up as we go along, even if we do so out of pre-existing templates. High achievement at school and university is strongly linked to self-education.[52] It is a function of voracious reading, listening and viewing outside of the formal curricula. The major contribution of formal instruction is to correct the vices of the autodidact. Anyone that is motivated to do so, and has a gift for higher-order thinking, should get to university. For this to be meaningful, though, a university has to provide abundant support for further self-education. Great libraries and laboratories are crucial. So also are encounters with faculty who can provide models of how the arduous work of connection and creation is done.

Any person who teaches in a university loves to communicate with bright students. If one-third or two-fifths of the cohort they teach cannot grasp the kinds of mathematical, physical or literary relations that are the university's stock in trade, then even with the best will in the world a university education is confounded.

---

52 Albert Nock 1932: 109 remarked that: 'We in the United States hear a great deal about the "average student," and his capacities, needs and desires. The Continental institution feels under no obligation to regard the average student as a privileged person. He is there on his own, if he be there at all, and he finds nothing cut to his measure, no organised effort to make things easy and pleasant for him, no special consideration for his deficiencies, his infirmity of purpose, or the amount or quality of intellectual effort that he is capable of making. Equality and democracy enjoin no such responsibility. In the Prussian schools … you will indeed see the shoemaker's son sitting between the banker's son and the statesman's son, over the same lessons … The three boys sit there because they are able to do the work.'

Some of these students will get a conceded pass, and others will either actively or passively drop out. Others will graduate to jobs not requiring degrees. If classes are filled with students out of their depth, the nature of those classes changes. Teachers lower the pitch of the class. It is not per se the size of classes that is the problem.[53] It is not even whether there are classes or even whether anyone attends class. The formal apparatus of instruction is not what matters. No one was ever instructed to genius. The English philosopher Michael Oakeshott put it beautifully when he said that the university is a place of education and what distinguishes it is the character of the place.[54] For him, a university education was the sort of education that is enjoyed by having the run of a place where the activity of thinking, conducted in its various modes, is going on.

To have the run of a place supposes that the student has an auto-didactic capacity. This capacity is given shape and form in a university. It is harnessed, refined and directed. Environment and atmosphere are the chief media of this transubstantiation. What matters in a great university is the nexus between the capacity of students for self-education and the correlated capacity of a university to provide deep, rich, resonant, and visible models of connection and creation.[55] Many, possibly now even most, contemporary students struggle with self-education. This is because they are either ill-suited to a university education or are in an institution that has either lost or else never had the subtle manner of enhancing and shaping the natural auto-didacticism of the gifted. The tight-fisted and yet peculiarly promiscuous resourcing of post-industrial universities ensured that the previous intimacy of brilliant staff and gifted students disappeared.[56] Institutions that were miraculously transformed by cabinet ministers from colleges and institutes into universities never acquired the vast libraries or the free-wheeling science laboratories that are the *sine qua non* of a superlative university, or the architecture that is an essential part of the context of inquiry and an endless source of morale and inspiration for students.[57]

---

53   Class sizes rose as the student:teacher ratio in Australian universities rose—from 1: 13 in 1990 to 1:22 in 2006 (Bradley 2008: 72). The figures apply to the 39 Australian universities represented by the 'Universities Australia' lobby body.

54   Oakeshott 1962: 311.

55   This applies to school as well. '[I]f the school itself rarely gets mentioned as a source of inspiration (by high-level creators—PM), individual teachers often awake, sustain or direct a child's interest. The physicist Eugene Wigner credits László Rátz, a math teacher in the Lutheran high school in Budapest, with having refined and challenged his own interest in mathematics ... as well as that of his schoolmates the mathematician John von Neumann, and physicists Leo Szilard and Edward Teller' (Csikszentmihalyi 1996: 174).

56   'Does that mean there will be more time for the academic to engage in small-group teaching, tutorials and one-to-one discussions? Not likely. The ratio of students to staff has risen to the point where in many areas this would be impractical' (Anderson, Johnson and Saha 2002: 6).

57   Allan Bloom expressed the point perfectly: 'When I was fifteen years old I saw the University of Chicago for the first time and somehow sensed that I had discovered my

For gifted students today, the lack of inspiration in the air is discouraging. They fight constantly, as they have all of their life, with boredom.[58] This is a small group. It rarely registers in the innumerable reports on the modern university. Nonetheless it is the group that embodies the essence of the university. From their numbers, come the leaders of the professions, the pioneers of business, and future researchers and professors. Most of these students are more talented than their teachers so it is difficult to keep them interested. There is an historic pattern that many of those who become high achievers in the arts and sciences later in life drop out—in the arts after second year, in the sciences in graduate school.[59] Some return, and some by circuitous routes. Others, like Bill Gates, Microsoft's co-founder, who scored 1590 out of a possible 1600 on his SAT, remain brilliant drop outs. Yet, as long as they are at university, they should encounter the kind of experience that will unleash their intellectual curiosity and draw out the best of their natural gifts for discovery.

---

life. I had never seen, or at least had not noticed, buildings that were evidently dedicated to a higher purpose' Bloom 1987: 243.

58   Collins 2001.
59   Simonton, 1984:72.

Chapter 5

The Social Mirage

Who should go to University?

With the onset of the post-industrial age, governments and political parties of all kinds across the OECD declared that the universities were now the principal means of upward social mobility. That was a fiction.[1] In 2012 more than 30 percent of young Australians went to university. But there were not graduate jobs for all of them or even for a majority of them. The majority had to be content with employment in retail, hospitality, and services. These were not jobs in the professions, let alone the learned professions. The promise of the post-industrial universities was that these institutions were a gateway to the high professions. For a minority of students this was true. For the rest this was spurious. Eight percent of jobs are in the learned professions like medicine, law, and engineering. A further 8 percent are in the associate professions like nursing and social work. This is a social ratio of long standing. It is persistent and unlikely to change.

What has changed though in the past 40 years has been the inflation of the classification of 'professional' and 'management' jobs. The social labelling of occupations has metastasized. Accordingly, the nominal number of jobs called 'professional' or 'management' in society has multiplied. In 1972, 19 percent of the American workforce was designated professionals and managers. That grew to 26.5 percent in 1992.[2] In 2013, it was 38 percent.[3] That it is a very large number. Yet much of that number is deceptive. The American Standard Occupational Classification (SOC) counts among managers the following: Funeral Service Managers, Food Service Managers, Farmers and Ranchers, Postmasters, Emergency Management Directors, Lodging Managers and Gaming Managers. We live in a world where everyone who directs something or coordinates something is now a 'manager.' But many such occupations are not management jobs in the sense of an occupation that manifestly requires or benefits in a major way from an arduous course of university studies. The following is a list of new-minted 2010 SOC occupation classifications. Only some of them are recognizably occupations where an advanced degree-length course of study is

---

1 Clark's 2014 study of 1000 years of long-term multi-generational social mobility data shows clearly that mass higher education did not increase the rate of inter-generational mobility even in countries like Sweden that provided free university tuition.

2 Kutcher 1993: 8, Table 4.

3 US Bureau of Labor Statistics, 'Employed persons by detailed occupation, sex, race, and Hispanic or Latino ethnicity' 2013.

essential to the work function: fundraisers; information security analysts; web developers; computer network architects; computer network support specialists; *community health workers*; special education teachers; exercise physiologists; nurse anesthetists; nurse midwives; nurse practitioners; magnetic resonance imaging technologists; *ophthalmic medical technicians*; hearing aid specialists; genetic counsellors; *orderlies*; *phlebotomists*; *transportation security screeners*; morticians, undertakers, and funeral directors; *financial clerks*; *solar photovoltaic installers*; wind turbine service technicians; *food processing workers*. Eight of the 23 classifications (those marked in italics) earned less than the 2010 US national average wage of $41,673.[4]

The most optimistic credible projection is that 20 percent of future jobs will require a degree. That is the outside upper limit. What happens to the rest in higher education? Twenty-five percent of incoming students drop out of university.[5] Another 25 percent of students who graduate will never work in a job that requires a degree. In the United States today 115,520 janitors have a bachelor's degree or higher. Twelve percent of parking lot attendants have a bachelor's degree. Seventeen occupations that require less than a high-school education have 50,000 US college graduates employed in them. In 1970, 1 in 100 taxi drivers or chauffeurs in the United States had a college degree. Today, 15 in 100 do. One in 20 sales clerks in the retail trade had college degrees in 1970. Today that figure is one in 4.[6]

---

4   BLS, 'Employment and wages for occupations identified as new in the 2010 SOC manual' May 2012.

5   In the case of Australia, Kemp and Norton in their 2014 report to government (34–5) repeat uncritically the view of the Bradley report (2008) that Australian job growth is disproportionately in professional and managerial occupations. According to the Australian Bureau of Statistics 2011 census, 12.9 percent of Australians are managers and 21.3 percent are professionals. That *sounds* impressive. However, consider the OECD *Skills Outlook Report of 2013*. Twenty-seven percent of Australian workers report that their qualification is higher than the qualification needed to get the job that they have today (171, Figure 4.25a). Fourteen percent report they are underqualified in terms of the qualification they would need to get the job today. Overqualified workers across the OECD on average earn only 4 percent more than appropriately qualified workers do in similar jobs (179). As Kemp and Norton report (34), the number of graduates going into professional and managerial jobs has declined by almost 10 percent between the early 1980s and 2013 (from 82 percent to 72 percent); the latter figure confirming that university is a waste of time and money for 28 percent of graduates. Yet the authors then conclude that there is no problem with over-education in Australia. This is the standard post-modern posture: just ignore that a third of graduates are over-educated (and this does not even include the almost-as-large non-graduating drop-out cohort). The Kemp and Norton report, written for a center-right government, interpolates the same assumptions as Bradley's report did for a left-of-center government. Across the OECD, on average 21 percent of employees today are over-qualified (OECD 2013b: 358, Table A4.25). Only Japan has a higher rate of over-education than Australia.

6   Vedder, Denhart and Robe 2013.

In spite of the phenomenon of massive over-education, governments encourage universities—and universities encourage themselves—to admit students who will not succeed in the graduate job market. Universities reduce their entry requirements and accept applicants with lower and lower entry scores—and less and less aptitude for university study. Thirty to 40 percent of university students have always dropped out.[7] Dropping-out is not a new phenomenon. What is new and what developed after 1970 was the mass scale of the university enterprise. Forty percent of a tiny number of enrollees in 1960 was fiscally and socially inconsequential. A quarter of a third of the age cohort in 2010 had acquired serious social and fiscal implications. Moreover, in 1960 university students dropped out into good jobs.[8] Many of the greatest entrepreneurs of the modern age were college drop outs.[9] They had talent with no need for certification of that talent. University is not for everyone. However most of those who dropped out of college in 2010 did not fall into something as good or better. Instead they competed with high school graduates for jobs in the large semi-skilled service sector.

So who should go to university? Post-industrial ideology wanted 'everyone' to go to university. The process of admitting students to university

---

7   The recurrence of the drop-out phenomenon brings with it a recurrence of the same inane solutions to the pseudo-problem of what is a natural corollary of (what the social scientist Charles Murray 2008: 84, rightly described as) the unnatural occupation of university study. Most human beings including a lot of intelligent ones are not so constituted as to want to sit down and read books all day. Those who are not bookish will either not read the books and materials set for them, or else they will fail or drop out. That does not stop a pointless 'completions' industry having grown up in higher education with faux recipes for solving a specious problem. It is striking how many of the formulas are simply re-badged over the decades. In 1957 Australia's Murray Committee was bemoaning that the failing student was not getting any pre-view 'examinations or other tests which will indicate to him the deficiencies of his understanding of the subject of these,' allowing the student to 'remain blissfully ignorant until the final examination' (37). The learning bureaucracies that emerged in the 1980s in Australian universities prescribed progressive assessments through the semester beginning in week five for the same reason. Yet nothing changed, except the absolute volume of students. The students still fail, many by virtue of never sitting any exam. Forty percent of 2 percent of 19 year olds could fail in 1960 and this was just the cost of a university education—it entailed no extravagant private or public costs. However when 30 percent of 30 percent of 19 year olds drop-out, this is a fiscal burden both for tax payers and fee payers that is pernicious and unjustifiable on any imaginable grounds.

8   The Murray Committee report on Australian universities in 1957 reported (35) 'of every hundred students who entered six universities in 1951 only 61 passed the first year examination, only 35 graduated in the minimum time, and only 58 have graduated or are expected to graduate at all.'

9   In 1957, the Murray Committee (32) noted that in Australian universities of the time 'some 30 percent of Commonwealth Scholarship holders fail to graduate.' Sixty years of reports on universities, faux-solutions, the rise of teaching and learning bureaucracies, and spiraling real costs of universities made not an iota of difference to this.

consequently changed. Rather than simply admitting those with scholastic aptitude and motivation, the focus turned to admitting as many applicants as possible. That meant increasing public spending on university places. It also meant focusing on those less likely to go to university. A sociological preoccupation with reasons why individuals don't go to university multiplied. Attention turned away from traditional entry factors—those of cognition and character—to matters of family income, parental qualifications, and the sociological profiles of applicants, their race, ethnicity, gender, and so on. The keywords became access, equity, minority participation, and first-generation college attendance. Measures of creativity, intelligence, and motivation were downplayed. Often strenuous efforts were made to side-step such measures in ways that made universities and colleges look like places where imagination, cognition and determination were irrelevant.

So, then, who should go to university? Today, two sets of criteria are usually invoked. One is the fashionable set of criteria invented by the diversity lobby, another redemptive bureaucracy of the post-industrial age. Diversity is mainly an American ideology.[10] It means handing out admissions points to persons who happen to have some officially-favored racial, ethnic or social background. It is an empty exercise in moral preening. The second set of criteria is meritocratic. It measures scholastic performance in high school or else general mental ability. For example, the most common method for selecting students for admission to Australian universities is a score based on final year secondary school assessment.[11]

---

10   And even more pointedly, a Californian ideology: Heather Macdonald 2013 observes of the University of California that today 'we can say that there are two Universities of California: UC One, a serious university system centered on the sciences (though with representatives throughout the disciplines) and still characterized by rigorous meritocratic standards; and UC Two, a profoundly unserious institution dedicated to the all-consuming crusade against phantom racism and sexism that goes by the name of "diversity." … It's impossible to overstate the extent to which the diversity ideology has encroached upon UC's collective psyche and mission. No administrator, no regent, no academic dean or chair can open his mouth for long without professing fealty to diversity. It is the one constant in every university endeavor; it impinges on hiring, distorts the curriculum, and sucks up vast amounts of faculty time and taxpayer resources. The university's budget problems have not touched it. In September 2012, for instance, as the university system faced the threat of another $250 million in state funding cuts on top of the $1 billion lost since 2007, UC San Diego hired its first vice chancellor for equity, diversity, and inclusion. This new diversocrat would pull in a starting salary of $250,000, plus a relocation allowance of $60,000, a temporary housing allowance of $13,500, and the reimbursement of all moving expenses.'

11   'Tertiary entrance rank derived from final year secondary school assessment (as in the Australian Tertiary Admissions Rank or ATAR) remains the most prominent criterion for undergraduate admission in Australian universities.' Palmer, Bexley and James 2011.

Another option is a test in the vein of the American Scholastic Assessment Test.[12] This is akin to an IQ *g*, or general mental ability, test.[13]

A common question is how valid are such tests in predicting performance at university compared to high school exams? Analyzing a sample of 151,316 students attending 110 American colleges and universities, the College Board that administers the SAT found that the correlation of predictors with first-year GPAs was 0.51 for SAT writing, 0.48 for SAT critical reading and 0.47 for SAT mathematics, all solid positive relations. The College Board also reported that high school GPA is a slightly better predictor (0.54) of first year GPA at college and university than SAT test scores.[14] Using both together, their predictive strength rises to 0.62. The predictive power of high school record plus SAT has remained essentially unchanged since the 1950s and 1960s.[15] The strongest correlation (0.67) occurs when high school record and SAT is used together to predict performance of students in small institutions.

In short, the predictive strength of the SAT overall is moderate. However, a different picture begins to emerge when we consider those who do well on the SAT tests. The SAT administrators have a measure of test proficiency. It is called college readiness. By readiness is meant a 65 percent likelihood of achieving a B- grade or higher in the first year of college or university. 'College readiness' means in effect a reasonably high probability of completing a degree.[16] In 2012 this required a combined SAT score of 1550 (out of 2400).[17] In 2012, only 43 percent of high school seniors who sat the SAT met the College Board's College and Career Readiness Benchmark. Those who do not meet this benchmark tend not to do well at college. Retention rates for students with an aggregate SAT score of less than 1550 are poor to very poor. Today more than 40 percent of

---

12   Australia had a scholarship system based on a general intelligence test. It was abolished in the 1970s by the Whitlam Labour Government in favor of a short-lived policy of free university tuition. The educational psychologist Godfrey Thomson pressed for IQ tests to choose students for the post-WWII selective secondary schooling in the United Kingdom. It was fairer than other selection methods, he argued. Floud and Halsey's classic study of Hertfordshire showed that when local authorities eventually dropped IQ tests from the 11+ exam, 'there was an immediate and significant decrease in the proportion of children from working class families entering grammar schools, and a comparable increase in the proportion of children from professional families' (Mackintosh 1998: 24).

13   http://research.collegeboard.org/programs/sat/data/validity-studies   Frey   and Detterman 2004 analyze the SAT as a test of general cognitive ability.

14   See also http://cshe.berkeley.edu/publications/docs/ROPS.GEISER._SAT_6.13.07.pdf.

15   http://research.collegeboard.org/sites/default/files/publications/2012/7/research report-2008-5-validity-sat-predicting-first-year-college-grade-point-average.pdf.

16   http://press.collegeboard.org/releases/2011/43-percent-2011-college-bound-seniors-met-sat-college-and-career-readiness-benchmark.

17   http://media.collegeboard.com/homeOrg/content/pdf/sat-report-college-career-readiness-2012.pdf.

four-year college entrants in the United States do not complete their degree.[18] Conversely, 78 percent of those who score 1550–1790 on their SATs will finish third year. This number rises to 87 percent for the 1800–2090 SAT band, and then to 92 percent for the 2100–2400 band. Simply put, proficient SAT scores predict academic achievement or at least doggedness. Less-than-proficient scores predict academic failure.[19]

So what percentage of the 17 year-old age cohort meets the college-readiness benchmark? Forty-eight percent of high school graduates and 37 percent of US 17 year olds took the SAT in 2012. Forty-three percent of SAT takers scored 1550 or more.[20] Not every college-bound American high school senior is obliged to sit the SAT but most in practice do even if they take other admissions tests as well. Given that then, we can conclude that 16 percent of 17 year olds in 2012 were college ready. This percentage of the age cohort aligns precisely with the percentage of the working population that traditionally has ended up in professional and para-professional employment. Individuals who are college-ready have a high likely-hood of finishing a degree.[21] Yet double that figure—30 percent or more—of 19 year olds are enrolled in four-year university and college systems in the United States and in most OECD countries. In short, only a half of those enrolled in higher education today have a genuine aptitude for university-level or college-level study. Without the aptitude for study, educational opportunity is simply a mirage. The students that have no aptitude for higher learning fail, drop out,

---

18   http://media.collegeboard.com/homeOrg/content/pdf/sat-report-college-career-readiness-2012.pdf.

19   Access to university without subsequent success is pointless. There is no way around this hard fact. The American Enterprise Institute (Rodriguez and Kelly 2014) did a study that asked the interesting question: which American universities or colleges offer applicants the golden combination of *access* (a good proportion of low-income students: more than 25 percent of Pell grant recipients), *affordability* (good prices for tuition: less than $10,000 per annum net price after grants and scholarships are factored in) and *success* (good graduation rates: better than 50 percent after 6 years). 1700 four-year colleges were surveyed. The research could only find 19 institutions that satisfied all three criteria, and as 11 of those had graduation rates in the 50–60 percent range, even the number of 19 out of 1700 institutions is questionable.

20   http://press.collegeboard.org/releases/2012/sat-report-only-43-percent-2012-college-bound-seniors-college-ready. Stille 2014 notes that, according to the ACT (American College Testing) and based on the 1,799,243 students who took the ACT college entrance test in 2013, only 26 percent of those test-takers were 'college ready' in all four areas of the test (English, Reading, Math and Science).

21   In Australia 35.2 percent of enrollees enter Australian universities on the basis of Australian Tertiary Admission Rank (ATAR) scores. Kemp and Norton (2014: 22, Table 5), looking at the status of bachelor-degree students 6 years after they commenced tertiary study, report that in 2013, 86.7 percent of students with an ATAR rank of 95–99 had completed their degree; while 56.7 percent of students with an ATAR of 60–69 had completed their degree.

or barely pass. Either way, they waste their time and money. Yet colleges and universities admit these applicants. They take their fees and organize loans for them. Their study is heavily subsidized by the state. The student pays; the state pays. The singular result of all of this is discontented students.

In Australia 30 to 40 percent of undergraduates consistently reported over the decade between 1999 and 2009 that they were unhappy or ambivalent at university.[22] Low academic achievement is strongly correlated with this dissatisfaction.[23] It is unsurprising, as a consequence, that a quarter or more of Australian undergraduates drop out of university. How could it be otherwise? Students that drop out, or who get a degree they never use, exit with debt that many find difficult to pay off. In 2012 Australian student debt totaled $23 billion. The annual interest on the debt was $600 million. In the United States in the same year student debt totaled $1 trillion, greater than all of the money owed on auto loans and greater than the US credit card debt.[24] The student loan market in the US had grown to a remarkable one-tenth of the size of the mortgage market. The volume of American student debt was fueled by tuition increases that rose 300 percent from 1990 to 2011. General inflation over the same period was only 75 percent. Even soaring health-care costs had risen a mere 150 percent by comparison over the period.[25] American students in 2010 were graduating with an average debt of $25,000.[26] In 2012, a survey of American 27 year olds revealed that 84 percent of them had started college and 60 percent of those had taken out loans. Of those in debt, 16 percent owed less than $10,000; 20 percent owed between $10,000 and $25,000. Thirteen percent owed between $25,000 and $50,000—and 11 percent owed more than $50,000.[27] In 2013, of the $11 trillion in American household debt, 8 percent was for auto loans, 6 percent for credit cards and 9 percent for student loans.[28] Consequently, many ex-students were delaying marriage and the purchase of a first home to pay off debts. Student debt was having a dampening effect on the housing market and retail markets, and was eating into capital for entrepreneurial business start-ups. Most of the student debt is backed by the government who collects it through the tax system. It is almost impossible to discharge. The US government can garnish wages, income tax returns and Social Security payments to make good on the

---

22 Bradley 2008: 74; ACER 2010: x; James, Krause, and Jennings 2010: 60.

23 ACER 2010: 43; James, Krause and Jennings: 61.

24 Laing 2012.

25 'As University of Michigan economics and finance professor Mark Perry has calculated, tuition for all universities, public and private, increased from 1978 to 2011 at an annual rate of 7.45%. By comparison, health-care costs increased by only 5.8%, and housing, notwithstanding the bubble, increased at 4.3%. Family incomes, on the other hand, barely kept up with the consumer-price index, which grew at an annual rate of 3.8%.' Reynolds, January 7, 2014.

26 The default rate on US student loans in 2009 was 8.8 percent. Saunders 2011.

27 Lauff, Ingels and Christopher 2014: Table 3.

28 The Federal Reserve Bank of New York, *Quarterly Report on Household Debt and Credit*, Third Quarter 2013.

current $67 billion in bad loans. What was meant to aid social mobility has turned into a constraint that now holds back many of its recipients. Student loans make sense for the 16 percent of the population who will end up in professional and semi-professional occupations. For them, it is a good investment—more expensive than a car but less expensive than a house. For others, rather than advantage, it disadvantages them.

No More How Green Was My Valley

The university is one of the most powerful imaginary institutions of modernity. The idolization of the university began before the post-industrial era, though it also accelerated and inflated during that period. The ideology of the university as an agency of social mobility has deep roots in the liberal-reformism of the nineteenth century.[29] A commonplace view of nineteenth-century liberals was that a university well managed was proof that persons without means could rise in society thanks to talent. Such a university would provide scholarships and other instruments of student support to ensure that those who were intellectually gifted but lacking in resources could study at university and improve their position in society.

This credo entered popular culture with Richard Llewellyn's 1939 novel *How Green Was My Valley*. It proved to be one of the most influential pop culture works of the twentieth century. Set in a poor Welsh coal mining town, and told from the standpoint of the academically-gifted Huw Morgan, Llewellyn's melodramatic tale popularized two ideas. The first idea was that great books symbolized the promise of emancipation from bleak lives lived in hardship and toil. The second idea was that, with education, the children of those who performed back-breaking work could become lawyers and doctors. John Ford's 1941 film of Llewellyn's novel shows the book shelf of young Huw's home lined with *Treasure Island*, Boswell's *Life of Johnson*, *Pickwick Papers*, and *Ivanhoe*. Huw is the first in his family to attend a 'National School.' When Huw graduates, he receives a certificate written in Latin, and is congratulated by his father for having achieved honors. 'What will it be?,' his father asks. 'To Cardiff to school? Then the University to be a lawyer, is it, or a doctor?'

'To be a doctor or a lawyer' was the promise of the university. It is always had been. This was its promise in the twelfth century. It was still its promise in the twentieth century. But the number of doctors and lawyers and other professionals

---

29   Of that reform mentality and its perpetual disappointments Albert Jay Nock in 1932 was to skeptically observe: 'Yes, yes, we kept saying, let us but just install this one new method in the secondary schools, or this one new set of curricular changes in the undergraduate college, or this one grand new scheme for broadening the scope of university instruction, and in a year or so it will prove itself to be the very thing we have all along been needing; and this, that or the other batch of pedagogical problems will be laid to eternal rest. Such, I think, is a fair summary of our 30 years' experience … '

in any society is inherently limited. It has a ceiling.[30] Yet a new class of professional in the second half of the twentieth century made a career out of defying that social fact. The post-industrial ideological imperative was to create a new universal class. This class defined itself in terms of 'social justice' and 'moral correctness.' It drew its authority as a class from two things. First from incessant acts of moralism; second from the claim that it could solve social problems by political reform. Accordingly, this new class translated all problems, even problems that were intellectual, ontological or technical, into social problems—and all social problems into questions of social mobility. The most potent ideology of the second half of twentieth century stated that social and geographical mobility was driven by education, culminating in going to university. What resulted was the system of mass higher education.

The early statements of this ideology make interesting reading in retrospect. Australia had a series of landmark reports on tertiary education after 1945. The first of these, by the Murray Committee in 1957, set the tone. Twenty-five years ago, the report declared, most countries produced many more graduates than, economically considered, their manner of life demanded.[31] It even seemed then that the pattern of the future might be industrial communities run by machines and unskilled labour—with the direction and control of the whole thing in the hands of a few brilliant experts.[32] But no, the Committee assured its readers, the opposite was true: 'the post war community calls for more and more highly educated people.'[33] Every subsequent government committee on the universities would say the exactly the same things that the Murray Committee went on to say: the machinery of modern society was increasingly 'complex,' there was a 'world-wide shortage' of graduates, and 'every young man or woman who wanted a university education and had the intellectual capacity to profit from it should have a fair chance of getting it.' By the time of Australia's 1964 Martin Committee Report on the universities, the knowledge society rhetoric was beginning to become well-honed: 'In the modern industrial and commercial society, people who have had a broad education contribute more to society's production than do those whose formal schooling has been limited and, generally speaking, they are remunerated accordingly; the literate are worth more than the illiterate, the highly skilled usually have larger incomes than the unskilled. Thus, even from the materialistic standpoint of the individual

---

30   Fifty-six percent of 2012 law graduates in the United States were unable to find regular, long-term employment in the law profession nine months after graduation.

31   Murray Committee 1957: 7.

32   That sounds actually a lot like the neo-feudal digital dystopia that the knowledge economy of Silicon Valley has become today, 55 years after the Murray Committee. Cf. Kotkin 2013.

33   The Murray Committee 1957: 16–19 reported needs for mathematics and science teachers, geologists, engineers, chemists and physicists. Fifty years later, in many of these same categories there were still shortages, even though the society was flooded with graduates. It may be the case that in the modern world there is an inherent scarcity of some employment types especially in occupations requiring high levels of mathematical and calculation abilities. The general expansion of education does not satisfy this demand.

income earner, the value of additional education becomes real.'[34] This would be repeated *ad nauseam* over the years—each time as if it was new coinage; what then were the other perceived benefits of minting ever-more graduates? There was the public good benefit: as 'when the individual makes some discovery of great benefit to mankind,' which assumed (wrongly as it turned out) that the average graduate of the mass university would make discoveries.[35] There were further (presumed) public goods: including the promise of 'a well-educated population capable of making reasoned judgments against a background of change,' 'the development of a responsible and enlightened community,' 'the raising of cultural standards,' and 'a greater and wiser use of leisure.' Well obviously that came to pass: the rampant taste for reality television 50 years later is unambiguous evidence, should any be needed, that the mass university, enrolling 30-to-40 percent of 19 year olds raised cultural standards. Just as it is equally evident that democratic citizens before the mass university were idiots who made terrible judgments and had no prudent way of deciding modern contingencies.

The Martin Committee went on to claim that 'statistics can be produced showing that there is a clear association between the proportion of the population engaged in full-time education and the annual production per head in various countries.'[36] In point of fact, as we have seen, the knowledge society (as it proceeded to unfold) was associated with lower levels of productivity, wealth creation and real increases in income. Maybe this was because the whole assumption of the knowledge economy that 'economic growth … depends … significantly upon education' was wrong. In fact the obverse is true: education depends on economic growth, not the other way round. Richer societies can afford to have the young in school longer. Schools, though, do not produce wealth. They do not even produce new knowledge. It is true that acquiring and applying knowledge does 'enable human and material resources to be used more effectively.' The wealth of industrial capitalism is a by-product of the application of natural science and social philosophy to economic ends. The discovery of electricity and the rule of law had exceptional economic effects. Those effects were felt without any additional persons going to school, college or university. The view of the Martin Committee was that education drove economic growth because more education meant a more skilled workforce, quicker modernization of capital, the faster introduction of new products and methods, and improved management.[37] Education addressed the challenge of

---

34   Martin Committee 1964 volume 1: 5.

35   Martin Committee 1964 volume 1: 6.

36   Martin Committee 1964 volume 1: 6.

37   The Murray Committee (1957: 15) talked about the growing need for 'leadership and expertise in the professions, in administration and in production.' Also in order to overcome Australia's three inherent disadvantages (small domestic market, lack of cheap labor, and its distance from other countries), it had to 'have more than its share of expertise and "know how" in all its enterprises.' Not the classic work ethic that had driven the economies of North-Western Europe and America, but 'know how' was the cure for disadvantage.

the complexity of large organizational units, complex pieces of equipment, complicated methods, and the need for innovation.[38] The doubtful presupposition of this was that education allowed the efficacious handling of 'change' and 'complexity'—as if humankind had never confronted these things before. Thus the hundreds of thousands of citizens with little formal education, who forged the American Revolution and pioneered the vast lands and the enormously energetic cities of the United States, were dummies by contrast with their brethren subject to 15 years of formal education in the knowledge society. The problem with this is that the economic, political and social achievements of the citizens of 1783 and 1883 were singularly more impressive than those of 1983 or 2013. The life-span of a large company today is much shorter than it was 100 years ago; the larger an organization grows the less efficient it becomes; the biggest area of contemporary jobs growth is in jobs for which a high school diploma or less is required. That is what the knowledge society and its 'improved management' achieved.

Today there is near-universal access to higher education in OECD countries.[39] Twenty-eight percent of Australians aged 25–64 have a university degree (1 percent has advanced research degrees);[40] another 10 percent has a vocational-type qualification.[41] As in all advanced economies, these figures have grown over the last century. In 1911, 0.7 percent of Australian males (aged 20–24) and 0.5 percent of females were in higher education. In 1921 the respective figures were 1.2 and 0.5 percent, in 1954 2.1 and 0.8 percent, and in 1961 3.7 and 1.2 percent.[42] In other words, by the beginning of the 1960s about 2.5 percent of the 19 year old cohort was engaged in some form of tertiary study.[43] This percentage was to grow by more than 10-fold in the next 50 years. Almost from the seedling-like historic start of the knowledge age, official Australian commissions predicted that 30 percent

---

38   Martin Committee 1957: 9.

39   Figures cited are for 2007 and are from the OECD's *Education at a Glance* report, 2009, unless otherwise noted.

40   The OECD also calculates 'graduation rates,' a prediction of the proportion of the young age cohort that will complete a degree in their life-time. The OECD projected (based on 2011 age cohort data) that 1.6 percent of young people will graduate with an advanced degree compared with 1 percent in 2000 (OECD 2013a: 58). In Australia the projective 'graduation rate' rose from 1.3 in 2000 to 1.9 in 2010. In the OECD as a whole it rose from 0.8 in 1995 to 1.6 in 2011.

41   OECD 2013a: 40, Table A1.5a; in 2007 the figures were 24 percent and 10 percent; see OECD 2009: 39, Table A1.3a. The OECD distinguishes between Type-A tertiary education and Type-B. Type A services elite and professional occupations; Type B technical and associate professional work.

42   Martin Committee 1964 volume 1: 9.

43   The Murray Committee (1957: 82) reported that in 1946 231-in-10,000 17–22 year olds attended university; in 1950 325, in 1951 383, in 1955 433. In 1957, 36,465 students were enrolled in nine Australian universities.

of the population would acquire a tertiary (a post-secondary school) qualification.[44] Official predictions of this kind were self-fulfilling. That said, the path to fulfilment went through some interesting twists and turns—in the 1950s, attending university in Australia was seen in life-long terms. Part-time evening or after-hours study for adults was commonplace.[45] University was not just for 19-year-olds.[46]

Early in the post-war period in Australia the majority of tertiary places were in universities, not in colleges.[47] The first two major post-war inquiries into higher education in Australia, the Murray report in 1957 and the Martin report in 1964, paved the way, starting in 1965, for a major expansion of Australia's college

---

44   Martin Committee 1964 volume 1: 15 expected that in the foreseeable future one-third of the male population and one-sixth of the female population would enrol at a tertiary institution 'sooner or later during their lifetimes.'

45   The Murray Committee 1957: 32 reported that: 'A distinctive feature of Australian universities is the high proportion of part-time students and particularly in two universities of external students. The opportunity offered to such students plays a significant part in the much higher university enrolments in Australia relative to population, than in the United Kingdom.' Part-time study was an efficient use of scare resources: 'Part-time courses result in the running of two shifts at a university, one during the day and another in the evening' (33). Canberra University College of the time, later absorbed into the Australian National University, had been created specifically to cater for part-time degree courses for Australian federal public servants. The knowledge society eventually eliminated after-hours study, reducing the space and time efficiencies of universities considerably.

46   The philosopher R.G Collingwood would begin his lectures on ethics to young Oxford undergraduates by telling them that he didn't think a person could usefully study ethics until at least the age of 25. Life experience is a condition of ethical understanding. Collingwood's rule could be extended to the university as a whole. University in large measure is wasted on the young who too often lack the maturity and discipline and purposefulness for advanced study. It is unsurprising then that a good predictor of the high-achieving creative individual is a person who drops out of university at the end of their second year. In part this is a function of the lack of challenge that universities offer high achievers. But it is also a sign of their own hesitation about their own vocation. The combination of breadth of understanding and disciplined focus required for high achievement of an original kind is difficult and it is a rare 19-year-old that has it. Collingwood was not alone in his view at the time. The Murray Committee, 1957, reported as common the view of Australian academics of the 1950s that enrolling university students were 'in general too immature to adapt themselves quickly to the university environment' (30). They may have been right. The Facebook-social-media obsessions and lax work-habits of the enrollees of the 2000s suggests even less maturity.

47   In 1963 69,000 students (58 percent) were enrolled at Australian universities, 14,600 at teachers colleges (12 percent) and 34,300 (30 percent) at technical and other institutions (Martin Committee, volume 1: 15). The Martin Committee (volume 2) recommended that 'technological and other non-university institutions should be strengthened' and accordingly that 'the proportion of university enrolments within the total tertiary enrolment' be scaled back 'from 58 percent in 1963 to about 50 percent in 1975' (15). By 1986 student load ('equivalent full-time student units' in the jargon) in the college sector exceeded that in the university sector (DEET 1993: 15).

sector.[48] What ensued was the development of a binary system of colleges and universities.[49] For two decades, colleges multiplied in Australia—many of them (as in the United States) small.[50] College enrolments (many of them diploma rather than degree students) grew larger than university enrolments, reversing the earlier weighting toward university study. The Murray and Martin reports were the product of a center-right policy climate in Australia. That changed with the election of the center-left social Australian Labor Party to power in 1983 and the subsequent higher education policy shift in 1989 that eliminated colleges, erased the distinction between college and university, created multiple new universities, expanded existing universities, amalgamated small institutions, and created a sector composed of large organizations.[51]

The result of all of this was that by 2007 34 percent of adult Australians had some kind of tertiary qualification. This compared with the OECD average

---

48   In 1957 Australia had nine universities and two university colleges. These were complemented by technical colleges, teachers colleges and agricultural colleges. Technical colleges offered certificate and diploma courses; teachers colleges mainly two-year diplomas. The Australian National University and Canberra University College were established under federal law; the other university institutions were established under state law. Funding was a different matter. In 1956, 50 percent of university income came from state governments, 29 percent from the federal government, and 15 percent from student fees. Murray 22–4. In 1939, 45 percent came from government grants, 31 percent from student fees, 16 percent from interest, rent, dividends and donations, and 8 percent from other sources. In 1991, 22 percent of the sector's income came from non-government sources. DEET 1993: 5. In 2011, 54 percent came from the federal government, 3 percent from state governments, 25 percent from student fees, and 14 percent from contract, royalty, grant, donations and investment income.

49   The Martin Committee volume 1: paragraph 5.137 made the serviceable and still perfectly valid distinction that '[the] objective of the education provided by a technical college is to equip men and women for the practical world of industry and commerce, teaching them the way in which manufacturing and business are carried on and the fundamental rules which govern their successful operation. The university course, on the other hand, tends to emphasize the development of knowledge and the importance of research; in so doing it imparts much information which is valuable to the practical man but which is often incidental to the main objective. Both types of education are required by the community, and in increasing amounts, but it is important that students receive the kind of education best suited to their innate abilities and purposes in life.'

50   Between 1965 and 1977 over 100 institutions were classified in legislation as colleges. By 1979 that had been reduced to 70. The system included institutes of technology, art colleges, teachers colleges, multi-purpose colleges, and agricultural and para-medical colleges. Forty-two of the eventual 70 colleges had less than 2000 students enrolled. DEET 1993: 14–15.

51   The number of institutions dropped from 87 in 1982 to 39 in 1992. Average enrolment size escalated from 4,300 to 14,000. DEET 1993: xxiv, 22.

of 27 percent.[52] The younger an adult was, the more likely they were to have a degree. Thus in 2007, 31 percent of Australians aged 25-to-34 had completed a university qualification; another 10 percent had finished a vocational type tertiary qualification. A total of 41 percent of the age cohort had attained a tertiary degree of some kind.[53] 2.1 percent of Australians in 2007 went on to enter a graduate research program.[54] In the same year across the OECD, 36 percent of 25-to-34 year olds had completed a tertiary qualification.[55] As a point of comparison, in 1997 the OECD figure was 20 percent. Participation rates in higher education across the advanced industrial economies exploded in the late 1990s and early 2000s. This reflected the continuously inflated demands generated by knowledge society lobbies. In the OECD and in Australia, the percentage of the population that was tertiary educated grew by 4.5 percent between 1998 and 2006. This remarkable bubble was the apotheosis of the long-term trend that took off in 1970.[56]

The End of the Post-industrial Era

The post-industrial era today is over. The Global Financial Crisis of 2008 was the first major indicator of a water-shed. We have entered a new era—though many social actors continue to behave as if nothing has happened. The Australian Government announced in March 2009 a policy to increase the number of university graduates to 40 percent of 25–34 year olds by 2025.[57] Coming just a few

---

52   Previously, the number of the Australian population aged 15 to 69 possessing an undergraduate or graduate degree had grown from 4.1 percent in 1982 to 8.7 percent in 1991. DEET 1993: xxiv, Table F.1.

53   In 1989, 10 percent of Australians aged 25–64 had a university degree and 21 percent had a non-university tertiary qualification. The Australian total of 31 percent was second highest in the world compared with the United States at 35 percent and the United Kingdom, number 14, at 9 percent. DEET 1993: xxv, Table F.2.

54   OECD 2009: 59, Table A1.1a. That figure for entering a research program compares with 2.8 percent across 20 OECD countries. Across 29 OECD countries in the same year, 1.5 percent of the population had obtained an advanced research qualification. In 1956, in Australia about 0.02 percent (2 percent of 1 percent of the population) were enrolled in research degree study, extrapolating from data from the University of Sydney which in that year had 108 full-course higher degree students enrolled, equal to 2 percent of its number of 5,761 first-degree students (Murray Committee: 43).

55   OECD 2009: 39.

56   In Australia, the years of notably big growth in student numbers in higher education include 1956, 1958–1960, 1965, 1973, 1990–1991, and 2008–2010. Data source: Australian Government, Higher Education Statistics Collection, 1992–2014.

57   Gillard 2009: 'I announce today that our ambition is that by 2025, 40 percent of all 25–34 year olds will have a qualification at bachelor level or above. Not just to have enrolled in higher education, but to have completed an undergraduate degree. Today that figure stands at 32 percent.' Julia Gillard, Deputy Prime Minister of Australia, March 4, 2009.

months after the GFC, this was akin to King Canute waving back the tide. The tide was profound and irreversible. This became clearer with the Sovereign Debt Crisis of 2010. The dramatic increase in university participation rates across the OECD in the late 1990s and early 2000s was mostly financed on national credit cards. Australia, which had sold off its public telecommunications operator, Telstra, and paid down its national debt in the late 1990s, was one of the few OECD countries facing the Global Financial Crisis and the Sovereign Debt Crisis that had a low national debt.

In this new era, no state can finance participation rates of 30 percent let alone 40 percent of young adults in university. This is partly—but not solely—a matter of economic feasibility. The Sovereign Debt Crisis underscored that such participation rates are not feasible. This is because they have to be purchased by unsustainable debt[58] or, as Australia did, by counter-productive penny-pinching. Secondly, the benefit of what is purchased, whether by sovereign debt and false economies, is pyrrhic. The post-modern higher education bubble did not deliver either the productive-economic-employment value or the pedagogic-intellectual-innovation value frequently attributed to it. Likewise the social equity value claimed for it was non-existent.

In 2011, the United Kingdom froze or reduced places in three-quarters of its universities. This was not a short-term trend. It was expected to take at least until 2025 for the global Sovereign Debt issue to be resolved. The scale and depth of the problem was vast and (consequently) generational. In the American case, for example, from the vantage-point of 2010, if no new industry sector emerged—that is, if there was no major leap in industry innovation and productivity—then to bring public debt back to sustainable levels required either a 50 percent increase in taxes or a 35 percent reduction in spending, or some combination of both.[59] Consequently, public spending on higher education started to trend downwards. As major US states, like California and Michigan, teetered on bankruptcy in 2010, their big and influential state university systems began to be scaled back. In 2013, US states were spending 28 percent ($2,353) less per student in higher education than they were in 2008.[60] Four-year institutions in response increased tuition fees by 27 percent ($1,850 per student) in the same period—in a self-defeating and petulant attempt to stave off reality. The accumulated endowments of the major

58   In 2013, America's publicly-held debt had reached 72 percent of GDP (CBO 2014: 2). According to the 2014 proposed budget of the White House, over the decade interest repayments on the debt were projected to rise from $223 billion to $800 billion per year, outstripping the size of defense spending by 2020.

59   Tully 2010.

60   Oliff, Palacios, Johnson and Leachman 2013. Reliance on state funding varies from university to university: the State University of New York system draws 36 percent from state sources; the University of Michigan, 5 percent. Boston Consulting Group 2014a.

US state research universities provided some lee-way for those institutions but even they faced having to do with less.[61]

Yet this was only a more visible part of a much longer trend.[62] The future of universities was not just about budget cuts in the context of economic stagnation. Post-2008 austerity in Spain, Italy, France, and elsewhere placed severe pressure on higher education spending but that was ultimately a symptom of the longer and deeper fiscal unaffordability of the post-industrial university. Unaffordability has seen various sleights-of-hand, with unsustainable public costs moved to private tuition (the United States) or sovereign debt (Europe) or alternatively reduced via the non-transparent systemic under-funding of domestic student places (Australia). But sleights-of-hand and elaborate shell-games cannot solve the problem of unaffordability. They just delay the day of reckoning. Australia's economy may have been one of the best in the OECD after the 2008 global downturn. But by 2014 it was moving in lock step with the rest in the matter of higher education.[63] This is because what we saw in 2008 was not only a financial crisis. It was also a turning point. It was the end of an era.

Financial crises on the scale of 2008 and 2010 are never just economic. They are the signal of a coming generational social shift. The sign of the end of Britain as the leading world power was the towering public debt it accumulated as a result of World War One and its chronic inability to reduce that debt during the 1920s and 1930s. The adjustments required of the new era will not just be economic—any more than the entry into the post-industrial age was. Even if the post-industrial epoch had a powerful fiscal and business aspect, it was also political, social and moral in character. Alternate conceptions of knowledge, innovation, education, participation, equity, and outcome will emerge in the new era. What accompanies a new era is a cultural shift. Thus many of the conventional assumptions of the past four decades will come into question and will be swept aside. Among them will be the dogma of ever-growing and unlimited participation rates in higher education.

Whenever governments in the post-modern era wished to expand participation by middle and upper social cohorts in education for electoral reasons, they

---

61   'Arizona's university system cut more than 2,100 positions; consolidated or eliminated 182 colleges, schools, programs, and departments; and closed eight extension campuses (local campuses that facilitate distance learning). The University of California laid off 4,200 staff and eliminated or left unfilled another 9,500 positions; instituted a system-wide furlough program, reducing salaries by 4 to 10 percent; consolidated or eliminated more than 180 programs; and cut funding for campus administrative and academic departments by as much as 35 percent.' Oliff, Palacios, Johnson, and Leachman 2013.

62   For data on the longer-term drop in US state government funding of universities, see Geiger and Heller 2011; State Higher Education Executive Officers 2012; Joint Legislative Audit and Review Commission 2013.

63   In 2010, the Dagong Global Credit Rating Company, China's leading credit rating agency, stripped America, Britain, Germany and France of their AAA credit ratings. Australia was rated AAA along with Norway, Denmark, Switzerland and Singapore.

used—as their justification—'the disadvantaged' viz. the lowest socio-economic status (SES) quartile or quintile. The presumption of governments was that the more students who came to university, the greater the percentage of low SES students who would enroll. The problem with this was that it simply was not true. A rise in the global rate of participation in higher education does not cause the percentage of students from low socio-economic backgrounds going to university to rise. With the matter of social inclusion firmly in mind, Australia's Federal Government commissioned the DEST/NBEET *A Fair Chance for All* Report in 1990. The report recommended the standard post-industrial phalanx of equity plans, objectives, targets, monitoring and measuring performance, and the tying of the funding arrangements of universities to these. What was the result when these were implemented? Participation by all disadvantaged groups in higher education in Australia remained unchanged between 1989 and 2007.[64] Interestingly, *A Fair Chance for All* reported that there had been little change in the socio-economic profile of students starting higher education over the period 1970–1985.[65] In 1974, Australia's Federal Labor Government even abolished student tuition fees and introduced a means-tested living allowance for university and college students in place of the pre-existing intellectually-competitive system of scholarship awards.[66] The assumption was that the changes would encourage 'participation' and 'access' by individuals from low SES backgrounds. In reality, the changes had zero effect.[67]

The short of this is that all of the post-industrial participation and inclusion policies are an illusion—even if an astonishingly expensive illusion. They are costly attempts to solve a problem that does not exist (except by fanciful definition). Already 90 percent of those in the top 10 percent of academic ability in the United States go to college.[68] Those who should go into higher education do go into higher education. Every attempt to use public policy to solve a non-problem generates its own problems. It pushes large numbers of people unsuited to university study into universities. They will drop out or else get nominal degrees that serve no vocational purpose. The only beneficiaries of public policy solutions to non-problems are those next on the rung of graduates of universities who are looking for cushy jobs. Jobs solving non-problems are great. As non-problems cannot be solved, their lack of solution gives lobbies in higher education endless excuses to press for more resources—hence the rise and rise and rise of the all-administrative university.[69] Between 1985 and 2005, the tertiary sector in the United States grew by 50 percent. That is to say, enrolments grew by 56 percent, faculty numbers

---

64 Bradley 2008: 28.

65 DEST/NBEET 1990: 15.

66 The left-of-center Labor Party had come to power in 1983 with 'participation and equity' as its primary education goals.

67 'Studies conducted before the end of the decade revealed no significant change in the social composition of the student population.' DEET 1993: 19.

68 Murray 2008: 112.

69 Ginsberg 2011.

by 50 percent, degrees granted by 47 percent and the number of degree-granting institutions by 50 percent. That is all more or less symmetrical and in lock-step until we look at numbers of administrators in the system. Their numbers rose by 85 percent and their collateral staff by 240 percent.[70] The historic ratio for universities of administrators to academics was 1:6; in the 1960s it was 1:5; today in some cases it is 1:1.[71] A phalanx of associate deans, vice-provosts, and bureaucratic helping units now exist to promote non-solutions to non-problems. The logic of the all-administrative university is that eventually no one there will be left to teach. Instead there will be a vast army of administrators writing unread documents setting out strategies and policies for overcoming low student performance and wondering why nothing ever results from these wonderful recipes.

In the middle of the twentieth century the argument about the gifted student at university was that there were many gifted students from poor backgrounds who couldn't get to university. Conversely there were upper class duffers at university for whom the institution was a social club. In reality 60 percent of University of Melbourne students in the 1950s were there on scholarships.[72] Twenty-five percent of the Australian population comes from postcode zones that are officially designated as having a low socio-economic status (SES). Seventeen percent of university students come from low SES postcodes.[73] Eleven percent of students enrolled in the high-status Group of Eight universities come from low SES backgrounds.[74] Despite large bureaucratic spending on low SES participation projects over decades, these figures have not changed over time. In 1985, 17 percent of students entering South Australian universities had fathers whose occupation was semi-skilled or unskilled (10 percent) or who were from a rural background (7 percent).[75] If government spending on increasing the rate of low SES participation in Australian universities had zero effect, it is even worse in the United States where low SES participation dropped as the university sector

---

70   Ginsberg 2011: 25, 28.

71   This is a long-term process. Take the case of the University of California. Gumport and Pusser, 1995, reported that '[the] ratio of spending on instruction to spending on administration [shifted] from roughly six dollars of instructional spending for each dollar spent on administration in 1966–67 to a ratio of about three dollars spent on instruction for each dollar spent on administration in 1991–92.' Additionally '[in] 1966–67 the ratio of permanently budgeted FTE administrators to academic positions at UC Berkeley was 0.1990 to 1. In 1971–72 it was 0.2803 to 1; in 1981–82, 0.4002 to 1; in 1991–92, 0.4170 to 1. For UCLA: 1966–67: 0.2696 to 1; 1971–72: 0.3390 to 1; for 1981–82: 0.3610 to 1; 1991–92: 0.4690 to 1.'

72   See for example the University of Melbourne *Calendar*, 1956. The university had 6,800 enrolled students in 1954 and 4,238 assisted students, of whom 337 had free places, 1,306 were on half fees, 322 were recipients of scholarships, 2,080 were recipients of Commonwealth Scholarships, and 193 were CRTS recipients (664–5).

73   Kemp and Norton 2014: 37.

74   James 2008: 23–4.

75   Power, Robertson and Baker 1986: 51.

expanded. When US federal support for students was scarce in 1970, 12 percent of college graduates came from the bottom-income quartile. Today the figure is 7 percent.[76] The more university education was subsidized, the more unaffordable it became for students from low-income backgrounds.[77] The real cost of higher education in the United States tripled between 1930 and 1990. The justification for universities at the same time stopped being pedagogic or intellectual and became social—extending 'opportunity,' enrolling 'the disadvantaged,' having 'the first person in their family attend university.'

The Price of a Degree

A contemporary college or university education is one of the most expensive goods (be it a public or private good) ever devised by human ingenuity. On one estimate since 1985 US college costs increased five times the rate of inflation.[78] Take US college textbooks as one example: between 1994 and 2005 they increased four times the CPI.[79] Health costs, notoriously inflated in the United States, in contrast rose only twice as fast as the CPI since 1978. In 1931 the average cost expended by American higher education institutions per student was $5,386 (in 2011 constant dollars). In 1956, the cost was $8,923; in 1989, $14,147.[80] By 2011, expenditure per student in American public universities was $37,976.[81] In 80 years annual cost per student in real terms had risen 7 times (and 4 times in the past 60 years). This escalating expenditure was matched by escalating fees. In 1964 at 4-year public institutions in the US students paid an average of $6,893 for tuition, fees, room and board (in 2011 constant dollars);[82] in 1981, the average figure was $9,554 at all 4-year institutions; by 2011 the average price at US public universities had risen to $23,066.[83] In short, prices in real terms had grown by a factor of 3.3 in 50 years. Was American higher education 7 times better compared to 1931 or 3 times as good as in 1964? The answer is no. Was the standard of research or teaching in American universities noticeably higher or the per capita quantity produced appreciably greater than in 1931 or 1964? The answer, again, was no.

---

76   Finley 2013.

77   The further consequence of escalating tuition costs is that it forced a large portion of the student population into permanent part-time work, gravely cutting into study time. State subsidy of university study is in large measure a subsidy of students working large numbers of hours in term time in service industries.

78   Higher Education *The Economist* 2012.

79   State Public Interest Research Groups 2005. The wholesale prices charged by textbook publishers increased 62 percent between 1994 and 2005, while prices charged for all finished goods increased only 14 percent.

80   US Department of Education, 1993.

81   US Department of Education, 2013, Table 334.10.

82   US Department of Education, 1990, Table 281.

83   US Department of Education, 2012 Table 381.

Unaffordability is not just a US phenomenon. In 1956 the *total* price of a four-year Bachelor of Arts with Honours degree at the University of Melbourne was £255 or $7,567 in 2013 inflation-adjusted dollar terms.[84] Sixty percent of University of Melbourne students in 1956 received University or Commonwealth government scholarships—these were based on academic merit. The *annual* price of the same degree in 2010 was $10,211 assuming the lowest Commonwealth government funding band. That is, one year of an Australian degree today costs more than four years of the same degree in 1956.[85] In 2013 the Australian government subsidized around 60 percent of the tuition price for students who were eligible for government support. So an Australian degree on average for a student after the government subsidy was factored in still cost about twice in real terms what the degree cost in 1956. All that government subsidization of tuition has done is pay for the administration costs that have been added over seven decades to what is at its core exactly the same good—and even then students still pay more than their predecessors did in 1950s. No Australian student today gains any benefit from the government subsidy compared with a student in 1956. In fact taking into account the scholarships that were available to students in 1956, low-income students in the 1950s were much better off than students are today. In short, the price of a degree in real terms today costs Australian society four times what it did in 1956 and students twice (or more) what it did in 1956. Yet the nature of a degree and the nature of departmental teaching and research are virtually unchanged in those 60 years.

Higher education's hyper real cost increases have been driven by a number of factors. The primary driver is the shift of focus of higher education since 1930 away from the historic core of 'instruction and departmental research' toward the phalanx of administratively-orchestrated pseudo-municipal add-ons and a managerially-devised money-hungry faux-research labyrinth. These structures include centrally-managed graduate scholarship and grant systems, the process-driven external-grant research complex, and the professionally-administered student experience industry. There are many chimeric solutions to the problem

84   University of Melbourne *Calendar* 1956: 209, 665; the 2013 price is calculated using the Reserve Bank of Australia pre-decimal inflation calculator. A single Arts subject cost £21 ($623 in 2013 dollars) in 1956; students did four subjects in first year and three each in their second and third years. A student today does eight subjects in each year. The cost to today's government-subsidized student is effectively double. As a point of comparison, in 1956 undergraduate engineering, architecture, dentistry and music subjects cost £90 each.

85   In 2011, Australian universities received $23 billion in income, including $13 billion of Australian government financial assistance. Total academic employee benefits (salaries, superannuation, leave, etc.) cost $6.7 billion ($138,644 per academic FTE). Before the post-modern age, universities ran on the model that academic costs were 60 percent of total costs. Applying that model, the cost of Australian universities in 2011 would have been $11.2 billion or half of the actual cost. Data source: Australian Government, Higher Education Statistics Collection, 1992–2014, cf. 'Adjusted Statement of Financial Performance for each HEP, 2011'; 'Selected Higher Education Statistics—Staff 2011.'

of tuition and university cost growth. One of them is the 'online university.'[86] It purportedly saves on 'brick and mortar' costs. But these are not the cost-drivers of the higher education bubble: non-departmental administrative and professional costs are. The online model has a number of educational down-sides as well as a number of strengths when wisely deployed.[87] But mainly it represents a further opportunity for the professional class to expand its power and its relentless price-gouging of the university. With online pedagogy comes an army of educational designers, information technologists, database administrators, learning and teaching developers, assistant deans, and pro-vice chancellors; that is, anyone but front-line academics devoted to the university's historic core of 'instruction and departmental research.' If the four-fold real increase in university costs in the past 60 years was stripped out of university and college spending, then most of the price ballooning would disappear. Tuition costs over time would arrest and plummet. That this has not happened previously is in part because the price of higher education has been subsidized by the state. The intent of state subsidies was to make higher education 'affordable.' The consequence of those subsidies was to make it very expensive.

An interesting case of how *not* accepting government subsidies reduces costs is that of the conservative Christian Grove City College in Pennsylvania. The college won a Supreme Court case (*Grove City College v. Bell*) in 1984, allowing it to refuse federal student aid. In 2014, the college offered tuition rates that were half of the national average of comparable highly-ranked private colleges. Independence of government has allowed the college to be prudent with its finances and avoid wasteful and pointless spending. Government subsidies rather than reducing costs cause them to rise. This is the result of multiple bureaucratic mandates that follow government grants. Government action to make higher education more affordable makes it greatly less affordable. Between 2001 and 2010 the cost of university education in the US increased from 23 percent of median annual earnings to 38 percent.[88] American universities and college could charge high prices because the prices were subsidized by state governments. Eventually this has proved too much

---

86   Reynolds 2014.

87   Online delivery of media-rich educational materials including online video lectures and portable document files is a positive thing. It is efficient and convenient and it allows for repeated viewing of downloaded materials. It reduces the considerable waste of time by students on travel to class in a time-poor age. What online delivery however cannot do is to deliver effective mentoring and advising of students by faculty. The decline of this in the age of mass higher education is worrying. 'Good advising with conscientious faculty participation is a goal that has eluded most colleges, especially those with large undergraduate enrollments.' (Bok 2009: 260) Overall in the final two decades of the twentieth century, American academics taught more class time and spent more time researching, but advised and mentored students less (Milem, Burger and Dey 2000). Students living in a social media burrow, even if they do down-load lectures and pdfs from time to time, constitutes neither a rounded nor an effective undergraduate education.

88   Higher Education *The Economist* 2012.

even for acquiescent state governments who responded to mendacious tuition increases by reducing subsidies.[89] Between 1990 and 2012, public subsidies for college in the US fell by 25 percent.[90] Prices though still did not fall. Instead universities and colleges aggressively pushed up prices. Students just paid more of the cost of universities. The professional-therapeutic-experience class in the universities knows what is good for students. It sets the prices in higher education. It expects students to pay, and pay very heavily, for the services that this class provides—even though these services have not slightest thing to do with core departmental teaching and research.

In spite of all of this we should not confuse higher education with a consumer good. A place at university is not a regular commodity. It cannot be consumed like a lettuce or used like a refrigerator. A university education is what a university student makes of it. This means that a student has to be 'college ready'—otherwise a university place is a waste of public and private money. As Vedder points out, cheap tuition is correlated with high drop-out rates in American higher education.[91] Low tuition prices encourage buyers of student places not to consider whether they are prepared and motivated for higher studies. That said, the term 'tuition' in tuition fees is today a misleading word. If universities and colleges were just organized classrooms they would still be expensive but they would not be the inordinately expensive public or private good that they are. But in fact they are no longer merely classrooms or even classrooms, labs and libraries.[92] They are just as much and even more so service bureaucracies, regulatory bureaucracies, therapeutic bureaucracies, external research management and research training bureaucracies, and transfer payment bureaucracies—functioning on pseudo-urban crypto-pastoral campuses along with a mass of auxiliary enterprises. 'Education' is a misnomer in contemporary higher education. The sector rather has become devoted to 'the managed transition to adulthood' in a therapeutic world that has seen fit to put off adulthood as long as it can. This higher tutelage is overseen by a phalanx of professionals and pseudo-professionals of all kinds. Academics are a

---

89   The College Board calculation is that real average tuition increased $5,500 for public colleges and $17,800 at private institutions from 1980 to 2010, while total student aid increased by $8,165. Saunders 2011.

90   Luzer 2013.

91   Vedder 2014. Drawing on data from Stille 2014, Vedder observes that higher education drop-out rates vary significantly between US states, from 68 percent in Alaska to less than 30 percent in states like New Hampshire and Pennsylvania. The difference, he concludes, is that the 'high failure states are low tuition states, while the low failure states charge high tuition fees.' This, he goes on to note, 'is consistent with a basic economic behavioural principle. When something is expensive, people use it carefully—the financial cost of failure is too high. When something is relatively cheap, incentives to use it prudently are reduced—the financial costs of dropping out are lowered.'

92   One measure of this is the ratio of academic salaries to total revenue (excluding auxiliary enterprises). The economist Richard Vedder estimates that this is about 25 percent in American universities. Vedder July 20, 2010.

side-show in this circus.[93] The number of non-faculty professional employees per 100 faculty members in the United States rose from 55 per 100 in 1976 to 98 in 2009.[94] The largest cost component of a university or college is salaries. The sector has a high proportion of top and second quintile income earners.[95] In the age of mass higher education an inverse relationship has operated: the more souls from the lower quintiles who sacrifice their income for a number of years, the greater the earning power of high quintile higher education professionals.

Table 5.1   CEO and Academic Remuneration

	CEO Compensation (AUD)		Professorial Salary (AUD)
Australian Vice-Chancellors	$721,607	*vs.*	$154,530
US Presidents (Top 100)	$480,409	*vs.*	$120,298
US Presidents (Top 37)	$572,578	*vs.*	$127,096
US Presidents (System)	$536,156	*vs.*	$114,343
UK Vice-Chancellors (Top 100)	$456,867	*vs.*	$116,463
UK Vice-Chancellors (Top 37)	$540,237	*vs.*	$126,463
Data Source: Devinney, 2013.			

93   'J. Paul Robinson, chairman of the Purdue University faculty senate, walks the halls of a 10-story tower, pointing out a row of offices for administrators. "I have no idea what these people do," says the biomedical engineering professor. Purdue has a $313,000-a-year acting provost and six vice and associate vice provosts, including a $198,000-a-year chief diversity officer. Among its 16 deans and 11 vice presidents are a $253,000 marketing officer and a $433,000 business school chief. The average full professor at the public university in West Lafayette, Ind., makes $125,000. The number of Purdue administrators has jumped 54 percent in the past decade—almost eight times the growth rate of tenured and tenure-track faculty. "We're here to deliver a high-quality education at as low a price as possible," says Robinson. "Why is it that we can't find any money for more faculty, but there seems to be an almost unlimited budget for administrators?"' Hechinger 2012.

94   Higher Education *The Economist* December 1 2012. Data source: National Centre for Education Statistics.

95   In comparable purchasing power parity dollar terms (US PPP$), full professors in Canada earn an average of $9,485 a month compared with those in Italy ($9,118), South Africa ($9,330), Saudi Arabia ($8,524), Britain ($8,369), Malaysia ($7,864), Australia ($7,499), India ($7,433), and the United States ($7,358). Altbach, Reisberg, Yudkevich,Androushchak and Pacheco, 2012. See the study's executive summary: http://www.uni-kassel.de/wz1/pdf/Day2/02_04_P.Altbach%20&%20M.%20Yudkevich.Executive%20Summary.pdf. See also Table 5.1 based on Devinney, 2013, http://www.modern-cynic.org/2013/05/08/university-leaders/.

What is a Degree Worth?

Surely though the income sacrifice of low quintile earners is worth it if they earn high incomes after graduation. But do they? In constant 2010 dollars, between 1947 and 2010, the real household income of the bottom quintile and second bottom quintile in the United States essentially doubled, rising from $13,525 to $26,695 and from $21,825 to $48,000 respectively.[96] Top-quintile income rose from $68,924 to $200,354, almost three-fold; second quintile income rose from $41,993 to $113,774, 2.7 times. The differential between the top and bottom quintile in 1947 was 1:5; in 2010 it was 1:8. The effort to create more educational equality helped to create a more unequal society. More qualifications did not reduce income inequality. How could it? Thirty or 40 percent of the population may end up in a university or a college but there are not 30 or 40 percent of jobs that require a degree or even a diploma. Between 25 to 40 percent of university and college students leave higher education only to work in jobs that do not require a degree.[97] These students pay a lot for essentially nothing.

In the United States, three occupations—retail sales, cashiers, and waiters and waitresses—employ more than 1.7 million college graduates. In the US today there are 28 million jobs requiring a college degree and 41 million employed graduates. Of around 136 million jobs in the US, the jobs that notionally require degrees make up about 20 percent of the total. Yet 30 percent of Americans in 2010 who were 25 years or older had a college degree. Consequently, around 37 percent of American graduates in 2010 worked in jobs that needed only a high-school diploma or less. In 1970, only one-in-ten did. For a person who graduates and then works in a job that does not require a degree, the two, three or four years that they spent in higher education are years outside the workforce—meaning years of income foregone and years of accumulating student debt to pay for tuition fees and living expenses.

But surely those who acquire a degree earn more than those who do not? The OECD calculated that in 2011 in the UK a university degree was worth up to £117,000 ($US180,000) in additional earnings. Assuming a 35-year working life of a graduate, that is a premium of $US5142 per year or $14 a day—a relatively modest amount. The modesty of the premium is clear when we consider that in 1950 a person with a 4-year degree in the United States earned 2.35 times average weekly earnings.[98] Estimates of the graduate income premium vary. The liberal US Brookings Institute estimates that a 4-year college graduate earns $570,000 more than a high school graduate over a life time for an average investment of $102,000 (the $48,000 cost of the degree plus the $11,600 per year opportunity

---

96   US Census Bureau. 2011 Table F-1 Income Limits for Each Fifth and Top 5 Percent of Families, Historical Income Tables.

97   Vedder, Denhart and Robe 2013; also Vedder, Denhart, Denhart, Matgouranis, and Robe 2010.

98   Ross 2013.

cost of not working for 4 years).[99] That's a premium of $13,371 a year or $36 a day in a 35-year working life. The economist Laurence Kotlikoff modelled the lifetime earnings of a plumber and a graduate of an elite private college and medical school, and concluded that the medical doctor was better off by a miniscule $423 a year than the plumber. Kotlikoff's analysis took into account educational costs, foregone earnings, annual federal and state income taxes, annual payroll taxes, Social Security benefits, and Medicare Part B premiums.[100]

The graduate premium model assumes that university students graduate. But there are significant numbers who pay tuition and fail to complete their degree. The rate of completion of a degree after six years ('150 percent of normal time') is 92 percent at the University of Virginia but only 15 percent at Utah Valley University.[101] At least 30 percent of Americans enrolled for a degree never complete their studies. Then there is the matter of student debt and the interest on that debt. At Princeton University the average graduating debt is $5,225 for the 23 percent of graduates who have any debt at all. The median starting salary of a Princeton graduate is $56,900. On the other hand, 85 percent of students from Ohio Northern University graduate with debt averaging close to $49,000 while the median starting salary for those graduates is $44,800.[102] Interest repayments on the loan will vary according to the level of interest rates and the term of the loan, but interest costs could be anywhere between $15,000 and $50,000. In 2012, 7-in-10 US college seniors graduated with student debt—with an average of $29,400 per borrower, implying interest payments roughly in the range of $10,000 to $30,000.[103]

There is a still more fundamental matter to take into account. This is the question of aptitude and ambition.[104] To put this in simple terms: those in group X today who have a degree would always have earned more money and will always earn more money on average than those in group Y without a degree. That would be true even if those in group X did not have a degree.[105] While students may

---

99   Greenstone and Looney 2011; based on data from Barrow and Rouse 2005.

100   Kotlikoff 2011.

101   http://collegecompletion.chronicle.com/table/.

102   Romeo 2013.

103   Data source: Project on student debt. http://projectonstudentdebt.org/state_by_state-data.php . Saunders 2011 calculated that the average debt was $25,000 in 2010.

104   Australia's Martin Committee (volume 1: 5) put it very well when it referred to some individuals' 'greater natural ability, application, energy or initiative.'

105   To its credit something like this was observed by the Martin Committee in 1964 in Australia. It noted the higher earning potential of graduates (volume 1: 5). In 1950 US census data indicated that an American male with 8 years elementary school typically earned 100 percent of average income, a male with 4 years high school 140 percent, and a male with 4 years or more of college 235 percent of average income. The Martin Committee, though it spruiked the earning premium of a degree, was sensible enough also to note that '[these] comparisons overstate the influence of additional education because individuals of greater natural ability, application, energy or initiative are more likely to continue their education to a higher level.' The absurdity of knowledge economy claims is apparent in

'invest' in education they do not acquire knowledge by the act of investing any more than they do so by acquiring 'a place' at university. Neither 'the money' nor 'the place' means anything without aptitude and ambition. Indeed many of the most successful and creative people who pass through universities drop out temporarily or permanently—because universities rarely challenge them sufficiently. Their success, whether in business, the arts or the academy, rests fundamentally on aptitude and ambition. Let us say group X, the top third of a high school cohort, go onto university. Their life-time earnings on average will be better than those who do not attend university. But let us say that we did not allow cohort X to go to university. Even if they only had high school diplomas, their life-time earnings would still be better than cohort Y. The academic performance of group X is really a proxy for generic capacities. The individuals in this group are more organized, they have better concentration and application, they are better at reasoning, writing and calculating than those in group Y. They are driven. They work harder. To be successful in most jobs, including in many well-paying jobs, only requires general intelligence plus initiative and character including responsibility, dedication and a capacity for hard work. No university can give a person such traits even though traits like reliability, trustworthiness, commitment, perseverance, resourcefulness and enterprise are essential to success at work.[106]

A number of occupations, not least of all those that used to be called the learned professions, do require a university education. Even then we should not forget that a great lawyer like Abraham Lincoln was self-taught. Self-taught or even apprenticed surgery though is unlikely to have happy results. On the other hand most office jobs, including most management jobs, do not require the study of philosophy or anatomy or any kind of organized higher learning. But they do require persons of good character who are generally intelligent. American majors that lead to high-earning careers include accounting, computer science, economics, electrical engineering, finance, international relations, mathematics, mechanical engineering, philosophy and statistics.[107] Materially-successful degrees on the whole are a modern variation of the traditional 'philosophy, politics, economics' kind of degree—updated with computing, finance and engineering.[108] There is a 'Platonic' thread in high-achieving contemporary degrees. In such degrees the

---

retrospect. What 4-year college graduate today will go on to earn 235 percent of average income? Not very many.

106   Cowen 2013 is right to point out that future labor market success, especially in mid-tier jobs, will depend increasingly on character traits like conscientiousness rather than paper qualifications. The mid-tier jobs don't really require a degree; but they do require honest and reliable employees.

107   Vedder, Denhart and Robe January 2013: 26, Table 4.

108   Cowen 2013: 21 defines the successful twenty-first-century employee as one who has strong math and analytic skills and is comfortable working with computers. My own view is that the serious twenty-first-century degree combines humanities-social-science, finance-economics, science-technology and arts-design disciplines—and develops the capacity to translate between these disciplines.

soaring demands of abstract philosophically-laced reflection meet the maxim that 'no-one without a knowledge of geometry should enter here'. Today there is deep self-destructive aversion to this in higher education.[109] A 2014 study of 29 elite American liberal arts colleges found that none of them had much interest anymore in the 'Platonic' disciplines that one might expect to dominate a serious system of higher education. The study looked at the key disciplines of Composition, Literature, Foreign Languages, US Government or History, Economics, Mathematics, and Natural or Physical Science.[110] It found that only six of the colleges in the study required students to take courses in three of these areas; nine of the colleges required exposure to only one or two of the great disciplines; five of the colleges required no exposure what so ever. Imagine trying to function at a high level without having had exposure to any of these or in fact without some exposure to all of these. Contemporary academia thinks that 'studies' (identity, gender, race,

---

109   Albert Jay Nock in 1932 noted how until around 1900 in the United States, when one of the now periodic progressive revolutions in curriculum occurred, the undergraduate college-type curriculum was more or less fixed and universal, and based on a centuries-long Great Tradition that pivoted on classic literature and history, mathematics and logic (61–2). This was initially set aside in favour of modern languages, English and the sciences, but the revolution swiftly devoured its children. Nock observed that the great question became: what is the use of sheer mathematics, or sheer Greek or Latin, a question that was put 'with an animus that precluded anything like rational consideration,' a tactic repeatedly used by curriculum revolutionaries. Looking back on this Nock concluded that the real motive for change was that higher education was trying to make a lot of people bear a curriculum for which they had no aptitude. A hundred years later this was a pervasive problem in American higher education. Yet, ironically, the core demand for those educated to a very high level in the durable Platonic disciplines had not changed even if the discipline of 'the classics' was long dead. For Harvard's entrance exam of 1869, a mix of Latin and Greek language, history and geography, and mathematics, see http://graphics8.nytimes.com/packages/pdf/education/harvardexam.pdf. The classical undergraduate curriculum, as Piereson and Riley 2014 note, was asphyxiated by Dewey's progressive educational ideology in the 1920s. It made a partial come-back with the Great Books programs pioneered by John Erskine, Robert Hutchins, Mortimer Adler, Jacques Barzun, and others. But this largely lacked the crucial computational and calculation component. By the 1980s Great Books programs had fallen out of fashion. Recently they have experienced a minor surge of interest yet still without the mathematics part that had survived from antiquity to the progressive era. The medieval seven liberal arts were composed of arithmetic, geometry, music, astronomy, grammar, logic, and rhetoric. Progressive education expelled the study of the Platonic-Pythagorean *quadrivium* of arithmetic, geometry, music, and astronomy from the liberal arts curriculum. The study of quantity and magnitude was viewed by progressives as suspect. In short, the reading represented by the Great Books has to be complemented by logic and mathematics otherwise it simply repeats the slow death of the humanities. Core scholastic aptitude is reading, reasoning, and reckoning. The 3 R's in fact represent a model for curriculum development in the future. It is possible to imagine a *trivium* of the future that uses the 3 R's as a structural or organizing principle for degrees. The PPE model is of that kind: philosophy (reading), politics (reasoning), and economics (reckoning).

110   American Council of Trustees and Alumni 2014.

global, and environmental 'studies') are a substitute for intellectual discipline. They are not. Ideology is not a substitute for serious demanding abstract inquiry.

Students spending minimal hours studying, reading little for their courses, and learning less than little in their degrees is simply a fake education. Courses on anti-capitalism, social justice and multiculturalism belittle and trivialize the humanities. Their professors may shower students with endless stories of oppression in 'studies' subjects but employers and the larger society are not in the slightest interested. Salaries are a social valuation of degrees. Degrees that lead at an undergraduate or graduate level to high incomes are a clear indicator of what the wider society thinks is worth studying. In 2012, high-earning ($70,000 p.a. or more for recent college graduates) degrees in the United States included logistics/transportation sciences, economics, finance, information management, engineering, construction sciences, mathematics, history, biology, biochemistry, area studies/international relations and political science.[111] With the exception of philosophy missing from the list, the list would not surprise Plato. Remember Plato's admonition: '*Mèdeis ageômetrètos eisitô mou tèn stegèn. Let no one ignorant of geometry come under my roof.*' That remains good advice for prospective students. If students wish to take courses on 'The Ethical Shopper' or 'The Rhetoric of Alien Abduction' by all means do so but they should not expect that the larger society will conclude that they have learnt anything for which it wishes to pay large salaries. Questions of war and peace, prosperity and depression along with the patterns of nature, and whether structures will stay up or fall down, have animated us for 2,500 years. Nothing is different today.

While in the university in the past 40 years everything has changed, then again nothing has changed. The 1950s knowledge economy promise was that 'a college degree' would offer above-average earnings, 2.35 times average income. Today a college graduate earns 2.5 times that of a person with 8 years education only.[112] 2011 US Bureau of Census data indicates that a graduate with a bachelor's degree will earn on average $2.4 million over a 40-year working life compared with

---

111   Carnevale and Cheah 2013. Over a career, liberal arts majors' earning power underperforms pre-professional and professional degrees at career outset and slightly outperforms them at career end. Both cohorts significantly underperform engineering and the physical and natural sciences and maths. (Humphreys and Kelly 2014) Occupations that increased their earning advantage during recessions across the period 1976 to 2011 in the United States in descending order of increased advantage were: economics, finance, computer programming, civil engineering, accounting, nursing, political science, international relations and marketing. (Miller,2014) The top-ten UK counterparts of the US top-earning degrees over a life-time are: Japanese studies, operational research, civil engineering, industrial relations, minerals technology, South Asian studies, chemical, process and energy engineering, general engineering, architecture, building and planning, and medicine and dentistry (University Education, 2014).

112   The OECD, 2009: Table A7.2A records a number of countries across the decade 1997–2007 where relative graduate earnings declined, including Canada, New Zealand, Norway, Spain, and Sweden.

a high school graduate who will earn $1.3 million, 1.9 times better. Compared with a person who has eight years of elementary education and earns a lifetime $936,000, the college graduate is 2.5 times better off.[113] Data from the 1950 US Census of Population indicated that the '4 year or more' college graduate was 2.35 times better off than a person of average income.[114] In 2005, median US income for those over 15 who worked was $28,567. Using the 1950's scale, graduates today would be earning $65,704. Yet in 2005 graduates over 25 working full-time earned $50,944, 1.8 times average earnings not 2.35 times.

What is also observable now is the very large spread of earning potential of a person with a bachelor's degree. The key question today is not whether a degree but what kind? Degree holders working in the fields of engineering, maths, science, management, finance, and media meet and often substantially exceed the average. Degree holders working in the fields of healthcare, sales, arts, resources and construction, transportation, education, community service, office support and services do not.[115] In fact the earnings of the latter look a lot like the 1950 outcome of someone in college for one-to-three years (aka a person with 'some college' education), who earned 1.6 times the elementary school graduate. The high school graduate today and in 1950 earns around 1.4 times the person with 8 years in elementary school. A large portion of the large number of 'college graduates' are very far removed from the graduates of the 'Platonic' disciplines whose aptitude for mathematics and socio-mathematical inquiry or for high-level reasoning, rhetoric and composition or for geo-strategic-calculation-married-with-linguistic abilities sets them apart both intellectually and in earning capacity.[116] Or to put this in sociologically-realist terms: if we look at the US figures for real median household income tracked by the educational attainment of the household head, we find that measured in 2010 constant dollar terms, households with a degree-holding head increased per annum earnings from $70,787 in 1974 to $75,586 in 2010, a 7 percent increase, while post-graduate-headed households went from $79,005 in 1974 to $98,663 in 2010, a 25 percent increase.[117]

Accordingly now in the United States, 11 percent of American adults (that is, most of the 16 percent of the population that is 'college-ready') track into higher

---

113   Julian 2012.

114   Martin Committee 1964 volume 1: 5. Data source: Denison 1962: 68.

115   Or as Glenn Reynolds in interview put it: 'Some students do better by going to college. Others do worse. Four out of 10 students, according to Gallup, wind up in jobs they could have gotten without a college degree. That makes the time, and money, spent in college a waste, at least as far as prosperity is concerned. And some students actually do worse by going to college, developing problems with drugs, alcohol, or sex that may plague them for years, or a lifetime. Then there's the debt, which can run into six figures, and isn't dischargeable in bankruptcy.' Lopez 2014.

116   As a prelude to the study of philosophy, Plato was of the view that a student should master arithmetic, plane geometry, solid geometry, astronomy, and harmonics.

117   Data Source: US Census Bureau 2011: Tables H-13 and H-14, Educational Attainment and Years of School Completed, Historical Income Tables.

degree (postgraduate coursework, professional degree or research Masters and PhD) programs.[118] The '11 percent' is a successful class. Yet it is also is a very discontented class. The '11 percent-ers' are a receptive audience for those who fashion voluble moralizing ideologies directed at the highest '1 percent' of income earners. The frustration of the '11 per-cent-ers' at not having the assets or the life-style of the '1 per-cent' class is palpable and pathetic. That this envy is dressed-up in 'social justice' rhetoric is pitiful. In part now because of its size, the post-graduate class is politically influential. It is strongly left-leaning. It was a key to Barack Obama's high-income-low-income, campus town-inner city electoral coalition in the American Presidential elections in 2008 and 2012. The professional class that constitutes the core of the post-graduate class is very ambitious. It wraps its material ambitions in moral rhetoric. These ambitions are reflected in its rising income which has grown steadily in real terms while middle-tier incomes in the United States have remained static.

Today 'going to university' is not the key to higher incomes. Rather it is the 'possession of a higher degree.' All that has happened in the 40 years of mass higher education was the replacement of 'the college degree' with the 'post-graduate degree.' University-driven social mobility is a mirage. It is a complete—vastly expensive and totally pointless—illusion. This makes the whole ambition of the mass university system completely futile. All that has happened in the past 40 years is that the measure of achievement has ratcheted upwards while the content of undergraduate education has been grievously watered down. Much thus has changed and yet the essence of the degree-income-reward-distribution system has not. It merely costs governments billions extra in taxpayer dollars and individuals billions in tuition costs in order to reach in a round-about way the same social outcome that prevailed in 1965. The only thing that the social change of the past 40 years has achieved is social continuity at a substantial private and public cost.

In short, an American who earns a degree and works in a service industry job for which a degree is not required will earn (not unusually) $1.8 million over a 40-year working career. That compares with $1.3 million for the average high school graduate. The differential of $500,000 in earnings is offset by income forgone for four years in the early years of earning ($50,000) and loans-plus-interest ($50,000), a net benefit of $400,000 over a life-time, that is $10,000 per year or $200 a week or $30 dollars a day.[119] This is a benefit but it is a minor or modest

---

118   Data source: US Census Bureau, Educational Attainment in the United States 2013. Eleven percent of the US population 25 years and older has a master's degree, professional degree or doctoral degree.

119   This is broadly consistent with the OECD estimate that the gross earning benefit of a degree over a life-time across OECD countries is $US330000 for men and $240000 for women. For men that represents a gross benefit of $210 a week over a 30 year working life. The calculation of a gross benefit does not include the costs to attain the benefit. See OECD 2013a: 127. The $30 a day figure is also broadly consistent with 2014 Payscale data for US states. Net Return on Investment (ROI) over 20 years by state ranges from $148,419 to $448,540 for graduates with financial aid, depending on the state where the student studied.

one.[120] The OECD in 2006 reported an average rate of return on university study of 13 percent.[121] More realistically, the compensation data provider PayScale's 2013 survey of 1486 American college and universities classified by in-state, out-of-state, not-for-profit, and for-profit programs indicated an annualized average rate of return on investment over 30 years of 5.09 percent (about the same as a long-term investment in US Treasury Bonds) and 6.51 percent with financial aid factored in.[122] Only a handful of top colleges in the US came close to a 13 percent ROI and only once financial aid was taken into account.[123] Twenty-six colleges (1.7

That is, it ranges from $20 a day ROI to $61 a day ROI. Abel and Deitz 2014 estimate graduate ROI is more than $1 million over a 40-year working life less $140,000 costs, the equivalent of more than $60 a day. That estimate sits at the highest end of the Payscale spectrum. Payscale data derives from surveys of graduate employees; Abel and Dietz rely on US Census Bureau, US Bureau of Labor Statistics, US Department of Education, and US College Board statistics.

120   Or as *The Onion* put it: '30-Year-Old Has Earned $11 More Than He Would Have Without College Education.' December 13 2013.

121   OECD 2006: Table A9.6. Private internal rates of return for an individual obtaining a university-level degree. Countries: Belgium, Denmark, Finland, Hungary, Korea, New Zealand, Norway, Sweden, Switzerland, United Kingdom, and the United States. In 2000 Borland, Dawkins, Johnson and Williams reported a 6 percent to 16 percent average premium for private individuals on investment in higher education, depending on various modelling and assumptions. Persons who spent the costs (of tuition and income forgone) had better average earnings over a working life, the report concluded. The premium though had declined with time. The study compared its findings of a 15 percent premium (based on 1997 data) with a previous study by Miller in 1982 (based on 1976 data) that had calculated a premium of 21 percent (2). This was a decline of a third in 20 years.

122   PayScale issues a College Return on Investment report for American colleges and universities. http://www.payscale.com/college-roi/. The data is for bachelor degree holders only, US employees, and full-time salaried employees only. The income data (the salary-earner's total cash compensation, which excludes stock and health care benefits) is self-reported. The investment includes tuition and fees, room and board, books and supplies. The calculation takes into account the variation between schools in the number of academic years it takes students to graduate. http://www.payscale.com/college-roi/c/ methodology.The cost of college (less financial aid) is calculated. That figure is compared with the net income of the graduate, which is their total graduate income across 20 years of working minus what the graduate would have earned as a high school diploma holder. In a larger sense, evaluating the rate of return on higher education involves a multi-step computation. It begins with a calculation of the real cost of higher education to a student at a college or university. It then takes that dollar cost and compares two scenarios: (a) where the prospective student invests the dollar amount in US treasury bonds (which averaged 5.2 percent annual return over the 1928–2013 period) and simply graduates high school and does not go to university, or alternatively (b) where the student goes to college or university, spends the dollars on higher education, and then generates earnings expecting them to be greater than what a high school graduate earns.

123   Payscale's survey data includes only graduates with a bachelor's degree and excludes graduates with higher degrees. Additionally it includes full-time employees only and excludes the self-employed and contractors. The 2014 survey reported on 1312

percent) delivered a negative rate of return (15 colleges or 1 percent, with financial aid). The long-term US inflation rate (1913–2013) is 3.22 percent. Of the 1486 providers, 196 (13 percent) secured a rate of return below that inflation figure and 96 (6 percent) did once financial aid was factored in. US treasury bonds averaged a 5.2 percent annual return over the period 1928–2013.[124] Excluding financial aid, almost half (700 or 47 percent) of US universities and colleges surveyed had a 30-year ROI that was less than the long-term bond rate.[125] Including financial aid, that figure scales to 352 institutions or 23 percent of the total surveyed. When financial aid is added in, half of all institutions provided a less-than-6.5 percent

---

university and colleges. The average sample size profiled per institution was 445 graduates. These institution samples were drawn from a data set that included 1.4 million bachelor graduates with no higher degrees. Abel and Deitz (2014 Chart 5) optimistically calculate that the return on bachelors degrees in the United States increased from 8 percent in 1970 to 14 percent in 2013. Like Payscale, they exclude college drop-outs from their calculations. But unlike Payscale, which directly surveys employees, Abel and Deitz relied for their ROI estimate on data from the US Census Bureau and U.S. Bureau of Labor Statistics, Current Population Survey, March Supplement; US Department of Education, Digest of Education Statistics 2012 and the College Board, Trends in College Pricing 2013 and Trends in Student Aid 2013.

124   http://pages.stern.nyu.edu/~adamodar/New_Home_Page/datafile/histretSP.html 1964–2013 the average was 6.97 percent; 2004–2013, 4.69 percent.

125   In 2014, Payscale changed its methodology to calculate 20-year ROI instead of 30-year ROI. Assuming that a student paid for on-campus housing and received financial aid, the Massachusetts College of Art and Design (instate) had the best annualized 20-year ROI for creative arts at 8 percent followed by the Rhode Island School of Design's 6.7 percent; Harvard was the best value private research university (15.1 percent); South Dakota School of Mines and Technology was the best value public out-of-state university (12 percent). The best value religious university was Brigham Young University with an annualized 20-year ROI of 12.6 percent; the best value research university (whether private, public in-state or public out-of-state) was the University of Virginia (17.6 percent); and the best value liberal arts college was Williams College with a 20-year ROI of 13.9 percent. At the other end of the ROI ladder, four universities tied for bottom with an annualized ROI of −10.6 percent. Thirty-two (2 percent) of 1312 institutions provided a less-than-1 percent ROI. Two hundred and seven institutions (15 percent) delivered less-than-5 percent. At the threshold of the bottom third of all institutions, the ROI was 6.2 percent, just 1 percent above the average 1929–2013 long-term ten-year US Treasury bond rate. Eighty-one percent of all institutions 20-year-ROIs met or exceeded however marginally the long-term bond rate; including 80 percent of liberal arts institutions; 85 percent of religious institutions; 87 percent of sports institutions; 91 percent of research institutions; 95 percent of business institutions, and 100 percent of engineering institutions; along with 5 percent of education majors, 29 percent of social work majors, 32 percent of arts majors, 52 percent of humanities majors, 75 percent of political science majors, 80 percent of life sciences majors, 87 percent of business majors, 98 percent of economics majors, 98 percent of nursing majors, 99 percent of computer science majors, and 100 percent of engineering majors. The Ivy League 20-year ROI ranged from 11.6 percent to 15.1 percent, all of them just exceeding the long-term return on the S&P 500 stock index.

average annualized return over 30 years. In short, the average return on a US college education hovers just above the long-term bond rate.

It ought to be noted as well that boosters of the graduate income 'premium' continually point to average returns on the investment in higher education but are silent on the matter of those graduates who enjoy less-than-average returns on their investment. Many graduates in a life-time of earnings routinely earn less than the average premium and in a significant number of cases earn less than had they never gone to college. There is no reason to think that a superior-performing high school graduate could not match in life-term earnings the US Treasury bond benchmark.[126] That is to say, higher ability individuals on average will choose more schooling; and those who don't on average will still earn higher wages unless we assume that the status of a degree, *viz.* its signaling capacity, leads to higher wages but then we are paying a lot for a status signaling system called higher education. Hanushek and Zhang report a correlation between cognitive ability (as measured by international literacy test scores) and increased earning capacity.[127] One standard deviation increase in the literacy score, they relate, increases annual earnings by from 5 percent in Italy to 24 percent in the United States.[128] One of the key things that matters in job success and university success is not the years of education but rather an individual's reading capacity. Yet, as recent studies indicate, university students read less and less. The sharp fall-off in the reading-heavy humanities in the post-industrial era was a symptom of this. Today a college graduate in a service industry or routine office job is in effect in the position of a superior-performing high school graduate. Society has invested a large amount of public money over 50 years ($346 billion in US federal and state subsidization in 2008)[129] to engineer minor pay premiums for graduates in employment sectors where for the most part university or college study is not necessary.

Eventually the consumers of higher education are going to resist this paltry outcome. They are not forever going to invest in a poor-return investment. The primary obstacle to a realistic consumer understanding is the universities themselves. They routinely make statements about the value of their product or good that are untrue, misleading, manipulative, and wrong. What other industry is allowed to get away with this? The long-term (1928–2013) return on the S&P 500 stock index is 11.5 percent. Payscale's 2013 survey reported that only eight US

---

126 'It has long been recognized that workers who attended school longer may possess other characteristics that would lead them to earn higher wages irrespective of their level of education.' Krueger and Lindahl 2001: 1103. '[A] considerable part of the estimated return to education ... appears due to classical ability bias from the more able also getting more schooling.' Hanushek and Zhang 2006: 19.

127 Drawn from the International Adult Literacy Survey conducted by the OECD in 1994, 1996 and 1998.

128 Hanushek and Zhang 2006: 19.

129 Digest of Education Statistics 2011: Tables 31 and 384.

institutions did better than that and only once financial aid was factored in.[130] In-state students who have the grades to get into SUNY Baruch College or Georgia Tech and who successfully graduate from these institutions acquire for themselves a real substantial material life-time benefit in so doing. This is not the case for most American college and university students.

Mobility (not)

Even if we assume all of the above, surely the phenomenon of being the 'first person in my family to get to university' has made all the state spending on universities worthwhile? Surely it must be the case that this vast public expenditure has increased social mobility between social strata? The answer, alas, is no. A long time ago scholarships did make the 'career open to talent' not just possible but routine and unexceptional. Australia's Martin Committee Report in 1964 noted that in 1963 about 49 percent of all university students received some financial assistance for the payment of fees.[131] After 1970 the rhetorical image of 'the student from a disadvantaged background' became a commonplace trope in official reports. But the role of this rhetoric was ideological not practical. It justified the expansion of the university system rather than the importing of hitherto overlooked talent into the university pool.

To put this matter another way: the problem of educational mobility, or the difficulty of getting to university, is frequently over-stated. The data from Australia is illustrative. While it is true that socio-economic background correlates to an extent with educational outcome, the correlation is far from dramatic. In Australia at the turn of the millennium, of the school leavers who selected university in preference to vocational education, 86 percent of girls and 79 percent of boys from the top end of the socio-economic scale were successful, compared with 76 percent of girls and 71 percent of boys from the low socio-economic end.[132] Once at university, the low SES cohort performed almost identically to the general student population.[133] On a world-historic scale, that was a very good outcome. It is likely that no society is ever going to achieve perfect mirror symmetry between

---

130   CUNY Baruch College, Georgia Institute of Technology, University of Virginia Main Campus, the College of William and Mary, Berkeley College NY, New Mexico Tech, SUNY Maritime College, Washington University Main Campus, and North Carolina State University. All are public in-state institutions, except one for-profit (Berkeley College). Annual ROI ranged from 15 percent (Baruch College) to 11.6 percent (NCSU). Five of the eight are research universities; three of the eight are engineering schools. Without financial aid, no institution matched or exceeded the S&P 500 long-term average.

131   19.7 percent of all students held Commonwealth scholarships; 18.3 percent of students held teaching-training awards. Martin Committee 1964 volume 1: 19.

132   Cook 2003.

133   Bradley 2008: 30; James 2008: 38–9.

socio-economic background and educational outcome; in short we are never going to see 25 percent of the students at university come from the low SES quartile. It is reasonable that societies continue to experiment with approaches to ensure careers open to talent. But such approaches also need to be conditioned by realism. In the first instance, this means that whatever ways we try should not be persisted with if they fail. 'More of the same' is not good public policy if the policy does not work. Secondly, it has to be recognized that families play a key role in turning the intellectual gifts of individuals into talents, and that, at the same time, there is a limited amount of influence that social policy has over family traits and behaviors. Spending money on social measures that do not work is a vain substitute for the role of the family.

After 1989, the Australian Government's principal way of increasing low SES participation in universities was to piggy-back on the total participation rate. Increasing the absolute number of students, it was assumed, would increase the relative number of students from low SES backgrounds. More students implied more low-SES students. This approach was a complete failure—as the government's own official inquiry in 2008, the Bradley Review, noted.[134] 'The belief that providing additional places would redress inequalities in participation without affirmative action has proven false,' it concluded. Nor is there any reason to think that with affirmative action anything would have been different unless university places were simply allocated on the basis of socio-economic status which would simply substitute ascription for achievement.[135] It would turn university into a patrimony—an ambition sometimes not so far from the surface of the equity lobby. So why then did Australia's Bradley Review into higher education recommend a major increase in the participation rate? It did so because of the circular assumptions of knowledge society advocates. The Review's consultant economist predicted that 'from 2010 the supply of people with undergraduate qualifications will not keep up with demand.'[136] But how could this be when even the OECD, a booster for qualification growth, plotted Australia across 1998–2006 as being on the borderline of 'slowing demand for higher educated individuals'?[137] As the Bradley Review noted, the 'core underlying assumption of the Access Economics (2008) modelling is that up-skilling of the workforce over time will

134 Bradley 2008: 38.
135 For example, the equity Commonwealth scholarship system in Australia, which targets low income groups, has had zero effect on the low SES participation rate, Bradley 2008: 36.
136 Access Economics, Bradley 2008: xi.
137 OECD 2009: 35, Chart A1.5. Notably, in 2007 the OECD average was in the over-supply quadrants, with countries ranging from Poland, France, Norway, Netherlands, United Kingdom, Israel, Czech Republic, Hungary, and so on, exhibiting slowing demand for the tertiary educated, and countries like United States, Denmark, Spain, and Australia on the borderline of over-supply. If the very generous assumptions of the OECD were altered in the direction of more rigorous ones, the picture of over-supply would be even more apparent.

be a major contributor to labor market demand.'[138] In other words, qualified labor called for more qualified labor. This is the typical of the circular reasoning of the post-industrial age. The resulting design, endorsed by Bradley, was to increase the participation rate in universities to 40 percent of the 25–34 year age cohort.[139] Though the Bradley Review may have refuted the notion, Australia's Labor Government in 2010 continued to link participation and social inclusion rates.[140] For every 4 places that the Federal Government added, it betted that 1 of those places would go to a student from a low SES quartile background. That strategy required either entrance scores to go down, grades to be inflated, assessment tasks to be diluted, or rubbery entry options to be created.[141] Financial incentives were waved in front of universities to get their compliance in this. Yet in 40 years, the percentage of those from a low SES quartile background at university had not changed. The Australian Labor government's 2010 ambition of raising the low SES cohort to 20 percent of total university enrolment failed. To achieve its target, the Labor government added 22 percent more undergraduate places in Australian public universities between 2009 and 2013. It still failed. In 2010 the low SES percentage was 16.5; in 2011, 16.8 percent; in 2012, 17.1 percent, where it was in the 1970s. Australian governments spend millions annually on 'higher education participation' financing schemes ($180 million in 2014) to no material effect whatsoever except to fund equity bureaucracies in universities. The only demonstrable achievement of the equity lobby has been to reduce the quality of university sector. It has subjected universities to ever-larger numbers of students

---

138   Bradley: 16.

139   Kemp and Norton, 2014: 4–5 report that in 2013 35 percent of 25–34 year olds had a bachelor degree; Commonwealth-supported, i.e. government subsidized, undergraduate places in Australian public universities increased by 22 percent between 2009 and 2013, from 444,000 to 541,000.

140   Referring to her political opponents, the preceding conservative government, the Australian Deputy Prime Minister of the day stated in 2010 that: 'The Howard government clearly did not care about participation or equity. During their time in government, participation by students from low socioeconomic backgrounds languished at about 15 percent while participation from rural and remote areas decreased ... Our move to uncap the number of university places is already having an impact in the community. Over-enrolment in 2010 is now estimated to be 44,495 places, or 9.9 percent above target. Students from disadvantaged backgrounds are also starting to see benefits as a result of our substantial new equity loading for institutions that enroll disadvantaged students. This loading is worth more than 15 times previous equity funding and will provide more support to regional and outer metropolitan institutions, given their student profile. This year university offers to low socioeconomic status applicants increased faster (8.8 percent) than offers to medium SES (7.8 percent) or high SES (5.8 percent) applicants, which puts us in good stead to meet our ambitious target to increase participation of low SES students to 20 percent by 2020.' Gillard 2010.

141   40 percent of Australian academics surveyed for Anderson, Johnson and Saha 2002: 38–9, reported the perception of an increase in the award of high grades.

with ever-lower entrance scores from all social quartiles whilst expanding the size and influence of equity and quality assurance bureaucracies that issue and audit 'access' and 'participation' policies. Universities and colleges reached and exceeded the optimal participation rate of 16 percent of the 19 year-old age cohort in the 1980s. A prudent policy of higher education would gradually re-raise entrance scores, reduce the waste of money and people's time and dreams represented by the post-industrial approach and over the medium term incrementally shrink the participation rate. The continuous expansion of the participation rate was justified by the promise of greater inclusion of students from low quartile and quintile SES backgrounds. Yet the primary beneficiaries of this policy were members of middle and upper quintiles and quartiles. A contrarian view of this inevitably begs the question: how would a lower global participation rate affect the participation by students from low SES backgrounds? Let us suppose for example that 15–20 percent of the 19–24 year old population got a university degree rather than 30 plus percent. In Australia the percentage of university students from low SES backgrounds has been constant over decades at around 17 percent. Participation in higher education has been indifferent to system changes. In short, any additional change would probably make zero difference.

Getting to University

Even Australia's experiment with free university tuition in the 1970s made no difference to low SES participation in higher education.[142] The material of society resists such social engineering. The gift of intelligence is broadly distributed through the human population. But broad distribution does not mean an abstractly equal distribution. After decades of meritocratic policy prescriptions we find that seventeen percent and not 25 percent of university students come from the lowest socio-economic quartile. What explains the gap? Gifts, including intelligence and character, are a natural lottery. So a gifted person will not necessarily have gifted children. That is commonly observed. It is also commonly inferred that those who are gifted and who accordingly have done well use their wealth or status to pass on advantages to the less gifted of their children. High status parents pay for better schools that deliver better exam

---

142   A classic example of misconceived policy is US affirmative action policy. This policy is very popular on American campuses. Universities and college with affirmative action policies reduce admission standards for applicants from preferred racial groups. This leads to higher-than-normal drop-out rates and poorer career prospects for those students than had they been accepted at a university or college where the applicant's admission scores matched the regular admission standard. Affirmative action policy does not reverse under-achievement but rather creates it (Sander and Taylor 2012; Sander 2005). Thus, ironically, race only becomes a predictor of attrition in college because affirmative action causes the systemic mismatching of students and institutions.

results. It is true that high quartile children do better on aptitude tests; yet test training only increases performance on these intelligence tests by a few points. So that does not explain the gap. It is not better schools or better tutors. Clark (2014) suggests a more nuanced answer, to the effect that the natural lottery does not distribute intelligence in a perfectly even or random fashion. Rather families skew the lottery. Families are a subtle mechanism for passing on intelligence across the long-term over multiple generations, often skipping a generation or two. Briefly put, successful families reproduce themselves not necessarily over the short term but rather over the epic long term, causing a certain crinkling of the social fabric. This subtle mechanism explains the gap—that is not vast, and should not be over-stated but nonetheless is persistent—between the 25 percent who make up the lowest SES quartile and the seventeen percent of their number at university. Nature, it seems, is not represented by the throw of the dice after all, and in its non-randomness is impervious to social policy.

This is also evident in the rather limited difference schools make in getting individuals to university. The gifts that an individual is endowed with have to be developed. Schools play a role in this but less than policy makers often think.[143] Schools arguably only make a marginal contribution to the latter-day Huw Morgans going to university.[144] The 'national school' push in the twentieth century delivered far less than its proponents expected and for a long time has been declining in efficacy.[145] This is because of what virtually every high achieving person in the arts, the sciences and the professions reports whenever they are asked 'what made the difference.' What made the difference to them was not their schooling. A majority report being bored by school.[146] Rather what made a difference was what happened at home, in particular their access to a home library and a model for reading books, viewing art and listening to recorded works.

---

143   Inflation-adjusted per-pupil spending on US schools increased 185 percent from 1970 to 2012 but SAT scores for reading, mathematics and science remained essentially flat over the period (Coulson, 2014: Figure 1).

144   High-performers (Hong Kong, Shanghai, Finland, Japan, and Singapore) on the OECD PISA (Programme for International Student Assessment) index, which measures international school student performance in mathematics and reading, share a common characteristic. OECD, 2011. High performing countries and cities retain strong home cultures where parents take an active interest in children's education at home. In Finland, 'seventy-five percent of parents read aloud to their children' (Aydt, 2012).

145   Boser 2011 reports that academic achievement per real school dollar dropped by 65 percent between 1971 and 1999. As with universities, the poorer their performance, the more that US schools spent on administration.

146   Goertzel, Goertzel and Goertzel 1978; Csikszentmihalyi 1996: 173–6; Simonton 1984: 74. Csikszentmihalyi 1996: 173 observes: 'It is quite strange how little effect school—even high school—seems to have had on the lives of creative people. Often one senses that, if anything, school threatened to extinguish the interest and curiosity that the child had discovered outside its walls.'

It has been long observed that self-education is the key to eminent creative achievement in the arts and sciences.[147] High achievers growing up tend to be voracious readers. They often read more than 50 books per year. The most pernicious trend today affecting educational achievement is the decline in reading at home. Home reading culture has a much greater positive effect on social mobility and educational achievement than do investments in public education (or institutionalized private education). Yet reading is on the decline. Between 1978 and 2005 book reading in American homes declined (see Table 5.2).[148] Surveyed in 2005 by Gallup, those reading zero books in a year rose from 8 to 16 percent of adults; those reading one to five books a year rose slightly; all other categories fell. Notable was the halving of readers who read more than one book a week—a rate of consumption of books to be expected of the literate professional and academic classes. The latter is a sign of the declining quality of elites.

Table 5.2   How Many Books a Year Do You Read? (US Gallup Survey)

	0 (%)	1–5 (%)	6–10 (%)	11–50 (%)	51 + (%)	No answer (%)
2005	16	38	14	25	6	1
1978	8	29	17	29	13	4
Source: Moore, Gallup News Service, 2005

The study of home scholarly culture across 27 nations by Evans, Kelley, Sikora and Treiman (2010) confirms what high achievers have long reported.[149] Books and other scholarly materials at home are the decisive determinant of educational attainment.[150] The development of intellectual endowments into talents is a form of self-making.[151] It is a function of the human capacity for self-determination.[152] It proceeds in a largely de-institutionalized manner. In their formal mode, schools

---

147   Simonton 1984: 73–7.
148   Moore 2005.
149   Evans, Kelley, Sikora, and Treiman 2010.
150   Evans, Kelley, Sikora, and Treiman 2010.
151   Heller 1987: 309–13.
152   Marginson 2010: 128–31. Sir Francis Galton in *Hereditary Genius* 1869 observed: 'It may be well to add a few supplementary remarks on the small effects of a good education on a mind of the highest order. A youth of abilities G, and X, is almost independent of ordinary school education. He does not want a master continually at his elbow to explain difficulties and select suitable lessons. On the contrary, he is receptive at every pore. He learns from passing hints, with a quickness and thoroughness that others cannot comprehend. He is omnivorous of intellectual work, devouring in a vast deal more than he can utilize, but extracting a small percentage of nutriment, that makes, in the aggregate, an enormous supply. The best care that a master can take of such a boy is to leave him alone, just directing a little here and there, and checking desultory tendencies.'

and universities have a qualified effect on learning. What matters most is the self-directed agency of reading, listening and viewing.[153] The effect of home libraries is to confer a very significant educational advantage, much more significant than either parent's level of education, parental income, father's occupation, or other background family characteristics. The study of Evans et. al. reports that the difference between a bookless home and one with a 500-book library is as great as the difference between having parents who are barely literate (3 years of education) and having university educated parents (15 or 16 years of education).[154] Thus, it is concluded, a home library is as important as parents' education, the most important variable in the standard educational attainment model, and is twice as important as a father's occupation.

The study found that the positive impact of a large home library is greater than the difference between being born into a society as poor as China and a society as rich as the United States. The latter amounts to just two years of education net of family background. This in fact is less than two-thirds the gap that separates children reared in bookless homes from those born into 500-book homes, all else being equal. As far as reaching university is concerned, the study found that a child growing up in a family with 500 books is 19 percentage points more likely to complete university than a comparable child growing up without a home library.[155] The figures of the study are controlled for parent's academic ability, occupational status and income.[156] If we begin with the case of children whose parents are almost illiterate, only 3 percent in bookless homes go to university compared to 13 percent where there is a large home library, an advantage of 10 percentage points.[157] The advantage rises to 15 percentage points for primary school parents, 21 percentage points for parents with incomplete secondary schooling, 28 percentage points for high school educated parents, and 37 percentage points for university educated parents. Home libraries are a more important factor than parents' education or any other influence in the standard attainment model.[158]

---

153   Australia's Murray Committee, 1957, astutely noted that 'what universities need above all in their students is general education and intellectual training, curiosity and a certain degree of maturity' (31) and pointed to the necessity of the high school graduate entering university to have developed the capacity for self-directed learning: 'undirected study which develops self-reliance and critical judgment' (36).

154   Evans, Kelley, Sikora and Treiman 2010: 180.

155   Evans, Kelley, Sikora and Treiman 2010: 179.

156   Evans, Kelley, Sikora and Treiman 2010: 186.

157   Evans, Kelley, Sikora and Treiman 2010: 182.

158   This may partly explain why home-educated children do better on standardized tests of performance. The evidence from independent, state and advocacy sources about non-institutionalized home schooling (which makes up close to 4 percent of the total US school population today) is clear. Compared with the institutionally schooled, they have higher college entrance scores, higher college GPAs, better college graduation rates and better pre-college academic performance (see for example Martin-Chang, Gould and Meuse 2011; Cogan 2010; Golden 2000; Klicka 1997). Home schooling is about a tenth of the cost of the

Pooling all the countries, the study reported that around 10 percent of respondents grew up with no books at home, 23 percent had around 10 books and 16 percent had about 25; some 33 percent had around 75 books and 18 percent grew up with hundreds of books. The international average was 112. Intriguingly, home libraries are a function of parental taste, not of parental income, class or occupation.[159] The prosperous, the academically able, and professional scholars buy a few more books than average but not that many. Similarly men buy a few more books than women do. But overwhelming home libraries are a function of families with a taste for books irrespective of the standard sociological markers. The implication is the opposite of Plato's view that if you wish to attain equality you have to abolish the family.

The Bradley Review observed that 'the most solidly based finding from research on school learning is that the largest source of variation in school achievement is attributable to differences in what students bring to school—their abilities and attitudes, and family and community background. Educational inequalities linked to family background tend to persist.'[160] That is correct. Yet, literally within the space of a few sentences, the Review proposed outreach, access, and entry programs across education sectors and learning support services for low SES groups as the means of boosting inclusion.[161] This, it recommended, be combined with 'trials of alternative approaches to the selection of students which use a broader range of criteria' and the inevitable 'monitoring and reporting framework to ensure that social inclusion is taken seriously' complete with 'targets and performance measures' and financial

---

institutionalized school system per student per year. In 2004–2005, the average expenditure per pupil in American public schools was $9,266, about a third of the college rate (US Department of Education, 2008). Between 1970 and 2006 real spending per school student in the US doubled (Lips, Watkins and Fleming 2008). Did education outcomes double? The answer is certainly not: reading scores remained flat over the period as did high school graduation rates. Drop-out rates for all ethnic groups in the system roughly halved over the period; the system successfully got its cohort to spend more time at school. That is all. In 2011, the average family income of American home educators was $40,000 to $50,000, which was notably lower than the median household income step of $50,000 to $60,000. A common response to this is to say that the success of home education is due to highly motivated parents, which is not a universal phenomenon. Perhaps so but that also unwittingly points to the problem of under-motivated institutionalized teachers in de-motivating bureaucratic school systems. It also misses the more fundamental point that there is no evidence that the level of actual knowledge of the general population is greater today than it was before the generalization of institutional schooling. It is not clear that either information or knowledge or creation can be effectively or efficiently transferred through the bureaucratic medium of institutionalized teaching. Like most institutions now, including universities, school systems are less knowledge conduits and more lobbies that constantly agitate to expand themselves. They exist in order to exist.

159   Evans, Kelley, Sikora and Treiman 2010: 186–7.
160   Bradley 2008: 41.
161   Bradley 2008: 42.

incentives for universities to meet targets.[162] All of these had been tried before and all had failed. A lengthy chapter of the Bradley Review proposed extensive tinkering with income support measures even though financial support and all other measures directed at low SES students had had no effect on inclusion rates in the 20 years since Australia's Federal Government had commissioned its *A Fair Chance for All* Report in 1990.[163]

Policies that encourage home libraries and reading, along with serious listening and viewing, are liable to have much more impact; expanding public libraries in low SES postcode neighborhoods is the logical corollary of this. Unfortunately, though, libraries—unlike schools or the universities—do not constitute a lobby group. Yet they have had many eminent supporters. Ralph Waldo Emerson once said that the real question is not what you will do with your library, but, rather, 'What it will do with you.'[164] That is the essence of the matter. Frances Spufford dubbed the effect of the home library *The Child That Books Built* (2002). Yet it is remarkable that in the entirety of the Bradley Review there was only one mention in passing of libraries.

How can going to university be a serious proposition without the mind having been developed? The Bradley Review, in a moment of carefully crafted cliché, said that 'higher education can transform the lives of individuals and through them their communities and the nation by engendering a love of learning for its own sake and a passion for intellectual discovery.'[165] In reality, the converse is true. Students bring such passions with them to university, already formed. They develop them, not in school, but through family scholarly culture. Thomas Jefferson declared to his friend John Adams, 'I cannot live without books.' Jefferson was an obsessive book collector from a young age. He amassed three home libraries in his lifetime,

---

162   Bradley 2008: 38, 39, 44–5. The report also suggested that 'the United Kingdom *Improving Retention* program has significant amounts of funding associated with it (£187 million) and allocates these funds based on student profile. This and the parallel *Widening Participation* initiative have, along with other measures, resulted in considerable improvement in participation rates of under-represented group students in a relatively short time' (35). This improvement, though, was in the recruitment of students, the easy thing, not in their retention and completion of a degree or their long-term prospects in the job market. The improvement, in other words, was quite meaningless. In 2007, at Bolton University in the United Kingdom, only 50 percent of first degree students completed their degree. In 2007 the *annual* attrition rate (of domestic students) for the worst performing Australian university, Central Queensland University, was 28 percent with the University of Technology Sydney not far behind at 25 percent (DEEWR 2008).

163   Bradley 2008: 47–67.

164   In an undated journal entry from 1873, Emerson wrote: 'Be a little careful about your Library. Do you foresee what you will do with it? Very little to be sure. But the real question is, what it will do with you? You will come here & get books that will open your eyes, & your ears, & your curiosity, and turn you inside out or outside in.' Emerson was the Chair of the Concord Free Public Library Committee from 1875 to 1882.

165   Bradley: 5.

and got himself periodically into debt doing so. When the Library of Congress was destroyed in 1814 in the war against the British, Jefferson sold his second book collection of around 6,700 items to the Library. Jefferson's endowment doubled the holdings of the Library of Congress. That did not stop him collecting books. When Jefferson died a few years later, he had more than 2,000 volumes in his home library.

Intensive reading is an essential preparation for university.[166] At university it is essential to doing well. Yet reading-heavy courses at university have become unpopular in the past 40 years. Take the case of humanities. It is sometimes contended that the humanities have become unpopular because they don't train people for a job. But humanities graduates from traditional demanding disciplines still compete effectively for high-paying occupations. A more likely explanation for the drop in humanities course numbers is that traditional humanities courses require high levels of reading and understanding.[167] This was not appealing to students enrolling in the post-industrial university. As the mass bureaucratic universities grew, traditional humanities disciplines shrank in relative terms. The big drop in numbers in the humanities came in the period 1971 to 1985, right at the outset of the post-industrial era.[168] The number of humanities students as a percentage of all US degree completions rose from 10 percent in 1951 to a peak of 17 percent in 1967. From 16 percent in 1971 numbers fell away sharply to 6 percent in 1985. They picked up in the late 80s and early 90s, echoing a minor intellectual revival in the humanities in the 1980s, falling away again to 7 percent in 2011.[169] Why was the post-industrial era so inhospitable for the humanities? Partly it was a function

---

166   So much so it is surprising that no admissions system has emerged based just on an applicants' record of reading.

167   This is required not just of students but of academic teachers as well. Of the latter, the size of their home libraries (or personal office libraries) might well be a measure of competence. What might be expected then of the personal libraries of academic faculty? 3,000 volumes or one book a week on average purchased between 15 years old and 65 years old. An academic starting employment at 30 could be expected to have already accumulated 750 volumes in a personal library. Steffens 2009 looks at the home libraries of 10 major architects: Allen, Cobb, Diller/Scofidio, Eisenman, Graves, Holl, Mori, Sorkin, Tschumi, and Williams/Tsien. The average size of the home library of the 10 architects was 2,742.

168   Humanities Indicators 2013. http://www.humanitiesindicators.org/content/hrcoImageFrame.aspx?i=II-1a.jpg&o=hrcoIIA.aspx_topII1.

169   Another way of measuring this is to look at the number of students majoring in the humanities. In the United States, from 1970/71 to 2003/4 the number of undergraduate students majoring in the humanities dropped from 30 percent to less than 16 percent. During that same period, business majors climbed from 14 percent to 22 percent of the undergraduate population. Chace 2009 calculates the specific discipline changes:

English majors: 7.6 percent to 3.9 percent

Foreign languages and literatures majors: 2.5 percent to 1.3 percent

Philosophy and religious studies majors: 0.9 percent to 0.7 percent

History majors: 18.5 percent to 10.7 percent

Business majors: 13.7 percent to 21.9 percent

of mass higher education. The core of the humanities—philosophy, literature and history—are difficult disciplines. Like mathematics and physics, they still produce employable high-earning graduates. But the obverse of this is that they only attract a relative handful of enrollees in the mass higher education market due to their difficulty. In absolute number terms, the humanities did not so much shrink as remain 'much the same size' yet in a much larger pool of undergraduates. Thus while the number of students in universities exploded after 1970, relative to population, the number of those studying philosophy, history and literature did not.[170]

To study the humanities means to read intensively. The larger contemporary culture is not comfortable with intense reading. The modern Enlightenment grew out of Protestantism which (in a manner of speaking) grew out of Gutenberg's book culture. Post-modern culture was the antithesis of the culture that Gutenberg and Luther spawned. It is ironic then that the intellectual descendants of the bookish culture of the Gutenberg-Protestant-Enlightenment embraced post-modern culture with alacrity. Having done so they then struggled to understand why students no longer wished to study the humanities (or in many cases simply no longer wished to study). Harvard University's 2013 report *Mapping the Future* addressed the pains of the humanities.[171] The report attributed the decline of the humanities to five factors:[172] The study of the humanities was an expression of empire; if the world today lacks empires then it has no need for the humanities. The humanities offered art as the glue of nations; that glue is now law and constitutions not books and paintings. The humanities offer interpretations rather than scientific conclusions in an age of science. Humanities graduates don't earn large incomes. The humanities are not technological but the surrounding world is. Having listed those big-picture causes of decline, the report then went on to flatly ignore them. The authors of the report chose instead to concentrate on something much more mundane: namely the high number of Harvard students who as 'pre-freshmen' indicate an intention to do Humanities and then change their mind. These would-be humanities students, it turns out, are much more likely to switch concentration than prospective science or social science students. In the mind of Harvard then, the way to fix the global problem of the decline of the humanities was to fix a very parochial problem. So instead of world-historical ambition, the report recommended tinkering with Harvard's first-year curriculum. It was left unclear how the 'pre-freshman' decision to drop the humanities might be affected

---

170   In 1970 in the United States, 96,771 students completed degrees in English, literature, languages, letters, philosophy, theology and linguistics; in 2011, 97,551 did so. US Department of Education 2013, Table 322.10.

171   Armitage et al. 2013. Top-tier private universities like Harvard are semi-immune from the fiscal reality of lean student numbers due to the depth of their pockets. But even in these institutions an obdurate reality is gradually intruding. Take Stanford as an example: 17 percent of students major in humanities but the humanities have 45 percent of faculty (Lewin, 2013). In the 1960s a third of Stanford students majored in the humanities.

172   Armitage 2013: 3–6.

by a pepped-up 'freshman experience' in first year. This sounded like the Titanic was sinking and the crew were righting the crooked pictures on the cabin walls. But not the worry: the report concluded on reflection that there was no 'crisis' of the humanities only a 'challenge'.[173] What Harvard needed to do to successfully reverse the historic decline of the humanities was target first-year students, add more faculty positions, 'interface' with social science, public health, business and law disciplines, and get 'special funding' so that extra-curricula student art activity could be integrated into the regular arts curriculum. In other words, repeat every failed self-serving institutional humanities strategy of the past 40 years. In step with these paint-by-numbers recommendations, Harvard's 'Curriculum Sub-Committee of the Humanities Project' proposed elegantly-devised framework courses, survey courses, and gateway courses to other divisions along with freshman advising and navigational tools to aid student subject selection. The sum result was admirably-classified, box-ticked, and pleasingly-rehearsed group work. Yet all the while the epic social, historical, and epistemological shifts at play in the decline of the humanities were ignored. The question of how such forces might be addressed was never raised. It was evidently best to disregard the ice-bergs.

Ignoring history, however, does not work. The broader post-modern culture does not like reading. Logic, mathematics, and literacy are side-stepped. This is not just an expression of popular culture. Elites are also affected by this. The home libraries that peppered the New England of the Protestant age have disappeared. This has created a paradox in its wake. The numbers of staff and students in traditional humanities fields have shrunk in relative terms to a minor place in the post-modern academy. Yet while they have been miniaturized these fields have remained intellectually robust, at least compared with their more recent peers.[174] This intellectual power however is a sign of weakness. For it is a residual

---

173 This and what follows Armitage 2013: 11, 52, 45.

174 The report of the 2012 Excellence in Research for Australia (ERA) national research review illustrated this neatly (Australian Research Council 2012). Fields of research in Australian universities were ranked 1–5 according to the strength of their research output, principally publications (measured by peer review for the social sciences excluding Psychology and citation analysis for the sciences excluding the Information Sciences and Mathematics: cf. ERA 2012 Discipline Matrix). The science fields with the largest portion (40 percent or more) of top (5) ranked research were Astronomical and Space Sciences, Macromolecular and Materials Chemistry, Theoretical and Computational Chemistry, Geochemistry, Geology, Geophysics, Ecological Applications, Evolutionary Biology, Forestry Sciences, Resources Engineering, Interdisciplinary Engineering, Nanotechnology, Medical Biochemistry, Immunology, Cardiovascular Medicine, Oncology, and Ophthalmology. The only fields in the peer-reviewed social sciences and humanities that approached these (with 20 percent or more 5-ranked) were Economic Theory, Econometrics, Transportation, Art Theory and Criticism, Archaeology, Philosophy, Literature, and History. Notably the latter two had re-defined themselves as 'studies' with a sizable 3-rank tail. (Tiny fields with less than 4 units of evaluation were excluded from the lists above.)

power. The strongest sources of modern academic culture have declined as their student numbers have slid. Nothing serious has superseded these sources. The new humanities hoped to take the place of the traditional humanities. These new programs were neither traditional social science nor the classic humanities. Rather they were a loose amalgam of both underscored by intense moralizing. They saw the traditional humanities as an expression of empire and an intellectual evil which the rise of 'studies' would smite. But all of this was parochial in-fighting. It was a function of the political shift of the universities to a mono-cultural left-liberalism. The larger culture took no heed of it. It had no interest in the battle of the books. In fact it didn't like books very much. That dislike was a function of the creative deficit in the larger culture. The contextual culture of the universities in the post-modern era was less interesting and less demanding than its predecessor culture. This was not just an issue for the humanities. It affected the sciences and the social sciences as well. But it was nonetheless very noticeable in the case of the humanities. Those disciplines were shunned right at the start of the post-industrial era. They were first to be dispensed with.

The culture critic F.R. Leavis observed this in 1967. He noted that when English Literature was forming as a discipline in the 1920s it had the great advantage that the 1920s was 'a creative period.'[175] This was the time of Lawrence, Joyce and Woolf. Thus 'something new and important, we could see ... was happening in English Literature,' and that 'impressive new creation' compelled 'an intense critical interest.' The interesting question that Leavis posed then was: 'What do we do in a present that is not strikingly creative'? That was a question for the whole of the post-industrial era. It was not that there were no interesting intellectual and cultural works created in the period. Yet there were many fewer of them in relative terms. This was not just a problem for literature. It affected most of the arts and sciences. From economics to physics, visual arts to music, philosophy to chemistry—in different ways, they all suffered an intellectual recession. In their place rose up mediocre faux-disciplines like media studies and leisure studies. Almost any of the 'studies,' from environmental studies to communication studies, were shallow and insubstantial. With their rise came a collapse of reading culture at university. The notion that a person went to university to 'read' a discipline, as J.K. Rowling the Harry Potter children series author did when she 'read' classics and French at the University of Exeter—or that a senior university academic might have been called a 'Reader'—or that academic faculty would possess large home libraries of their own, or that bright students might want to borrow books from those libraries—fell into abeyance.[176]

175　Leavis 1969: 69–70.

176　Rowling recalls not doing much work at university but spending time while there listening to *The Smiths* and reading Dickens and Tolkien, probably a useful preparation for her future career (Parker 2012).

Conclusion

The Academic University

The Fordist Dinosaurs

Universities were supposed to be the herald of the post-Fordist information age. They turned out instead to be among the most entrenched Fordist dinosaurs in the post-industrial era. They promised innovation, creativity and discovery but delivered a lot less of that than their institutional predecessors. Business Fordism failed in the 1960s. University Fordism failed 50 years later. The universities became a singular example of why not only companies but large organizations in general fail.[1] Such organizations often appear outwardly to be unbeatable. But inwardly their discovery quotient is considerably less than their delivery capacity.[2] They run on empty—and eventually their delivery quotient declines. That happened to the universities. Incrementally, almost invisibly, their facility for discovery flagged. It did not disappear. Nonetheless it shrank. That was followed by a decrease in their ability to deliver knowledge to students—and to tempt students to study and think. On the whole students stopped listening and learning. Most students today at university study little, read little, observe little and write little. They drop out in large numbers. A large proportion of those who do graduate will never work in a job that requires a degree. University graduates once earned markedly more than median earnings. The typical university graduate today earns only a modest and decreasing increment above the social median.

Sixty years ago university students studied the great disciplines that demanded much of them. Today only a hand-full of students do so. These students are abundantly rewarded by society and employers. The rest of the student population is not. Yet the great disciplines are disappearing in the universities. The great majority of students do not want to enroll in them. They require too much reading, writing, calculating and thinking. Students prefer to enroll in 'studies' courses, which are a parody of university inquiry. So the great disciplines shrink and the intellectual power of the university abates. Modern society has a surfeit of professionals and managers. Many of these jobs carry inflated titles. They do not belong to the world of the learned professions nor do they entail much in the way of leadership or responsibility. But even these pseudo-professional positions are out of the reach for many university graduates today who end up in low-paying service jobs after spending years on the university merry-go-round. They graduate with debt that they find difficult to pay off. Debt default is rising. Graduates are

---

1 Christensen 2003.
2 Dyer, Gregersen and Christensen 2011.

putting off marriage, delaying the purchase of a home, and struggling to find capital for business start-ups due to the debt burden.

The universities continue to promise social mobility but they cannot deliver it. The percentage of students from the lowest social quartile attending university today is no greater than it was in 1970. In some cases it is proportionately less today than it was in 1970. State subsidization of universities fuelled the growth of tuition prices. In real terms, prices today are four times what they were in the 1950s. Likewise university costs per student are 2-to-4 times what they were then. It is much more expensive for a low-income student to go to university today with a state subsidy than it was in 1960 or 1970 without a state subsidy. Government subsidies have functioned solely to allow universities to charge more to cover the perpetual expansion of marginal functions staffed by a well-rewarded, academically irrelevant, post-industrial professional and adminodemic class. The equity industry in universities is part of that class. While it has completely failed to create social mobility it has succeeded handsomely in promoting its own self-interest. This is not an isolated problem. Increasingly none of the claims made by the mass university system to justify its existence are credible. It is clear that the days of the post-industrial university are numbered. It is like the Soviet Union in the 1980s. Its denizens repeat formulas for which there is neither evidence nor even belief. The size of the university sector will shrink. This is not a matter of whether the university 'ought' to shrink or whether it 'should' shrink or even whether it 'must' shrink. Rather, more simply, it will shrink. The glory days of the mass university are long behind it. In order to survive, the sector has to lose at least 1-in-3 of its students and eliminate the 30 cents in the dollar that it spends on unnecessary and self-defeating professional services. The modern university is obese. It has to slim down. That is not just a consequence of the global downturn after 2008, though the downturn has played its part as a trigger for change. Rather it is a function of a system that does not deliver what it claims to deliver and that does not discover what it says it discovers. Universities do not live up to their own mythologies. The scholastic emperor has no clothes. The small children who see that naked reality are beginning to say so.

The parallel with the newspaper industry is instructive. Over the past decade or two, newspaper revenues have fallen by more than half, employment in the industry has dropped by nearly 30 percent, and more than 700 institutions have shut their doors.[3] The contemporary university system will eventually go the way of the railroad industry and the newspaper industry. None of these disappeared entirely—yet each shrank dramatically. The implied logic of this is that the mass university in its turn will lose numbers, students, status, staff, influence and revenue. So even if new providers enter the marketplace, the market will still be shredded. It is not unreasonable to think that across the next 20 or 30 years, university revenue in the OECD will decline by a half and university employment by a third in real terms. That is Joseph Schumpeter's creative destruction at work.

---

3   Economist 2014a.

The university at its greatest is a discovery institution. In order to continue to be so, the sector has to shrink the number of Goliaths and expand the number of Davids. After decades of compulsive expansion of the size of institutions, it is time to look at the benefits of the small academic university, the *microversity*. Mass scale along Fordist lines led the universities into a dead-end. The megaversities and multiversities become less, not more, efficient. They discovered less in real terms; they transmitted less knowledge than they claimed to; they prepared their graduates less adequately by advising, mentoring and shaping them less well.[4] Instead universities administered ever-more: eventually to the point where administration and professional services and adminodemics now appear to be the point of the university. They consume 70 cents in the dollar of university income. That is 20 cents in the dollar more than in 1970 and 30 cents in the dollar more than in 1930. Yet the core business of a university—departmental instruction and research—today is identical to what it was then. Academic salaries in real terms have not changed over the years. Technology is less costly. Yet university costs have spiraled. For the low income student, university is much less affordable today than it was in the 1950s and 1960s, even while government subsidies have multiplied. Today the university is more unaffordable for everyone—including the taxpayer. The sole reason for this is the unwarranted explosion of administrative and professional functions, processes and costs.

Rethinking the University

The single greatest challenge in rethinking the model of the contemporary university is to conceive a functional model of a university that is not bureaucratic in nature. The larger part of resources in a university today is commanded by the class of adminodemics, managers, administrators and professionals. The engorged scale of university administration is staggering. That said administration is a necessary component of any university. Finance, personnel, legal, facilities and technology services were there at the birth of the modern university. The question is not their necessity but rather their scale and ethos. Administration can be modest, lean, and

---

4 Academics teach and research more than ever but they encourage, advise, and inspire students ever less because of the claims of professional bureaucracy on their time and attitudes. A Gallup-Purdue University (Ray and Kafka 2014) survey of 30,000 US graduates reports that graduates are 2.3 times more likely to be engaged at work and 1.9 times more likely to experience general well-being in life if they had a college mentor, a professor who took a personal interest in them, and a professor who was an inspirational teacher. Today only 14 percent of graduates report having had this kind of mentor. The liberal professionalized procedural university hates these old-fashioned university types in the same way that contemporary hospitals despise nurses who care. The whole thrust of bureaucratic culture is toward impersonal procedure and codification. This is the nature of legal-rationality. The cost of legal-rational culture is its chronic inability to inspire or motivate.

helpful. Contemporary university administration is the converse. It is possessed by a bureaucratic spirit to expand and command. In Australian universities, there are 1.3 non-academic staff members to every academic staff member. That is the median figure across the sector. Any company would be drummed out of business operating on such a bloated ratio. Most non-academic staff members today are back office central administration staff, not front office departmental staff. Since the beginning of the 1980s, revenue has flowed away from academic departments to Faculties, Colleges and Central administrations at a rate of about one half of one percent per year. Today 70 percent of university income is distributed to university administration.

In Adam Smith's day, and for a century or more thereafter, administration was around 20 percent of university costs, no more. Professors did much of the administration themselves, and did it effectively. Adam Smith himself was an outstanding professor-manager in his time at the University of Glasgow.

> during the 1750s he became an experienced and successful academic administrator with something of a taste for management. In his first year as a professor he was put in charge of moving the library into a new problem-ridden building designed by William Adam. From 1755 he was to be effectively in charge of the library as Quaestor and responsible for its accounts—which he kept meticulously—and for purchases ... By 1754 Smith had also gained a reputation for property management. He was responsible for the protracted and intricate negotiations involved in rebuilding the Principal's house, in building a new natural philosophy classroom, for accommodating the Academy of the Fine Arts, and for housing James Watt's workshop. By the late 1750s he was in charge of the university's accounts and the university's dealings with the town council on property matters and the students' tax liability.[5]

Smith managed to be twice Dean of Faculty, Vice-Rector and Quaestor of the university and still teach one hour five days a week on moral philosophy for 32 weeks of the year to classes of 70 or 90 students, followed by a one hour discussion of the lecture with the lecture class, plus one hour of lectures on rhetoric five days a week for 12 weeks, and three hours of smaller classes with 20 students three hours a day five days a week for 32 weeks of the year—a teaching load of 30 hours a week for 13 weeks and 25 hours a week for 20 weeks. Smith's teaching load was at the upper end of today's eftsl (equivalent full-time student load) measures—around 25 eftsl per annum—and his hours of teaching were two to three times today's lengths. The lecture course on moral philosophy, which included outlines of both his *Theory of Moral Sentiments* and *The Wealth of Nations*, cost students one and a half guineas (£1.57) to enroll, in today's money £2,630. Assuming a student attended three courses of this kind, with attendant tutorial discussions, during the teaching year—that is an annual fee of £7,890. Glasgow's course structure and fee

---

5   Phillipson 2010: 131.

structure was comparable with the University of Melbourne's in the mid-1950s. In contrast, the unsubsidized annual tuition fees for international undergraduate students at the University of Glasgow in 2014 ranged from £13,750 in the Arts to £31,250 in Medicine with Science programs costing £17,250.

Each year incrementally the portion of university revenue appropriated by central administration grows. Universities have repeatedly claimed that centralizing administration and professional services is more efficient—but it is not. Australian universities began the era of its 'unified national system' in 1996 with 1.3 non-academic staff to 1 academic staff member. The ratio was the exactly same 15 years later in 2011.[6] There were many claims about improvement but no actual administrative efficiency gain in that whole time. The administrative productivity gain of centralized databases, the relocation of professional staff to central offices, and the amalgamation of departments into Schools, Schools into larger Schools, and larger Schools into Colleges was zero. In terms of efficiency, centralization was a complete failure. While most Australian universities in 2011 converged around the ratio of 1.3 non-academic staff members to 1 academic staff member, there were outliers. At the nightmare end, the ratio at Victoria University in Melbourne was 1.9:1. In contrast, the ratio at the University of New South Wales was 0.5:1 and at the University of Notre Dame 0.6:1. Lean administration was possible. But these were the exceptions, not the rule.

To achieve a state of modest administration is not easy. Everything in a bureaucratic world is urgent, imperative, necessary, and must be done now. There is little evidence-based reason for bureaucratic expansion, but much huffing-and-puffing. The way to begin to reverse this is simple enough though for state universities. It requires legislatures to cap administrative spending in universities. A start (for example) in the case of Australian universities would be to cap the ratio of non-academic to academic staff at 0.5:1.[7] One front office administrator at departmental level for every four academic staff is appropriate, along with one back office central administrator for every four academic staff. That tallies to 0.5:1. No more is necessary to support the core business of teaching and research in a university. And considerably less is conceivable.

A second step would be to remove extraneous functions from universities. Bureaucracies spread by inventing superfluous processes and dubbing them essential. Many of these are ideological. All of them, arguably, could and should go. Universities do not need convoluted application processes for tiny dollops of incentive money and pointless awards, or teaching and learning development that develops nothing but regulation, or 'low SES' support bureaucracies that have left

---

6 Data source: Australian Government, Higher Education Statistics Collection, 1996–2011.

7 The University of Melbourne in 2014 announced the taking of baby steps in this direction, reducing its professional and administrative staff cohort by 15 percent (500 staff) and increasing its academic staff by 200–300, with the aim of creating a 1:1 administrative: academic staff ratio. Trounson 2014.

the low SES enrolment percentage in universities unchanged for 40 years, and on and on. An epidemic of adminodemic functions spread in universities during the last 25 years. These need to be phased out. Most assistant and associate dean, sub-vice-chancellor, director, and vice-provost offices have no place in a lean university. This requires shrinking the scope of university service and professional departments. Many of their functions can be eliminated. Others can be outsourced or devolved back to department level. University departments are close to those who use services. This avoids the massive transaction costs of centralized back-office managers and administrators who constantly handball queries rather than execute tasks. It has long been observed that bureaucracies lack information to make effective decisions. Today in universities they spend their time on email—distracting other staff by asking for information they lack because of their central location.

A third step would be to reduce the prolix paperwork and multiplication of steps now attached to all functions in universities, even the necessary ones. The 'ease of doing business' is a watchword for future universities. The five page application document can be shrunk to one page, the five sign-offs authorizing activity cut to one, the cumbersome five steps in the badly-designed finance database reduced to one. 'One step compared to five steps' is the difference between modest administration and bureaucratic administration. Approvals need to be given, expenditure needs to be checked, leave taken needs to be reported, and so on. By making each procedure short and quick, the pathologies of bureaucracy are reduced. Replacing the tortured, insincere and often demented language of bureaucratic administration with language that is honest, plain and sincere is a start.

One argument against doing all of the above is that governments place large regulatory burdens on universities. One recent Australian analysis calculated the burden of reporting to government, itself merely one component of contemporary regulation. PhillipsKPA estimated that there were 46 separate requirements for Australian universities to report to government.[8] The report analyzed the recurrent costs of 18 of those reports (and estimated the working days spent in each university preparing the reports). The estimate was that the university sector in 2011 allocated 66,000 working days and spent $26 million dollars satisfying government reporting requirements, almost 1 percent of the sector's cost. Overall, it was estimated that the sector allocates up to 3 percent of its costs for reporting purposes.[9] That is the tip of the proverbial ice-berg which includes the much larger costs of compliance with manifold legislation covering insurance, safety, transport, building, and so on. The transformation of universities into pseudo cities brought with it vast compliance costs yet no tax base that would allow universities to pay for this compliance. So while governments do impose ever-expanding regulatory burdens on universities, universities amplify these with their own attempts to become a fake metropolis. But while they might imagine themselves as cities from time to time, mostly they are overly mature Fordist organizations

---

8   PhillipsKPA 2012.
9   The Australian government conceded this in Emerson and Bird 2013.

bulging with techno-structures that delight in every opportunity to expand process. Governments afford these structures endless opportunities to devise ever-more complicated processes.

When Australia's hyper-bureaucratic 'unified national system' promised 'efficiency' in 1990s, in reality it created a hot house for the universities to develop rules, codes, and an army of adminodemics to promulgate and apply them. The temptation of government is to equate public good with the state with regulation and bureaucracy. Yet governments everywhere today are also under pressure to move away from this model. This is because government funding of the mass universities is not sustainable in the long term.[10] Public funding has dropped in Australia from 60 percent to 56 percent of university costs.[11] It is difficult to see

---

10   In 2011, 9 of 39 Australian universities had a net operating result expressed as a percent of total income that was less than 5 percent. Data source: Australian Government, Higher Education Statistics Collection, 1992–2014.

11   Australia spent $23 billion on its universities in 2011. $13 billion of that came from the federal government. Most of the remainder from student tuition fees (Data source: Australian Government, Higher Education Statistics Collection, 1992–2014.) In 1995 Australia spent $10.8 billion in 2011 dollar terms, and the federal government kicked in $6.4 billion of that. Over the period 1995–2011, the federal government share of total spending on higher education reduced from 60 percent of the total to 56 percent, unsurprisingly for as student numbers rose so did the government's fiscal burden, encouraging prudent governments to spend less as they spent ever-more on universities. Public funding of universities in real 2011 dollar terms doubled in Australia between 1995 and 2011. That kind of funding expansion happened across the OECD. It was unsustainable. Governments did it mainly by borrowing. The sovereign debt they accumulated ended by crucifying them financially. In Australia the sovereign debt route was largely avoided (until after 2008). Instead the federal government under-funded domestic student places and shifted costs to students. That temporarily ceased when in 2012 the government contributions rose again to an average of around 60 percent of tuition costs. Subsidies ranged between 17 percent and 78 percent of course fees—depending on the perceived public benefit of each course. The approach to the 'base funding' of each full-time domestic student in higher education in Australia illustrates the technique of under-funding. This component of higher education financing rose to a peak in 1994 (the early days of Australia's 'national unified system') and then significantly declined between 1994 and 2003. (Lomax-Smith 2011: see especially Figure 1.1.) It rose again to 1994 levels by 2010 as government fiscal control loosened and sovereign debt financing increased. The decline in the 'base funding' of Australian domestic student places was partly cross-subsidized with international student tuition fees. The peak of Australia's foreign student market was 2007. It declined irreversibly after that. Under-funding was a strategy that piggy-backed on legacy resources (like buildings). It could not persist forever. Another technique deployed to shrink government funding of student places was to incrementally whittle away the government's contribution to domestic student places, and shift costs back to students. In 1994 Australian students on average contributed in constant 2010 dollar terms $2,700 of an education costing $14,500. In 2010 students contributed $4,000 of an education worth $14,500. The student contribution increased 150 percent while the larger government contribution decreased by 9 percent—dropping from

it not dropping to 40 percent at some foreseeable future point.[12] Australia's is a mainly state university system.[13] As is the case globally, students will progressively pay for a larger portion of state-subsidized higher education. The Australian case is just one among many. Each national funding system is distinct but the broad trend is similar. The long-term incremental decline in the portion of university spending that is publicly funded is a common phenomenon. Across the OECD, mainly outside of Europe, public financing of tertiary institutions of all types declined from 77 percent in 1995 to 76 percent in 2000 to 71 percent in 2005 to 68 percent in 2010.[14] A steady incremental kind of erosion occurred. In Australia the public share of *all* tertiary education spending dropped from 64 percent in 1995 to 46 percent in 2010.[15] Similarly in the United Kingdom spending fell from 80 percent to 25 percent; Demark 99 to 95 percent; the United States 38 to 36 percent; Sweden 93 to 90 percent; Italy 82 to 67 percent; Israel 62 to 54 percent; France 85 to 81 percent.

To date, fee-raising has had little direct impact on enrolment. In the past 40 years, the responsiveness or sensitivity of prospective students to price has generally been low.[16] Driven by the post-industrial expectations of governments,

---

81 percent to 72 percent of 'base funding.' In short, Australia's federal government spent more on education (due to greater student numbers) by spending less (reducing its subsidy of student fees). In 2011 compared with 1995, it spent twice as much on universities in real terms while still funding a declining portion of university costs.

12   Lomax-Smith 2011: Table 2.1 sets out in US dollars international comparisons of 'base funding' per student—the state and student contribution to the funding of 'teaching and learning informed by scholarship and a base capability in research' (viii). Australia funded students at public universities $10,314 per head, including a $6,142 government contribution and a $4,172 student contribution. The United States average figure for public higher education institutions was the inverse of this: $10,732 overall including $4,321 from government and $6,451 from students. The Lomax-Smith data also provides two further useful comparisons: Denmark's base funding for students was $10,500 provided by the government entirely. Top-tier UK research universities (Cambridge and University College London) split contributions between government and students $7,962:$5,752 (total: $13,714) and $7,944:$6,196 (total: $14,140) respectively. A tier-one American research university, the University of Michigan Ann Arbor, received $12,841 from the state and $12,590 from students (total: $25,431) for its basic activity. 'Base funding' of Australian students represents about 35 percent of income to Australian universities. On top of this is income from a range of sources including other government funding, government research grants, state government sources, full fee-paying international students, full-fee paying domestic students, research, contracts, charges, and bequests. Lomax-Smith 2011: Figure 1.2.

13   Australia in 2014 had 37 public universities, 4 private universities and 131 other higher education providers (Kemp and Norton 2014: 95).

14   OECD, 2013a: 201.

15   OECD, 2013a: 208, Table B3.3.

16   Australia abolished university fees in the 1974 and then re-introduced them in 1985. Re-introduction of fees had no impact on numbers of students from low socio-economic backgrounds enrolling in universities.

schools and parents, students have enrolled en masse in universities and colleges to date without much regard for price. Student loan schemes—which put off payment into the future or allow forgiveness of debt—encouraged this. But the atmosphere of the market is changing. Growing consumer resistance to student debt and a growing understanding of the shrinking return on investment in higher education is evident. That said, the level of income is not the major problem of universities. On the contrary, universities in the major economies do not suffer from a lack of income but rather from an excess of it.

In 1995 there were 30,000 full-time equivalent academics (excluding casual staff) in Australia and Australian universities that year received operating revenue of $7.5 billion, the equivalent of $250,000 per academic in 1995 dollars or $381,000 per academic in 2011 dollars. In 2011, Australia had 48,325 full-time equivalent academics while universities received $23 billion in operating revenue, the equivalent of $476,000 for each academic. This represents a 25 percent cost increase in real terms over sixteen years. In 1995, academic salaries and benefits averaged $78,000 per academic, or $119,000 in 2011 dollar terms. In 2011, academic salaries and benefits totaled $6.7 billion for 48,325 FTE staff, or $138,644 per capita, a 16 percent cost increase in real terms. Over the same period, the number of students taught per academic rose by 33 percent, so academics were vastly more efficient as a cost unit. This simultaneously implies that the non-academic segment of the Australian university was vastly less efficient. In 1960 there were 3,034 full-time academic staff members in Australia and around 800 part-time staff, or 3,800 FTE.[17] The operating revenue for the universities was £31.3 million or $812,367,973 in 2011 dollars, the equivalent of $213,781 for each academic.[18] On this measure, Australian universities in 2011 consumed 2.22 times the operating revenue that they did in 1960. What cost $23 billion in 2013 would have cost the equivalent of $10.4 billion in 1960. In a nutshell this is the story of the post-modern university. It takes more than twice and in many cases three or four times the resources to do what the modern pre-1970s university did.

Contemporary universities—both public and private—need to do more with less income. The clear path to this is to reduce the central administration and professional bloat—and spend less. In 2011, Australia's federal government paid for $13 billion of the $23 billion operating cost of Australian universities. Students contributed around $6 billion. Academic salaries cost $6.7 billion. Academics salaries have not been a major factor, or even a factor, in the cost explosion of Australian universities. An Australian professorial salary in 1956 was £4250 or in 2013 dollars $126,000, roughly what associate professors were paid in 2013.[19] As everywhere, the primary upward driver of costs is administration. Australia's non-academic salaries cost $5.9 billion in 2011. In 1960 it cost 2.2 less in real terms to deliver a higher quality of university education in Australia: that is,

---

17 Based on Martin, 1964: 90 and on Martin's figures for 1963 part-time staff: 92.
18 Martin, 1964: 13.
19 Murray: 60.

a putative $10.4 billion compared with the actual $23 billion spent in 2011. If hypothetically in 2011 Australian universities had spent a constant $6.7 billion on academic remuneration and an additional 35 cents in the dollar on administration that would have added up to $10.4 billion. Practically the sole difference between 1960 and 2011 is the level of expenditure by universities on generic professional functions of questionable benefit and on the *nomenclatura*, the bureaucratic class of vice-presidents, deputy vice-chancellors, associate deans and directors who command the generic apparatus. The last refuge of a Soviet-style command economy is university systems across the OECD. It makes no difference whether a university is public or private. They all spend vast amounts on the production of gratuitous functions, labyrinthine administrative processes, pointless marketing, failed competition, spurious plans, useless strategies, vacuous documents, inane branding, dysfunctional databases, needless committees, tendentious grant-seeking, comic institutional ambitions, vain rhetoric, inaccurate metrics, shell-game budgets and brittle self-justification. Today 70 cents in every dollar that a student or the taxpayer hands over to a university goes to the *nomenclatura* and its myriad of offices.

Today in Australia if non-academic costs were reduced by 60 percent—bringing them in line with the 0.5:1 ratio of professionals to academics—a $3.54 billion salary productivity saving would follow.[20] That putative saving is no different from the academic teaching productivity saving produced by the 1990s 'unified national system' in Australia: the sole efficiency of that system. A $3.54 billion salary productivity saving would equate around 27 percent of federal spending on Australian universities. In the post-2008 environment it would not be surprising if federal spending on Australian universities reduced over the medium term from $13 billion to $9 billion in constant 2011 dollar terms. That is consistent with probable long-term international fiscal constraints. A significant portion of that could be achieved by reducing administrative super-sizing and by the de-regulation of public and private universities. Ideally, tuition fees should be devoted to meeting the real costs of departmental teaching and research. To achieve this requires governments to apply strict budget caps on the use of public funds by universities for professional, administrative and adminodemic services.[21] Conversely it requires universities to over-come their addiction to bureaucratic spending and to the endless proliferation of policy and rules and non-academic functions that drives the ceaseless need for more and more professional staff.

---

20   Reducing 70 cents-in-the-dollar administrative costs by 60 percent would reduce costs to what they were between 1930 and 1970, namely to the 40 cents-in-the-dollar range. Universities would have match staff size with a scaling back of professional-administrative-managerial functions. Functional reduction is the key to creating lean organizations.

21   A simple budget cap that restricted university spending on professional and administrative staff to no more than 40 cents in the dollar would immediately end the cost and tuition spiral of the sector.

None of this is easy. It entails not just institutional adaptation but also a cultural re-think. Everyone in universities complains about bureaucracy, even the professional administrator class, and yet everyone is also hopelessly addicted to its narcoleptic allure. Could universities do without research management, graduate administrations, and teaching and learning development? If they disappeared tomorrow, teaching and research would go on competently as they have for the last century. Could universities administer in one step rather than five steps? Countries have learnt to institute ease of doing business. Why not universities? Yet this is not just about functionality. For bureaucracies are lobbies. They agitate to expand. They will agitate furiously against shrinkage. But we have come to the point where arguably we have no choice but to rein them in.

Reversing the Tide

The key to reversing the administrative tide is for the university to focus once again, after 50 years of distraction, on its core business of 'instruction and departmental research.' The universities have confused environment and system. Over the past half century, the 'environment' of the university department (the administrative faculty; the professional service division; the external grant body) mutated to become the 'system.' This needs firm correction. The time that is devoted to the procedures and policies of the mass bureaucratic university and the parallel bureaucracies of government needs to be shrunk. Along with the bureaucracies has come the proliferation of professional and pseudo-academic functions and services. Together these have caused the quiet growth of entropy in the universities. University energies have been wound down—exhausted by a non-academic legal-rational compulsively procedural environment-turned-system. A revitalization of energies requires smaller organizational units focused on the kind of grass-roots delivery and discovery that once characterized thriving academic departments.

This then raises the question: what is a viable size for universities in the future? How much will national university systems in leading countries have to contract before they reach a point of proper equilibrium between state funding, private expenditure, the job market, learning and discovery? The answer is that the university and college sector needs to be about half the size in per capita terms of what it is today. Society and citizens benefit clearly from a university and college sector that has places for 16 percent (and an outside maximum of 20 percent) of 19 year olds. About 16 percent of jobs in society are professional or para-professional in nature; and about 16 percent of high school graduates are 'college ready'. Of the 16 percent who are college ready universities can usefully educate around half of them. There is no point in students going to university to learn little or nothing, to fail or graduate and then work in service jobs that do not require a degree. All that universities are doing for large numbers of students is charge them fees. The students get no evident personal or social benefit from their education. Students who receive little or no benefit from a university education need alternatives. Principally they need jobs in high-growth, employment-generating economies. This is the great failure of the post-industrial era. It did not create sufficient middle-tier jobs: the kind of employment that is skilled, well-paying but does not require a degree, and that can be undertaken by able high school graduates. The corollary of this is a system of apprenticeships, paid internships and cadetships that provide structured entry for high school graduates into the workforce. Nonetheless no amount of training or certification can substitute for a lack of jobs. Education and skills-formation follow job creation; they do not create jobs. Job-poor economies are failures. Post-industrial economies have been big failures at generating mid-tier skilled employment. The call to 'go to college' provided political cover for that failure. But universities cannot create job-rich economies. That is the function of business and government economic policy—not of higher education. The one exception to that rule concerns innovation. Universities do have a role to play in high-level economic innovation. Serious research does lead to lead to ideas that grow economies. Yet the mass bureaucratic university proved less not more able to contribute to that than its predecessors did.

Colleagues who read this book in manuscript asked me if I had any confidence that our contemporary political class will be able to address these issues. I do have some skepticism about whether they can—not least because the political class is now uniformly the product of higher education. However that is more to do with the rhetoric of the political class than with the realities that they face. The political class en masse has learnt the post-industrial script. Despite this it will over-see a shrinking of the universities. This will not happen swiftly. It has taken 40 years to get to the current miserable point and it will take 40 years to undo it. But the undoing has already started. US states have shrunk funding to US state universities by 28 percent since 2008. Australia in 2014 signaled the intent to de-regulate its higher education market—removing pseudo-market planned economy style growth targets.[22] In 2012 the US higher education market shrank by 2 percent, after previously having risen from 15.2 million in 1999 to 20.4 million in 2011. First-year enrolments in UK universities which were 445,415 in 2009–2010 averaged 440,225 across the 2009–2013, a 2 percent drop also.[23]

---

22   Kemp and Norton 2014: 5. Reflecting on government attempts to plan the number of persons with a degree, the authors observe that there 'is no basis for saying whether such a rate would be too low, too high or just right for the needs of students and the economy at the time or in any particular place.'

23   The US figure is cited by the *Economist*, 2014b; the UK figure is calculated from data on UCAS acceptances by institution 2009–2013; a handful of universities that did not report data for every year of the period were excluded from the calculation. In October 2010, the UK Browne Review recommended major tuition fee increases. First-year enrolment in UK universities has ranged from 445,415 (2009–2010) and 461,605 (2010–2011) to 408,815 (2011–2012) and 445,065 (2012–2013). Boston Consulting Group 2014a reported that for 2011–2103 in the US there was an annual growth of only 0.4 percent in enrolment for all public and private universities. This was down from an annual growth

A market stripped of government targets and incentives might still grow but equally in a world of expanding consumer resistance to student debt and a declining return on the investment in degrees, the market for university places is just as likely to decrease. In 2013 and 2014 a noticeable number of US colleges and universities began to go out of business.[24] OECD figures on long-term public funding of tertiary education since 1993 show that the state portion everywhere has shrunk—even in Denmark, Sweden and France.[25] It will probably continue to shrink. Australia in 2014 indicated a plan to reduce its government subsidy of university tuition fees from 59 percent of the total cost to 45 percent.[26] It was also considering deregulating university fees—allowing the public universities to set their own fees (high or low) in place of a government cap on fees. That said, market solutions to date have shown no ability to contain the chronic over-spending by universities on marginal and irrelevant functions. In the United States in fact the most excessive spenders on pointless functions are the private universities. The current problems of the university transcend the public-private, state-market divide. They go to the heart of the question: 'what is a university'? Universities no longer can answer this question.

If it is a choice between hospital beds and university places, the political class will choose hospital beds. The political class does not care about universities except as an occasional political talking point. The political class does care about hospitals because voters care about hospitals. The real obstacle to the proper rescaling of the university sector is the universities themselves. They have become a giant lobby group intent on perpetuating and growing a legal-rational apparatus and parking-policing-service machine. This machine arrogates to itself multiple pseudo-municipal functions. What politicians are already doing, and what they will continue to do, quietly, is to privatize tuition and living costs by one means or another. Deferred payment income-contingent loan schemes allow them to do

---

of 3.6 percent from 1990 through 2010. For-profit college enrolments in the US fell by 7 percent across 2011–2012. This might be an effect of the post-2008 economic and fiscal climate (combined with diminishing state funding, rising tuition costs, growing student debt, and demographic changes); though universities previously have been a refuge from bad job markets and dismal economies, and rising price signals have rarely discouraged enrolment. Higher education is a pseudo-market, fortified and ring-fenced by easy loans and/or government subsidies. Then again the enrolment decline might equally represent the start of a longer-term eroding of the market. In other words it is unclear whether the post-2008 wilting represents just the temporary decline of an ever-growing market or whether it is the sign of a mature market, past its prime, that is beginning to be shredded as the forces of creative destruction start to take hold. Of course, one ought to be cautious about all such predictions. Predictions often fail; Ken Olson, who was President and Founder of the Digital Equipment Corporation, declared in 1977 that 'there is no reason anyone would want a computer in their home.' Predicting the future is difficult.

24   Macdonald 2014.
25   OECD, 2013a: 208, Table B3.3.
26   Shepherd 2014: 153–4.

this—and still say that the outcome is fair. Most of these loan schemes are classic post-industrial pseudo-market arrangements. They are structured to readily forgive debt; they price interest at sub-market rates, and they delay borrower repayment until generous income thresholds are reached. This encourages enrolment in degrees that offer little or no real return on investment—either intellectual or material.

The primary problem of contemporary universities is that the university market is corrupted. Many universities sell useless products at exorbitant prices to naive consumers—and consumers increasingly de fault on the loans given to them to pursue something that they will never achieve.[27] One of the reasons why the public funding of university places has proved unsatisfactory in the long term is that it hides this problem. But private funding of places has not proved automatically any better. Both tax-financed places and student-purchased places have turned out in many or even most instances to be poor value, and sometimes atrocious value, for the university place holders. Nor does deregulation of the fees of public universities guarantee better value for money: at any tier in the system. The problem of the universities is not just one of public versus private financing. It is rather about the nature of the product or the good: that poses again the question what is a university? What are students paying for when they pay for a university place? Are they paying for municipal services like policing or parking—or are they paying for the lectures of professors? Do buyers understand that the value of a university place is not the getting of it but whether the buyer has the motivation and aptitude to leverage that place to learn things and to develop the intellectual capacities and knowledge that lead to serious professional careers? Without that, both the cheapest and the most expensive places are equally worthless. Eventually legislatures will pass laws that oblige colleges and universities to disclose the rate of return on student investment in institutional fees and costs. Alternatively consumers will start to consult the league tables that matter. Either way, the charade will not go forever. What cannot last, will not last. The mass university tulip bubble at some point will burst.

A university education is not just, solely or even mostly about the material return on the investment in education—even though governments throughout the post-industrial era have pumped up expectations of big returns in order to artificially inflate the higher education market. So what about those students who go to university to study and learn? They do exist—even though they are barely half of university enrollees today. The 2012 American Freshman Survey asked nearly 200,000 American freshman students what they thought was essential

---

27   Or else, as in the United States during the Obama administration, students are increasingly forgiven their loan debt, which simply adds to unsustainable tax-payer costs, which will be shaved off in other ways, such as the reduction in tuition subsidies. What the right hand giveth, the left hand taketh away.

about university or college education.[28] Of the university students interviewed, unsurprisingly 80 percent wanted to be well-off financially. Of the 20 standard answers offered by the survey a good financial future was what was most often cited as being important to students. The next most common thing was raising a family. The life of the mind ranked low on the survey. Twenty-six percent cited making a theoretical contribution to science; 15 percent rated writing original works (novels, poems, etc.) and creating artistic works (painting, sculpture, etc.) as important. These survey questions are not especially incisive ones. But they do give a rough indication of the numbers of students coming into university today who are interested in creative and intellectual things. It is somewhere between 40 and 50 percent of first-year students all told. That is about the same percentage of students entering university in the United States who are 'college ready'—meaning that they have an aptitude for higher learning. Most of the rest (up to 40 percent of them) will not complete their degrees. They are enticed into university by an institutional system that knows full well that they will fail or drop out. Even chronic grade inflation cannot stop that happening. The individual and social costs of this are enormous. The social benefit of it is zero. Those who are motivated to learn and who have an aptitude for learning sit in classes with an equal number who are neither intellectually motivated nor gifted. No one benefits from this; everyone is harmed by it.

The system of higher learning is vastly over-extended. It urgently needs scaling back. In any event, it already seems to be heading in this direction, with a substantial number of universities in 2013 in financial trouble. In January 2013, Moody's Investors Service declared a negative outlook for the entire US higher education sector, citing mounting pressure on all key university revenue sources. The negative outlook forecast was repeated in July 2014.[29] Across 2002–2008, long-term debt at not-for-profit universities grew at 12 percent per year; between 2006 and 2010 there was a significant weakening of the cash-flow and balance sheets of a large number American universities and colleges. This might prove to be a short-term phenomenon, the view of most university administrators, but not necessarily so. The Boston Consulting Group 2014a identified five forces transforming US higher education: 1. Revenue sources are falling, often severely; 2. Demands are rising for a greater return on investment in higher education; 3. Along with demands for greater transparency about student outcomes; 4. New business and delivery models are gaining traction; and 5. The globalization of

---

28   Pryor, Eagan, Blake, Hurtado, Berdan and Case 2012, based on data from 192,912 first-time, full-time students entering 283 US four-year colleges and universities.

29   In fall 2013, over half of US public universities reported either no growth or declines in enrolment. Total net tuition revenue declined for 25 percent of regional public institutions and 4 percent of flagships and systems. For private US universities, total revenue fell 20 percent, with universities most reliant on tuition revenue feeling the greatest strain. Most at risk were lower-rated private colleges and smaller, regional public universities. Moody's Investors Service, July 2014.

higher education is accelerating. Except for point 5, all of these are symptoms of a looming cycle of creative destruction for universities and colleges. If this does happen, and it proves to be not just a short-term event, then it is possible that a lot of these institutions, perhaps as many as a third, will not survive the head-winds of this creative destruction. Arguably, a Cambrian Era of change is looming for the university and college sector. The forces that are driving it are not understood by institutional actors. 'Leveraging shared services' and other bureaucratic centralist devices will not fix the problem that these ageing arthritic institutions face. 'Cloud computing' will not fix the problem either. Economies of scale are not the solution. Rather small scale is. Universities think that by continuing to move away from decentralized staffing at the small-scale departmental level to generic staffing at the large-scale central level, they will cut costs and increase productivity. They won't. They don't. Their problem is large-scale central operations.

In addition to a smaller scale, the higher education sector also needs an infusion of honesty. Good markets and good publics both need transparent information. Instead the higher education sector constantly pretends to itself and to others. Honesty begins with honest claims about life-outcomes. This requires direct, clear, public *caveat emptor* statements from all institutions as to their drop-out rate, graduation rate, rate of employment of graduates in jobs requiring a degree, and the long-term return on investment in their degrees and majors.[30] If institutional honesty begins there then it concludes with the honest naming of institutions. A much more candid naming of universities, colleges and institutes of technology is long over-due. The inflation of institutional titles needs puncturing. The modern university claimed that a university is an institution that combines research with teaching. It is a discovery institution. Yet most contemporary universities do little research. To bridge the gap between claim and reality, some 'universities' have distinguished themselves from colleges and technological institutes on the grounds that they have graduate research 'training' programs. The 'teaching' of researchers though is a fig-leaf that covers the embarrassment that these institutions in reality do little research. Other institutions don't care even for the fig-leaf. They have simply seized the title university. It does not matter, it seems, if a university only teaches students. It doesn't even matter if that teaching is second fiddle to administration. In response to the inflation of the term 'university,' the more traditional discovery universities have claimed the title 'research university.' That name is tautological. But in an age of excess, such tautology is understandable.

If we wanted to coin a new name in defiance of such excess then the term 'academic university' might be a fitting designation for an institution of higher learning that was prepared to drop all the accumulated peripheral functions of the past century and devote itself to 'departmental teaching and research.' In an

---

30   This proposition accords with Christensen's (2013) view that: 'We can use capital with abandon now, because it's abundant and cheap. But we can no longer waste education, subsidizing fields that offer few jobs. Optimizing return on capital will generate less growth than optimizing return on education.'

era of shrinking public subsidies for universities and increasing private consumer resistance to bloated tuition fees that are spent on everything but tuition, an 'academic university' is the kind of institution that is capable of returning to the lean cost structures of the 1930s and 1940s—when 40 cents not 70 cents in the dollar was spent on administration and professional services. The simplest fix for ailing contemporary universities is to eliminate 30 cents in the dollar of wasteful spending on generic professional services.[31] While the mainstream bureaucratic university will shrink and sink under its own weight, there are great prospects for academic universities that are small and lean with old-fashioned cost structures; that focus on departmental research and teaching; that are managed by professorial academics active in research and teaching rather than by sham adminodemics; and that have curricula that incorporate the reading of demanding texts in programs of study that are intellectually coherent; and that incubate serious research carried out autonomously, free of external bureaucratic imperatives and time wasting.

We see today a series of interesting collegial experiments. These are teaching programs based on liberal arts, Christian, classical, and Great Books themes. These though are not really models for the academic university—as they rarely look to the systemic integration of research with teaching. Such experiments principally belong to the collegiate teaching world rather than the university world of unified research and teaching, though they have some application to lower-division undergraduate university teaching.[32] The reinvigoration of the idea of the university requires more than just intensive collegiate reading programs—though those would be a good start. They have two qualities—intensive reading and academic focus—that universities need. Both the new knowledge that the contemporary research university creates and the old knowledge that it transmits suffer from a lack of systematic integration. The former today is a motely array of specialized, fragmented sub-disciplines and fields that never talk to each other (and often despise each other); the latter is a grab-bag of elective subjects and cobbled-together majors. The best exception to this is the PPE (Politics, Philosophy and Economics) type of university degree. This kind of program is

---

31   The simplest way to achieve this is for legislatures to cap (by law) university and college spending on professional and administrative services at no more than 40 cents in the dollar. That requires one line in annual budgets passed by legislatures or one sentence inserted in all university legal charters.

32   For example, the nascent Benedictus College (London), Campion College (Sydney), the planned Ralston College (Savannah, Georgia), the online LibertasU helmed by the philosopher Roger Scruton, the New College of the Humanities (London) founded by the philosopher A.C. Grayling, and various Great Books programs including at Mercer University (Macon, Georgia), the University of Texas at Austin's Thomas Jefferson Center for the Study of Core Texts and Ideas run by Thomas and Lorraine Pangle, and at Thomas Aquinas College (Santa Paula, California). Grayling's New College model with its £18000 annual student fee in 2012 was broadly comparable with the combined government-student contribution of other leading UK institutions but it certainly did not break with the excessive fee structure of the post-modern university.

serious and systematic. It is the research university equivalent of the collegiate-style Great Books program. The extension of PPE-type tripartite structures in new ways (such as degrees in 'Mathematics, Physics and Chemistry' or 'Finance, Engineering and Design') offers the promise of serious discipline depth combined with trans-discipline breadth. Being able to combine discipline depth and trans-discipline breadth is part of the challenge for academic universities in the future.[33] Alasdair Macintyre has pointed out that the modern research university can talk about the parts of creation but not about the whole.[34] That is no model for a Catholic university, as Macintyre stresses. Yet it is also no model for serious thought in general. As the analytic dissection of knowledge has grown, and the unified, integrated, synthetic and cohesive aspect has waned, so has the intellectual power of the research university. The research fecundity of the research university accordingly has diminished.

As for the pretend universities, it remains to seen what can be done with them. Having pirated the name 'university,' what institution would now give it up? And yet those institutions owe society a fundamental duty of honesty. At a minimum they have a duty to be honest about what kind of 'university' they are. This suggests the need for a lot more explicit and a lot more rigorous public labelling of universities—whether as research universities, doctoral teaching universities or comprehensive teaching universities. Institutions that cannot meet even those thresholds more properly ought to be called a college or an institute.[35] What's in a name? The answer is: sometimes nothing at all and sometimes a lot. If higher education institutions cannot call themselves what they are and not what they would like to be or what they pretend to be, how can they begin to teach, research or communicate about the world as it actually is and not as it is in some cheap fantasy? To the rationality of the real, we ought to tip our hat.

---

33   Take as an example the studio arts. These were the basis of the nineteenth and twentieth-century art school. Along with most social science and humanities disciplines, interest in the studio arts has shrunk dramatically in the past 40 years. None of these disciplines have disappeared entirely yet their weight and influence has visibly shriveled. In contrast, the media arts discipline has been a rare (if modest) growth area in the broader arts domain. This is due to the fact that the media arts (if done well) are much closer in character to STEM disciplines than to either the studio arts or the twentieth-century humanities. The media arts are computer-based and integrate digital technology with pattern thinking. In contrast, attempts to reinvent the humanities as the digital humanities, humanities computing, or computational humanities have all failed to gain any real traction among shrinking humanities student and staff cohorts—even while the syncretic act of bridging the arts-science divide remains key to the reinvention of the university, assuming that is at all possible.

34   Macintyre 2009: 174–6.

35   Kemp and Norton 2014: 63 report the latest naming fad: providers of further and technical education in Australia, having systemically failed at delivering high-quality technical education, today are lobbying to re-name themselves 'polytechnic universities.' What next? Is it the hospitality-recreation-sports university?

References

Abel, J.R. and Deitz, R. 2014. Do the Benefits of College Still Outweigh the Costs? *Federal Reserve Bank of New York Current Issues in Economics and Finance*, Volume 20, Number 3.

Access Economics. 2010. *Australia's Future Research Workforce: Supply, Demand and Influence Factors*. Canberra, Australia: Department of Innovation, Industry, Science and Research.

Access Economics. 2003. *Exceptional Returns: The Value of Investing in Health R&D in Australia*. Canberra.

ACER Australian Council for Educational Research. 2010. *Australasian Survey of Student Engagement, Australasian Student Engagement Report*. Camberwell, Vic: ACER.

Alberge, D. 2010. Feted British authors are limited, arrogant and self-satisfied, says leading academic. *The Guardian*, July 28.

Allen Consulting Group. 2003. *A Wealth of Knowledge: The return on investment from ARC-funded research*. Report to the Australian Research Council, September 4.

Allgood, S. and Walstad, W. 2007. *Faculty Time Allocations to Teaching, Research and Other Work*. Paper for American Economic Association annual meeting. http://www.aeaweb.org/annual_mtg_papers/2007/0105_1430_0503.pdf.

Altbach, P.G., Reisberg, L., Yudkevich, M., Androushchak, G. and Pacheco, I.F. (eds). 2012. *Paying the Professoriate: A Global Comparison of Compensation and Contracts*. New York: Routledge.

Altonji, J.G., Kahn, L.B. and Speer, J.D. 2013. *Cashier or Consultant? Entry Labor Market Conditions, Field of Study, and Career Success*. Yale University, September 16.

American Academy of Arts and Sciences. 2013. *Humanities Indicators*.

American Council of Trustees and Alumni. 2014. *Education or Reputation? A Look at America's Top-Ranked Liberal Arts Colleges*. Washington DC: ACTA, January.

Anderson, D., Johnson, R. and Saha, L. 2002. *Changes in Academic Work—Implications for Universities of the Changing Age Distribution and Work Roles of Academic Staff*. Canberra: Department of Education Science and Training.

Anderson, J. 2007. *Space, Time and the Categories: Lectures on Metaphysics, 1949–50*, edited by C. Cole. Sydney: Sydney University Press.

Arbesman, S. 2012. *The Half-life of Facts: Why Everything We Know Has an Expiration Date.* New York: Penguin.

Arbesman, S. and Christakis, N.A. 2011. Eurekometrics: Analyzing the Nature of Discovery. *PLoS Computational Biology* 7: 6, June.

Arum, R. and Roksa, J. 2011. *Academically Adrift: Limited Learning on College.* Chicago, University of Chicago Press.

Astin, A.W. 1993. *What Matters in College: Four Critical Years Revisited.* San Francisco: Jossey-Bass.

Australian Research Council. 2012. *Excellence in Research for Australia 2012 National Report.* Canberra: Commonwealth of Australia.

Australian Research Council. 2009. *ARC–supported research: The impact of journal publication output 2001–2005.* Canberra: ARC.

Autistic Spectrum Disorders. N.D. Did Einstein and Newton have Asperger's Syndrome? *Fact Sheet.* http://www.autism-help.org/points-%20aspergers-einstein-newton.htm.

Aydt, R. 2012. Finland, Where Reading is a Superpower. *Publishing Perspectives,* October 17.

Bahrampour, T. 2013. Baby Boomers are Killing Themselves at an Alarming Rate, Raising Question: Why? *The Washington Post,* June 3.

Baird, L.L. 1991. Publication Productivity in Doctoral Research Departments: Interdisciplinary and Intradisciplinary Factors. *Research in Higher Education,* 303–18.

Ball, P. 2012. *Curiosity: How Science Became Interested in Everything.* London, Bodley Head.

Ball, P. 2009. *Shapes: Nature's Patterns.* Oxford: Oxford University Press.

Barlow, T. 2008. *Full Funding for Research.* Background paper for Review of Australian Higher Education. Sydney: Barlow Advisory.

Barrow, L. and Rouse, C.E. 2005. Does College Still Pay? *The Economists' Voice,* 2: 4.

Battu, H., Belfield, C.R. and Sloane, P.J. 1999. Overeducation among graduates: A cohort view. *Education Economics* 7, 21–38.

Bauerlin, M. 2008. *The Dumbest Generation: How the Digital Age Stupefies Young Americans and Jeopardizes Our Future (Or, Don't Trust Anyone Under 30).* New York: Penguin.

Baum, S., Ma, J. and Payea, K. 2013. *Education Pays: The Benefits of Higher Education for Individuals and Society.* New York: College Board.

Becker, G. 1964. *Human Capital: A Theoretical and Empirical Analysis with Special Reference to Education.* New York, National Bureau of Economic Research.

Begley, C.G. and Ellis, L.M. 2012. Drug development: Raise standards for preclinical cancer research. *Nature* 483, 531–3, March 29.

Beglinger, M. 2012. Hauptsache Bürokratie. *Das Magazin.* 22, 14–21.

Bell, D. 1973. *The Coming of Post-Industrial Society.* New York: Basic Books.

Bettencourt, L.M.A., Lobo, J., Strumsky, D. and West, G.B. 2010. Urban Scaling and Its Deviations: Revealing the Structure of Wealth, Innovation and Crime across Cities. *PLOS One*. 5:11.

Bettencourt, L.M.A., Lobo, J., Helbing, D., Kuhnert, C. and West, G.B. 2007. Growth, innovation, scaling, and the pace of life in cities. *PNAS: Proceedings of the National Academy of Sciences of the United States* 104:17, 7301–6.

Bills, D. 2003. *Characteristics associated with research degree student satisfaction, completion and attrition at the University of South Australia.* Adelaide: University of South Australia.

Bloom, A. 1987. *The Closing of the American Mind.* New York: Simon and Schuster.

Bok, D. 2006. *Our Underachieving Colleges: A Candid Look at How Much Students Learn and Why They Should Be Learning More.* Princeton, NJ: Princeton University Press.

Borland, J., Dawkins, P., Johnson, D. and Williams, R. 2000. *Returns to Investment in Higher Education: The Melbourne Economics of Higher Education Research Program Report No. 1. Report to the Vice Chancellor, the University of Melbourne.* Parkville: The University of Melbourne.

Boser, U. 2011. *Return on Educational Investment A district-by-district evaluation of U.S. educational productivity.* Washington, DC: Center for American Progress.

Boston Consulting Group. 2014a. *Five Trends to Watch in Higher Education,* April 10.

Bourke, P. and Butler, L. 1998. *The Concentration of Research in Australian Universities: Six Measures of Activity and Impact, Higher Education Series.* Report No. 32. July.

Bourke, S., Holbrook, A., Lovat, T. and Farley, P. 2004. *Attrition, Completion and Completion Times of PhD Candidates.* AARE Annual Conference, Melbourne, 28 November–2 December.

Bradley, D. (Chair). 2008. *Review of Australian Higher Education Report.* Canberra: Commonwealth of Australia.

Brand, S. and West, G.B. 2011. Why Cities Keep on Growing, Corporations Always Die, and Life Gets Faster. *The Long Now Foundation*, July 25.

Brenner, S. 2014. Frederick Sanger (1918–2013). *Science* 343: 6168, 262.

Brody, N. 1992. *Intelligence.* 2nd ed. San Diego, CA: Academic Press.

Brown, D. 2011. An Economist's Take on the Art Market and the Gulf Region's Pivotal Role In It. *InMotion*, February 28.

Bureau of Labor Statistics. 2012. *National Longitudinal Survey of Youth 1997.* http://www.bls.gov/nls/nlsy97.htm

Burnham, J. 1960 [1941]. *The Managerial Revolution.* Bloomington, IN: Indiana University Press.

Carnevale, A.P. and Cheah, B. 2013. *Hard Times: College Majors, Unemployment and Earnings,* Washington DC: Center on Education and the Workforce.

Carroll, J. 2008. *Ego and Soul: The Modern West in Search of Meaning.* Melbourne: Scribe.

Carroll, J. 2004. *The Wreck of Western Culture*. Melbourne: Scribe.

Castoriadis, C. 2011. *Postscript on Insignificance: Dialogues with Cornelius Castoriadis*. London: Continuum.

Castoriadis, C. 1997 [1992]. The Retreat from Autonomy: Postmodernism as Generalised Conformism. *World in Fragments*. Stanford: Stanford University Press.

Castoriadis, C. 1991a. The Greek *Polis* and the Creation of Democracy. *Philosophy, Politics, Autonomy*. Oxford: Oxford University Press.

Castoriadis, C. 1991b. The Crisis of Culture and the State. *Philosophy, Politics, Autonomy*. Oxford: Oxford University Press, 219–41.

Castoriadis, C. 1979. Transformation sociale and creation culturelle. *Sociologie et Sociétés* 11:1, 33–48.

Cattell, R. and Butcher, H.J. 1970. Creativity in Personality. In P.E. Vernon (ed.), *Creativity*. Harmondsworth: Penguin.

Cavendish, C. 2011. Nurse Training has Eroded the Caring Ethos. *The Times*, September 22.

Chace, W.M. 2009. The Decline of the English Department. *The American Scholar*, Autumn.

Charlton, B. and Andras, P. 2005. Medical Research Funding may have Over-Expanded and be due for Collapse. *QJM: An International Journal of Medicine*, 98, 53–5.

Christensen, C. 2013. We are living the capitalist's dilemma. *CNN*, January 21.

Christensen, C.M. 2003. *The Innovator's Dilemma*. New York: HarperCollins.

Clark, G. 2014. *The Son Also Rises: Surnames and the History of Social Mobility*. Princeton, NJ: Princeton University Press.

Clarke, P. and Graves, N. 2010. In most forms a waste of time. *The Australian* January 20.

Coates, H., Dobson, I., Edwards, D. Friedman, T. Goedegebuure, L. and Meek, L. 2009. *The attractiveness of the Australian academic profession: A comparative analysis*. Melbourne: L.H. Martin Institute, Educational Policy Institute and ACER.

Cockburn, I.M. 2007. Is the Pharmaceutical Industry in a Productivity Crisis? *Innovation Policy and the Economy*, Volume 7, Josh Lerner and Scott Stern (eds) Cambridge, MA: MIT Press, 1–32.

Cogan, M.F. 2010. Exploring Academic Outcomes of Homeschooled Students. *Journal of College Admission*, Summer.

Cole, J. 2009. *The Great American University*. New York: Public Affairs.

Coleman, P. 2010. I Thought of Archimedes. *The Last Intellectuals*. Balmain: Quadrant Books.

Collins, J. (Chair). 2001. *The education of gifted children: Inquiry into the education of gifted children*. Canberra: Senate Employment, Workplace Relations, Small Business and Education References Committee.

Collins, N. 2013. 1820s Best Decade for British Innovation. *Daily Telegraph*, January 8.

Collins, N. 2012. Higgs Boson: Prof Stephen Hawking Loses $100 bet. *Daily Telegraph*, July 4.

Congressional Budget Office. 2014. *The Budget and Economic Outlook, 2004–2014*. http://www.cbo.gov/publication/45010.

Cook, M. 2003. Finding a Place in the Tertiary World. *The Age*, February 26.

Coulson, A.J. 2014. State Education Trends, Academic Performance and Spending over the Past 40 Years. *Policy Analysis*, No. 746.

Cowen, T. 2013. *Average Is Over: Powering America Beyond the Age of the Great Stagnation*. New York: Penguin.

Cowen, T. 2011. *The Great Stagnation*. New York: Penguin.

Cox, C. 1926. *Genetic Studies of Genius, Volume II, The early mental traits of three hundred geniuses*. Stanford: Stanford University Press.

Crews, C.W. 2013. *Ten Thousand Commandments: An Annual Snapshot of the Federal Regulatory State*. Washington DC: Competitive Enterprise Institute.

Csikszentmihalyi, M. 1996. *Creativity: Flow and the Psychology of Discovery and Invention*. New York: Harper.

Dawkins, J.S. 1988. *Higher Education: A Policy Statement*. Canberra: Australian Government Publishing Service.

Dawkins, J.S. 1987. *Higher Education: A Policy Discussion Paper*. Canberra: Australian Government Publishing Service.

Day, M. 2011. Royal Society's Knowledge, Networks and Nations report: Would Einstein get funded today? *Daily Telegraph*, March 29.

DEET Department of Employment, Education and Training Higher Education Division. 1993. *National Report on Australia's Higher Education Sector*. Canberra: Australian Government Publishing Service.

DEET Department of Employment, Education and Training. 1990. *A Fair Chance For All: National Institutional Planning for Equity in Higher Education: A Discussion Paper*. Canberra: Australian Government Publishing Service.

DEEWR Department of Education Employment and Workplace Reform. 2008. *Attrition Rate for Domestic Commencing Bachelor Students by State and Higher Education Provider, 2001 to 2007*. Canberra: Australian Government.

Deloitte Access Economics. 2011. *Higher Education Teaching and Learning Costs*. Canberra: Department of Education, Employment and Workplace Relations.

Denison, E.F. 1962. *The Sources of Economic Growth in the United States*. New York: Committee for Economic Development.

Dennis, W. 1955. Variations in Productivity among Creative Workers. *Scientific Monthly*, 80: 277–8.

Dennis, W. 1954. Predicting Scientific Productivity in Later Maturity from Records of Earlier Decades. *Journal of Gerontology*, 9:4, 465–7.

Desrochers, D.M. and Wellman, J.V. 2011. *Trends in College Spending 1999–2009*. Washington DC: Delta Cost Project.

De Tocqueville, A. 2003 [1835/1840]. *Democracy in America*. London, Penguin.

DETYA Department of Education, Training and Youth Affairs. 1997. *Education Participation Rates Australia 1997*. Canberra: Australian Government.

Devinney, T. 2013. Are University Leaders Really Overpaid? *The Modern Cynic*, May 8.

Dhar, V. 2014. Caught Between a Rock and a Hard Place. *Financial Times*, March 23.

Dickie, C. 2010. *Photography: The 50 Most Influential Photographers of All Time*. Hauppauge NY: Barron's Educational.

Diep, F. 2014. Stanford University To Open A Center For Studying Bad Science. *Australian Popular Science*, March 22.

DIISR Department of Innovation, Industry, Science and Research. 2011. *Focusing Australia's Publicly Funded Research Review*. Canberra: Australian Government.

Donnelly, L. and Sawer, P. 2013. 13,000 Died Needlessly at 14 worst NHS Trusts. *Daily Telegraph*, July 13.

Dorsey, E.R., Roulet, J.D., Thompson, J.P., Reminick, J.I., Thai, A., White-Stellato, Z., Beck, C.A., George, B.P. and Moses, H. 2010. Funding of US Biomedical Research, 2003–2008. *Journal of the American Medical Association*. 303:2, 137–43.

Dyer, J., Gregersen, H. and Christensen, C.M. 2011. *The Innovator's DNA*, Boston, MA: Harvard Business Review Press.

Dzeng, E. 2014. How Academia and Publishing are Destroying Scientific Innovation: A Conversation with Sydney Brenner. *King's Review*, February 24.

Economist. 2014a. Creative Destruction. *The Economist*, June 28.

Economist. 2014b. The Future of Universities, The digital degree. *The Economist*, June 28.

Economist. 2012. The College-cost Calamity. *The Economist*, August 4.

Economist Intelligence Unit. 2005. *The Future of the Life Sciences Industries: Ageing Pharmaceuticals and Growing Biotech*. *The Economist* Magazine.

Elgar, F. 2003. *PhD Completion in Canadian Universities*. Final report. Halifax, Nova Scotia: Graduate Students Association of Canada.

Elliot, J. 1997. *Early Student Withdrawal: The Reasons Students Give for Leaving the University*. Teaching and Learning Forum 97 conference. https://otl.curtin.edu.au/events/conferences/tlf/tlf1997/elliott.html.

Ellis, K. 2008. *Business Analysis Benchmark: The Impact of Business Requirements on the Success of Technology Projects*. New Castle, DE: IAG Consulting.

Emerson, C. and Bird S. 2013. *Assuring Quality while reducing the Higher Education Regulatory Burden*. Canberra: Australian Government.

Eubersax, J. 2009. College Tuition Inflation. *Satyagraha—Cultural Psychology* blog.

Evans, M.D.R., Kelley, J., Sikora, J. and Treiman, D.J. 2010. Family Scholarly Culture and Educational Success: Books and Schooling in 27 Nations. *Research in Social Stratification and Mobility* 28, 171–97.

Feist, G. 1999. The Influence of Personality on Artistic and Scientific Creativity. In R. Sternberg (ed.), *Handbook of Creativity*. Cambridge: Cambridge University Press.

Finley, A. 2013. Richard Vedder: The Real Reason College Costs So Much. *Wall Street Journal*, August 23.

Flexner, A. 1967 [1930]. *Universities: American, English, German*. New York: Teachers College Press.

Florida, R. 2002. *The Rise of the Creative Class*. New York: Basic Books.

Fogel, R.W. 2004. *The Escape from Hunger and Premature Death, 1700–2100*. Cambridge: Cambridge University Press.

Food and Drug Administration. 2013. Summary of NDA Approvals and Receipts, 1938 to the present. *US Food and Drug Administration* website http://www.fda.gov/default.htm.

Fosse, E. and Gross, N. 2012. Why Are Professors Liberal? *Theory and Society* 4, 127–68.

Frey, M.C. and Detterman, D.K. 2004. On the Scholastic Assessment or g? The Relationship Between the Scholastic Assessment Test and General Cognitive Ability. *Psychological Science*15:6, 373–8.

Friedman, M. 1991. Gammon's Law Points to Health Care Solution. *The Wall Street Journal*, November 12.

Friedman, M. 1977. Gammon's 'Black Holes.' *Newsweek*, November 7.

Gallagher, M. 2009. *Australia's research universities and their position in the world*. Address to the Financial Review Higher Education Conference 2009, Sydney, March 10.

Galton, F. 1874. *English Men of Science: Their Nature and Nurture*. London: Macmillan.

Galton, F. 1869. *Hereditary Genius*. London: Macmillan.

Gammon, M. 2005. Gammon's Law of Bureaucratic Displacement: A note from Dr Max Gammon with some quotes from Milton Friedman. *Australian Doctors Fund*, January.

Gammon, M. 1993. Among Britain's Ills, a Health Care Crisis. *Wall Street Journal*, September 8.

Gammon, M. 1988. Growth of Bureaucracy in the British National Health Service. *Journal of Management in Medicine* 3:1, 55–66.

Gammon, M. 1975. *UK NHS Hospital Service: Manpower and Number of Beds Occupied Daily, 1965–1973*. London: St. Michael's Organization.

Garwin, L. and Lincoln, T. (eds) 2003. *A Century of Nature*. Chicago: University of Chicago Press.

Geiger, R.L and Heller, D.E. 2011. *Financial Trends in Higher Education: The United States*. Working Paper No. 6. Pennsylvania State University: Centre for the Study of Higher Education.

Gilder, G. 1981. *Wealth and Poverty*. New York: Basic Books.

Gillard, J. 2010. On Track to Deliver World-Class Tertiary Learning for All. *The Australian*. June 19.

Gillard, J. 2009. *Speech*. Universities Australia Conference, Canberra. March 4.

Ginsberg, B. 2011. *The Fall of the Faculty: The Rise of the All-Administrative University and Why it Matters*. Oxford: Oxford University Press.

Ginsburg, T. and Miles, T.J. 2014. The Teaching/Research Tradeoff in Law: Data from the Right Tail. *Coase-Sandor Institute for Law and Economics Working Paper* No. 674 (second series).

Goertzel, M.G., Goertzel, V. and Goertzel, T.G. 1978. *Three Hundred Eminent Personalities*. San Francisco: Jossey-Bass.

Golden, D. 2000. Home-Schooled Kids Defy Stereotypes, Ace SAT Test. *The Wall Street Journal*, February 11.

Golden, R. 1999. *Masters of Photography: A Complete Guide to the Greatest Artists of the Photographic Age*. London: Carlton.

Gordon, R.J. 2012. *Is US Economic Growth Over? Faltering Innovation Confronts the Six Head-Winds*. National Bureau of Economic Research (NBER) Working Paper Series.

Greene, J.P. 2010. *Administrative Bloat at American Universities: The Real Reason for High Costs in Higher Education*. Goldwater Institute, Policy Report No. 239, August 17.

Greenstone, M. and Looney, A. 2011. Where is the Best Place to Invest $102,000—In Stocks, Bonds, or a College Degree? *The Hamilton Project*, June 25.

Guardian Newspaper. 2012–2013. *A guide to contemporary classical music*. http://www.theguardian.com/music/series/a-guide-to-contemporary-classical-music.

Gumport, B. and Pusser, B. 1995. A Case of Bureaucratic Accretion: Context and Consequences. *Journal of Higher Education*, September-October.

Hanson, V.D. 2014. The Outlaw Campus. *National Review Online*, January 7.

Hanushek, E. and Zhang, L. 2006. *Quality-Consistent Estimates of International Returns to Skill*. NBER Working Paper 12664. Cambridge, MA: National Bureau of Economic Research.

Harmon, L.B. 1961. The High School Backgrounds of Science Doctorates. *Science* 133, March 10.

Harrell, T.W. and Harrell, M.S. 1945. Army General Classification Test Scores for Civilian Occupations. *Educational and Psychological Measurement* 5, 229–39.

Harris, G.T. and Kaine, G. 1994. The Determinants of Research Performance: A Study of Australian University Economists. *Higher Education* 27, 191–201.

Hartley, J.E., Monks, J.W. and Robinson, M.D. 2001. Economists' Publication Patterns. *The American Economist* 45:1, Spring, 80–85.

Hauser, R. 2002. *Meritocracy, Cognitive Ability, and the Sources of Occupational Success*. Center for Demography and Ecology Working Paper No. 98–07. University of Wisconsin-Madison.

Hechinger, J. 2012. The Troubling Dean-to-Professor Ratio. *Business Week*, November 21.

Heilman, K.M., Nadeau, S.E. and Beversdorf, D.O. 2003. Creative Innovation: Possible Brain Mechanisms. *Neurocase* 9: 5, 369–79.

Heller, A. 1999. *A Theory of Modernity*. Oxford: Blackwell.

Heller, A. 1992. Modernity's Pendulum. *Thesis Eleven* 31, 1–13.

Heller, A. 1987. *Beyond Justice*. Oxford: Blackwell.

Heller, A. 1985. *The Power of Shame: A Rational Perspective*. London: Routledge and Kegan Paul.

Henle, M. 1962. The Birth and Death of Ideas. In H. Gruber, G. Terrell and M. Wertheimer (eds), *Contemporary Approaches to Creative Thinking*. New York: Atherton.

Hernstein, R.J. and Murray, C. 1994. *The Bell Curve: Intelligence and Class Structure in American Life*. New York: Free Press.

Herper, M. 2011. The Decline Of Pharmaceutical Research, Measured In New Drugs And Dollars. *Forbes*, June 27.

Higher Education. 2012. Not What It Used To Be: American Universities Represent Declining Value for Money to their Students. *The Economist*, December 1.

Higher Education Council. 1989. *Review of Australian Graduate Studies and Higher Degrees*. Canberra: Australian Government Publishing Service.

Hille, K. 2011. China searches for the Next Steve Jobs. *Financial Times*, October 21.

Hohman, J. 2010. States with More College Grads don't have Better Economies. *Mackinac Centre for Public Policy*, June 3. http://www.mackinac.org/12895.

Horrobin, D.F. 2000. Innovation in the Pharmaceutical Industry. *JRSM: Journal of the Royal Society of Medicine* 93, 341–5.

Hugo, G. 2011. *The Future of the Arts, Humanities and Social Sciences Academic Workforce: A Demographic Perspective*. Presentation to Australasian Council of Deans of Arts, Social Sciences and Humanities (DASSH) Conference, Magnetic Island, Queensland, September 29.

Hugo, G. 2008. *The demographic outlook for Australian universities' academic staff*. Council for Humanities, Arts and Social Sciences (CHASS).

Hugo, G. 2005. *The Demography of Australia's Academic Workforce: The ATN Universities*. Australian Technology Network of Universities (ATN) Conference on Building Partnerships: Finding Solutions—The ATN Workforce in Profile. Melbourne.

Humphreys, D. and Kelly, P. 2014. *How Liberal Arts and Sciences Majors Fare in Employment: A Report on Earnings and Long-Term Career Paths*. Washington, DC: Association of American Colleges and Universities.

Ioannidis, J.P.A. 2005. Why Most Published Research Findings Are False. *PLoS Medicine* 2:8, 696–701.

Jacob, B. and Lefgren, L. 2011. The Impact of Research Grant Funding on Scientific Productivity. *Journal of Public Economics* 95, 1168–77.

James, R. 2008. *Participation and Equity: A review of the participation in higher education of people from low socioeconomic backgrounds and indigenous people*. Parkville, Vic: Centre for the Study of Higher Education, University of Melbourne.

James, R., Krause, K.L. and Jennings C. 2010. *The First Year Experience in Australian Universities: Findings from 1994 to 2009*. Parkville, Vic: Centre for the Study of Higher Education, University of Melbourne.

James, W. 1880. Great Men, Great Thoughts, and the Environment. *The Atlantic Monthly* 46:276, 441–59.

Jencks, C. 1972. *Inequality: A Reassessment of the Effect of Family and Schooling in America*. New York: Basic Books.

Jiranek, V. 2010. Potential Predictors of Timely Completion among Dissertation Research Students at an Australian Faculty of Sciences. *International Journal of Doctoral Studies* 5.

Johnson, J.A. 2013. *Brief History of NIH Funding: Fact Sheet*, Washington DC: Congressional Research Service, December 23.

Joint Legislative Audit and Review Commission. 2013. *Trends in Higher Education Funding, Enrollment, and Student Costs, Report to the Governor and General Assembly of Virginia*. Richmond: Commonwealth of Virginia.

Jones, B.F. and Weinberg, B.A. 2011. Age Dynamics in Scientific Creativity. *Proceedings of the National Academy of Sciences* 108:47, November.

Jones, C.I. 2005. Growth and Ideas. *Handbook of Economic Growth*, Volume 1B. Edited by Philippe Aghion and Steven N. Durlauf. Amsterdam: Elsevier, 1064–1108.

Jones, C.I. 2000. Sources of US Economic Growth in a World of Ideas. *American Economic Review* 92:1, March.

Jones, J.M. 2010. Americans Say Jobs Top Problem Now, Deficit in Future. *Gallup*, March 12.

Joyner, J. 2012. Administrative Bloat at America's Colleges and Universities. *Wall Street Journal*, December 30.

Julian, T. 2012. *Work-Life Earnings by Field of Degree and Occupation for People with a Bachelor's Degree: 2011*. Washington DC: US Department of Commerce.

Jump, P. 2010. Ignore us at your Peril, Warn the Champions of Curiosity. *Times Higher Education*, November 11.

Karlgaard, R. 2013. Gilder's Triumph: Knowledge and Power. *Forbes*, July 15.

Kemp, D. 1999. *Knowledge and Innovation: A Policy Statement on Research and Research Training*. Canberra: Australian Government.

Kemp, D. and Norton, A. 2014. *Review of the Demand Driven Funding System—Final Report*. Canberra: Australian Government.

Kerr, C., 1966 [1964]. *The Uses of the University*. New York: Harper and Row.

Kiley, K. 2011. Where Universities Can Be Cut. *Inside Higher Ed*, September 16.

Kim, K.H. 2011. The Creativity Crisis: The Decrease in Creative Thinking Scores on the Torrance Tests of Creative Thinking. *Creativity Research Journal* 23:4, 285–95.

Kim, K.H. 2008. Meta-analyses of The Relationship of Creative Achievement to Both IQ and Divergent Thinking Test Scores. *Journal of Creative Behavior* 42, 106–30.

Klein, D.B. and Stern, C. 2007. Is There a Free-market Economist in the House? The Policy Views of American Economic Association Members. *American Journal of Economics and Sociology* 66:2, 309–34.

Kler, P. 2005. Graduate Overeducation in Australia: A Comparison of the Mean and Objective Methods. *Education Economics* 13, 47–72.

Klicka, C. 1997. *Home Schooling in the United States: A Legal Analysis*. Paeonian Springs, VA: Home School Legal Defense Association.

Kotkin, J. 2013. California's New Feudalism Benefits a Few at the Expense of the Multitude. *The Daily Beast*, October 5.

Kotlikoff, L. 2011. Study This to See Whether Harvard Pays Off. *Bloomberg*, March 9.

Kristol, I. 1979. The New Class Revisited. *Wall Street Journal*, May 31.

Krueger A. and Lindahl, M. 2001. Education for Growth: Why and for Whom? *Journal of Economic Literature* 39, 1101–36.

Kutcher, R.E. 1993. The American Work Force, 1992–2005 Historical Trends, 1950–92, and Current Uncertainties. *Monthly Labor Review*, November.

Laing, J.R. 2012. What a Drag! *Barron's*, April 14.

Lakatos, I. 1978. *The Methodology of Scientific Research Programmes: Philosophical Papers Volume 1*. Cambridge: Cambridge University Press.

Lane, R. 1966. The Decline of Ideology and Politics in a Knowledgeable Society. *American Sociological Review*, October.

Larsen, P.O. and Ins, M. 2010. The Rate of Growth in Scientific Publication and the Decline in Coverage Provided By Science Citation Index. *Scientometrics* 84, 575–603.

Lauff, E., Ingels, S. and Christopher, E. 2014. *Education Longitudinal Study of 2002 (ELS:2002): A First Look at 2002 High School Sophomores 10 Years Later*. Washington DC: National Center for Educational Statistics, Institute of Education Sciences.

Laurance, W.F., Useche, D.C., Laurance, S.G., and Bradshaw, C.J.A. 2013. Predicting Publication Success for Biologists. *BioScience* 63: 10, 817–23.

Leavis, F.R. 1969. *English Literature in our time and the university: Clark Lectures 1967*. London, Chatto and Windus.

Lee, L.C., Lin, P.H., Chuang Y.W. and Lee, Y.Y. 2011. Research Output and Economic Output: A Granger Causality Test. *Scientometrics*. 89:2, 465–78.

Le Fanu, J. 2012. *The Rise and Fall of Modern Medicine*. Revised edition. New York: Basic Books.

Leher, J. 2010. A Physicist Solves the City. *New York Times*, December 17.

Lewis, C.S. 2000. The Hobbit. *Essay Collection and Other Short Pieces*. London, HarperCollins.

Lewis, C.S. 1972. The Humanitarian Theory of Punishment. *God in the Dock: Essays on Theology and Ethics*. Grand Rapids: Wm B. Eedermans.

Li, I.W. and Miller, P.W. 2013. The Absorption of Recent Graduates into the Australian Labour Market: Variations by University Attended and Field of Study. *Australian Economic Review* 46:1, 14–30.

Lindsey, B. 2013. Why Growth Is Getting Harder. *Policy Analysis*. No. 737, October 8.

Link, A., Swann, C. and Bozeman, B. 2008. A Time Allocation Study of University Faculty. *Economics of Education Review* 27: 4, 363–74.

Lips, D., Watkins, S. and Fleming J. 2008. Does Spending More on Education Improve Academic Achievement? *Backgrounder #2179 on Education.* Washington DC: Heritage Foundation.

Lomax-Smith, J. (Chair). 2011. *Higher Education Base Funding Review.* Canberra: Commonwealth Government of Australia.

Lopez, K.J. 2014. The School of the Instapundit: Interview with Glenn Reynolds. *National Review Online*, January 7.

Lotka, A.J. 1926. Statistics—The Frequency Distribution of Scientific Productivity. *Journal of the Washington Academy of Sciences* 16:12.

Lovitts, B.E. and Nelson, C. 2000. The Hidden Crisis in Graduate Education: Attrition from Ph.D. Programs. *Academe* 86:6, 44–50.

Ludwig, A. 1995. *The Price of Greatness.* New York: Guilford.

Luzer, D. 2013. Can we make College Cheaper? *Washington Monthly*, April.

MacDonald, H. 2014. Neo-Victorianism on Campus. *Weekly Standard*, October 20.

MacDonald, H. 2013. Multiculti U. *City Journal*, Spring.

MacDonald, M. 2014. Small U.S. Colleges Battle Death Spiral as Enrollment Drops. *Bloomberg*, April 14.

Mach, E. 1896. On the Part Played by Accident in Invention and Discovery. *The Monist* VI:2, January, 161–75.

Macintyre, A. 2009. *God, Philosophy, Universities.* Lanham, MA: Rowman and Littlefield.

Macintyre, A. 1981. *After Virtue.* London: Duckworth.

Mackintosh, N.J. 1998. *IQ and Human Intelligence.* Oxford: Oxford University Press.

Maddison, A. 2003. *The World Economy: Historical Statistics.* Paris: OECD Publishing.

Mandel, M. 2009. The Failed Promise of Innovation. *US Business Week*, June 3.

Marginson, S. Forthcoming. Challenges for Australian higher education in the Asian century. In C. Johnson, V. Mackie and T. Morris-Suzuki (eds), *The Social Sciences in the Asian Century.*

Marginson, S. 2011. Higher Education in East Asia and Singapore: Rise of the Confucian Model. *Higher Education* 61:5, 587–611.

Marginson, S. 2010. Space, Mobility and Synchrony in the Knowledge Economy, in Simon Marginson, Peter Murphy and Michael A. Peters, *Global Creation: Space, Mobility and Synchrony in the Age of the Knowledge Economy.* New York: Peter Lang, 117–49.

Martin, L.H. 1964–1965. *Tertiary Education in Australia, Report of the Committee on the Future of Tertiary Education in Australia.* Melbourne: Australian Universities Commission, volumes 1–3.

Martin, Y.M., Maclachlan, M. and Karmel, T. 2001. *Postgraduate Completion Rates. Occasional Paper Series.* Canberra: Higher Education Division, DETYA.

Martin-Chang, S., Gould, O.N. and Meuse, R.E. 2011. The Impact of Schooling on Academic Achievement: Evidence from Homeschooled and Traditionally Schooled Students. *Canadian Journal of Behavioural Science* 43: 3, 195–202.

Martyr, P. 2014. Should the Commonwealth Fund Medical Research? *Quadrant*, July 1.

Marx, K. 1972. *Economic and Philosophical Manuscripts of 1844* in *The Marx-Engels Reader*, edited by R. Tucker. New York: Norton.

McCall, R.B. 1977. Childhood IQ's as Predictors of Adult Educational and Occupational Status. *Science* 197, 482–3.

McCloskey, D.N. 2010. *Bourgeois Dignity: Why Economics Can't Explain the Modern World*. Chicago: University of Chicago Press.

McInnis, C., Hartley, R., Polesel, J. and Teese, R. 2000. *Non-Completion in Vocational Training and Higher Education*. Parkville, Vic.: Centre for the Study of Higher Education, The University of Melbourne.

McInnis, C. 1999. *The Work Roles of Academics in Australian Universities*. Canberra: DETYA.

Mead, W.R. 2010. The Crisis of the American Intellectual. *Via Media*, December 8.

Mendham, T. 2011. Degrees of woo. *The Sceptic* 31, 20–25.

Milem, J.F., Berger, J.B. and Dey, E.L. 2000. Faculty Time Allocation: A Study of Change over Twenty Years. *Journal of Higher Education* 17, 454–75.

Miller, C. 2014. A College Major Matters Even More in a Recession. *The New York Times*, June 20.

Moles, A. 1958. *Information Theory and Esthetic Perception*. Urbana, IL: University of Illinois Press.

Moody's Investor Service. 2014. Negative outlook continues for US higher education, although signs of stability are emerging. *Global Credit Research*, July 14.

Moore, D. 2005. About Half of Americans Reading a Book. *Gallup News Service*, June 3.

Motl, L. 2006. IQ in different fields. *The Reference Frame*, March 13.

Mueller, B. 2014. Pay Increases for Academic Professionals Outpace Inflation. *The Chronicle of Higher Education*, May 3.

Murphy, P. Forthcoming 2015. Discovery and Delivery: Time Schemas and the Bureaucratic University. In R. Barnett, C. Guzmán-Valenzuela, O.H. Ylijok and P. Gibbs (eds), *Time and Temporality in the University*. London: Routledge.

Murphy, P. 2014. The Aesthetic Spirit of Modern Capitalism. In P. Murphy and E. de la Fuente (eds), *Aesthetic Capitalism*. Leiden, Brill.

Murphy, P. 2013. Beautiful Minds and Ugly Buildings: Object Creation, Digital Production, and the Research University—Reflections on the Aesthetic Ecology of the Mind. In M.A. Peters and T. Besley (eds), *The Creative University*. Rotterdam: Sense Publishers, 33–48.

Murphy, P. 2012. *The Collective Imagination: The Creative Spirit of Free Societies*. Farnham: Ashgate.

Murphy, P. 2010. Discovery. In Peter Murphy, Michael A. Peters, and Simon Marginson, *Imagination: Three Models of Imagination in the Age of the Knowledge Economy*. New York: Peter Lang, 87–138.

Murphy, P. and De la Fuente, E. (eds) 2014. Introduction: *Aesthetic Capitalism*, Leiden: Brill.

Murphy, P. and Roberts, D. 2004. *The Dialectic of Romanticism*. London: Continuum.

Murphy, P. 2001. *Civic Justice: From Ancient Greece to the Modern World*. Amherst, NY: Humanity Books.

Murray, C. 2012. *Coming Apart: The State of White America, 1960–2010*. New York: Crown Forum.

Murray, C. 2008. *Real Education*. New York: Three Rivers Press.

Murray, C. 2003. *Human Accomplishment*. New York: HarperCollins.

Murray, K.H.A. (Chair). 1957. *Report of the Committee on Australian Universities*. Canberra: Commonwealth Government Printer.

National Survey of Student Engagement. 2012. *Promoting Student Learning and Institutional Improvement: Lessons from NSSE at 13 Annual Results 2012*. Indiana University School of Education: Center for Postsecondary Research.

National Survey of Student Engagement. 2004. *Pathways to Collegiate Success, 2004 Survey Results*. Indiana University School of Education: Center for Postsecondary Research

Nie, N.H, Golde, S. and Bulter, D.M. 2007. *Education and Verbal Ability over Time: Evidence from Three Multi-Time Sources*. Working Paper, Stanford University.

Nightingale, P. and Martin, P. 2004. The Myth of the Biotech Revolution. *Trends in Biotechnology* 22:11.

Nock, A.J. 1932. *The Theory of Education in the United States*. New York: Harcourt, Brace.

Oakeshott, M. 1962. *Rationalism in Politics and other essays*. London: Metheun.

Odlyzko, A. 1995. The Decline of Unfettered Research, October. http://www.math.washington.edu/Commentary/science.html.

OECD. 2013a. *Education at a Glance*. Paris: OECD.

OECD. 2013b. *OECD Skills Outlook 2013: First Results from the Survey of Adult Skills*. Paris: OECD Publishing.

OECD. 2011. *Lessons from PISA for the United States, Strong Performers and Successful Reformers in Education*. Paris: OECD.

OECD. 2009. *Education at a Glance*. Paris: OECD.

OECD. 2006. *Education at a Glance*. Paris: OECD.

Oliff, P., Palacios, V., Johnson, I. and Leachman, M. 2013. Recent Deep State Higher Education Cuts May Harm Students and the Economy for Years to Come. *Center on Budget and Policy Priorities*, March 19. http://www.cbpp.org/cms/?fa=view&id=3927.

Paglia, C. 2012. How Capitalism Can Save Art. *Wall Street Journal*, October 5.

Palmer, N., Bexley, E. and James, R. 2011. *Selection and Participation in Higher Education*, March 2011. University of Melbourne: Centre for the Study of Higher Education.

Pammolli, F., Laura Magazzini, L. and Riccaboni, M. 2011. The Productivity Crisis in Pharmaceutical R&D. *Nature Reviews Drug Discovery* 10, June, 428–38.

Parker, I. 2012. Mugglemarch, J.K. Rowling Writes a Realist Novel for Adults. *The New Yorker*, October 1.

Paton, G. 2012. University Drop-Out Rate Soars by 13pc in a Year. *Daily Telegraph*, March 29.

Paton, G. 2008. One in Seven Students Drop Out of University. *Daily Telegraph*. June 5.

Phillips, N. 2013. Scientists Spent '500 years' Grant Chasing. *The Age*. March 22, 2013.

Phillips, K.P.A. 2012. *Review of Reporting Requirements for Universities*. Richmond, Vic.

Phillipson, N. 2010. *Adam Smith: An Enlightened Life*. Penguin.

Piereson, J. and Riley, N.S. 2014. The Great Books Make a Comeback. *Minding the Campus*, May 27.

Poincaré, H. 1913. *The Foundations of Science*. New York, The Science Press.

Powell, M. 2010. Illinois Stops Paying Its Bills, but Can't Stop Digging Hole. *New York Times*, July 2.

Power, C., Robertson, F. and Baker, M. 1986. *Access to Higher Education: Participation, Equity and Policy*. Canberra: Commonwealth Tertiary Education Commission.

Poynard, T., Munteanu, M., Ratziu V., Benhamou, Y., Di Martino, V., Taieb, J. and Opolon, P. 2002. Truth Survival in Clinical Research: An Evidence-Based Requiem? *Annals of Internal Medicine* 136:12, 888–95.

Price, D.J.S. 1970. Citation Measures of Hard Science, Soft Science, Technology, and Nonscience. In C.E. Nelson and D.K. Pollock (eds), *Communication among Scientists and Engineers*. Lexington, MA: Heath, 3– 22.

Price, D.J.S. 1965. The Scientific Foundations of Science Policy. *Nature*, 206, 233–8.

Price, D.J.S. 1963. *Little Science, Big Science*. New York: Columbia University Press.

Price, D.J.S. 1961. *Science Since Babylon*. New Haven: Yale University Press.

Pringle, P. 2003. College Board Scores With Critics of SAT Analogies. *Los Angeles Times*, July 27.

Pryor, J., Eagan, H., Blake, L.P., Hurtado, S., Berdan, J. and Case, M.H. 2012. *The American Freshman: National Norms Fall 2012*. Los Angeles: Higher Education Research Institute, UCLA.

Rahmin, S. 2010. English Examinations: Have they got easier? *Daily Telegraph*, June 11.

Ray, J. and Kafka, S. 2014. Life in College Matters for Life after College. *Gallup Economy*, May 6.

Redner, S. 2005. Citation Statistics from More Than a Century of Physical Review. *Physics Today*, June.

Research Universities Future Consortium. 2012. *The Current and Future Well Being of the American Research University*, June.

Reynolds, G.H. 2014. *The New School: How the Information Age Will Save American Education From Itself*. New York: Encounter Books.

Reynolds, G.H. 2014. Degrees of Value: Making College Pay Off. *The Wall Street Journal*, January 7.

Reynolds, G.H. 2014. Higher Education, Lower Standard. *USA Today*, January 14.

Reynolds, G.H. 2006. *An Army of Davids: How Markets and Technology Empower Ordinary People to Beat Big Media, Big Government, and Other Goliaths*. Nashville, TN: Thomas Nelson.

Rodriguez, A. and Kelly, A.P. 2014. *Access, Affordability, and Success: How Do America's Colleges Fare and What Could It Mean for the President's Ratings Plan?* Washington DC: American Enterprise Institute.

Rojstaczer, S. and Healy, C. 2012. Where A is Ordinary: The Evolution of American College and University Grading, 1940–2009. *Teachers College Record* 114: 7.

Rojstaczcr, S. and Healy, C. 2010. Grading in American Colleges and Universities. *Teachers College Record*, March 4.

Romeo, N. 2013. How to Reinvent College. *The Daily Beast*, May 13.

Romer, C. and Bernstein, J. 2009. *The Job Impact of the American Recovery and Reinvestment Plan*, January 9.

Ross, T. 2013. £117,000 Boost from a Degree 'far outweighs tuition fees.' *Daily Telegraph*, June 26.

Roy, A. 2013. *How Medicaid Fails The Poor*. New York: Encounter.

Rudolph, F. 1990 [1962]. *The American College and University: A History*. Athens: University of Georgia Press.

Sander, R. 2005. A Systematic Analysis of Affirmative Action in American Law Schools. *Stanford Law Review*. 57, 367–482.

Sander, R. and Taylor, S. 2012. *Mismatch: How Affirmative Action Hurts Students It's Intended to Help, and Why Universities Won't Admit It*. New York: Basic Books.

Sanger, F. and Dowding, M. 1996. *Selected Papers of Frederick Sanger*. Singapore: World Scientific Publishing.

Saunders, D. 2011. Student Loans—Forgive and Forget. *RealClearPolitics*, October 30.

Scannell, J.W., Blanckley, A., Boldon, H. and Warrington, B. 2012. Diagnosing the decline in pharmaceutical R&D efficiency. *Nature Reviews Drug Discovery*, Volume 11, March, 191–200.

Schneider, J. and Hutt, E. 2013. Making the Grade: A History of the A–F Marking Scheme. *Journal of Curriculum Studies*, May 16.

Schneider, S.J. (ed.) 2008. *501 Movie Directors. A Comprehensive Guide to the Greatest Filmmakers*. Hauppauge NY: Barron's Educational.

Schuck, P. 2014. *Why Government Fails So Often*. Princeton: Princeton University Press.

Schwartz, N.D. 2013. Where Factory Apprenticeship Is Latest Model From Germany. *New York Times*, November 30.

Scruton, R. 1998. The Aesthetic Endeavour Today. *The Aesthetic Understanding*, South Bend, Indiana: St Augustine's Press.

Shepherd, A.F. (Chair). 2014. *Towards Responsible Government: The Report of the National Commission of Audit Phase One*. Canberra: Commonwealth of Australia.

Simkin, M.V. and Roychowdhury, V.P. 2005. Stochastic Modeling of Citation Slips. *Scientometrics* 62, 367– 84.

Simkin, M.V. and Roychowdhury, V.P. 2003. Read Before You Cite! *Complex Systems* 14, 269–74.

Simmel, G. 1971. Subjective Culture. *On Individuality and Social Forms*. Chicago: University of Chicago Press.

Simon, C.C. 2012. Major Decisions. *New York Times*, November 2.

Simonton, D.K. 2013. Scientific Genius is Extinct. *Nature* 493, January 31.

Simonton, D.K. 1999. *Origins of Genius: Darwinian Perspectives on Creativity*. New York: Oxford University Press.

Simonton, D.K. 1994. *Greatness*. New York: The Guilford Press.

Simonton, D.K. 1984. *Genius, Creativity and Leadership*. Cambridge, MA: Harvard University Press.

Snyderman, M. and Rothman, S. 1988. *The IQ Controversy: The media and public policy*. Brunswick, NJ: Transaction.

Social Science Research Council of Australia. 1966. *Bibliography of research in the social sciences in Australia, 1960–1963*. Canberra: Social Science Research Council of Australia in association with Australian National University Press.

Spearman, C. 1927. *The Abilities of Man, Their Nature and Measurement*. London: Macmillan.

Spufford, F. 2002. *The Child that Books Built: A Life in Reading*. London: Faber.

State Higher Education Executive Officers. 2012. *State Higher Education Finance FY 2012*. Boulder, CO: SHEEO.

State Public Interest Research Groups. 2005. *Ripoff 101*, second edition. Washington DC: State PIRGs.

Steffens, J. (ed.) 2009. *Unpacking My Library: Architects and their Books*. New Haven: Yale University Press and Urban Center Books.

Stepan, P. 2010. *50 Photographers You Should Know*. New York: Prestel.

Stille, H.C. 2014. *A Continuing National Scandal: Non-graduating Student Cost to the Public at Public Senior Higher Education Institutions*. South Carolina: Higher Education Research/Policy Center.

Stone, R. 1966. A Model of the Education System. *Mathematics in the Social Sciences and other essays*. Cambridge: MIT Press.

Storr, A. 1972. *The Dynamics of Creation*. London: Secker and Warburg.

Synder, S.H. 2005. The Audacity Principle in Science. *Proceedings of the American Philosophical Society*, 149:2, 141–58.

Tang, R. 2008. Citation Characteristics and Intellectual Acceptance of Scholarly Monographs. *College Research Libraries* 69: 4, 356–69.

Teichholz, N. 2014. The Questionable Link Between Saturated Fat and Heart Disease. *The Wall Street Journal*, May 2.

Theil, P. 2014. *Zero to One: Notes on Start-ups, or How to Build the Future.* London: Penguin Random House.

Thornton, S. and Curtis, J.W. 2012. *A Very Slow Recovery: The Annual Report on the Economic Status of the Profession, 2011–12.* Washington DC: American Association of University Professors.

Tinto, V. 1982. Limits of Theory and Practice in Student Attrition. *Journal of Higher Education*, 53, 687–700.

Tonta, Y. and Ünal, Y. 2005. Scatter of Journals and Literature Obsolescence Reflected in Document Delivery Requests. *Journal of the American Society for Information Science and Technology*, 56:1, 84–94.

Toutkoushian, R.K., Porter, S.R., Danielson, C. and Hollis, P.R. 2003. Using Publication Counts to Measure An Institution's Research Productivity. *Research in Higher Education*, 44: 2, 121–48.

Trounson, A. 2014. Old and New Cuts put Uni Jobs at Risk, says Melbourne University VC Glyn Davis. *The Australian*, June 6.

Tully, S. 2010. The Best Stimulus? Spend Less, Borrow Less. *Fortune*, June 25.

Uebersax, J. 2009. College Tuition Inflation. *Satyagraha* Blog, July 14.

UNESCO Institute for Statistics. 2000. *Transition Characteristics at Ages 15, 16, 17, 18, 19 and 20.*

University Education. 2014. Graduate Jobs: Top 10 Degree Subjects by Lifetime Salary. *Daily Telegraph*, October 12.

University of California, Berkeley and Bain and Company. 2010. *Achieving Operational Excellence at University of California, Berkeley Final Diagnostic Report—Complete Version*, April.

Urquhart, D.J. 1958. Use of scientific periodicals. *International Conference on Scientific Information*, National Academy of Sciences-National Research Council, Washington DC, 287–300.

US Department of Education. 2013. *Digest of Education Statistics.* Washington DC: National Centre for Education Statistics.

US Department of Education. 2012. *Digest of Education Statistics.* Washington DC: National Centre for Education Statistics.

US Department of Education. 2011. *Digest of Education Statistics, 2011.* Washington, DC: National Centre for Education Statistics.

US Department of Education. 2008. *Digest of Education Statistics.* Washington DC: National Centre for Education Statistics.

US Department of Education. 1993. *120 Years of American Higher Education: A Statistical Portrait.* Washington DC: National Center for Education Statistics.

US Department of Education. 1990. *Digest of Education Statistics.* Washington DC: National Centre for Education Statistics.

Valadkhani, A. and Worthington, A. 2006. Ranking and Clustering Australian University Research Performance, 1998–2002. *Journal of Higher Education Policy and Management* 28:2, 189–210.

Veblen, T. 1921. *The Engineers and the Price System*. New York: Heubsch.

Vedder, R. 2014. Dropouts Cost More Than $12 Billion a Year. *Minding the Campus*, February 11.

Vedder, R. 2010. Learning From Socrates and Adam Smith on Financing Universities. *The Chronicle of Higher Education*, July 20.

Vedder, R. and Denhart, C. 2007. Michigan Higher Education: Facts and Fiction. *Mackinac Center for Public Policy*, June 20. http://www.mackinac.org/8647.

Vedder, R., Denhart, C. and Robe, J. 2013. *Why Are Recent College Graduates Underemployed? University Enrollments and Labor-Market Realities*. Center for College Affordability and Productivity, January.

Vedder, R., Denhart, C., Denhart, M., Matgouranis, C. and Robe, J. 2010. *From Wall Street to Wal-Mart: Why College Graduates Are Not Getting Good Jobs*. Center for College Affordability and Productivity, December.

Vernon, P.E. 1947. Research on Personnel Selection in the Royal Navy and the British Army. *American Psychologist* 2, 35–51.

Westervelt, E. 2013. The Online Education Revolution Drifts Off Course. *All Things Considered*. National Public Radio (NPR), December 31.

Williams, R. 2013. Strokes Fall by 40 Percent due to Increased Statin Use. *Daily Telegraph*, October 12.

Woelert, P. and Millar, V. 2013. The 'Paradox of Interdisciplinarity' in Australian Research Governance. *Higher Education* 66, 755–767.

Wolf, A. 2002. *Does Education Matter? Myths about Education and Economic Growth*. London, Penguin.

Wright, T. and Cochrane, R. 2000. Factors Influencing Successful Submission of PhD Theses. *Studies in Higher Education* 25, 181–95.

Wurtman R.J and Bettiker, R.L. 1995. The Slowing of Treatment Discovery, 1965–1995. *Nature Medicine* 1, 1122–5.

Zhao, H. and Jiang, G. 1985. Shifting of World's Scientific Center and Scientist's Social Ages. *Scientometrics* 8, 59–80.

Zickuhr, K. and Rainie, L. 2014. E-Reading Rises as Device Ownership Jumps. *Pew Research Internet Project*, January 16.

Zimbler, L.J. 2001. *Background Characteristics, Work Activities, and Compensation of Faculty and Instructional Staff in Postsecondary Institutions: Fall 1998*. Washington, DC: National Center for Education Statistics, US Department of Education.

Index

For Product Safety Concerns and Information please contact our EU
representative GPSR@taylorandfrancis.com Taylor & Francis Verlag GmbH,
Kaufingerstraße 24, 80331 München, Germany

Printed and bound by CPI Group (UK) Ltd, Croydon, CR0 4YY
01/05/2025
01858355-0006